D0321807

**Accompanying
CD/CDs in the pocket
at the front/back of
the book**

EDINBURGH NAPIER UNIVERSITY LIBRARY

3 8042 00809 7865

Essentials for the Improvement of Healthcare Using Lean & Six Sigma

D.H. Stamatis

CRC Press
Taylor & Francis Group
Boca Raton   London   New York

CRC Press is an imprint of the
Taylor & Francis Group, an **informa** business

A PRODUCTIVITY PRESS BOOK

CRL
362.10685 STA
7dy

Productivity Press
Taylor & Francis Group
270 Madison Avenue
New York, NY 10016

© 2011 by Taylor and Francis Group, LLC
Productivity Press is an imprint of Taylor & Francis Group, an Informa business

No claim to original U.S. Government works

Printed in the United States of America on acid-free paper
10 9 8 7 6 5 4 3 2 1

International Standard Book Number: 978-1-4398-4601-8 (Hardback)

This book contains information obtained from authentic and highly regarded sources. Reasonable efforts have been made to publish reliable data and information, but the author and publisher cannot assume responsibility for the validity of all materials or the consequences of their use. The authors and publishers have attempted to trace the copyright holders of all material reproduced in this publication and apologize to copyright holders if permission to publish in this form has not been obtained. If any copyright material has not been acknowledged please write and let us know so we may rectify in any future reprint.

Except as permitted under U.S. Copyright Law, no part of this book may be reprinted, reproduced, transmitted, or utilized in any form by any electronic, mechanical, or other means, now known or hereafter invented, including photocopying, microfilming, and recording, or in any information storage or retrieval system, without written permission from the publishers.

For permission to photocopy or use material electronically from this work, please access www.copyright.com (http://www.copyright.com/) or contact the Copyright Clearance Center, Inc. (CCC), 222 Rosewood Drive, Danvers, MA 01923, 978-750-8400. CCC is a not-for-profit organization that provides licenses and registration for a variety of users. For organizations that have been granted a photocopy license by the CCC, a separate system of payment has been arranged.

Trademark Notice: Product or corporate names may be trademarks or registered trademarks, and are used only for identification and explanation without intent to infringe.

Library of Congress Cataloging-in-Publication Data

Stamatis, D. H., 1947-
  Essentials for the improvement of healthcare using Lean & Six Sigma / Diomidis H. Stamatis.
    p. ; cm.
  Includes bibliographical references and index.
  Summary: "By using theories of Six Sigma and Lean methodology, this text presents solutions to fundamental problems in healthcare. This text breaks the system down into three fundamental areas: primary care, hospitals, and managed care. The author identifies the four critical issues that affect healthcare as it relates to efficiency and cost by addressing the specific issues. The book discusses the application of IT in healthcare as a tool of improvement, and how to select the best project for improvement. The author also includes a discussion of ISO and the Malcolm Baldridge award. Case studies are included to illustrate successes"--Provided by publisher.
  ISBN 978-1-4398-4601-8 (hardcover : alk. paper)
  1. Medical care--Quality control. 2. Six sigma (Quality control standard) I. Title.
  [DNLM: 1. Quality Assurance, Health Care--organization & administration--United States. 2. Delivery of Health Care--standards--United States. 3. Efficiency, Organizational--United States. 4. Outcome and Process Assessment (Health Care)--methods--United States. 5. Quality Assurance, Health Care--methods--United States. W 84.4 AA1]

RA399.A1.S727 2011
610.68--dc22   2010038121

Visit the Taylor & Francis Web site at
http://www.taylorandfrancis.com

and the Productivity Press Web site at
http://www.productivitypress.com

For Jessica and Caitlyn

Contents

Preface

The U.S. healthcare system, as good as it might be, is inadequate to meet future demands. The future for improvement is in the areas of tort reform, insurance portability, elimination of preexisting conditions as a reason for denying healthcare insurance, cost efficiency and effectiveness, error-free delivery systems, improved diagnostics and treatments, and accurate computational technologies for medicine (billing and records).

The United States has the best overall healthcare system in the world. However, when we talk about being the best, we must recognize that "best" has many interpretations. For example, no one will deny the fact that we have the "best" access to healthcare; no one will deny that we have the "best" treatment in healthcare; no one will deny that we have the "best" care in healthcare; and no one will deny that we have the freedom to choose our doctor, hospital, and insurance and to be part of the decision making in our own health situation. On the other hand, no one will deny that the cost for our healthcare is very high and no one will deny that many unacceptable errors occur in the practice and delivery of healthcare.

Much discussion is taking place to remedy healthcare as a whole system. However, the discussion is not really about improving healthcare but rather on how government can take control of our individual rights. After all, healthcare is one-sixth of our total economy. To be sure, there is a political agenda in the wind of improvement. However, in this book, we are going to address some concrete issues and concerns that can be done without government intervention or, at the least, minimum intervention. We will simply mention political and legal issues because nothing can be done unless the citizenry speak through the ballot box.

We are fortunate to live in an era that provides medical science at its best. New discoveries are constantly making diagnosis and treatment options easier and less invasive. Access to this level of sophisticated and effective medical care comes at a cost. The healthcare industry has tried in multiple ways to manage the cost burden of healthcare delivery while attempting to provide reasonable access to all levels of medical care. The industry as a whole, however, is faltering due to its own high cost and regulations imposed on it by government.

It is failing because it is focusing its efforts on implementing reactive controls instead of requiring proactive efficiency. Instead of controlling costs, the healthcare model is adding to the expense due to practicing defensive medicine. Instead of allowing open access, the model is becoming more and more restrictive due to local insurance restrictions. Instead of insurance spreading the individual risk and cost burden among policyholders, insurance companies are struggling to remain financially competitive in the general marketplace. This, of course, is a direct relationship of what government is doing to restrict healthcare in state-by-state policies rather than having an open policy of competition between states.

At this rate, healthcare will be the next industry bailout. It is time for reform. It is time for simplification of an overly complicated system. It is time to update a healthcare model that adds financial burden to itself by excessive regulation and ineffective use of technology. It is time to embrace and utilize electronic systems to store and access demographic, insurance, and medical data instantaneously and to employ algorithms to process claims in real time. It is time to offer national competition versus state-specific coverage. It is time to offer simpler and more transparent coverage and payment. It is time to leverage advances in other industries to add efficiency and cost savings to our healthcare industry. The time is now!

Specifically, we are going to address the issues of efficiency and effectiveness and how quality initiatives may help to improve the overall healthcare system.

Chapter 1 introduces four critical issues and the opportunities that we have to improve the areas of concern.

Chapter 2 discusses the directions of improvement. Specifically, it identifies the indicators for primary care, managed care, and hospital care.

Chapter 3 introduces the mechanics of change. Specifically, we address the concept of working together for a common goal of improvement. We do this by introducing the concepts of teams and specific tools that can be used to address and understand change.

Chapter 4 focuses on the transition of groups to teams. Specifically, the issues of the administrative process in team development are addressed and we give a cursory explanation of the internal development and transition of individuals to a team.

Chapter 5 emphasizes that the concept of teams and meetings is always present in every quality improvement initiative. Specifically, here we provide some of the logistical issues that teams go through and must be aware of as they move toward improvement of the organization

Chapter 6 focuses specifically on the effects of change in healthcare.

Chapter 7 focuses on customer satisfaction (CSat). Specifically, it addresses the rationale for understanding the CSat and explains some of the measurement characteristics in the process of improvement.

Chapter 8 addresses the process and what we must be aware of so that we may improve it. Specifically, we introduce the definition of a process and then proceed to present some specific methodologies to understand and improve it further. These methodologies are failure mode and effect analysis (FMEA), advance practice quality planning (APQP), project management, and process flow.

Chapter 9 focuses on the Six Sigma methodology and how it may be used in healthcare. We introduce the DMAIC (define, measure, analyze, improve, control) and DCOV (design, characterize, optimize, verify) models and we also discuss the healthcare-specific DMAIIC model.

Chapter 10 focuses on Lean methodology and how it may be used in healthcare. Specifically, we address the philosophy of Lean and present some key tools and methodologies that may be used in healthcare.

Chapter 11 focuses on measurement. Specifically, we explain why measurement is important and how it can be used in the healthcare industry.

Chapter 12 discusses the issues of primary care. Specifically, it addresses how to define the process, redesign it, and define metrics for true improvement. A very detailed example of a process flow of a physician's practice is included.

Chapter 13 offers immediate applications for computer technology (information technology [IT]) in healthcare. This chapter discusses IT as it is and as it should be applied in healthcare at large. Specifically, we address issues concerning (1) billing and administration, (2) electronic documentation, and (3) patient care.

Chapter 14 introduces the concept of project selection in the improvement process and details development through the DMAIC model.

Chapter 15 summarizes the ISO 9000 standards as they apply to healthcare and also addresses the issues and concerns of the National Integrated Accreditation for Health Organizations (NIAHO). It presents a cursory overview of ISO 13485—Medical Devices.

Chapter 16 provides an overview of the Malcolm Baldrige National Quality Award Program as it applies to healthcare.

In addition, the following appendices can be found on the companion CD to this book:

Appendix A offers additional information on Six Sigma, providing specific forms and formulas for this methodology.

Appendix B provides additional tools and methodologies used in the Lean approach to improvement.

Appendix C offers additional tools used in the improvement process. This appendix provides over 30 specific tools that may be used in any improvement initiative.

Appendix D suggests some change ideas, providing an outline of questions that may help a practitioner in healthcare improve and facilitate the process of change.

Appendix E contains a typical patient health questionnaire (PHQ) checklist for depression as an example of preventive interaction.

Appendix F lists frequent symbols for value stream mapping (VSM) or sometimes called value stream process (VSP) and provides a fast reference to the most frequent symbols used in the VSM process.

Acknowledgments

No book is the complete product of one individual. This book is no different. I am in debt to many individuals and I feel bad that I will forget to thank quite a few who have helped me toward the completion of this book:

By far the most important individual has been my physician, Dr. R. Russ, who has given me many hours of his time to discuss some of the issues of healthcare, especially outcomes and measuring improvement of chronic diseases.

Thank you to Dr. T. A. Khalifa from American University of Cairo, Egypt, for his suggestions in measuring improvement in healthcare, especially using Lean and Six Sigma methodologies.

I thank Dr. P. Mitsas from Henry Ford Health System for his generous comments on earlier drafts.

Special thanks go to A. Hyduke, S. Jagiela, K. Seyed, K. Sharp, and B. Versage from the Lehigh Valley Network Hospital for their suggestions and thought-provoking issues regarding Lean in a hospital environment.

R. M. Steiner, RN, program manager for AIAG Healthcare and state director for Michigan IPIP/PCMH, offered valuable suggestions and recommendations for improving the manuscript.

M. Mroz from the AIAG group, in Southfield, Missouri, kept me abreast with the latest information in the IPIP (improving performance in practice) development for primary care in Michigan.

Quality Digest granted me permission to use (1) the partial wheel with goals added, and (2) the hospital-based performance model.

J. Stamatis, PA-C, offered thought-provoking arguments and discussions on the various issues of primary care, emergency care, and, especially, electronic record technology.

I thank the editors of the book for making a rough manuscript into a presentable final product.

Finally, my chief editor and critic, Carla, offered excellent suggestions throughout the book. Her background as a registered nurse served as a check for many of the ideas in this book.

Introduction

In 1996, when *Total Quality Management in Healthcare* was published, I said that "it takes more than the latest technology to stay competitive ... and quality must be viewed as a customer determination." I wrote about the need to internalize quality and its concepts of improvement in all health institutions as well as private physicians' practices. My focus then was the "process" and the critical characteristics that define that process (Stamatis 1996). I was and continue to be convinced that quality methodology is one way to improve quality in many areas of healthcare.

I began writing this book 12 years later to reemphasize the importance of outcomes and process measures in any environment that delivers healthcare. The major difference between my first book and this one is that I am much more cognizant of *emotional intelligence* and the role that it plays in discussing any issue or concern about healthcare. The concept of emotional intelligence was first defined in 1990 by P. Salovey and J. Mayer. It involves the ability "to perceive accurately, appraise, and express emotion; the ability to access and/or generate feelings when they facilitate thought; the ability to understand emotion and emotional knowledge; and the ability to regulate emotions to promote emotional and intellectual growth" (Elksnin and Elksnin 2003). Why am I mentioning emotional intelligence? Because the healthcare discussion is very charged up and quite often individuals, as well as groups, do not make sound decisions based on fact or data. Rather, they make decisions based on their views of data and their emotions.

With all the high-tech and expensive medical care available in the United States, one may assume that Americans are among the healthiest people in the world. But that is not true. An oxymoron of sorts exists: The United States spends more than any other country (about 17% of its gross domestic product) on healthcare, but ranks 12th among 13 industrialized nations in measures of overall health, such as life expectancy. This statistic, however, has to be explained by the fact that it is measured by the World Health Organization (WHO), which measures all deaths including soldiers and city murder deaths (homicides). Another very fundamental reason for this discrepancy may be the fact that other countries have very homogeneous populations and their norms are very consistent, whereas the United States is a "melting pot" of different ethnicities that bring their own norms. If you exclude these aberrations, the United States has the best system in the world by far.

Why is the U.S. healthcare system perceived to be in such bad shape? Medical practices and hospitals are designed to care for patients, but they are also businesses. Doctors are reimbursed by insurers for services such as medical procedures and surgeries that the doctors recommend and order. As a result, many doctors order too many tests, perform too many procedures, and prescribe too many medications. Some doctors also provide excessive medical care to protect themselves against malpractice lawsuits. Much of this is not in the best interests of the patient. However, most of this practice is because the doctors want to feel safe from frivolous lawsuits. It is called *defensive medicine.*

What role do patients play? Often, they go to their doctors asking for specific treatments that they have heard about from friends, read about on the Internet, or seen in a drug company or advocacy group ad on TV or in a magazine. Doctors want happy customers, so after a while it is easier to acquiesce than to argue. Americans are conditioned to believe that more is better, but that is not always the case; in fact, sometimes it is worse. How so? All medical procedures and even some tests and medications carry risks for side effects or complications. For example, angioplasty, which uses a catheter and balloon to open a narrowed artery—and is sometimes followed by the placement of a stent (a tube to keep it open)—carries risks for heart attack, blood clots, kidney problems, or stroke.

Similarly, some degree of brain damage (loss of cognitive functions that can last up to 12 months, such as memory or judgment) can occur with coronary bypass surgery. Yet, many of these patients' symptoms, especially those with stable angina (chest pain), could have been treated with medication that has far less risk for side effects. In many cases, patients do not really need the stent or the surgery (Gottfried 2009).

Then why were these procedures performed? Gottfried (2009) claims that, to a large degree, doctors create their own demand. For example, Miami has a lot more cardiologists than the Minneapolis area. And recent research found that annual Medicare spending on healthcare for Miami seniors was nearly 2.5 times higher than it was for statistically matched older adults in Minneapolis. The Miami healthcare costs included 6.5 times more visits to specialists, compared with Minneapolis healthcare expenditures.

Do doctors create their own demand in other areas of medicine? In general, more specialists mean more expensive healthcare—and poorer health. We need specialists to have a good healthcare system. But, based on several studies, including research by investigators at Dartmouth Medical School, regions in the

United States that have a greater proportion of primary care physicians (such as family physicians and general internists) than specialists provide better care at lower costs (Gottfried, 2009).

However, in the United States, medical students want to be specialists because they make more money and usually can arrange less demanding schedules than generalists can. Also, there is more prestige. For example, brain surgeons are referred to often for their intellectual abilities, but one never hears that about pediatricians. But do specialists not provide better care when treating serious conditions? Not necessarily. Studies by Dartmouth Medical School researchers and others show that, as the number of specialists increases, healthcare improves—up to a point. Increasing the availability of primary care doctors is associated with lower costs and better healthcare quality (Gottfried 2009).

This occurs perhaps because the extra procedures that specialists perform increase the odds that something will go wrong. Primary care doctors more often follow a "watchful waiting" philosophy. They put more emphasis on preventive medicine and may know the patient well enough to recognize when stress or other medical conditions are worsening symptoms. Should we avoid consulting specialists? Certainly not. We just should not see them unless we have to. We should go to our primary care doctor first and rely on his or her judgment as to whether specialist care is needed.

When it is necessary to go to a specialist, we should choose a busy one. Because they typically have enough medically indicated work to do, such specialists are less likely to recommend marginal or unnecessary procedures. Also, whenever any doctor—generalist or specialist—recommends a procedure, we should not be shy about asking, "Is it really necessary?" This query is particularly important when elective procedures that may carry risks, such as most orthopedic surgeries or elective cardiac surgeries, are recommended. If we are not convinced, we should get another opinion.

Does the same advice apply to medication? Yes. Medication can be effective and even lifesaving. For example, drugs for elevated cholesterol and high blood pressure have played a substantial role in preventing heart disease and stroke. If we need them, we should take them. But we should make sure that we really need them. In general, weight loss, salt reduction, and exercise should be given a chance before using drugs to reduce blood pressure. The early stages of type 2 diabetes are often treatable with diet and exercise alone, but doctors frequently skip this step.

Even if medication is taken for a chronic illness, such as high blood pressure, heart disease, or diabetes, it is necessary to maintain a healthy lifestyle. Patients have responsibility for their own health. However, when doctors prescribe a medication, they do not always choose wisely among available drugs. Because drug companies market new drugs heavily to patients and doctors, many physicians opt for these expensive medications when older, cheaper, generic alternatives would do just as well—if not better. Only 10% of new drugs are really new; the rest are molecular variations on existing ones, which are more profitable for the manufacturers but no more effective (Gottfried 2009).

Gottfried (2009) described a patient with gastroesophageal reflux disease (GERD) who came to his office and asked for "the little purple pill" that she had seen advertised on TV. He explained that the generic heartburn drug he had prescribed was nearly identical, but she insisted. She was sufficiently impressed by the flashy graphics on the TV ad to pay substantially—out of pocket—for the medication. Should patients not have access to newer drugs if that is what they want? Yes, but they need to understand that when a drug is approved, it has generally been tested on several thousand people. Serious problems often are not discovered until the drug has been prescribed hundreds of thousands of times. That is why the cholesterol drug cerivastatin (Baycol), the diabetes medication troglitazone (Rezulin), and the heartburn drug cisapride (Propulsid) are no longer available.

Serious—sometimes deadly—side effects have been discovered after medications had been on the market for a while. Such side effects are unlikely with drugs that have been around for several years. Cheaper drugs are sometimes more effective, too. Several large studies have shown that diuretics ("water pills")—among the oldest and cheapest drugs for high blood pressure—reduce heart failure and stroke more effectively than newer compounds. If someone has high blood pressure and his or her doctor is not prescribing a diuretic, the patient should ask why. If two or more drugs are needed (about 70% of the time, this is necessary), a diuretic usually should be one of them.

References

Elksnin, L. K., and N. Elksnin. 2003. Fostering social-emotional learning in the classroom. *Education* 124 (1): 63–75. Retrieved on July 1, 2004, from InfoTrac OneFile database.

Gottfried, D. 2009. Are you getting too much medical care? *Bottom Line* September: 5–6.

Salovey, P., and J. D. Mayer. 1990. Emotional intelligence. *Imagination, Cognition, and Personality* 9: 185–211.

Stamatis, D. H. 1996. *Total quality management in healthcare: Implementation strategies for optimum results.* New York: McGraw–Hill.

Chapter 1

The Four Critical Issues in Healthcare

Introduction

In both the Preface and Introduction, we emphasized that the overall system (see Figure 1.1) of healthcare in the United States is the "best" in the world. However, we also pointed out that there are areas where improvement may be implemented. These areas are in four categories: (1) occurrence of errors or mistakes in delivery of treatment, (2) the recognition of the uninsured, (3) cost of delivery of healthcare, and (4) efficiency.

In addition to these four categories, three items of concern must be pointed out. However, they all deal with our legal system and not much can be done unless the citizenship is courageous enough to bring its concerns forth in respective state and federal legislatures with commitment and involvement to bring about real reform for the better:

- Tort reform: litigation issues
- Insurance portability: preexisting conditions and carrying over the insurance of choice from employer to employer
- Free market accessibility to purchase insurance across state boarders: to be able to buy the insurance of choice in the open market regardless of residency

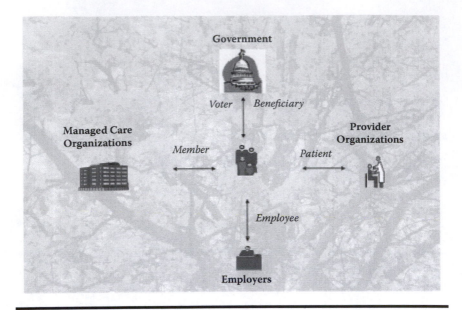

Figure 1.1   U.S. healthcare system.

Occurrence of Errors or Mistakes in the Delivery of Treatment

Let us examine the four categories in a little more detail, since we can do something about them. We begin with the errors. In healthcare, just like in manufacturing, we consider an error to be a flaw or omission in the design, standard, or specification. On the other hand, a mistake happens even though there was correct planning in the design phase, due to procedures that were not followed or made known. What is a mistake or error in the delivery system of healthcare? A glaring example of this is surgery (Ridge 2008; Norton 2007; Dillon 2008; Edwards 2008). With 2,700 cases of wrong-site surgeries continuing to occur annually, experts recommend more consistent adoption of the universal protocol (UP) or, in this case, a defined alternative process when site-marking is impractical.

To be sure, this is a very good approach, but the fact is that we still have problems. A recent review of the National Practitioner Data Bank and additional closed claims databases for wrong-site procedures estimated that wrong-site surgery continues to occur approximately 1,300–2,700 times annually in the United States, despite the Joint Commission (TJC) requirement for a UP 5 years ago. In addition, up to 30% of all wrong-site and wrong-patient procedures have their genesis before patient admission to the hospital from scenarios such as inaccurate clinic note dictations or mislabeling of radiographs, thus reinforcing the need for the UP to prevent error. (The reader here will notice that the TJC statistics in this area were drawn from electronic databases.)

The UP was introduced by TJC in July 2004 as a national patient safety goal and consists of three components: a preprocedure verification process, surgical site marking, and a surgical "timeout" immediately prior to starting the procedure. In the language of quality, this may be thought of as *advanced quality planning.*

It is very interesting that the timeout was recently expanded to include the verification of correct patient positioning; availability of relevant documents, diagnostic images, instruments, and implants; and the need for preoperative antibiotics and other essential medications (e.g., the use of beta-blockers). Some disagree with an expanded approach, believing that it dilutes the original intent. However, many hospitals have found it to be helpful to improving all the processes of care (Dillon 2008; Harrington 2009).

Less widely publicized are wrong-site invasive procedures performed outside the operating room, highlighting the reason that this protocol should be applied equally to clinical settings outside the operating room for any invasive procedure that requires a patient's consent. Inadequate or inaccurate surgical site-marking represents a major risk factor for wrong-site surgery. Examples that have led to error include site-marking by a junior member of the surgical team who will not be present during the procedure, using an "X" that may be misunderstood as "not this side," the use of nonpermanent markers that wash off during surgical prep, residual markings from previous surgery, or inability to mark the site (e.g., mucosal surfaces, teeth, visceral surgery). For some typical examples, see Table 1.1. In the language of quality this may be thought of as *mistake proofing.*

What is very intriguing about all this planning and verification that currently exist is that there are still problems in the process. For example, in the preprocedure verification process, we encounter a significant statistic of about 20–30% of all wrong-site and wrong-patient procedures originating before patient admission to the hospital. Potential scenarios include inaccurate clinic note dictations related to a wrong side, the mislabeling of radiographs or other diagnostic tests, or a mix-up of patients with similar or identical names. This happens even with the sound rationale for conducting these precautionary measures to confirm (1) patient identity, (2) the nature of the planned procedure, and (3) the exact surgical site. Each patient is unequivocally identified by an identification bracelet that includes the patient's name, birth date, and a medical record number, yet errors occur.

Table 1.1 Serious Reportable Surgical Events ("Never-Events"), as Defined by the National Quality Forum

1. Surgery performed on the wrong body part
2. Surgery performed on the wrong patient
3. Wrong surgical procedure performed on a patient
4. Unintended retention of a foreign object in a patient after surgery or other procedure
5. Intraoperative or immediate postoperative death in an ASA class 1 patient[a]

Source: NQF consensus report, update 2006.

[a] ASA stands for American Society of Anesthesiologists. In 1963, the ASA adopted a five-category physical status classification system for assessing a patient before surgery; a sixth category was later added: (1) a normal healthy patient, (2) a patient with mild systemic disease, (3) a patient with severe systemic disease, (4) a patient with severe systemic disease that is a constant threat to life, (5) a moribund patient who is not expected to survive without the operation, and (6) a declared brain-dead patient whose organs are being removed for donor purposes.

Five years after the launch of the UP, an editorial in the July 2009 issue of *Patient Safety in Surgery* reviewed the obstacles that have limited the effectiveness of UP and that need to be addressed to improve the process. These included:

- There was no consistent method for documenting correct procedure for the patient, during preadmission workup.
- Adoption of UP was lacking across all specialties, not just surgical specialties.
- Site-marking methods varied greatly.
- Agreement to abort the process and start over if any objections or inconsistencies occurred was lacking.
- There was no repeated "timeout" for every additional procedure on the same patient.
- The patient was not involved in the site marking.
- There was no alternative site-marking process for sites unable or impractical to be marked.
- The Centers for Medicare and Medicaid Services (CMS) stopped payment for wrong-site surgery. Most would agree that hospitals should not be reimbursed for performing wrong-site surgery, which is exactly what CMS announced in 2008. However, experts caution that specifically defining wrong-site, wrong-patient, and wrong-procedure surgery is needed before

reimbursement is withheld. An example is when the site of the surgery is changed during the procedure because additional information is obtained during the procedure, necessitating a change in surgical procedure or site. Premier Inc. urged CMS to better define wrong-site surgery by setting clear boundaries of what is and is not included and to consider an appeal process on a case-by-case basis (Pugliese 2009).

In addition to the major errors in surgery, preventable trivial errors, mistakes, or oversights happen in healthcare. For example, *Reader's Digest* (2008) reported the following statistics:

- Sixty percent of doctors do not follow hand-washing guidelines.
- Ninety-six percent of doctors agree that they should report impaired or incompetent colleagues or those who made serious mistakes, but....
- Forty-six percent of doctors admit to having turned a blind eye at least once.
- Ninety-four percent of doctors have accepted some kind of "freebie" from a drug company.
- Forty-four percent of doctors admit that they are overweight.
- Fifty-eight percent of doctors would give adolescents contraceptives without parental consent.

Finally, to put the errors in perspective, consider statistics from the U.S. Department of Health and Human Services:

- The number of physicians in the United States is about 700,000.
- Accidental deaths (medical error) caused by physicians per year are 120,000.
- Deaths due to medical error per physician are 0.171.

Recognition of the Uninsured

The second issue of healthcare is the concern of the true count of the "uninsured." No single statistic drives the healthcare reform debate like the number of uninsured Americans, variously characterized as 45, 46, 47, or even 50 million. Unfortunately, though, most of what we think we know about the uninsured is wrong. For the record, in 2007 the Census Bureau reported 45.6 million Americans lacked health insurance and in 2008 the Bureau reported that 46.3 million were uninsured. Also see *Income, Poverty, and Health Insurance Coverage in the United States: 2008. U.S. Census Bureau. Issued September 2009.* In both years (2007 and 2008) the number is actually down slightly from the 47 million who were uninsured in 2006.

However, these numbers do not tell the whole story. For example, roughly one-quarter of those counted as uninsured, or 12 million people, are eligible for but have not enrolled in Medicaid or the State Children's Health Insurance Program (S-CHIP). This includes 64% of all uninsured children and 29% of uninsured parents. Since these people would be enrolled in those programs automatically if they went to a hospital for care, calling them "uninsured" is misleading. Also, it is a fact that, upon visiting an emergency facility in the United States, NO ONE—with or without any type of insurance, whether legal or illegal resident—may be turned away due to government regulations.

An additional 10 million uninsured Americans are not American citizens. Approximately 5.6 million of them are illegal immigrants. An additional 4.4 million are legal immigrants who have not been naturalized.

Nor are the uninsured necessarily poor, as one might assume. A study by former Congressional Budget Office (CBO) director June O'Neill found that 43% of the uninsured have incomes above 250% of the poverty level, making at least $55,125 for a family of four. Slightly more than a third have incomes above $66,000. Another study, by Mark Pauly of the University of Pennsylvania and Kate Bundorf of Stanford University, concluded that nearly three-quarters of the uninsured could afford coverage but have chosen not to purchase it. Most of the uninsured are young and in good health. According to the CBO, roughly 60% are under the age of 35, and fully 86% report that they are in good or excellent health (Tanner 2009).

Finally, when we hear about the 45 million Americans without health insurance, the suggestion is that they were all born without health insurance and will die without health insurance. But the reality is that most of them are uninsured only for a relatively short period of time. No more than about 30% of the uninsured remain so for more than a year; 16% go without insurance for at least 2 years and less than 2.5% for 3 years or longer. About half are uninsured for just 6 months or less. Because health insurance is too often tied to employment, the working poor who cycle in and out of the job market also cycle in and out of health insurance (Tanner 2009).

None of this is meant to suggest that those without health insurance do not face severe hardship in many cases, or that we should not try to expand health coverage. But it does mean that we might be able to deal with this problem in a much more targeted way, rather than with a huge, expensive new government program. For example, young, healthy, and well-off people might be more inclined to buy insurance if it cost less. This could be achieved by eliminating regulations that increase the cost of insurance for younger, healthier workers, eliminating costly benefit mandates, and creating more competition by allowing people to purchase insurance across state lines.

Because people are losing their insurance when they lose their jobs, we should move away from a healthcare system dominated by employer-provided insurance. This means changing the tax treatment of health insurance. The current system excludes the value of employer-provided insurance from a worker's taxable income. However, a worker purchasing his or her own health insurance must do so after paying taxes on income. This gives a significant advantage to employer-provided insurance.

Workers should receive a standard deduction, a tax credit, or, better still, large health savings accounts for the purchase of health insurance, regardless of whether they get insurance through their employers or purchase it on their own. After all that, we can begin to look at those who may need some kind of subsidy to afford insurance.

As *all* doctors know, if a diagnosis is not correct, the right treatment will not be prescribed. This also holds true for healthcare reform. So, before we start expanding coverage to those who need it, let us make certain we understand who they are. It is necessary to make sure that the count is the correct one so that we do not react emotionally to a need that perhaps is not necessary and as critical as we may think it is.

Cost of Delivery of Healthcare

The third critical issue is the concern of high cost throughout the healthcare. To begin with, when we view cost in healthcare we must recognize that the total cost is the sum of the doctor's fee, insurance fee, medication, technology, and hospital costs.

Doctor's Fee

Physicians and surgeons held about 633,000 jobs in 2006; approximately 15% were self-employed. About half of wage-and-salary physicians and surgeons worked in offices of physicians, and 18% were employed by hospitals. Others practiced in federal, state, and local governments, including colleges, universities, and professional schools; private colleges, universities, and professional schools; and outpatient care centers.

Reader's Digest (2008) reports the following breakdown for a bill of $100 that a doctor charges for taking 30 minutes to investigate a typical stomach pain. After paying the bills, he gets less than half:

- $3.50 for malpractice insurance
- $3.50 for equipment, repairs, and maintenance
- $6.00 for supplies, including gowns, tongue depressors, and copy paper

- $7.00 for rent and utilities
- $11.00 for office expenses, such as telephones, accounting fees, advertising, medical journals, licenses, and taxes
- $28.00 for secretary, office manager, and medical assistant salaries and benefits
- $41.00 into the doctor's paycheck

Over the course of the year, all these costs add up to $155,000, the annual salary of the average family physician. The number rose just 3.3% between 2002 and 2006, while expenses increased nearly 25% over the same period. As one can see, the doctor's fee is not as bad as people make it out to be.

Another issue of individual doctors' fees is the notion of specialty. Increasing the number of primary care physicians—as opposed to specialists—can reduce the rate of hospitalizations as well as the fee structure. Primary physicians can focus on preventable conditions much better because good outpatient care can potentially thwart the need for hospitalization, and early intervention can curb complications or more severe disease. An example of this is the report by University of Texas researchers who studied bacterial pneumonia, which often strikes the elderly after a bout of flu or a cold. Researchers Lemus, Freeman, and Tan (2009)

> found that hospitalizations for bacterial pneumonia from 1999 to 2000 were three times the national rate in the 32 Texas counties that border Mexico. Additionally, hospitalization rates for Hispanic elders (aged 65 or older) were 41% higher than for white elders. However, *an increase of 1 primary care provider per 1,000 people reduced pneumonia-related hospitalizations by a third in these largely Hispanic communities.* (emphasis added)

The authors noted that "this finding reinforces the importance of primary care physicians in reducing hospitalizations for preventable conditions." The researchers also found:

> Each $1,000 increase in county median household income was associated with a 3.36% increase in the hospitalization rate for bacterial pneumonia. They expected that people with health insurance would be less likely to be hospitalized for bacterial pneumonia, but nearly 96% of Hispanic and white elders were covered by Medicare or Medicaid.
>
> These findings suggest that placing additional primary care physicians in communities may lower the hospitalization rates for this

preventable condition. This measure would, in turn, reduce public health care costs and improve elders' quality of life. This study used hospital discharge, U.S. Census, and Healthcare Cost and Utilization Project data and was funded in part by the Agency for Healthcare Research and Quality (HS16381 and HS11618).

The distribution of doctors in the United States is found in Table 1.2.

There is no question that doctors in the United States have a high salary (see Table 1.3), especially compared with their counterparts abroad. American doctors make, on average, four times what French doctors earn. And it is not just because everyone in America makes more money: The gap between doctors' incomes and those of professionals is far bigger in the United States than elsewhere. In the 1990s, the ratio of the average American doctor's income to the average American employee's income was about 5.5. In Germany, it was 3.4; in Canada, 3.2; in Australia, 2.2; in Switzerland, 2.1; in France, 1.9; in Sweden, 1.5; and in the United Kingdom, 1.4 (Beam 2009).

American doctors' salaries are high for several reasons. The first is the cost of education. In France and Great Britain, students go directly to medical school

Table 1.2   Distribution of Doctors

Percent Distribution of Active Physicians in Patient Care by Specialty, 2005	
Primary care	**40.4**
Family medicine and general practice	12.3
Internal medicine	15.0
Obstetrics and gynecology	5.5
Pediatrics	7.5
Specialties	**59.6**
Anesthesiology	5.2
Psychiatry	5.1
Surgical specialties, selected	10.8
All other specialists	38.5
Total	**100.0**

Source: American Medical Association, Physician Characteristics and Distribution in the U.S., 2007.

Table 1.3 Median Compensation for Physicians, 2005

Specialty	Less than 2 Years in Specialty ($)	Over 1 Year in Specialty ($)
Anesthesiology	259,948	321,686
Surgery: general	228,839	282,504
Obstetrics/gynecology: general	203,270	247,348
Psychiatry: general	173,922	180,000
Internal medicine: general	141,912	166,420
Pediatrics: general	132,953	161,331
Family practice (without obstetrics)	137,119	156,010

Source: Medical Group Management Association, Physician Compensation and Production Report, 2005.

Notes: Salary, bonus and incentive payments, research stipends, honoraria, and distribution of profits were included in total compensation. Self-employed physicians—those who own or are part owners of their medical practice—generally have higher median incomes than salaried physicians. Earnings vary according to number of years in practice, geographic region, hours worked, skill, personality, and professional reputation. Self-employed physicians and surgeons must provide for their own health insurance and retirement. Bureau of Labor Statistics. (Ed.). (August 20, 2009). http://www.bls.gov/oco/ocos074.htm (retrieved on September 12, 2009).

after high school, and their entire educations are free. In the United States, students must first get a bachelor's degree before attending medical school, and the average medical student's debt is $155,000. At least 3 years of residency, which usually pays less than $50,000 a year, follow medical school. After all that, it is no wonder that doctors feel entitled to six-figure salaries.

Another reason that U.S. doctors get paid a lot is market forces. In a single-payer system like the United Kingdom's, the government can bargain down the prices of treatments, which leads to lower income for doctors. No such entity exists in the United States; Medicare is big, but not that big.

Finally, there is the notion of opportunity costs. Presumably, many doctors could have opted for jobs on Wall Street or in management consulting instead of choosing to go to medical school. They could have chosen positions in major companies with starting salaries of $150,000. Instead, most doctors go to medical school to take on $35,000 a year in debt. This leads to a kind of hunger for money to catch up.

But none of this really matters because doctors' salaries are not a large enough chunk of healthcare spending in the United States to make a difference. Beam (2009) reports that the Reinhardt study shows that doctors' net take-home pay (that is, income minus expenses) amounts to only about 10% of overall healthcare spending. (It was originally stated that doctors' take-home pay amounts to 1% of overall healthcare spending. In fact, it is about 10%). So, if that amount were cut by 10% in the name of cost savings, only about $26 billion would be saved—a drop in the ocean compared with overhead for insurance companies, billing expenses for doctors' offices, and advertising for drug companies. The real savings in healthcare will come from cutting these expenses (Beam 2009).

That said, it appears that healthcare reform will have some leveling effect on doctors' salaries. Primary care doctors, for example, make significantly less than specialists. While the median salary of a family doctor is $137,000, the median anesthesiologist salary is $260,000. If one boosts Medicare payments to primary care physicians by about 10%, the theory is that refiguring payment incentives will attract more primary care doctors, which would promote prevention and front-end treatment and reduce the flow of patients to specialists.

The inevitable result: Beam (2009) points out that primary care doctors should get paid a little more and specialists a little less. But even that could be a tough sell. "Whenever you're talking about cutting specialists' pay, you're going to have a lot of resentment," says Kevin Pho, a primary care physician in New Hampshire who writes the blog *KevinMD*. That is why the bills do not explicitly cut specialists' payments. "It's not necessarily that I'm paying this doctor $2 more and this one $2 less," says Ellen-Marie Whelan, a health policy analyst at the Center for American Progress. "It will come from savings within the system." Beyond that, however, it is hard for the government to set physician income. It cannot dictate the costs of treatments as in France or the United Kingdom. It can only negotiate lower prices through Medicare and hope that the rest of the industry follows suit. (It often does.)

That might be a good thing. After all, it is possible to pay doctors too little. In the same way in which many Americans complain about low teacher salaries, chatter about low doctors' salaries is common in France, Greece, Japan, and the United Kingdom. Some would say that it is best to err on the side of overpaying doctors than underpaying them. Moreover, Americans do not seem to mind paying doctors a lot—especially if insurance companies are the ones paying (Beam 2009).

This is why economists do not tend to focus on how much doctors get paid but, rather, on how they are paid. For example, many doctors are paid on a fee-for-service basis: Every time they prescribe a treatment or a test, they get a cut, which incentivizes overspending. If doctors were paid a flat rate for every patient they saw plus a bonus for positive outcomes, this would incentivize better health rather than more spending. None of these solutions is perfect. Fisher (2009) cites Harvard's David Himmelstein and Steffie Woolhandler's report that even paying doctors based on quality measures (using data from medical records that the doctors create) can be fudged. Plus, whichever payment method is used, it does not change the fact that someone, somewhere, will be paid less and will not be happy about it.

Insurance Fee

In the United States, health insurance is regulated by government. Each state controls the offerings and therefore the premiums. This means in no uncertain terms that state bureaucrats approve insurers to their satisfaction. This is very unfortunate because competition is stifled. America's Health Insurance Plans, the industry group generally known as AHIP, says on its Web site that nearly 1,300 insurance providers in the United States cover more than 200 million Americans. But this number includes many plans with the same parent company. Even though the aggregate number is large, in reality, because of regulation, it is not uncommon to have only one or two providers of insurance in a particular state. This causes prices to go higher.

The regulated atmosphere throughout the country has forced insurers to consolidate. In fact, according to the American Medical Association, there have been 400 corporate mergers among insurance providers in the last dozen years. The reader should not be surprised at this because we do operate in a capitalistic economy and insurance companies are in the business to make a profit. So when the supply is not available to accommodate the demand, price goes up.

Price Waterhouse Coopers (PWC) (2006) studied this and found that in the last 20 years, benefit costs have risen 8.7% every year. During the same period, premiums have gone up the same amount, so there was a correlation in the increase of premiums and the cost of the services that are provided. Specifically, the most significant drivers of the increase were consumer demand, new treatments, and more intensive diagnostic testing.

People in developed countries are living longer. The populations of these countries are aging, and a larger group of senior citizens requires more intensive medical care than a younger, healthier population. Advances in medicine and medical technology can also increase the cost of medical treatment. Lifestyle-related factors can increase utilization and therefore insurance prices such as increases in obesity caused by insufficient exercise and unhealthy food choices, excessive alcohol use, smoking, and use of street drugs. Other factors noted by the PWC (2006) study included the movement to broader access plans, higher priced technologies, and cost shifting from Medicaid and the uninsured to private payers.

The U.S. healthcare system relies heavily on private (for-profit) and not-for-profit health insurance, which is the primary source of coverage for most Americans. The U.S. Census Bureau reports that approximately 84% of Americans have health insurance; some 60% obtain it through an employer, while about 9% purchase it directly (Center for Sensible Finance [CSF] 2009). Various government agencies provide coverage to about 27% of Americans (there is some overlap in these figures) (U.S. Census Bureau 2007).

Public programs provide the primary source of coverage for most senior citizens and for low-income children and families who meet certain eligibility requirements. The primary public programs are Medicare, a federal social insurance program for seniors and certain disabled individuals; Medicaid, which is funded jointly by the federal government and states but administered at the state level and covers certain very low-income children and their families; and SCHIP, also a federal–state partnership that serves certain children and families who do not qualify for Medicaid but who cannot afford private coverage. Other public programs include military health benefits provided through TRICARE and the Veterans Health Administration and benefits provided through the Indian Health Service. Some states have additional programs for low-income individuals (U.S. Census Bureau 2008).

Furthermore, the U.S. Census Bureau (2007) reported that, in 2006, about 47 million people in the United States (16% of the population) were without health insurance for at least part of that year. About 37% of the uninsured lived in households with an income over $50,000.

The insurance industry is also exercising a very political presence as a significant lobbying group in the United States. In 2008, insurance was the eighth among industries in political contributions to members of Congress, giving $28,654,121, of which 51% was given to Democrats and 49% to Republicans (healthinsurance.org 2008).

Medication (Prescription Drugs)

The cost of prescription medication keeps rising while consumers' wallets are emptier than ever. There are ways to save on medication or afford a prescription that was previously unaffordable. Many pharmacies now offer low-cost prescription programs, especially for antibiotics. Like everything else in today's world, it is worth the time and energy to shop around and look at all options.

Communicating with the prescribing physician may help in determining whether a more affordable alternative to the medication or samples are available. Doctors can often prescribe a generic medication that is much more cost effective and works just as well as the name-brand medication.

tic medicines are being used more often. However, in some cases, the patient must take the initiative to ask for them because doctors quite often benefit from prescribing costly medicines. Databases now make it possible for pharmaceutical companies to track how often local doctors prescribe their most costly medicines. Then the companies often award them with vacations, lecture fees, research grants, and consulting contracts.

Technology also can play a role in the dispensing of medication. Studies have shown that computerized prescriptions can save lives; the National Institute of Medicine recently reported that prescription errors cause at least 7,000 deaths each year and that electronic prescriptions can reduce those mistakes by catching misdosing and drug–drug interactions. E-prescribing can also cut costs; in 2008, a study from Brigham and Women's Hospital showed that prescribing software that can identify both generic drug options and medications covered by a patient's insurer has the potential to save up to $845,000 for every 100,000 patients each year (Park 2009).

Technology

Proponents of digital medical records say that the issue goes beyond saving paper and money. Technology can save money and many unnecessary tests, and at the same time improve diagnostics. On the other hand, some of the technology is very expensive. For example, among common diagnoses with which technology has had a tremendous success, nonstroke neurologic illnesses such as multiple sclerosis have been associated with the highest out-of-pocket expenditures (mean: $34,167), followed by diabetes ($26,971), injuries ($25,096), stroke ($23,380), mental illnesses ($23,178), and heart disease ($21,955) (Park 2009).

By default, technology has to play a major role in the healthcare industry. The challenge in the twentieth century was a shortage of patient information; on the other hand, now and in the future the challenge will be to handle an overabundance of patient information. Compounding matters is the fact that the human brain, even a physician's brain, cannot keep up with the exponential growth in medical knowledge that will occur in forthcoming years. The ability of most humans to memorize things has remained flat, but the medical knowledge that needs to be assimilated is increasing geometrically.

We already know that suboptimal medical care often is provided to patients because of the failure to access all the data necessary to make the right decision. Now, with technological innovations and breakthroughs, we can improve not only the diagnostics but also the delivery of treatment.

Researchers at the Harvard Law and Medical Schools as well as at Ohio University have reported in the *American Journal of Medicine* that medical bills are involved in more than 60% of U.S. personal bankruptcies—an increase of 50% in just 6 years. More than 75% of these bankrupt families had health insurance but still were overwhelmed by their medical debts. Using a conservative definition, the same researchers found that 62.1% of all bankruptcies in 2007 were medical.

Hospital Costs

Overall spending on medical malpractice litigation comes to about $30 billion a year, or just over 1% of our healthcare spending (Wang 2009). This, of course, is part of the hospital cost, which is passed on to all of us. However, most of the increases in hospital costs are government regulations and are due to the hospitals' inefficiencies throughout their own systems. On the other hand, we must all recognize that hospitals are money machines because, in most cases, they gain a "charity" tax deduction for the difference between what they collect and their "list" prices. If they can actually collect the money, which they often do by threatening collection lawsuits, they make a tremendous profit. If not, then they deduct from taxable income their phantom losses from patients who do not pay.

For example, an ambulance ride with a list cost of $1,000 could bring in $1,000 from a patient who pays or a tax deduction of $1,000 because of the patient who does not, which then can be deducted against other income. Furthermore, the list prices inflate other medical costs. Rooney and Perrin (2008) describe an example of the inflated cost in the case of a Denver hospital patient who tracked down the charges for his treatment paid by Medicare and health insurance companies; these totaled $6,000 compared to the $67,000 the hospital demanded.

How did the current situation happen? The system evolved over recent years as collection methods improved and credit ratings became important for most Americans. The well-meaning tax deduction was legislated when hospitals could not collect from many uninsured patients. Now, however, aggressive pursuit and greater difficulty in declaring personal bankruptcy under new bankruptcy reform laws have made it far easier for hospitals to enforce collections.

Utley (2008) writes that almost no other business in America has such abusive pricing power, including the power to keep charges secret from customers until they get their bills. He continues by quoting the *Wall Street Journal (WSJ)*, describing how "nonprofit" hospitals have accumulated billions of dollars of untaxed profits on the theory that they are providing a public service. The *WSJ* pointed out that many of these hospitals provide very little care to the uninsured, while many of their CEOs earn salaries in the millions. Equally, they have little incentive or competitive pressure to be competent or cost effective.

The "solution" is either socialized medicine (with government control over costs and availability) or competition and transparency. The latter should be the American solution. However, federal and state governments often make competition very difficult. Still, it is slowly appearing. New services advertise basic heart and blood tests for about $200, as compared to more than $2,000 in most hospitals. A new system of "Minute Clinics" is appearing in some CVS drug stores for $59 per visit, and Walmart is starting up similar clinics with $4 generic medicines. These clinics are staffed by nurses and backed up by doctors and databases. They can handle some 80% of common ailments.

However, many states restrict such clinics and the American Medical Association (AMA) is now attacking them. This action may backfire for the AMA and others that attempt to dwarf the trend because the legislators and their constituents have been demanding accessible and affordable healthcare for years. And that is exactly what retailers are delivering as a supplement to the primary care physician. Such systems could provide major savings for many children's sicknesses and save parents immense amounts of time spent waiting for doctor's appointments (Goldstein 2007).

Hospital costs may be reduced by individual health savings accounts, which offer an alternative for some; however, groups are not large enough to challenge hospital costs, especially for emergencies. A major reform would allow health insurance companies to (1) offer insurance without limits of preexisting conditions, and (2) operate nationally across state lines and offer selective coverage or catastrophic coverage (e.g., excluding certain very costly and unlikely diseases or covering extreme diseases or surgeries). In fact, Florida has a new law allowing health insurance choice. A surplus government insurance fund for rare illnesses would reduce insurance costs enormously and cost far less than our current system.

Medicare fraud is another immense waste. Johnson (2008) detailed a report where just one thief with a laptop computer succeeded in stealing $105 million. The report also showed that fraud costs taxpayers some $60 billion yearly because Medicare pays most doctor bills without review. Back (2008) has reported how doctors have incentives to buy expensive equipment and then charge Medicare even more for often unnecessary tests or procedures. Even without fraud, the system encourages older patients to seek out specialists for every ache and prompts doctors to order masses of costly tests to shield themselves from lawsuits. Many operations are also considered unnecessary, with numbers varying tremendously all over the country for the same ailments. Medicaid is another multibillion dollar scandal of waste and fraud.

Yet another contributing factor of increasing costs in the hospital environment is the issue of patients who leave the hospital before they are properly discharged. Stranges et al. (2009) report that the number of hospital stays that ended with patients leaving against the advice of medical staff increased from

264,000 cases to 368,000—about 39%—between 1997 and 2007. The report used statistics from the 2007 Nationwide Inpatient Sample, a database of hospital inpatient stays that is nationally representative of inpatient stays in all short-term, nonfederal hospitals. The data are drawn from hospitals that comprise 90% of all discharges in the United States and include all patients, regardless of insurance type, as well as the uninsured. For cases in which patients left against medical advice in 2007, the federal agency also found the following:

- The top five diagnoses of those leaving early were chest pain with no determined cause (25,600), alcohol-related disorders (25,300), substance-related disorders (21,000), depression or other mood disorders (13,900), and diabetes with complications (12,500).
- Medicaid and Medicare patients each accounted for about 27% and privately insured patients accounted for 19% of those leaving prematurely. About 22% of the cases in 2007 involved uninsured patients.
- Men were roughly 1.5 times more likely to leave against medical advice than women were.
- In the Northeast, patients left hospitals against medical advice at twice the rate of that of the rest of the country: 2 per 1,000 population versus an average of 1 per 1,000 population in all other regions.

Why is all this not being debated? For one reason, some of the richest and most powerful lobbies in the states and Washington, D.C., are run by the medical, insurance, and pharmaceutical establishments. They do not want a competitive system. Democrats do propose forcing everyone to "buy" high-cost insurance, while continuing with the current system, and then having taxpayers subsidize premiums for the poor. But they also oppose tort reform, which would hurt their trial lawyer political allies. On the other hand, many Republicans benefit from the same medical, insurance, and pharmaceutical lobbies and do not want to change the status quo.

Efficiency

We need to rethink healthcare reform. For sure, looking at doctors' fees, insurance premiums, cost of covering the uninsured, introduction of technological innovations, medical prescriptions, and other items is not enough. The future focus must be on developing cost-effective and error-free delivery systems, improved diagnostics and treatments, and efficient and accurate computational technologies for medicine, in addition to accessibility and insurance practices. Table 1.4 shows some areas where improvement may be pursued.

Table 1.4 The 11 Best Practice Tracks

Healthcare	Quality
Safety—personal and process safety	Safety—personal and process safety
Management systems	Management system (quality manual, procedures, and instructions)
Performance measurement	Key process characteristics
Change management (behavior)	Change management
Human error	Mistake proofing
Root cause analysis	Problem solving
Corrective action program	Corrective action
Operations excellence	International standards or national awards (i.e., ISO or Baldrige)
Training (personnel and trainers)	Training
Elimination of sentinel events[a]	Mistake proofing and/or design robustness
Equipment reliability and maintenance	Measurement system analysis and overall equipment effectiveness

[a] A sentinel event is an unexpected occurrence involving death or serious physical or psychological injury, or the risk thereof. Serious injury specifically includes loss of limb or function. The phrase, "or the risk thereof," includes any process variation for which a recurrence would carry a significant chance of a serious adverse outcome. Such events are called "sentinel" because they signal the need for immediate investigation and response (Joint Commission: Joint Committee on Accreditation of Healthcare Organizations—JCAHO).

Medical cost reform is just one of many areas where state and federal representatives are corrupt and paralyzed, in particular because of the gerrymandered power structure, whereby sitting congressmen are almost invulnerable to defeat. They then legally collect millions in campaign contributions from the pertinent lobbies. Reform will only come if Americans become better informed through better and complete media coverage about health costs.

Reform depends also upon major corporations attacking the current system, such as Walmart and others who have started to do this with in-store clinics. But most companies are silent and afraid to tackle the medical power structure. The Chamber of Commerce and National Federation of Independent Businesses seem reluctant to challenge both the monopolies and the current system. Lessons from the experiences of other nations are certainly available, and then can be used to improve our healthcare to be even better than it is now.

Promoting competition and explaining to Americans how choice and disclosure will lower costs and provide greater accessibility, especially for the uninsured, is a vote-getting issue. Current medical costs already absorb twice the percentage of gross domestic product as they do in Europe. They are helping to bankrupt America.

Summary

In this chapter, we have discussed the critical issues of healthcare and elaborated on some of the difficulties for improvement. We separated the issues based on those about which we can do something as opposed to those that need legal intervention through either federal or state government. In the next chapter, we will focus on the direction of improvement in the three major categories of healthcare.

References

Back, P. B. July 24, 2008. Paying doctors to ignore patients. *The New York Times*. http://www.nytimes.com/2008/07/24/opinion/24bach.html?_r=4&partner=rssuserland&emc=rss&pagewanted=all&oref=slogin&oref=slogin (retrieved on September 7, 2009).

Beam, C. September 10, 2009. Let's pay doctor: Couldn't we fix the health care system by paying doctors less?" http://www.slate.com/id/2227965/?gt1=38001 (retrieved on September 12, 2009).

Center for Sensible Finance. July 2009. http://www.sensiblefinance.org/?page_id=46 (retrieved on September 3, 2009).

Dillon, K. A. 2008. Time out: An analysis. *AORN Journal* 88 (3): 437–442.

Edwards, P. 2008. Ensuring correct site surgery. *Journal of Perioperative Practice* 18 (4): 168–171.

Fisher, E. S. June 18, 2009. Doctors' pay, a key to health care reform. *New York Times*. http://roomfordebate.blogs.nytimes.com/2009/06/18/better-medical-care-for-less/ (retrieved on September 14, 2009).

Goldstein, J. June 26, 2007. AMA calls for investigation of retail clinics. http://blogs.wsj.com/health/2007/06/26 (retrieved on September 4, 2009).

Harrington, J. W. 2009. Surgical time outs in a combat zone. *AORN Journal* 89 (3): 535–537.

Health-insurance.org. April 2008. Health care and insurance dominate the Washington lobby. http://www.health-insurance.org/health-insurance-lobbyists (retrieved on September 3, 2009).

Johnson, C. June 13, 2008. Medical fraud a growing problem: Medicare pays most claims without review. *The Washington Post*. http://www.washingtonpost.com/wp-dyn/content/article/2008/06/12/AR2008061203915.html (retrieved on August 31, 2009).

Lemus, F. C., J. L. Freeman, and A. Tan. March 18, 2009. Correlates of bacterial pneumonia hospitalizations in elders, Texas border. *Journal of Immigrant and Minority Health* (e-pub). http://www.ahrq.gov/research/sep09/0909RA17.htm (retrieved on July 6, 2009).

Norton, E. 2007. Implementing the universal protocol hospital-wide. *AORN Journal* 85 (6): 1187–1197.

Park, A. March 14, 2009. The move to digital medical records begins in Tampa. http://eflorida.com/uploadedFiles/Innovation_Center/Innovation_Buzz/E-MedicalRecords-Tampa-TIME.pdf (p. 24).

Price Waterhouse Coopers. 2006. The factors fueling rising healthcare costs 2006. Price Waterhouse Coopers for America's Health Insurance Plans http://www.ahip.org/redirect/PwCCostOfHC2006.pdf (retrieved on August 31, 2009).

Pugliese, G. 2009. Transforming healthcare. http://www.premierinc.com/quality-safety/tools-services/safety/safety-share/08-09-full.jsp#downloads-5#downloads-5 (retrieved on September 7, 2009).

Reader's Digest. 2008. Healthcare. July: 125–126.

Ridge, R. A. 2008. Doing right to prevent wrong-site surgery. *Nursing* 38 (3): 24–25.

Rooney, J. P., and D. Perrin. 2008. *America's health care crisis solved.* New York: John Wiley & Sons.

Stranges, E., L. Wier, C. T. Merrill, and C. Steiner. August 19, 2009. Patients increasingly leaving hospitals against medical advice. *AHRQ News and Numbers*. Agency for Healthcare Research and Quality, Rockville, MD. http://www.ahrq.gov/news/nn/nn081909.htm (retrieved on September 7, 2009).

Tanner, M. August 20, 2009. *The Philadelphia Inquirer.* http://www.philly.com/inquirer/opinion/20090820_A_true_count_of_the_uninsured_html (retrieved on August 26, 2009).

U.S. Census Bureau. 2007. Income, poverty, and health insurance coverage in the United States: 2006. Issued August 2007. http://www.census.gov/prod/2007pubs/p60–233.pdf (retrieved on September 4, 2009).

———. 2008. CPS health insurance definitions. http://www.census.gov/hhes/www/hlthins/hlthinstypes.html (retrieved on September 3, 2009).

———. May 10, 2009. http://www.factcheck.org/2009/03/uninsured-us-citizens/ (retrieved on March 3, 2010).

———. September 29, 2009. http://www.census.gov/prod/2009pubs/p60-236.pdf (retrieved on February 14, 2010).

———. 2009. *Income, Poverty, and Health Insurance Coverage in the United States*: 2008. Issued September 2009.

U.S. Department of Health and Human Services. http://www.ahrq.gov/qual/errorsix.htm (retrieved on January 15, 2010).

Utley, J. B. August 4, 2008. How hospital costs ran amok. http://www.reason.com/news/show/127821.html (retrieved on September 1, 2009).

Wang, S. S. September 3, 2009. Putting a price on defensive medicine. http://blogs.wsj.com/health/2009/09/03 (retrieved on September 4, 2009).

Selected Bibliography

Anon. 2006. Wrong site surgery and the universal protocol. *Bulletin of the American College of Surgery* 91 (11): 63.

Catalano, K. 2008. Have you heard? The saga of wrong site surgery continues. *Plastic Surgery Nursing* 28 (1): 41–44.

Clarke, J. R., J. Johnston, and E. D. Finley. 2007. Getting surgery right. *Annals of Surgery* 246 (3): 395–403.

Clarke, J. R., J. Johnston, D. P. Martindell, and M. Blanco. 2008. Wrong-site surgery: Can we prevent it? *Advances in Surgery* 42: 13–31.

Hunter, J. G. 2007. Extend the universal protocol, not just the surgical time out. *Journal of the American College of Surgeons* 205 (4): e4–5.

Jhawar, B. S., D. Mitsis, and N. Duggal. 2007. Wrong-sided and wrong-level neurosurgery: A national survey. *Journal of Neurosurgery: Spine* 7 (5): 467–472.

Seiden, S. C., and P. Barach. 2006. Wrong-side/wrong-site, wrong-procedure, and wrong-patient adverse events: Are they preventable? *Archives of Surgery* 141 (9): 931–939.

Trott, B. n.d. Medical bills underlie 60 percent of U.S. bankruptcies. *Health and Science.* http://www.thefreelibrary.com (retrieved on August 15, 2009).

van Hille, P. T. 2009. Patient safety with particular reference to wrong site surgery—A presidential commentary. *British Journal of Neurosurgery* 23 (2): 109–110.

Chapter 2

Directions of Improvement in Healthcare

Introduction

In the last chapter, we introduced and discussed the critical issues of healthcare. In this chapter, we discuss the three directions of improvement within healthcare. Reforming healthcare has been discussed by many for a very long time. However, not too much has happened because government regulations and quality principles of improvement have not really been at the core of the *improvement* discussion. Fundamentally, three areas of concern should be examined in the journey of improvement:

- Primary care
- Hospital care
- Managed care

Primary Care

So far we have indicated that by improving and providing access to primary care, we can definitely improve both cost and satisfaction. But what exactly is improvement in primary care? Many states, including Colorado, Pennsylvania, North

Carolina, Michigan, Washington, Minnesota, and Wisconsin, have started programs to help individual practices incorporate quality tools and methodology in solving some of their problems. The objectives of these programs are to

- Improve the patient experience in primary care, including engaging patients in self-management activities
- Improve primary care quality and outcomes using collaborative activities, educational resources, and coaching within the practice
- Apply evidence-based guidelines consistently in care of patients
- Use technology to improve practice processes, with an emphasis on use of the patient registry
- Reduce waste in the medical practice, with the outcome of increasing clinician time with patients
- Improve pay-for-performance metrics
- Move practices toward the patient-centered medical home concept

In the state of Michigan, for example, a formal program has been developed through the Michigan Partnership for Community Caring (MPCC) and the Automotive Industry Action Group (AIAG) that recruits Michigan-based primary care medical practices to participate in the Michigan improving performance in practice (IPIP)/patient-centered medical home (PCMH) project. This initiative is a state-based quality improvement approach and it is funded in large part by the Robert Wood Johnson Foundation and sponsored by the American Board of Medical Specialties. The program was developed in collaboration with the national primary care specialty societies to help physicians improve chronic disease and preventive care in the office-practice setting. It focuses on the following:

- Disease registries
- Work flow analysis
- Chronic care model
- Team building and communication
- Implementation of systems change
- Quality improvement principles
- Advanced access scheduling
- Population-based care management

A practice participating in this type of a program benefits in many ways, including:

- Assistance to practices in maximizing their physician group incentive program (PGIP) incentives and pay-for-performance (P4P) requirements

- Increased efficiency in office processes
- Improved care of chronically ill patients, as well as increased patient and staff satisfaction
- Advance practices toward PCMH designation
- Help to physicians in maintenance of certification (MOC) and continuing medical education (CME) credits and to others on the practice staff with continuing education credit, offering a positive economic impact

Michigan IPIP/PCMH is unique; it involves physicians from multiple-specialty organizations, as well as government stakeholders. It engages improvement teams within the practice that will be coached by quality experts from industrial settings. The coaches receive special training in the healthcare culture and assist the practice to implement quality principles and ultimately improve the physician's practice. The focus of this training is to identify value-added processes and eliminate waste, therefore streamlining the overall cost of the practice. While the focus is initially on the practice's chronic diseases, such as diabetes and hypertension, over time it will expand to apply to all patients and will include asthma as well. The training of the quality coach is provided on a volunteer basis and at no cost to the practice.

Hospital Care

In the last chapter, we addressed some of the hospital issues as they relate to cost and quality. We are not unique in our observations. However, here we are addressing some of the items that hospitals can do or address in a prevention mode to curtail their cost and improve overall quality and customer satisfaction. The basis for our discussion can be found on the Internet site http://www.qualityindicators.ahrq.gov/pqi_download.htm.

The items of concern are called the *prevention quality indicators* (PQIs) and are a set of measures that can be used with hospital inpatient discharge data to identify quality of care for "ambulatory care–sensitive conditions." These are conditions for which good outpatient care can potentially prevent the need for hospitalization or for which early intervention can prevent complications or more severe disease. They have been identified by the Agency for Healthcare Research and Quality (AHRQ). *Quality indicators* (QIs) expand the original Healthcare Cost and Utilization Project (HCUP) QIs. The PQIs were released in November 2001 and they were revised in 2004, 2006, 2007, 2008, and in June 2009. The *inpatient quality indicators* (IQIs), the second set, were released in May 2002. The third set, the *patient safety indicators* (PSIs), was released in March 2003.

The prevention quality indicators represent hospital admission rates for the following 14 ambulatory care–sensitive conditions. The items in parentheses are the specific numerical indicators:

■ Diabetes, short-term complications (PQI 1)
■ Perforated appendicitis (PQI 2)
■ Diabetes, long-term complications (PQI 3)
■ Chronic obstructive pulmonary disease (PQI 5)
■ Hypertension (PQI 7)
■ Congestive heart failure (PQI 8)
■ Low birth weight (PQI 9)
■ Dehydration (PQI 10)
■ Bacterial pneumonia (PQI 11)
■ Urinary infections (PQI 12)
■ Angina without procedure (PQI 13)
■ Uncontrolled diabetes (PQI 14)
■ Adult asthma (PQI 15)
■ Lower extremity amputations among patients with diabetes (PQI 16)

With high-quality, community-based primary care, hospitalization for these illnesses often can be avoided; therefore, costs and improvement can be realized in real terms since they are all measurable. Although other factors outside the direct control of the healthcare system, such as poor environmental conditions or lack of patient adherence to treatment recommendations, can result in hospitalization, the PQIs provide a good starting point for assessing quality of health services in the community. Because the PQIs are calculated using readily available hospital administrative data, they are easy to use and an inexpensive screening tool. They can be used to provide a window into the community—to identify unmet community healthcare needs, to monitor how well complications from a number of common conditions are being avoided in the outpatient setting, and to compare performance of local healthcare systems across communities.

Obviously, these QIs provide an overview of the methods used to identify, select, and evaluate the AHRQ QIs, a summary of the literature-based evidence, empirical rates based on the state inpatient databases, and detailed definitions for each PQI. Potential users of these data include hospitals, state data organizations, and hospital associations because they are (1) population based and adjusted for age and sex, and (2) publicly available without cost. Specifically, they can be used as

■ Screening tools to help flag potential healthcare quality problem areas that need further investigation

- Tools to provide a quick check on primary care access or outpatient services in a community by using patient data found in a typical hospital discharge abstract
- Databases to help public health agencies, state data organizations, healthcare systems, and others interested in improving healthcare quality in their communities

On the other hand, the inpatient quality indicators are a set of measures that provide a perspective on hospital quality of care using hospital administrative data (see Table 2.1). These indicators reflect quality of care inside hospitals and include inpatient mortality for certain procedures and medical conditions; utilization of procedures for which there are questions of overuse, underuse, and misuse; and volume of procedures for which there is some evidence that a higher volume of procedures is associated with lower mortality. Generally, IQIs

- Can be used to help hospitals identify potential problem areas that might need further study
- Provide the opportunity to assess quality of care inside the hospital using administrative data found in the typical discharge record
- Include 15 mortality indicators for conditions or procedures for which mortality can vary from hospital to hospital
- Include 11 utilization indicators for procedures for which utilization varies across hospitals or geographic areas
- Include six volume indicators for procedures for which outcomes may be related to the volume of those procedures performed
- Are publicly available without cost

In addition to the IQIs, AHRQ has identified two other areas of monitoring and/or measure for improvement: *patient safety indicators* and *pediatric quality indicators*. A summary of the PSIs and PQIs is shown in Table 2.2.

The patient safety indicators' QIs measure healthcare quality by using readily available hospital inpatient administrative data. The PSIs are a tool to help health system leaders identify potential adverse events occurring during hospitalization. To do that, they include (1) 20 indicators for complications occurring in hospital that may represent patient safety events, and (2) 7 indicators with area-level analogs designed to detect patient safety events on a regional level.

The PSIs were released in March 2003. In February 2006, the fourth QI module, the pediatric quality indicators, was added and the pediatric population was removed from the other modules. Both are free and publicly available. The PSIs provide a perspective on patient safety events using hospital administrative data, which are readily available and relatively inexpensive to use. The PSIs can be used to

Table 2.1 The Inpatient Quality Indicators

IQIs	Individual Measures
Mortality rates for medical conditions	• Acute myocardial infarction (AMI) (IQI 15) • AMI, without transfer cases (IQI 32) • Congestive heart failure (IQI 16) • Stroke (IQI 17) • Gastrointestinal hemorrhage (IQI 18) • Hip fracture (IQI 19) • Pneumonia (IQI 20)
Mortality rates for surgical procedures	• Esophageal resection (IQI 8) • Pancreatic resection (IQI 9) • Abdominal aortic aneurysm repair (IQI 11) • Coronary artery bypass graft (IQI 12) • Percutaneous transluminal coronary angioplasty (IQI 30) • Carotid endarterectomy (IQI 31) • Craniotomy (IQI 13) • Hip replacement (IQI 14)
Hospital-level procedure utilization rates	• Cesarean section delivery (IQI 21) • Primary Cesarean delivery (IQI 33) • Vaginal birth after Cesarean (VBAC), uncomplicated (IQI 22) • VBAC, all (IQI 34) • Laparoscopic cholecystectomy (IQI 23) • Incidental appendectomy in the elderly (IQI 24) • Bilateral cardiac catheterization (IQI 25)
Area-level utilization rates	• Coronary artery bypass graft (IQI 26) • Percutaneous transluminal coronary angioplasty (IQI 27) • Hysterectomy (IQI 28) • Laminectomy or spinal fusion (IQI 29)

Table 2.1   The Inpatient Quality Indicators (Continued)

IQIs	Individual Measures
Volume of procedures	• Esophageal resection (IQI 1)
	• Pancreatic resection (IQI 2)
	• Abdominal aortic aneurysm repair (IQI 4)
	• Coronary artery bypass graft (IQI 5)
	• Percutaneous transluminal coronary angioplasty (IQI 6)
	• Carotid endarterectomy (IQI 7)

- Help hospitals identify potential adverse events that might need further study
- Provide the opportunity to assess the incidence of adverse events and in-hospital complications using administrative data found in the typical discharge record

On the other hand, the PQIs are a set of measures that can be used with hospital inpatient discharge data to provide a perspective on the quality of pediatric healthcare. Specifically, PQIs screen for problems that pediatric patients experience as a result of exposure to the healthcare system that may be amenable to prevention by changes at the system or provider level. The PQIs provide a perspective on patient safety events using hospital administrative data, which are readily available and relatively inexpensive to use. Specifically, they

- Apply to the special characteristics of the pediatric population
- Screen for problems that pediatric patients experience as a result of exposure to the healthcare system that may be amenable to prevention by changes at the provider level or area level
- Help to evaluate preventive care for children in an outpatient setting (most children are rarely hospitalized)

Managed Care

The term *managed care* is used to describe a variety of techniques intended to reduce the cost of providing health benefits and improve the quality of care (managed care techniques) for organizations that use those techniques or provide them as services to other organizations (managed care organizations [MCOs]), or to describe systems of financing and delivering healthcare to

Table 2.2   Patient Safety Indicators and Pediatric Quality Indicators

Patient Safety Indicator	Measurement	Pediatric Quality Indicator	Measurement
Hospital-level patient safety indicators (20 indicators)	• Complications of anesthesia (PSI 1) • Death in low mortality DRGs (PSI 2) • Decubitus ulcer (PSI 3) • Failure to rescue (PSI 4) • Foreign body left in during procedure (PSI 5) • Iatrogenic pneumothorax (PSI 6) • Selected infections due to medical care (PSI 7) • Postoperative hip fracture (PSI 8) • Postoperative hemorrhage or hematoma (PSI 9) • Postoperative physiologic and metabolic derangements (PSI 10)	Provider-level pediatric quality indicators (13 indicators)	• Accidental puncture or laceration (PDI 1) • Decubitus ulcer (PDI 2) • Foreign body left in during procedure (PDI 3) • Iatrogenic pneumothorax in neonates at risk (PDI 4) • Iatrogenic pneumothorax in non-neonates (PDI 5) • Pediatric heart surgery mortality (PDI 6) • Pediatric heart surgery volume (PDI 7) • Postoperative hemorrhage or hematoma (PDI 8) • Postoperative respiratory failure (PDI 9) • Postoperative sepsis (PDI 10) • Postoperative wound dehiscence (PDI 11) • Selected infections due to medical care (PDI 12) • Transfusion reaction (PDI 13)

Table 2.2   Patient Safety Indicators and Pediatric Quality Indicators (Continued)

Patient Safety Indicator	Measurement	Pediatric Quality Indicator	Measurement
	• Postoperative respiratory failure (PSI 11)		
	• Postoperative pulmonary embolism or deep vein thrombosis (PSI 12)		
	• Postoperative sepsis (PSI 13)		
	• Postoperative wound dehiscence in abdominopelvic surgical patients (PSI 14)		
	• Accidental puncture and laceration (PSI 15)		
	• Transfusion reaction (PSI 16)		
	• Birth trauma— injury to neonate (PSI 17)		
	• Obstetric trauma—vaginal delivery with instrument (PSI 18)		

(Continued)

Table 2.2   Patient Safety Indicators and Pediatric Quality Indicators (Continued)

Patient Safety Indicator	Measurement	Pediatric Quality Indicator	Measurement
	• Obstetric trauma— vaginal delivery without instrument (PSI 19) • Obstetric trauma— cesarean delivery (PSI 20)		
Area-level patient safety indicators (seven indicators)	• Foreign body left in during procedure (PSI 21) • Iatrogenic pneumothorax (PSI 22) • Selected infections due to medical care (PSI 23) • Postoperative wound dehiscence in abdominopelvic surgical patients (PSI 24) • Accidental puncture and laceration (PSI 25)	Area-level pediatric quality indicators (five indicators)	• Asthma admission rate (PDI 14) • Diabetes short-term complication rate (PDI 15) • Gastroenteritis admission rate (PDI 16) • Perforated appendix admission rate (PDI 17) • Urinary tract infection admission rate (PDI 18)

Table 2.2   Patient Safety Indicators and Pediatric Quality Indicators (Continued)

Patient Safety Indicator	Measurement	Pediatric Quality Indicator	Measurement
	• Transfusion reaction (PSI 26) • Postoperative hemorrhage or hematoma (PSI 27)		

enrollees organized around managed care techniques and concepts (managed care delivery systems). According to the National Library of Medicine, the term "managed care" encompasses programs

> intended to reduce unnecessary health care costs through a variety of mechanisms, including: economic incentives for physicians and patients to select less costly forms of care; programs for reviewing the medical necessity of specific services; increased beneficiary cost sharing; controls on inpatient admissions and lengths of stay; the establishment of cost-sharing incentives for outpatient surgery; selective contracting with health care providers; and the intensive management of high-cost health care cases. The programs may be provided in a variety of settings, such as health maintenance organizations (HMOs) and preferred provider organizations (PPOs). (Gartner 2009)

As one can see, the possibility of improvement is great in any one of the defined scopes that the term *managed care* encompasses. The issue now becomes whether the people involved in these decisions are willing and able to drive these improvements into the system.

The growth of managed care in the United States was spurred by the enactment of the Health Maintenance Organization Act of 1973. While managed care techniques were pioneered by health maintenance organizations, they are now used by a variety of private health benefit programs. Managed care is now nearly ubiquitous in the United States, but it has attracted controversy because it has largely failed in the overall goal of controlling medical costs. Proponents and critics are also sharply divided on managed care's overall impact on the quality of U.S. healthcare delivery.

One of the most characteristic forms of managed care is the use of a panel or network of healthcare providers to provide care to enrollees. Such integrated delivery systems typically include one or more of the following:

■ A set of selected providers that furnish a comprehensive array of healthcare services to enrollees
■ Explicit standards for selecting providers
■ Formal utilization review and quality improvement programs
■ An emphasis on preventive care
■ Financial incentives to encourage enrollees to use care efficiently (Kongstvedt 2001; Lynch 1992; Insurance Association of America 1995; DesRoches et al. 2008; Miller et al. 2005)

Provider networks can be used to reduce costs by negotiating favorable fees from providers, selecting cost-effective providers, and creating financial incentives for providers to practice more efficiently (Kongstvedt 2001; Insurance Association of America 1995). A survey issued in 2009 by America's Health Insurance Plans found that patients going to out-of-network providers are sometimes charged extremely high fees (Kolata 2009; America's Health Insurance Plans 2009; Insurance Association of America 1995; Lynch 1992). Other managed care techniques include disease management, case management, wellness incentives, patient education, utilization management, and utilization review. These techniques can be applied to both network-based benefit programs and benefit programs that are not based on a provider network. The use of managed care techniques without a provider network is sometimes described as "managed indemnity."

The overall impact of managed care remains widely debated. Proponents argue that it has increased efficiency, improved overall standards, and led to a better understanding of the relationship between costs and quality. They argue that there is no consistent, direct correlation between the cost of care and its quality, pointing to a 2002 Juran Institute study that estimated that the "cost of poor quality" caused by overuse, misuse, and waste amounts to 30% of all direct healthcare spending (Price Waterhouse Coopers 2008). The emerging practice of evidence-based medicine is being used to determine when lower cost medicine may in fact be more effective.

Critics of managed care argue that "for-profit" managed care has been an unsuccessful health policy because it has contributed to higher healthcare costs (25–33% higher overhead at some of the largest HMOs), increased the number of uninsured citizens, driven away healthcare providers, and applied downward pressure on quality (worse scores on 14 of 14 quality indicators reported to the National Committee for Quality Assurance) (Himmelstein et al. 1999; *U.S. News and World Report* 1997; Kuttner 1999).

The most common managed care financial arrangement, *capitation,* places healthcare providers in the role of micro health insurers, assuming the responsibility for managing the unknown future healthcare costs of their patients. Unfortunately, large health insurers manage such risks better, in the sense of predictable costs, than small insurers do. Small insurers, like individual consumers, tend to have annual costs that fluctuate far more than those of larger insurers. Cox (2006) and Blakely (1998) explain the term "professional caregiver insurance risk" as the inefficiencies in healthcare finance that result when insurance risks are inefficiently transferred to healthcare providers who are expected to cover such costs in return for their capitation payments. As Cox further demonstrates, providers cannot be adequately compensated for their insurance risks without forcing managed care organizations to become price uncompetitive vis-a-vis risk-retaining insurers. A health insurance plan with the same features as traditional indemnity coverage except for limited implementation of cost containment or managed care concepts is an option.

Summary

In this chapter, we have given an overview of the three fundamental directions of improvement in healthcare by addressing the issues of primary care, managed care, and hospitals. In the next chapter, we begin the discussion of change and the requirements for understanding it.

References

America's Health Insurance Plans. August 2009. The value of provider networks and the role of out-of-network charges in rising health care costs: A survey of charges billed by out-of-network physicians. America's Health Insurance Plans. http://www.ahipresearch.org/PDFs/ValueSurvey/AllStatesReport.pdf

Blakely, S. July 1998. The backlash against managed care. *Nation's Business.* http://findarticles.com/p/articles/mi_m1154/is_n7_v86/ai_20797610/pg_2/ (retrieved on September 14, 2009).

Cox, T. 2006. Professional caregiver insurance risk: A brief primer for nurse executives and decision makers. *Nurse Leader* 4 (2): 48–51.

DesRoches, C., E. Campbell, et al. 2008. Electronic health records in ambulatory care—A national survey of physicians. *New England Journal of Medicine* 359: 50–60.

Gartner, I. T. February 24, 2009. Spending to grow 2.6%. Health data management. http://www.healthdatamanagement.com/news/I.T._spending27781-1.html? (retrieved on June 20, 2009).

Himmelstein, D., U. S. Woolhandler, I. Hellander, and S. I. Wolfe. (1999). Quality of care in investor owned versus non profit HMOs. *Journal of the American Medical Association* 282: 159.

Insurance Association of America. 1995. *Managed care: Integrating the delivery and financing of health care—Part A. Health.* Washington, D.C.: Insurance Association of America.

Kolata, G. August 11, 2009. Survey finds high fees common in medical care. *The New York Times,* p. 1.

Kongstvedt, P. R. 2001. *The managed health care handbook,* 4th ed. Aspen, CO: Aspen Publishers, Inc.

Kuttner, R. 1999. The American healthcare system: Wall Street and healthcare. *New England Journal of Medicine* 340: 664.

Lynch, M. E., ed. 1992. *Health insurance terminology.* Washington, D.C.: Health Insurance Association of America.

Miller R., C. West, et al. 2005. The value of electronic health records in solo or small group practices. *Health Affairs* 24 (5): 1127–1137.

National Library of Medicine. n.d. Managed + care. http://www.ncbi.nlm.nih.gov/sites/entrez?db=mesh&term (retrieved on February 2, 2009).

Price Waterhouse Coopers. December 2008. The factors fueling rising health costs 2008. Report prepared by Price Waterhouse Coopers for America's Health Insurance Plans. http://www.americanhealthsolution.org/assets/Reform-Resources/Cost-Trends-and-Cost-Shifting/risinghealthcarecostsfactors2008.pdf (retrieved on September 14, 2009).

U.S. News and World Report. 1997. HMO honor roll. October 23, p. 62.

Selected Bibliography

American Medical News. November 3, 2008. Slow adoption of e-prescribing forces Medicare to try hard sell. http://www.ama-assn.org/amednews/2008/11/03/gvl21103.htm (retrieved on February 2, 2009).

———. December 10, 2007. Tax credits for EMRs. http://www.amaassn.org/amed news/2007/12/10/edsa1210.htm (retrieved on September 9, 2009).

America's Health Insurance Plans. 2008. Fast facts. HealthDecisions.org. http://www.healthdecisions.org/LearningCenter/Facts.aspx (retrieved on July 7, 2009).

Chute, C. November 1995. Moving toward international standards in primary care informatics. www.ahrq.gov/research/pcinform/dept3.htm (retrieved on August 15, 2009).

Crosson, J. C., P. A. Ohman-Strickland, K. A. Hahn, B. DiCicco-Bloom, E. Shaw, A. J. Orzano, and B. F. Crabtree. 2007. Electronic medical records and diabetes quality of care: Results from a sample of family medicine practices. *Annals of Family Medicine* 5 (3): 209–215.

Gill, J. M., Ewen, E., and Nsereko, M. 2001. Impact of an electronic medical record on quality of care in a primary care office. *Delaware Medical Journal* 73 (5): 187–194.

Henry J. Kaiser Foundation. June 2004, 2006, 2008. Kaiser public opinion spotlight: The public, managed care and consumer protections. http://www.kff.org/spotlight/managedcare/index (retrieved on October 10, 2009).

———. August 2007. *Health care costs: A primer.* Menlo Park, CA: Kaiser Family Foundation Health Care Marketplace Project.

Jollis, J. G., M. Ancukiewicz, E. R. DeLong, D. B. Pryor, L. H. Muhlbaier, and D. B. Mark. 1993. Discordance of databases designed for claims payout versus clinical information systems: Implications for outcomes research. *Annals of Internal Medicine* 119 (8): 844–850.

Kaiser Family Foundation Health Care Marketplace Project. September 2007. Trends in health care costs and spending. http://www.kff.org/insurance/7692.cfm (retrieved on March 24, 2009).

Linder, J. A., Ma, J., et al. 2007. Electronic health record use and the quality of ambulatory care in the United States. *Archives of Internal Medicine* 167 (13): 1400–1405.

Peabody, J. W., J. Luck, S. Jain, D. Bertenthal, and P. Glassman. 2004. Assessing the accuracy of administrative data in health information systems. *Medical Care* 42 (11): 1066–1072.

Phillips, R., and M. Klinkman. May 20, 2008. Health IT to support the patient-centered medical home. www.ncvhs.hhs.gov/071127p1.pdf (retrieved on July 28, 2009).

Schellhase, K. G., T. D. Koepsell, and T. E. Norris. 2003. Providers' reactions to an automated health maintenance reminder system incorporated into the patient's electronic medical record. *Journal of the American Board of Family Practice* 16 (4): 350–351.

White, K. 1967. Improved medical care statistics and the health services system. *Public Health Reports* 82 (10): 847–854.

Chapter 3

The Mechanics of Change

Introduction

In the last two chapters, we addressed the fundamental issues of healthcare and discussed some of the specific areas of improvement. In this chapter, we introduce the mechanics of change. Whereas change may be instituted by one individual, the most effective way to change and keep that change in place is through teams. Specifically, here we are going to address the concept of working together for a common goal of improvement.

Any type of improvement in any organization means change. The change may be simple or complex, small or large. In simple terms, change implies that something will be different from the status quo. However, that change may be better or worse than the status quo.

Hopefully, by using quality principles, change will result in improvement and, consequently, in better results across the organization. The change concept is a general notion or approach that has been found to be useful in developing specific ideas for change in many organizations that have indeed resulted in improvement. Using this change concept in healthcare will provoke new ways of thinking about the problem at hand.

One of the basic principles in the journey of improvement is the concept of cross-functional and multidisciplinary teams. It is the root of a system that, if understood and implemented correctly, will benefit the organization at any level. A summary of the approach of doing work with teams is shown in Table 3.1. It

Table 3.1 Beliefs about Work

Traditional Beliefs about Work	New Beliefs about Work
Power structure is from top down	Power is shared and not based on position
Supervision/control is necessary	People can manage themselves
Respect for authority is expected	Outcome/accomplishment is respected
Postponement of gratification is the norm	Short-term reward is more important
Sacrifice for the organization is expected	Individual needs are important
Work is work	Work can and should be satisfying
People like "being taken care of"	People prefer to be in control of themselves
Mode is one of being cautious, safe, compliant	Growth requires risk; mistakes are acceptable

is beyond the scope of this book to have an exhaustive discussion on teams; how-ever, we are going to give a general overview of the main attributes of what a team is, how it can be used, and the ingredients that will make it successful. The reader is also encouraged to read other sources on teams, such as Stamatis (2002).

In simple terms, a team is people working together to accomplish common goals—indeed, a simple definition, but a very powerful one. In order for this to work, the following three criteria are essential:

- Individual members share the same goals and see themselves as part of the team working together on a specific project with a definite time duration.
- The team is small enough (five to nine people) so that members can com-municate regularly, face to face. Team members should be able to talk to all other members.
- Members should be from different functions, such as billing, medical records, scheduling, and so on (cross functional), and from different disci-plines, such as physicians, registered nurses (RNs), certified physician assis-tants (PA-Cs), practical nurses, and so on (multidiscipline).

Typical Participants in a Healthcare Team

A typical team is made up of individuals for a particular task. The membership of the team generally is made up of the following:

- Committee persons are individuals who will be part of the core team. Another usual name for a committee person is simply a team member.
- The supervisor is the person in charge of the office or department. He or she must have some managerial responsibility.
- The team coordinator is the leader of team members, staff, RNs, PA-Cs, clerical, medical records, etc.
- Support and resources comprise individuals from different areas who may participate as the need arises. They may be representing functions or positions such as
  - Education training coordinator
  - Employee resources coordinator
  - Health and safety representative
  - Quality liaison
  - Work standards
  - Sourcing representative
  - JCM representative
  - Billing
  - Material handling
  - Human resources
  - Quality office
  - Medical doctor(s)

Boundary Conditions

The team members are the core of the improvement initiative. However, their responsibility may be extended or adjusted to reflect absenteeism, lack of specialty participation, relief allocation, need of specific tools to address specific problems, and others as needed. All improvement initiatives are dependent on several conditions, which become constraints. Some are corporate policy, office policy, legal agreements, OSHA regulations, environmental requirements, national agreements, and governmental regulations.

Sample Roles and Responsibilities of Team Members

As we already have mentioned, the idea of creating a team is to make sure that work is effective and productivity is increased as well as profitability. Therefore, teams work to accomplish daily zone/area goals based on effective communications all across the work environment, as well as to promote all the time an environment of teamwork and trust through individual and collective effort in the following areas:

- Quality
  - Check or follow up operation problems
  - Collect data for analysis
  - Maintain quality work habits
  - Ensure quality workmanship
  - Troubleshoot

- Cost/productivity schedule
  - Always look for continual improvement
  - Assign people to jobs
  - Be readily accessible
  - Control indirect material cost/scrap/waste
  - Distribute workload evenly
  - Ensure tool and material availability
  - Ensure team participation
  - Locate/deliver stock
  - Maintain tools
  - Make sure equipment/tools are available
  - Ensure punctuality

- Safety
  - Foster safe environment
  - Manage housekeeping
  - Maintain safe work area/environment
  - Make sure all are working safely
  - Work safely
  - Work smart

- Effective communication with all customers (internal and external)
  - Coach
  - Explain "why" we do "what"
  - Give recognition for job well done/idea or solution attempt
  - Implement company policy
  - Listen to ideas
  - Maintain positive attitude
  - Pass information on to team members, next shift, other teams

    – Recognize accomplishments
    – Relay management information

■ Promotion of an environment of teamwork and trust
    – Build trust
    – Assist others
    – Be a "team player"
    – Be a working member
    – Be open toward ideas of the team
    – Coordinate team effort
    – Coordinate time off with team or teams
    – Establish productive norms
    – Follow up team projects
    – Help team members
    – Know all team members
    – Know versatility and limitations of the team
    – Know all jobs, as required
    – Lead by example
    – Participate in decision making
    – Support other members of the team
    – Support the team
    – Take charge of your job
    – Teach others
    – Think positively—build morale
    – Train and rotate team members
    – Be willing to get involved with a job

In the process of their development, team members also develop their own rules. Typical rules are to

■ Be on time
■ Be prepared
■ Be committed to the team purpose
■ Listen actively
■ Focus on the subject
■ Do your fair share and help others
■ Be nonjudgmental rather than negative; look for something worthwhile
■ Understand cultural differences
■ Tolerate disagreements
■ Not be defensive
■ Question and clarify what is not understood

- Share information
- Establish responsibilities
- Determine accountability
- Treat members as equals despite titles or positions
- Share the glory; share the defeats
- Develop a reward system that all members share equally
- Identify and work within organizational norms (for example, chain of command and processes for sharing/obtaining information, getting approval to take action, communicating within and outside the organization)
- Encourage and support each other
- Avoid cliques (for example, sit next to different people each time you meet)
- Commit to team decisions through consensus
- Implement team decisions
- Interface with other teams

As important as these rules are, they become useless unless there is respect for and trust of each other. During the active sessions of the team, whether or not members agree and whether or not there is a volatile subject as part of the discussion, the appropriate courtesy and etiquette must be adhered to. Some rules for such behavior include:

- Pay attention (do not live your life on "automatic pilot").
- Acknowledge others (do this by at least saying "good morning" or "hello").
- Think the best (assume innocence; thinking well of others can improve them *and* yourself).
- Listen (be here now).
- Be inclusive (appreciate differences).
- Speak kindly (people are fragile; handle with care).
- Do not speak ill of others (this is especially cowardly when done behind someone's back).
- Accept and give appreciation and recognition.
- Respect even a subtle "no."
- Respect others' opinions (your opinion is *only your* opinion).
- Mind your body (practice good hygiene and avoid wearing heavy perfume or cologne).
- Be agreeable (you do not know it all and you are not always right).
- Keep it down (prevent noise pollution).
- Respect other people's time (be on time and do not be in a hurry to leave).
- Respect other people's space (applies to physical space, privacy, and property).
- Apologize earnestly (an insincere apology is just plain rude).
- Assert yourself (respect yourself—you do not have to be a wimp to be nice).

- Avoid personal questions (respect privacy).
- Care for your guests (care for patients and customers as though they were guests in your home).
- Be a considerate guest (consider whether you would like it if someone did "that" in *your* house).
- Think twice before asking for favors (requests should not be imposing or unnecessary).
- Refrain from idle complaints (consider whether you are unhappy with the circumstances or with yourself).
- Accept and give constructive criticism (help yourself and others to improve).
- Respect the environment (the big picture).
- Practice accountability (do not be quick to blame others).

Before we close this general section on teams, let us address the criteria for good teams. There are a number; however, we believe that the following are perhaps the most critical. As a consequence, always keep in mind what a well-functioning team does (hint: excellent performance):

- The work team has a sense of purpose, based on common goals that members willingly work toward accomplishing.
- The team has norms and rules of conduct that describe how it wants to work.
- Members care about each other as people, not just as group members.
- Members talk to and listen to each other. When members disagree, they are willing to handle the conflict in positive ways.
- Members identify and establish resources to use when needed.
- While the team has a formal leader, leadership is sometimes shared based on who has the most knowledge and can get the task done with the best results.
- The team focuses on positive problem solving—completing tasks—rather than on destructive interpersonal issues and feelings.
- Mistakes that are made due to risk-taking behavior are seen as opportunities for learning and growth.
- The work team is aware of the needs of its members and its customers and works to meet those needs.
- The work team is committed to producing quality work and measures itself honestly against set standards.
- The work team is a way to grow in the job and as a person.
- Each work team member has clear basic roles and work assignments, as well as backing up other group members.
- The climate of the team is informal, comfortable, and relaxed. There are no signs of underlying tension, boredom, or lack of interest.
- There is plenty of discussion; everyone is encouraged to participate.

- The team evaluates itself every few months, checking to see how well its members are working together and how well the job is getting done.
- Team decisions are made by consensus after openly discussing everyone's ideas.
- Members agree to disagree.
- Members cannot make it personal or take it personally.

Implementation of the Team

The idea of continual improvement is to form a team in the work environment so that the people in that environment together can accomplish common goals of improvement. This improvement may be in any area, such as cost, efficiency, morale, safety, and so on. The implementation team will be formed in each area of the facility as the specific teams are formed. The design committees will have the responsibility of the implementation process, reporting directly to the steering and planning committees. Typical membership for a design committee is five to seven members. Note here that the selection is in odd numbers to avoid ties in the decision-making process:

- Facility coordinator (required)
- Selected trainers
- Supervisor
- Medical staff (physician, RN, etc.)
- Union representatives (if available)
- Scheduler
- Appropriate team member or members
- Comptroller representative
- Employee resource coordinator

Continual improvement teams are small (no more than seven to nine core members and extended members as needed). They are formed within specific areas of the office or organization to solve specific issues. Depending on the size of the office or organization, the number of teams will vary. However, regardless of the number of teams, success depends on communication, which involves:

- Biological systems: mouth for speaking and ears for hearing
- Cognitive systems: brain and how we think
- Social and psychological systems: culture, experience, how we feel about ourselves

To understand the communication process, one must understand its components:

Sender → Filter → Message → Filter → Receiver → Listening → Feedback

- The *sender* is the person with a message to deliver. The sender needs to consider:
    - The receiver: internal or external to the company, level of familiarity with the information
    - The purpose of the message: to inform, entertain, direct, or persuade
    - The organization of the message: logical order to help the receiver understand
    - The size and length of the message: number of words used or ideas presented
    - The ability of the message to get the receiver's attention: word choice, ability to depict action through illustration, picture, or diagram
    - The selection of the appropriate channel: written, spoken, or electronic
- The *receiver* is the person or group for whom the message is intended.
- The *message* is what the sender wants the receiver to understand.
- The *feedback* is the response of the receiver to the sender based on the understanding of the message. The feedback may be positive (agreement) or negative (disagreement).
- The *filter* is something that is placed between the source and the receiver. All of us have filters and use them in our own ways. There are several types of filters and each one may be used to clarify the sending message. Typical filters may include:
    - Physical filters such as the ability to hear or see
    - Stereotype filters such as race, gender, age, education, culture, or physical ability
    - Tone of voice that does not agree with the message ("Darling" said in an angry tone of voice is not a loving word. Sometimes, how things are said can make a difference in how the message is heard. If a person is aware of the receiver's filters, he or she can avoid them.)
    - Body language (including facial expressions, posture, gestures, or eye contact) that does not agree with the message

Yet another issue in the implementation and sustainment processes of teams is invariably conflict. No matter how well the team learns to make decisions by consensus, a team will have conflict. Conflict is usually seen as negative and something to be avoided. When handled well, however, conflict is positive.

In fact, it is essential to the life of the team and specifically in the effective decision-making and problem-solving processes. Conflicts are needed to help the team grow. If managed well, conflicts can increase the quality of a team's work and make members feel proud of their work in the team. There are three main benefits to be gained by well-managed conflict:

- By *listening* to diverse ideas and points of view, it is possible to gain a broader understanding of a problem.
- By *encouraging* different ideas on an issue, the team has more alternatives from which to make a final decision.
- The energy produced by conflict stimulates interest in the team and the shared problem. It can even make members more committed to the final decision.

To be sure, conflict is considered natural and it can be dealt with in a positive way for good results. Team members see conflict, disagreement, and different ideas as part of a successful team. If there is creativity, there is the chance of conflict. Typical positive ways of viewing conflict include:

- Conflict is resolved through openness. Since conflict is natural, it is dealt with openly, not "pushed under the rug."
- Conflicts happen over issues, not over personalities. People may be part of the conflict, but they are not the issue. You may disagree with another member of the team, but you do not put that person down or embarrass him or her. *Do not make it personal!*
- Conflict means that the team must look for alternatives. Members of the team do not try to pin the blame on someone for a problem or failure. The team says, "We don't like the way things are now; what do we want as an alternative?"
- Conflict resolution is focused on the present. *Discussion* of the conflict is kept to what is happening now. Disagreements, conversations that have taken place with others outside the team, and behaviors of members in other situations are not part of working through the present conflict.
- Conflict is a team issue. Disagreements that affect certain members become issues with which the whole team must deal because they affect the work of everyone in the team. Therefore, members do not have to settle differences on their own. The team pitches in to help.

If conflict is left alone or dealt with in a negative way, it fosters negativity and ultimate failure for the team. The following are some negative ways in which we deal with conflict:

- Avoidance (denial or withdrawal). With this approach, we try to get rid of conflict by denying that it exists. We simply refuse to acknowledge it. Usually, however, the conflict does not go away, but rather grows to the point at which it becomes all but unmanageable.
- Suppression (smoothing over). "We run a happy ship here." "Let's not deal with that just now." A person using suppression plays down differences or delays confrontation until another time and does not recognize the positive aspects of handling the conflict openly. Again, the source of conflict rarely goes away.
- Confrontation:
  - Power dominance. Power is often used to settle differences. The source of the power may be authority or position. Power could also take the form of a majority vote. Power strategies have winners and losers, and the losers do not support a final decision in the same way that winners do. Future meetings of the team may be disturbed by the conscious or unconscious renewal of the struggle previously "settled" by the use of power.
  - Compromise or negotiation. Although compromise ("You give a little, I'll give a little, and we'll meet each other in the middle") is usually seen as a virtue, it has some serious drawbacks. The compromise position may be watered down or weakened to a point at which it will not be effective. There is often little commitment made by either side.

Is there anything that can be done to deal with conflict? Yes, there is. We probably will never eliminate conflict, but we can diffuse it or minimize it. After all, it is hard not to react defensively when we feel that our ideas are under attack. Someone disagrees with us and our faces get hot, our palms get sweaty, and our voices rise in pitch and volume. Being defensive is natural. The problem is that when we are defending ourselves, we do not listen very well and probably have a hard time thinking through what others are saying.

So, what can you do? Keep these ideas in mind:

- The person disagreeing with you has a point of view that is just as reasonable to him or her as yours is to you.
- The other person is probably just as uncomfortable with the conflict as you are. Try to relax. Sit back in your chair. If you look calm and sure of yourself, the other person is more likely to stay calm too.
- Start by identifying the things that you can agree on. The other person usually wants to resolve the conflict too, so start with the positives.
- Stick to the issues and avoid personal arguments.
- Do not dwell on who is to blame for the conflict, but rather focus on what can be done to solve the problem or find an alternative to the situation.

- Accept the fact that others have a right to disagree with you. *Show that you accept by the expression on your face and the words that you speak.* Instead of saying, "Where did you come up with that?" say, "I hadn't thought about that."
- Ask how others in the team feel about the issue. Then keep quiet and give others a chance to give their thoughts.
- If the team discussion does not cover all the issues, you may want to respond. Be sure to talk to the whole team, not just the person who disagrees with you.
- *Listen* to what is said and who is saying it. Do not interrupt. Pay attention to show that you value other opinions. The following tips may help for good listening:
  - First, you must really want to listen!
  - Show that you are paying attention.
  - Listen for content and then for meaning.
    - What I heard you say was …
    - What that means to me is …
    - How I react to that is …
    - My thoughts on that are …
  - Try not to interrupt too often.
  - Try not to argue mentally.
  - Feelings are not right or wrong, so avoid telling the person that he or she should not feel that way.
  - Remember to whom you are responding and take his or her needs into account.
  - When you do make a judgment statement, separate what you think of the person from what you think of the person's behavior or opinions.
  - Watch for nonverbal signals.
  - Clarify things. Check things out instead of making assumptions.
  - Sometimes it is helpful to report your feelings. This can create a supportive and open atmosphere. However, beware of tendencies to steal the spotlight.
  - Remember that you will never be a perfect listener. However, this does not mean that you should not make a significant effort to improve your listening abilities.
- Why is listening important?
  - Listening is a key to relationship building.
  - Listening is a key to problem solving.
  - Listening is a key to learning.
  - Listening is the most important element of communication.

Decision Making

Before the team can make a decision, it needs to make sure that the decision is its to make. This implies that there must be criteria for an optimum decision. Essential criteria must be addressed (See Table 3.2). The reader will notice that the more "yes" answers there are to these criteria, the more involvement the work team has in the decision or the activity. The more "no" answers there are, the more involvement of management will be required. Essential criteria include:

Table 3.2   Decision-Making Criteria Flowchart

Does the Team Have	No	Action	Yes
Authority?	X	Forward to the proper authority	Go to next criterion
Time?	X	Schedule time	Go to next criterion
Information?	X	Get the information	Go to next criterion
Skills?	X	Get the skills or get someone who has the skills	Go to next criterion
Support?	X	Discuss until consensus is reached	Go to next criterion
Scope?	X	Meet with other teams to make sure there is no overlap and share ideas. Try to be as specific in your scope as possible	Go to next criterion
Cost?	X	Look at all possibilities and alternatives to cost because they may affect the problem at hand	Go to next criterion
Common purpose?	X	Discuss until consensus is reached	Go to next criterion

Edinburgh Napier University Library

- *Authority:* Does the team have the authority to make the decision or to take on the project or task?
  - Not restricted by
    - Master agreement
    - Local agreement
    - Corporate policy
    - Steering committee
  - Not restricted by predefined standards
- *Time:* Does the group have the time?
- *Information:* Does the group have the information that it needs?
  - Is the information obtainable?
  - Is the team authorized to have access to that information?
- *Skills:* Does the group have the skills?
  - Do the skills exist in the organization or do the members have to be trained elsewhere?
- *Support:* Is management supporting decision making by a team?
  - Is there consensus that the team should be involved and can improve results?
- *Scope:* Is the boundary of the problem within the jurisdiction of the team?
  - Is the impact of the decision or activity limited to the work group's area?
- *Cost:* Is cost an issue?
  - Are funds available?
- *Common purpose:* Do management and the team believe that the activity or decision is important for the team to perform or make?
  - Is there a commitment for a positive resolution?

Decision-Making Tools

To make a decision in any endeavor there are three fundamental issues with which everyone should be familiar. The first by far is a basic understanding of financial information for teams, the second is an understanding of the power of data, and third is a systematic way to problem solving.

Financial information is important because sooner or later in any project there is going to be a discussion of benefit versus risk as it relates to cost. The team should be familiar with at least a minimum understanding of return on investment, cost, and budget.

Understanding data and their power is inherent in any decision making. The reason is that, with data, the team members will be able to decide on a particular action so that they can say with confidence that these are indeed "data-driven decisions." However, unless they understand what appropriate data are, how they can be collected, and how they can be analyzed, any discussion about results may be questionable.

The issue of systematic problem solving is also very important because, through this process, a rational decision may be reached that can be repeated. Furthermore, it is a major advantage for everyone to use a specific method rather than a random one or an approach that depends on the knowledge of the leader of the team. Notice that here we are talking about the process of deciding on a resolution of a problem rather than an individual tool. Obviously, one can use many different tools, depending on the situation.

The team will be faced with opportunities for many decisions. Hopefully, these decisions should be reached by *consensus,* which, by definition, is a decision that everyone can support. This is very important because it does not mean that the decision is everyone's first choice; rather, it is one with which each person can live and support completely. Consensus is not a majority vote. It is not a unanimous decision. Consensus is said to be 70% agreement and 100% support. It may take longer to reach consensus, but it is time well spent. More alternatives are considered, and the combined thinking power of the group is greater than that of any single individual. This is the notion of *synergy.* Some guidelines to use in reaching consensus include:

- Never make it personal.
- Avoid arguing for your own ideas. Present your position as clearly and logically as possible.
- Avoid win/lose situations in your discussions. Let go of the notion that someone must win and someone must lose.
- Avoid changing your mind only to avoid conflict or to reach agreement and peace. Change your mind if you can truly "buy in" to the proposed solution, but do not do it if it means that you are "giving in."
- Avoid conflict-reducing techniques such as majority vote, averaging, bargaining, coin-flipping, and such. Treat differences as an opportunity to get more information.
- View differences of opinion as both helpful and natural rather that as hindrances. Generally, the more ideas expressed, the greater is the chance of disagreement, but this is also a better way to use resources.
- Make sure that people have reached similar conclusions for the same basic reasons.
- Avoid trying to influence people's positions with trade-offs. For example, when people finally agree, do not feel that they must be rewarded by having their way on some point later.
- Be willing to consider the possibility that your work group can do well in making a decision instead of saying something like, "We'll never be able to decide on this one!"

To appreciate consensus and the advantages over majority rule, we must be cognizant of the following criteria that make teams effective and the decisions that come out of them very powerful. In other words we must always keep in mind what a well-functioning group does. The following are some criteria:

- The work team has a sense of purpose, based on common goals that members willingly work toward accomplishing.
- The team has norms and rules of conduct that describe how it wants to work.
- Members care about each other as people, not just as team members.
- Members talk to and listen to each other. When members disagree, they are willing to handle the conflict in positive ways.
- Members identify and establish resources to use when needed.
- While the team has a formal leader, leadership is sometimes shared based on who has the most knowledge and can get the task done with the best results.
- The team focuses on positive problem solving—completing tasks—rather than on destructive interpersonal issues and feelings.
- Mistakes that are made due to risk-taking behavior are seen as opportunities for learning and growth.
- The team is aware of the needs of its members and its customers and works to meet those needs.
- The team is committed to producing quality work and measures itself honestly against set standards.
- The team is a way to grow in the job and as a person.
- Each team member has clear basic roles and work assignments, as well as backing up other team members.
- The climate of the team is informal, comfortable, and relaxed. There are no signs of underlying tension, boredom, or lack of interest.
- There is plenty of discussion; everyone is encouraged to participate. There is no hidden agenda.
- The team evaluates itself every few months, checking to see how well its members are working together and how well the job is getting done.
- Group decisions are made by consensus after openly discussing everyone's ideas.
- Members agree to disagree.
- Members cannot make it personal or take it personally.

Many tools can be used in any problem identification and decision making. In Appendix C (on the accompanying CD), we have identified over 30 specific tools and Stamatis (1996) contains an extensive discussion of many tools as applied to healthcare. Here, we limit ourselves to the following most often used tools for decision making—whether to identify a problem or to solve one.

8D

This method reduces or eliminates the root cause of the problem through the use of the following steps. Even though it is called 8D for the eight disciplines, in actuality, the methodology has nine. It is based on the scientific method, but extended to cover the following:

1. Preparation for the 8D. Not all problems need a formal problem-solving methodology. Thus, the first step is to evaluate the situation and decide whether or not a formal approach is necessary.
2. Formation of the team. This step of the methodology calls for the selection of the appropriate and applicable individuals who will be the main participants for the resolution of the problem at hand. These individuals must be in some way responsible for their process and therefore must have a direct interest in the outcome. In other words, they must be owners of what is going on. This is very important because they are the ones that will call and include all activities that can help define the problem and causal factors and implement corrective action, verification, validation, and prevention.
3. Problem description. All indicators should be utilized to identify and quantify the problem as completely as possible in customer terms or symptoms. In this step you must be as specific as possible.
4. Problem isolation. Now that you have identified and understood the problem, you must be able to isolate it so that it does not infiltrate other items or, even worse, get to the next process or customer.
5. Cause identification. Ask the question "why" as many times as required to drive to a definition of the underlying root cause. You know that you have arrived at this point when you make the root cause disappear and appear at your discretion.
6. Test programs. This step calls for verification of all the solutions that have been identified. You need to have proof that you have accounted for the risks and that the solution will work.
7. Corrective action. This step is a three stage process. The first one is to eliminate the root cause and implement ongoing control actions as appropriate and applicable. The second is to verify the effectiveness of actions in quantifiable terms. The third is to go back and correct the defective product produced.
8. Problem prevention. Modify management and operating systems, practices, procedures, and processes to prevent recurrence of similar problems.
9. Team recognition. Recognize the cooperative contribution of the team members.

For an exhaustive discussion on this process, see Ford Motor Company (2002) and Stamatis (2002). For additional information, see Brassard and Ritter (1994) and Bens (1999).

When to Use 8D

The 8D methodology may be used to resolve an existing problem in any area of the organization. The magnitude of the problem is of no consequence. The 8D is very flexible and easy to use. However, it needs a true commitment from the team to apply it diligently and to investigate each of its steps thoroughly without any fear of retaliation if data uncovered are contrary to what management has thought. Table 3.3 shows a typical matrix of appropriate use of the 8D methodology.

The 5 Whys

This is a methodology and tool that helps to identify underlying causes by asking sequential questions starting with the word "why" to get to the core of the problem. It may take more or less than five questions to get to the problem; however, five is a good general rule with which to start. The 5 Whys approach is one of the simplest tools for problem investigation. A simple form that may be used is shown in Table 3.4. It focuses on three fundamental questions to start the investigation:

- What is wrong with what?
- Do you know why the problem occurs on this particular stage or service?
- Test the operational definition by asking, "Do you know why?"

Table 3.3 Appropriate Use of the 8D Process

If	Then
100% certain about the cause of the problem	Do not use the 8D process
Fairly sure about the cause of the problem	Test (D5) before you implement the solution (D6)
Several possible causes of the problem exist	Describe the process (D2), identify the cause (D4), and test the solution (D5)
Clueless about the cause of the problem	Use the entire 8D problem-solving process

Table 3.4   A Typical, Simple "5 Whys" Form

Why	Answer	Comments/Action

An example may demonstrate the principle. A microbiology specimen is not fully incubated by 8:00 a.m. Using the 5 Whys methodology, the following questions can be asked:

- First why: *Why does this happen?* Specimen sits on tray outside the hood for a long period.
- Second why: *Why?* The technician is not working at the hood when specimen arrives.
- Third why: *Why?* Ova and parasite tests are always performed first.
- Fourth why: *Why?* Current work flow prioritization puts ova and parasite testing ahead of specimen incubation.

In this case, only four *whys* are necessary, but the problem is identified nevertheless: It is an issue of prioritization.

There are five general steps for developing this tool or form:

- Describe the problem.
- Ask why the problem occurred.
- Continue asking why until a clear answer is reached.
- Take appropriate corrective actions and document these actions. If the problem is eliminated, no further action is needed.
- If the problem continues or recurs, repeat the process or use another problem-solving technique.

IS/IS NOT

This is a method of narrowing down or focusing on the "true" problem by successively asking what it is and what it is not. For example:

It is a supplier's problem; it is not an internal problem.
It is a problem from a different department.
It is not a billing problem.
It is not an internal stocking problem.
It is a supply problem with syringes; it is not a supply problem with medications, etc.

We generally use IS/IS NOT when we define a problem to decide what is in scope and what is not going to be considered at this time. It helps to focus on the problem at hand. Sometimes it is also useful to use it when we are part of the way through a problem and are not sure what we are trying to do and what is not so important. Quite frequently, it is used when planning a solution to help decide what to include and what to exclude in terms of

- Quick versus long
- Logical versus psychological
- Individual versus group

A typical form used in the analysis of IS/IS NOT is shown in Table 3.5.

Measuring Effectiveness of a Team

There are many tools and techniques that the team may use to measure how well it is working as a team. Here, however, we will address three basic ones that every team should consider in its practice: (1) work team effectiveness, (2) team member evaluation, and (3) self-assessment.

The idea of work team effectiveness is to measure the working dynamics of the team as a whole. The core objective is to find out whether or not everyone is moving in the right direction and whether or not the objective is being met. A typical evaluation instrument is illustrated in Table 3.6. Everyone in the group can fill out the opinion survey so that everyone has a chance to give an opinion. Another approach is to have someone outside the team fill out the form after spending at least 30 minutes observing the team at work or in a meeting.

The idea of team member evaluation is to measure the working dynamics of the individual team member in the team. The core objective is to find out whether or not the individual is working effectively toward the common purpose. A typical evaluation instrument is found in Table 3.7. Everyone in the group can fill out the opinion survey so that everyone has a chance to give an opinion or someone outside the team can fill out the form after spending at least

Table 3.5   Typical Form of the IS/IS NOT Method

Questions to Ask to Describe a Problem (Every Question May Not Apply to Every Problem)	
IS	IS NOT
What	**What**
What is the object with which you are having a problem? What is the problem (defect)?	What similar object or objects could have the defect but does or do not? What could be the problem (defect), but is not?
Where	**Where**
Where do you see the defect on the object? Be specific in terms of inside to outside, side to side, end to end, one object to another. Where (geographically) can you take me to show me the problem? Where can you first see it?	Where on the object is the problem not seen? Does the problem cover the entire object? Where else (geographically) could you have observed the defective object, but did not?
When	**When**
When in time did you first notice the problem? Be as specific as you can about the day and time. In a process-flow diagram, at what step do you first see the problem?	When in time could it have been first observed, but was not? Where else in the process flow, life, or operating cycle might you have observed the defect, but did not?
Since you first saw it, when have you seen it? Be specific about minutes, hours, days, weeks. Can you plot any trends or patterns?	What other times could you have observed the defective object, but did not?
How big	**How big**
How much of each object has the defect?	How many objects could have had the defect but did not?

(*Continued*)

Table 3.5   Typical Form of the IS/IS NOT Method (Continued)

Questions to Ask to Describe a Problem (Every Question May Not Apply to Every Problem)	
IS	*IS NOT*
What is the trend? Has it leveled off? Has it gone away? Or is it getting worse? How many objects have the defect? How many defects do you see on each object? How big is the defect in terms of dollars, people, time or other resources? What percentage in relation to the total?	What other trends could have been observed but were not? How many defects per object could there be, but are not? How big could the defect be, but is not?

30 minutes observing the team at work or in a meeting. The idea here is to find out if there are any barriers and, if so, to remove them.

The idea of self-assessment is to measure the working dynamics of individuals as they perceive their participation in terms of the entire team. This is different from the team member evaluation in the sense that this specifically addresses the issues of perception of the individual as a member of the team. The core objective is to find out whether or not the individual has a positive perception of belonging to and participating in the team environment. A typical evaluation instrument is shown in Table 3.8. Everyone on the team can fill out the opinion survey so that all have a chance to give their opinions. The idea here is to determine how often certain behaviors are used in participating in a work team meeting. The goal is personal improvement and it is accomplished by checking off three areas and working to improve them.

Once the areas that need to be improved are determined, then the team can tackle how to make these areas better. Is there an opportunity for coaching or training or extra practice? Is there information that would make the team work better and get more done? Does an "expert" need to be called in to improve the situation? If this is the case, then members of the team should

- Be willing to admit that some help is needed
- Know where to go for help

Table 3.6   Teamwork Effectiveness

	Rating				
	Rarely (1)	Sometimes (2)	Usually (3)	Often (4)	Almost always (5)
Members listen to each other					
Members ask each other questions if they do not understand how someone feels or what is said					
Members go to the right place to find information					
Members talk to each other					
Members are comfortable and relaxed with each other					
Members try to help one another succeed					
Members appear to care about each other					

(Continued)

Table 3.6 Teamwork Effectiveness (Continued)

	Rating				
	Rarely (1)	Sometimes (2)	Usually (3)	Often (4)	Almost always (5)
Members care about the quality of their work					
Members are proud to be a part of the team					
Total					
Scoring	After you have completed the form, add the numbers together for each response. For example, if you gave a rating of 2 to the first question, 3 to the second question, and 3 to the third, your total for these three questions would be 8.				
Score interpretation	If the total score is (1) between 34 and 45: the group is effective and no special training is called for, so keep up the good work; (2) between 22 and 33: the group is somewhat effective, but some development and reinforcement are needed; (3) 21 or below: your group needs lots of training and practice.				

- Be aware of available training opportunities in the plant
- Be aware of available training opportunities within other areas of the community

When all is said and done, the team will only be successful if every individual is successful. Here are some points to live by as a team member for a successful team:

- Help each other to be right, not wrong.
- Look for ways to make new ideas work, not for reasons why they will not.
- If in doubt, check it out! Do not make negative assumptions about each other.
- Help each other win; take pride in each other's victories.

Table 3.7 Team Member Evaluation for Identification of Barriers

Concern	Yes	No
Goals and objectives are clear		
Group roles are clear		
Decisions are made efficiently		
There is an opportunity for all views to be expressed before decisions are made		
Members seem to share their beliefs openly		
Members appear to understand that their behavior has an impact on the entire group		
The group is flexible		
Group members look for ways to help each other		
The group sets priorities		
The group keeps the priorities in mind even when reacting to crises		
Interpersonal issues are dealt with openly		
The resources of group members are used effectively		
The group works together to make a decision—not in competition		
Creativity is encouraged		
Conflict is dealt with openly and honestly		
Work group roles are shared		
The work group considers planning essential to doing business		
All members participate openly in the planning process		
The environment of the work group encourages member growth and creativity		
Members listen carefully		
Members are highly committed to the group's effort		
Members avoid quick judgments		

Table 3.8 Self-assessment

When I participate in a team meeting, I …	Rating				
	Rarely (1)	*Sometimes (2)*	*Usually (3)*	*Often (4)*	*Almost always (5)*
Stay focused on the purpose and objectives of the session					
Offer opinions and ideas focused on the subject only, not on other people or personalities					
Am honest and straightforward when dealing with others					
Offer information in a positive way					
Take the initiative to act or help without being asked					
Communicate clearly					
Show respect by listening to others					
Keep an open mind and consider all options					

Table 3.8   Self-assessment (Continued)

When I participate in a team meeting, I …	Rating				
	Rarely (1)	Sometimes (2)	Usually (3)	Often (4)	Almost always (5)
Avoid quick judgments					
Total					

- Speak positively about each other and about the organization at every opportunity.
- Keep a positive attitude, no matter what.
- Act as if it all depends on you.
- Do everything with enthusiasm; it is contagious.
- Do not lose faith.
- Have fun!

Relationships between Internal and External Teams

Continual improvement is not an option; it is an absolute necessity. Change is one of the certainties of life and, unless we understand its mechanics, we will fail. Conversely, continual improvement must be a way of life for everyone everywhere. It is everyone's responsibility. Not only must that be true, but it also must be readily apparent to customers. If customers do not see constant change toward continual improvement as a norm, they will not remain loyal to our product or service. Both internal and external customers have a stake in the products and service we provide.

Internal. Are there other teams and/or work groups in the office or clinic or hospital? How do those teams or work groups communicate with, interact with, and feel toward one another?

The idea here is to self-evaluate the progress of improvement. Learn from successes and mistakes. How do they apply that learning? From time to time, a team or work group needs to take a break from "business improvement as usual" and take a look at how well the team is doing. Is the team or work group accomplishing what it is supposed to? Are team members working together? Do members feel like they are part of the team? Is there room for improvement in certain areas? The only way to get better is to take *getting better* seriously. Ask the team to identify what has gone well in the group and what has gone not so well, or even wrong. If we identify "things gone right/things gone wrong," we can begin to learn from our experiences.

Are there systems in place for working toward continual improvement? Already established systems need to be utilized for the continual improvement process. Examples of common current systems that are already established and used in many healthcare facilities include but are not limited to the following:

■ Quality operating system (QOS)
■ Maintenance operating system (MOS)
■ Training operating system (TOS)
■ Quality deployment system (QDS)
■ Health and safety system
■ Safety operating system

Within these various systems, supporting information can be found, such as

■ Waste reduction information
■ Housekeeping issues
■ Process improvement information
■ Cost
■ Quality indicators

Customers. Communicate with and treat the next job station, zone, area, or department as a buying customer.

Suppliers. Communicate with

■ Other members of the office, clinic, or hospital as suppliers
■ Pharmaceutical suppliers
■ In-house supplier departments

Summary

In this chapter, we discussed the mechanics of change from a somewhat unique perspective. We introduced the concepts of teams and specific tools that can be used to address and understand change. Key points were the 8D, 5 Whys, and IS/IS NOT methodologies and recognition of the different levels of customers. In the next chapter, we will focus on the transition of the group to a team.

References

Bens, I. 1999. *Facilitation at a glance.* Salem, NH: AQO/Participative Dynamics/Goal/QPC.

Brassard, M., and D. Ritter. 1994. *The memory jogger II.* Salem, NH: Goal/QPC.

Ford Motor Company. 2002. *Global 8D.* Dearborn, MI: Ford Motor Company.

Stamatis, D. H. 1996. *Total quality management in healthcare: Implementation, strategies for optimum results.* New York: McGraw–Hill.

———. 2002. *Six Sigma and beyond: Problem solving and basic mathematics.* Boca Raton, FL: St. Lucie Press.

Selected Bibliography

http://healthit.ahrq.gov (retrieved on August 5, 2009).

http://healthit.ahrq.gov/portal/server.pt/gateway/PTARGS_0_1248_661809_0_0_18/AHRHIT_Primary_Care_July07.pdf (retrieved on September 18, 2009).

http://www.hhs.gov/healthit/ (retrieved on August 5, 2009).

Langley, J., and C. Beasley. July 2007. Health information technology for improving quality of care in primary care settings. Prepared by the Institute for Healthcare Improvement for the National Opinion Research Center under contract no. 290-04-0016. AHRQ Publication 07-0079-EF. Rockville, MD: Agency for Healthcare Research and Quality.

Chapter 4

The Transition of Groups to Teams

Introduction

In the last chapter, as part of the discussion of the mechanics of change, we discussed the importance of teams and the contribution that they make to any problem-solving process. However, putting individuals to work together does not create a team; rather, this is a group. The transition from group to team is time consuming, and quite often the participants need training to make the transition. This chapter focuses on this transition.

A vital part of the quality improvement initiative effort is to establish a formal organization of teams to implement and maintain the quality management system effectively, including specific methodologies such as Six Sigma and Lean. These teams are responsible for managing the quality effort at all locations and within all functions. This may sound simple, but it involves a great deal of work. It is important to consider the entire organizational structure when establishing these teams. In a typical service organization—especially healthcare—the various types of teams that will function at the different management levels must be defined.

For example, the management committee sets the policy for the organization. This committee is assisted in this effort by the director of quality, who reports to the management committee. Advice is provided to the management committee by the quality council. The council is chaired by the director of quality. It is the responsibility of these two bodies to provide overall direction and guidance to the organization. This includes providing resources, scheduling and coordination of education, and other areas as the need arises. (In some organizations, there is no management committee and the quality council is the same as the steering committee.)

The next level in the formation of teams in typical service organizations is the steering committee. This group should be created to provide similar guidance and direction and to maintain consistency of purpose within the organization. It is important that the members of these committees do not normally interact functionally in their day-to-day operations but rather are a part of the same business team. An administrative team in a hospital environment may serve as an example. This team would comprise legal, personnel, control, communications, development, and planning departments. The leaders of each of these functions would comprise the steering committee.

Whereas the quality council and steering committee address general problems within the entire organization, the divisional quality improvement team, the location and functional quality improvement team, and the business quality improvement team focus on more specific areas of the organization.

The divisional quality improvement team is a typical staff-level team that is responsible for implementing the quality system in the staff functions and support areas of the division. This team also provides guidance and support to the location and functional quality improvement team as well as the business quality improvement team. The location and functional quality improvement team is, as the name implies, responsible for implementing the quality system in a given location or function. A radiology department is a good example of a location and a billing department is a good example of where a functional team is needed.

A business team may be created in service organizations that have a matrix-type management structure. These organizations are organized around service types, and the teams have the same responsibility as the location and functional quality improvement team. Service industries that may have a need for business teams are the hospitality, healthcare, legal, and construction industries.

Membership of any of the quality improvement teams (QITs) should represent every function involved. These functions normally interact with each other in order to accomplish their tasks. This interface is where many of the problems arise and are thrown over the imaginary wall within the organizational structure. The first time through the quality system, the QIT members should be from the highest level possible for that entity. At a branch site, for example, the staff reporting to the branch manager should form the QIT. This gives the QIT the authority and decision-making power that it needs and emphasizes the importance of the program to the rest of the supervisors and employees.

Each QIT must have a chairperson (sometimes called a leader), who is either appointed or elected. Caution must be exercised here, particularly if a senior executive or the quality manager is being considered. If the quality manager is chosen, the quality management system (QMS) could be perceived to be "just another quality program." If an executive is chosen, he or she may dominate discussions and totally control the direction of the process. The intent of the QMS is to get people involved and participating so that they will own the system. If the leader dominates the action, this may not happen. When a leader is selected, several other characteristics need to be considered. The leader should be well respected and must also understand and firmly believe in the system. This person should be open minded, objective, and results oriented.

The next organizing activity that must be accomplished is the selection of a QIT administrator. This position requires a person with many of the same characteristics as the leader. In addition, he or she should be a good organizer. The person should also be somewhat "thick skinned" because some of the duties of the position could be discouraging. The administrator (sometimes called the secretary) is the support person for the leader. It is this person's job to handle the administrative details of the QIT's activities. The administrator should be in charge of minutes and agendas for meetings, be an information resource for the QIT, and be responsible for the support needs of the QIT. For example, if the QIT decided on a procedure and measurement chart format, it would be the administrator's duty to have the procedures printed and distributed and the charts ordered and available. The administrator would also help the chairperson follow up on any action items prior to meetings. The duties of the administrator may require a full-time position. On the other hand, the position of the leader may not.

Once the QIT has been formed, its first agenda item should be to ensure that all members are educated in tasks to be addressed and quality tools of improvement. Then, the team can proceed to develop its charter and plan the program. The charter should define the structure and membership of the QIT, define the authority and responsibilities (duties) of the QIT and its members, and provide for the records that will be maintained. Among the responsibilities that might be addressed in the charter is the need to develop and implement the quality system, including schedules for the action items. Members represent their functions to the QIT and represent the QIT to their functions. They are responsible for carrying out the decisions of the QIT in their departments. That is, they are responsible for implementing the QMS actions in their departments. The QIT must also monitor the effectiveness of the system and report to management on its progress. Member participation in training will demonstrate commitment to and importance of the quality system.

As the QIT starts developing the plan, it should distribute responsibility for each action to the members, who act as sponsors. This allows them to concentrate on the details for implementing the intent of the action. They will provide the preliminary plan for the action to the QIT for approval. If the action is complex, they may choose to establish a subcommittee to assist in the effort.

This will spread the workload to other members of the organization and let others participate in the quality system at an early stage, which ensures ownership and facilitates implementation. Typically, the sponsor assists in instructing the management QIT and supervisors in the proper method of implementing the actions and monitors progress in all departments.

At first, QIT meetings should be held every week to speed up the initial implementation. Meetings should not normally exceed 1 hour in length, and most of the legwork should be done between meetings. This will allow the members to deal with decisions at the meetings and assign action as necessary. The meetings should be carefully planned. An agenda should be established for each meeting with a time schedule assigned. Minutes must be kept and should include action assignments with names and dates.

Finally, planning for the QIT in healthcare should provide for the flow of information throughout the organization. Minutes of meetings, data, successes, and problems should be shared with other QITs. This will assist them in solving the same or similar problems that may have already been solved by the originating QIT. A forum should be provided for the QIT leaders, administrators, and managers to meet periodically (depending on the organization and problems) to share these ideas. This would be in addition to the normal vertical paper communication flow in the organization.

Typical implementation steps:

- Conduct the first organizational meeting (review policy, principles, and quality management action system)
- Select a leader
- Select an administrator
- Educate team members
- Write the team charter
- Assign element sponsorship
- Appoint subcommittees
- Develop an implementation plan
- Hold meetings routinely to implement the plan and monitor the results

The intent of the action is met when

- Quality improvement teams are in place and functioning
- Plans and objectives have been documented
- Formal implementation plans have been developed
- Regular meetings are held and formal minutes are issued to monitor progress

Internal Development of the Team

Now that we have addressed the issues of the administrative process in team development, let us also summarize the internal development and transition of individuals to a team. Whether we are on a sports team, in a community group, or another work group, the group grows and develops over time. Many studies show us that groups go through five stages of development as they learn to work together to become a team. The stages happen every time the group comes together. As time goes on, the group will pass through these stages more rapidly depending on the personalities involved and the time the group spends together. When members leave the work group or new people join the group, the group may go back to an earlier stage.

Stage 1: Forming

People start a group by getting acquainted with each other to learn the following:

- Each person's place in the group
- How others can contribute to the group
- Where and when members can depend on each other
- The goals of the group

Members are optimistic, but somewhat anxious. Though polite and sociable, they tend to be somewhat nonexpressive and keep their real feelings private. Members tend to be followers and want to be told what to do. This period can be thought of as the "honeymoon" stage.

Frustrations that may be encountered:

- No clear assignments
- Lack of action or progress
- Poor communication
- No buy-in to the group's mission or task
- High frustration level
- Low trust level

Things to do:

- Share expectations (e.g., ask, "What do you expect to be different?")
- Develop (or revisit) the group's mission statement (what the work of the group is and how well the group plans to do it)

■ Focus on the process, rather than the task or the people
■ Begin to identify group norms—the "OK" behavior for the group

The goal of this stage is *acceptance of and commitment to the group.*

Stage 2: Storming

At this stage, resistance begins and arguments surface. Members begin to

■ Argue more freely for their own opinions, beliefs, thoughts, or ideas
■ Compete for attention and influence
■ Challenge any leaders that try to emerge
■ Reject task responsibilities and leave action items incomplete

"The honeymoon is over." Personality disputes erupt and, because members are uncomfortable, attendance drops off. During this stormy stage, the group must learn to manage conflict if it is to be effective.

Frustrations that may be encountered:

■ Rehashing the same issues over and over
■ Good data generation but no action taken
■ High frustration from playing win/lose
■ Norms not followed
■ Negativism and distrust apparent
■ Subcommittees crossing lines and "banging heads"

Things to do:

■ Agree to disagree
■ Not make it personal
■ Decide how the group is going to handle conflict, and then handle it
■ Stop to look at the group's process, goals, objectives, and mission
■ Stick to the ground rules and norms
■ Shuffle committee members
■ Reduce meeting time
■ Take some action (risk taking)

The goal of this stage is *clarification of the group's major activities and a sense of belonging as group members.*

Stage 3: Norming

Group norms and boundaries are now in place and the work group begins to function more effectively. The first signs of teamwork are that members

- Become more sensitive to each other's needs
- Share ideas, information, opinions, a feeling of togetherness, and pride in the team
- Accept the team structure and support each other
- Manage conflict
- Concentrate on a common goal instead of working as individuals

Team spirit builds, cliques dissolve, and a team identification emerges (characterized by private jokes and jargon). Real progress is made toward achieving goals because committees are working well, risk taking is supported, creativity is rewarded, and members willingly accept tasks and assignments. Attendance is high and everyone contributes. The trust level increases.

Frustrations that may be encountered:

- Team possibly not open to external resources and stakeholders
- High activity with low productivity
- Overuse of consensus
- Competition with other, similar teams

Things to do:

- Invite guests (managers and others) to meetings
- Present to outsiders (reality test) and get feedback from stakeholders
- Visit other teams and look at external resources
- Examine alternative processes and decision-making methods
- Review accomplishments in light of objectives

The goal of this stage is to *gain external involvement and internal support.*

Stage 4: Performing

The team is now working at full capacity. Leadership is shared or meetings seem to run without a formal leader. Team members

- Know their roles and follow team norms and ground rules
- Work well together

- Have a high degree of commitment to the goals of the team
- Are proud of the work accomplished by the team

Frustrations that may be encountered:

- Resting on the team's laurels
- Not moving on with new projects
- Lack of planning
- No adjustment of the mission
- Projects seen as being beneath the team
- Totally independent action by team members
- Diminishment of risk taking, innovation, creativity

Things to do:

- Plan for transition
- Look at the process
- Rearrange responsibilities and subcommittees
- Bring in other teams and resources
- Reexamine the mission
- Redo structure

The goal of this stage is to *take pride in team achievements.*

Stage 5: Ending

This stage is not always included in the stages of team development because it means that the team is changing. After all, at this stage, the tasks have been completed and the team is ready to move on to something new. The team may be given a new set of goals to accomplish or may react this way if several members leave at one time or after an extended period of downtime, like the break between Christmas and New Years or facility changeovers. Members feel disoriented or at loose ends because they have lost the team association. If the team is to continue with another project, its members will probably go through most of the earlier stages of team development, though more quickly now since some of the members have been exposed to the process. In this stage, the team also celebrates, pays attention to lessons learned (both positive and negative), and gives praise to those who deserve it.

Frustrations that may be encountered:

- Failure of transition to occur
- Loss of focus; no sense of direction

- Members drop out; attendance decreases
- Members feel that they do not fit in anymore
- Team spirit degenerates

Things to do:

- Declare victory and celebrate
- Set new goals
- Search out new projects
- Plan for the transition
- Seek external recognition
- Get new stakeholder expectations for the team

The goal of this stage is *satisfaction with and recognition of a job well done.*

Now that we understand the transition, let us address some additional general points. First, the advantages of teams include:

- A new way of working
- Greater freedom for employees to do a better job
- Improved cooperation between management and union
- Improved communication
- Improved productivity and quality
- Creating a competitive edge

Second, there are four key elements imperative for team formation:

- Shared goals
- A work team with a reason for working together
- Interdependence
- Team members' ability to depend on each other:
  - Every member has some experience, knowledge, and ability to help meet the goals of the team.
  - There must be commitment to complete the goal of the team.
  - Members of the team must be committed to the idea that working together as a team leads to better work tasks than working as individuals would.
  - Each member must be accountable and responsible for completing the items assigned to him or her.
  - The team fails or succeeds together.
  - Members are accountable to the team as well as to the larger organization.

Summary

In this chapter, we addressed the issues of the administrative process in team development, and we gave a cursory explanation of the internal development and transition of individuals to a team. In the next chapter, we continue the discussion but the focus now is on the logistical issues that teams face once they have been formed.

Selected Bibliography

Blanchard, K. 2005. *Go team! Take your team to the next level.* San Francisco, CA: Berret-Koehler Publishing, Inc.

Kimble, C., B. Alexis, and F. Li. 2000. Effective virtual teams through communities of practice. Department of Management science research paper series, 00/9. University of Strathclyde, Strathclyde, UK.

Richards, T., and S. T. Moger. 1999. *Handbook for creative team leaders.* Aldershot, Hants, England: Gower Publishing.

————. 2000. Creative leadership processes in project team development: An alternative to Tuckman's model. *British Journal of Management* 4: 273–283.

Tuckman, B. 1965. Developmental sequence in small groups. *Psychological Bulletin* 63 (6): 384–399.

Chapter 5

Logistical Issues
of Teams

Introduction

In the last chapter, we introduced the administrative process in team development and a summary explanation of the internal development and transition of individuals to a team. In this chapter, we emphasize that in every quality improvement initiative—whether it is total quality management or the current wave of interest in Six Sigma or Lean—the concept of teams and meetings is always present. Specifically, here we will provide some of the logistical issues that teams go through and must be aware of as they move toward improvement of the organization.

Everyone that has dealt with teams has experienced a moment or two of frustration, boredom, confusion, unresponsiveness to the issues, lack of commitment of management and team members ... and the list goes on. On the other hand, many have experienced totally different outcomes, such as productivity, collaboration, high emotional activity, satisfaction, completion of tasks, and certainly an aura of sharing open information, to name a few. Let us examine some of the items that we must consider in the team environment to be successful.

To Meet or Not to Meet

Perhaps one of the most important questions that all of us have to answer is whether a team needs to meet or not. Here, we provide some guidelines:

- ■ When to meet
  - – To provide information and ask for feedback
  - – To demonstrate a process
  - – To provide opportunity for teamwork
  - – To gather and share input on projects
  - – To gain acceptance for an idea
  - – To make a decision
  - – To brainstorm, pool ideas, and discuss options
  - – To reconcile conflicting views

- ■ When not to meet
  - – When providing information with no opportunity for feedback
  - – When a memo or phone call would achieve the same result
  - – When there is insufficient time to prepare
  - – When expected results do not warrant spending time and money to hold the meeting

- ■ Meeting quiz
  - – Ask the following questions when deciding to hold a meeting. If two out of three questions are answered with "yes," then most likely a meeting is the best strategy.
    - • Do I need a team? ___Yes ___ No
    - • Does someone else agree a meeting is needed? ___Yes ___ No
    - • Is this really my issue? ___ Yes ___ No

There will be times when a decision may need to be made quickly. It may be appropriate for a leader to make a decision without the benefit of input from others. Communicate the decision to others as soon as possible. On the other hand, if the meeting is strictly for communication purposes, then the following may be more effective:

- ■ One-on-one conversation
- ■ Phone call
- ■ Social gathering
- ■ Memo
- ■ Electronic mail

After determining when, why, and how long to hold a meeting, decide on the type of meeting:

- *Information:* The focus of this meeting is the flow of information down from management, up and across from work groups, and across from department to department. Presentations are common at such meetings, as are question and answer sessions.
- *Team building:* The focus of this type of meeting is on how a group of individuals is working together and what they can do to improve their relationships with each other.
- *Transition:* During times of change, the culture of an organization under-goes stress and even crisis. Meetings can bring together both those causing the change and those affected by it.
- *Orientation:* The focus of this meeting is to orient individuals to a new job, task, work team, etc. This provides individuals with an opportunity to learn about the job at hand.
- *Problem solving:* The focus of this meeting is to focus on a problem or opportunity for improvement and to share information and brainstorm solutions. Often a problem-solving method such as the 8D or the PDSA (plan-do-study-act) methodologies will be used.

Once the determination has been made that a team is required and the type of meeting decided upon, the next item of concern is where to meet and how long the meeting should be. Where a meeting is held makes a difference because it sets the tone. Table 5.1 identifies some of the considerations that have to be addressed when deciding on the place to meet.

Setting Objectives

A good meeting depends upon having a good objective to support it. If there is a good, clear objective, what needs to be accomplished will be clear and processes that will help to get there can be chosen. When a meeting is being set up, first ask:

- Are the operational definitions clear to everyone?
- Does this meeting have a clear objective? Does the objective require a meeting?
- What do I want to accomplish with this meeting?
- Is this purpose worth the cost of holding a meeting?

Table 5.1 Typical Considerations for Deciding Where to Meet

Location	Advantages	Disadvantages	Length of Meeting
Formal location such as a supervisor's office	Good for visibility Usually quiet and provides privacy from distractions	May intimidate participants and impede information sharing May not be free from distractions such as ringing phones	Average meeting lengths vary between 1 and 2 hours. It is important to keep in mind the following points: The length of the meeting is clearly stated on the agenda
Home turf (conference room)	Relaxed atmosphere, familiar	Distraction to participants, noise level	The meeting starts on time
Off site	Neutral atmosphere, no interruptions	Timing of meeting could be put off, inconvenient Chance of lack of participation Room availability	The time to be spent on each agenda item is specified next to the item The timing on the agenda items is kept without making participants feel rushed The meeting ends on time

Effective objectives should be:

- Specific
- Measurable
- Results oriented

A good check for self-evaluation as to whether good objectives are in place is to ask:

- Why am I holding this meeting?
- What do I want to achieve in this meeting?
- What do I need to accomplish after this meeting is over?

The format for an objective is "to [action] [measurable result] and [condition].) The condition may be placed anywhere in the objective. An example of an objective would be "to select [*action*] a course of action to increase our efficiency in registration of walk-in patients at the ER [*condition*] by 10% by the end of the year [*measurable result*]."

Selecting Participants

How many times have you attended a meeting at which the people needed to accomplish its purpose were not there? Have you ever been at a meeting and wondered why you or someone else was invited, since there was nothing that you or he or she could add? This topic helps to identify who should be invited and why.

Once a purpose has been set, the next task is to identify those people who have the skills and knowledge that will help to achieve that purpose. Meeting participants are as important to consider as meeting logistics. There are different types of people who will take part in a meeting—for example:

- Deciders
- Doers
- Getters

In selecting the meeting participants, remember the old saying that the number of people invited is directly proportional to the length of any meeting. Here, we provide a small list of general selection criteria. Our recommendation is to invite those who

- Have necessary knowledge or skills
- Are responsible for or must approve any decision
- Must carry out decisions
- May oppose decisions
- Are new and need some exposure to a topic

Creating an Agenda

An agenda is essential for informing each of the participants on what will take place in the meeting, what prep work is necessary prior to the meeting, and how long the meeting will last. The agenda details the

- Purpose
- Items to be covered
- Background information necessary to prepare for the meeting
- Time to be spent on each agenda item

For the agenda to be most effective, participants should receive it 24 hours before the meeting occurs. Agendas may vary in format according to the topic of the meeting. However, some elements are essential for a good agenda and should appear in some form. The following are typical agenda items:

- Meeting participants (listed in alphabetical order)
- Objective (stated with an action and a measurable result)
- Meeting date
- Meeting time (start and ending times)
- Location (including room number and directions if necessary)
- Agenda items (Make sure they are in a form of an action plan that leads to the objective. The agenda may list the person responsible for that item and the time allocated. By listing the agenda items with times for each, participants do not need to stay for the whole meeting if they are required for only one agenda item.)
- Prior knowledge that participants should have and preparation required so that everyone comes prepared and the meeting can run smoothly

Establishing Meeting Roles and Ground Rules

Establishing effective meeting roles is an essential part of a successful work team. The challenge for a work team is to establish a way of operating that will support all the roles and responsibilities that the team members need to fill. Roles, responsibilities, and ground rules help define how the work team will work together.

Key items here are jointly to define how the group will function within a meeting framework. New or already formed work teams could benefit from investing time in talking about some of the following key issues:

- How should we function as a team?
- How should we make decisions?
- What do we expect from one another as members?
- How will we track our progress?
- What are the roles and responsibilities of an effective work team such as ours?

Work teams that become cohesive and maintain their effectiveness balance their focus between task and process issues. Effective work team members monitor both task and process issues and openly discuss continual improvement.

Meeting Leader

The meeting leader is a spokesperson for the team, calls the meetings, establishes a meeting time, and directs the meeting to follow the agenda. He or she is the day-to-day authority responsible for the overall coordination and helps the team to achieve its goals and objectives. The role of the meeting leader may rotate from person to person. The person who is the leader of one meeting or series of meetings may be a participant or facilitator in another meeting. Specific leader responsibilities include:

- Preparing a detailed agenda in advance
- Introducing the participants
- Presenting the agenda
- Inviting team participants
- Establishing ground rules with participants
- Bringing closure by summarizing and stating conclusions clearly
- Developing final review and wrap-up by reviewing a list of open issues
- Gaining quick resolution when possible and/or assigning responsibility
- Summarizing accomplishments
- Reviewing follow-up activities
- Conducting an evaluation of the session

Facilitator

The facilitator monitors the team's interaction to help keep members focused on their goal and ensures that all members get an opportunity to participate. The facilitator needs to be neutral in terms of content and is looked upon as the process expert. We must make a key point here: Within the team meeting, a facilitator will probably not always be necessary. The group leader can keep the meeting flowing using the agenda, and he or she will often have facilitation skills, along with other group members. On the other hand, if there are too many experts (two or more) on the team, it is a very good idea to have a facilitator to make sure that the experts do not monopolize the discussion.

Participants

The participants are team members responsible for carrying out assignments given to the team. They accomplish this by being receptive to consensus decision making, listening actively to other members, keeping an open mind, and being committed to following the steps of the problem-solving process. Specific responsibilities of participants include:

- Contributing ideas
- Providing requirements
- Stating preferences
- Challenging ideas
- Defending ideas
- Participating in reaching consensus

Recorder

The recorder is a team member responsible for taking notes during the meeting and for writing, publishing, and distributing the minutes. The recorder often works with the leader to coordinate logistics. He or she does not write down everything that is said and does not record the name of the speaker. The recorder is responsible for supporting the facilitator. The primary responsibilities include recording and displaying each conclusion, decision, or open issue of the team within easy view or with rapid retrieval throughout the session. The recorder also will provide the supplies and equipment as needed by the facilitator. The recorder

- Captures notes about the discussion
- Documents only what the team decides

Ground Rules

Prior to beginning a facilitated meeting, the establishment of ground rules needs to occur. In order to have ground rules that will be adhered to by the team, it is important that the facilitator involve the participants in the development of their ground rules. This will help create an effective working environment. Generally, team development of ground rules leads to team enforcement of the rules. Some typical rules include:

- Treat others as equals, not as inferiors.
- Be sincere, not manipulative and sneaky.
- Genuinely care about others, rather than being indifferent or uncaring.
- Keep an open mind rather than being certain and dogmatic.
- Be descriptive and specific rather than evaluative and vague.
- Concentrate on solving problems rather than on blaming others.
- Assume others have good intentions rather than assuming that they are devious.

- Explain the "what" and the "why"; do not assume that purpose or intentions are automatically understood.
- Listen for the other person's point of view; we do not always share the same reality.
- Encourage everyone to give input; do not dominate.
- Accept and appreciate the differences in others; do not let stereotypes run the meetings.
- Watch and respond to the way people interact at every meeting; how people work together affects the outcome.

Room Setup

The room in which a meeting is held should be convenient for all participants. Different furniture arrangements can change the atmosphere dramatically. Before a room is reserved, think about the atmosphere to be created and select a room that conveys that atmosphere. When planning for and selecting facilities, the following issues should be addressed:

- Room
- Equipment
- Supplies

Room

Participants are seated so that they are able to see each other and the facilitator easily. There are many ways to set up a room for a meeting. Some of the most common setups are listed here:

- U-shaped tables
  - Limited interaction
  - Emphasize importance of leader
  - Work well for viewing most visual aids
  - Invite formation of teams

- Small tables
  - Encourage strong team identity and discussion for each table
  - Reduce importance of leader
  - Reduce likelihood of table-to-table discussion
  - Make viewing of visual aids awkward
  - Set an informal, restaurant-like tone for a meeting

- Rectangular tables
  - Emphasize the importance of the leader
  - Encourage discussion

- Circular tables
  - De-emphasize the importance of the leader
  - Make viewing of visual aids awkward
  - Invite participant-to-participant discussion

- Oval tables
  - Emphasize importance of leader and, at the other end of the table, the leader's chief cohort or antagonist
  - Invite formation of teams, with one side of the table opposed to the other side
  - Encourage some participant-to-participant discussion, especially across the table
  - Work well for viewing most visual aids

Other Considerations

In addition to the previous issues, other items should also be considered for a smooth and effective meeting:

- Chairs need to be comfortable and provide necessary support.
- A table should provide ample writing space for each participant.
- Wall space should be ample if charts need to be posted.
- There need to be sufficient numbers of flip charts and markers; flip charts need to be placed in locations for everyone to have access and visibility.
- Check where electrical outlets are located and that they are working.
- The computer and/or projector in the room should work and not be placed on the wrong side of the room. It is generally a good idea to arrange meeting equipment so that it is near the front of the room. That way it is easy for the leader, facilitator, and recorder to get to it.

Equipment

In our modern technological world, one should consider the appropriate and applicable equipment for delivery and presentation. High on the list of equipment should be:

- Computer
- Applicable software for presentation, *i.e.* PowerPoint, etc.

- Projector
- Other miscellaneous items as described in the below supplies list

Supplies

In many team meetings, supplies are always an issue. It is very hard for all involved if, in the middle of the meeting, the appropriate supplies are not available. Obviously, no two meetings are alike and therefore the appropriate supplies depend on the meeting type. What is important here is to make sure that supplies are ample and available for all participants. The following is a list of typical meeting supplies:

- Speaker or presenter
  - Blackboard
  - Flip chart stand
  - Overhead sheets (colors)
  - Slide projector and remote control
  - Chalk (colors) and eraser
  - Overhead projector
  - Overhead pens (colors)

- Participants
  - Writing pads
  - Highlighters
  - Name cards on table
  - Pens
  - Binders or folders

- Facilitator
  - Flip charts
  - Masking tape (1 inch)
  - Overhead projector
  - Overhead pens
  - Chalk and eraser
  - 16 mm Projector
  - Computer projector
  - Screens
  - Microcomputer or terminals
  - Markers (colors)
  - Magnets
  - Overhead sheets
  - Blackboard
  - Tape recorder
  - Extra bulbs
  - VCR (format?)
  - Monitor
  - Extension cords

Facility Considerations

It is important to make sure that the meeting room will meet needs. These are some important points to keep in mind:

- Main room
  - Seating/size
  - Flexibility in setup
  - Ventilation/acoustics audiovisual capabilities

- Ease of access
  - Fire and emergency exits and procedures
  - Transportation
  - Handicapped participants
  - Message system

- Breakout room
  - Availability at all times; numbers/sizes
  - Equipment
  - Proximity to main room

Starting a Meeting

Starting a meeting on time helps to set a tone and is as important as the location and setup of the room. Starting on time keeps the meeting focused. To help make the start of a meeting as effective as possible, keep these tips in mind:

- Post the agenda on a flip chart or wall so that everyone can see it.
- Introduce all of the participants.
- Restate the objectives and agenda items.
- Bring extra copies of the agenda and past meeting minutes to every meeting.

Establishing Team Strategies and Objectives

It is important at the beginning of a meeting to establish the strategies and objectives. This will help the meeting start effectively, stay on track, and end with a successful outcome. Every meeting needs to have an objective. The meeting facilitator's role is to make sure that everyone understands and agrees with that objective. If the objective is stated in the agenda, make sure everyone knows what the objective is. Also make sure that everyone agrees that this is an important objective that can be accomplished by those who are attending the meeting. If the objective is not stated in the agenda, this is a good topic to start the meeting with. Use a brainstorming process to get input on what the objective is and then use a consensus process to get agreement on the objective. Furthermore, make sure that all operational definitions have been identified, explained, understood, and agreed upon.

Establishing ground rules for a meeting is very important, especially if the team has not met before. Use a brainstorming process to get participants to identify the ground rules for

- Interruptions
- Critique and criticism
- Handling differences of opinion
- Participation
- Interpersonal conflict

It is critical that all participants be comfortable with each ground rule.

Involving All Team Members and Building Team Consensus

Involvement of all members is an essential element of an effective work team. Without total involvement, consensus may not be reached. Various situations arise in work team meetings that keep involvement from being less than 100% effective. Two of the most common situations include:

- Team members who do not give any input
- Low participation by the team as a whole

If one or both of these situations are encountered, the following may help:

- Utilize active listening techniques to encourage people to speak.
- Call on people who have not spoken—for example, "Fred, you have been kind of quiet. What do you think?"
- Go around the room and ask each individual to voice an opinion.

Team consensus holds the work team together and makes it easy for its members to carry out their decision. It is important that all team members are on board and that they own and understand the decision. Team consensus is reached when all members can say that they agree with the decision, that they can live with the disagreement, or that they have had their "day in court." It is imperative that, when consensus is reached, all participants say, "We have agreed to …." as opposed to "They have agreed to …." Three approaches are useful when trying to obtain team consensus:

- Compromise. After listening to all of the different opinions, the team tries to find a way to incorporate parts of all opinions so that each party agrees. A good rule of thumb for compromise is the 70% agreement to 30% disagreement.
- Very active discussion (simulated debate). Individuals are asked to make the strongest case they can for their positions. The debate, or contest

between opinions, may bring out unexpected or unrecognized advantages to one position or another that may help the team to make a decision. A variation on this process is to ask the meeting participants to switch sides and debate in favor of someone else's idea.

■ Forced decision (used as a last choice and not recommended). This leaves the decision up to the team leader, but should only be used after the team has tried both compromise and simulated debate but found them to be unsuccessful.

Applying Active Listening Skills

Listening sounds like an easy task, but even when one intends to listen, distractions or barriers can cause receipt of inaccurate or distorted messages or even missing the message. For example, if there are distractions, such as people having a lively conversation nearby while one is on the phone, it is quite difficult to concentrate fully on the phone conversation.

Most listening problems are not caused because we miss one small detail, but rather because we fail to listen between the lines and pick up what the speaker is truly saying. Active listening is especially important in helping one to go beyond behavior and begin to understand thoughts and feelings. Understanding provides what is "really" being said. The goal of active listening is to receive cues from the whole person.

Listening skills allow one to go beyond the verbal message to hear

■ The content of what is being said
■ How the individual feels about what is being said

Good listening skills include:

■ Maintaining eye contact with the speaker
■ Asking questions to clarify what is being said

Listening can also help in hearing what is not being said. During a session, listen and try to understand others' verbal and nonverbal messages. This can also be critical in building rapport. Nonverbal behavior includes tone of voice, rate of speech, body posture, and facial expressions. At times, nonverbal messages may not match the verbal message. Researchers have found that up to 95% of the meaning in a message comes from nonverbal cues. However, to interpret the nonverbal cues, it is necessary to consider them in their proper context. A gesture in itself rarely has a standard meaning. Like words, gestures can have many meanings. The correct meaning is understood by the context in which it is used. For example, it is important to be aware of and read nonverbal messages in active listening. The following are examples of nonverbal messages:

- Speaking in a monotone or slow speed and low pitch, which might indicate boredom or depression
- Nervous speech and loud tone, which may indicate anger

On the other hand, verbal messages include statements about

- How an individual perceives a situation
- The feelings that the individual is experiencing
- Details about the situation at hand

Carefully listening to what an individual says and does not say will help form a clearer picture of the situation. Be aware of "trigger words" that an individual may use. Trigger words cause us to listen subjectively rather than objectively and, as a result, our listening efficiency drops to zero. For example, the words "deadline," "budget," and "overtime" may trigger an emotional response within an organization. It may not be possible to stop this from happening, but one may be able to listen more effectively if one knows which words are likely to evoke such a response.

Leading a Brainstorming Session

A very common approach to discussing a problem or a solution in a variety of situations is the brainstorming technique. A facilitator will often lead brainstorming sessions. Here are some tips:

- Brainstorming is used to generate a large number of ideas on any given subject. The idea behind brainstorming is that ideas generated by an uninhibited group are likely to be much more numerous and creative than those generated by one individual.
- Brainstorming can be used to identify problems, the causes of problems, and their solutions.

The following guidelines should be used as "ground rules" or standards that the whole group follows when taking part in this activity:

- Everyone in the group should understand the problem to be addressed.
- All ideas are good ideas.

- Free-wheeling and building on previous ideas is encouraged.
- No idea is criticized.
- Everyone is encouraged to participate.
- All ideas are recorded.
- All members have equal opportunity to participate.

Two types of approaches can be used when facilitating a brainstorming session:

- Structured. The advantage of using this approach is that it allows all the individuals in the group to give their ideas as their turn arises in the rotation or pass until the next round. It also allows every member of the group an equal chance to participate. On the other hand, using this approach risks decreasing the creativity of the group, due to increased structure.
- Unstructured. The advantage of using this approach is that it allows the group to give ideas quickly and easily as they come to mind. It also creates a more relaxed atmosphere. On the other hand, using this approach risks unequal participation from the group.

Now that the ground rules have been established and the method of participation determined, the brainstorming session can start. Next steps include:

- Stating the purpose of the brainstorming session and establish all the ground rules
- Telling the team which method of participation will be used
- Having the team members generate a large number of ideas
- Recording all ideas on a flip chart and posting them so that everyone can see what has been recorded
- Letting ideas incubate (Note: Once brainstorming has started, the ideas will come much more quickly. Do not stop brainstorming too soon. Let some time go by to allow ideas to surface by themselves.)
- After all ideas have been recorded, reviewing and clarifying the ideas and determining what action needs to be taken

We hope that the preceding information gives the reader a good idea as to what steps to follow when facilitating a brainstorming session. However, that is not the end of the process. A successful brainstorming session will produce a large amount of feedback, but often not in a clear, concise manner because

- The participant has a hard time expressing his or her idea
- The idea is not completely thought through
- The idea is badly stated

In the event that any of these three things occurs, the following facilitation actions should be taken:

- Use active listening skills and encourage the speaker to elaborate.
- If necessary, ask questions to clarify.
- Restate the idea in more concise form without changing the participant's meaning.
- Thank the participant for being willing to contribute.

Handling Difficult Situations

Not every brainstorming session or meeting is "a piece of cake." Often, participants' feelings and personalities get in the way of an effective brainstorming session. But there are ways around this issue. Following are five common situations and facilitation actions that can be taken to help eliminate or diffuse a difficult situation.

SITUATION 1: ONE INDIVIDUAL DOMINATES THE WHOLE GROUP AND CONVERSATION

Facilitation actions may include:

- Intervening to regain control without embarrassing the individual
- Involving other members of the team in the discussion; if necessary, using the ground rules, which might include: "Do not speak again until someone else has spoken"
- If necessary, going around the room and asking each individual to voice an opinion

SITUATION 2: TWO OR MORE PARTICIPANTS GET STUCK IN A CONFLICT OF OPINIONS

Facilitation actions may include:

- Commenting on what has been observed
- Reminding participants of the purpose of the meeting
- Expressing confidence that agreement can be reached
- Identifying or listing items on which participants can agree
- Identifying or listing items on which participants disagree
- Resolving disagreements
- Refocusing the group

SITUATION 3: TWO OR MORE PARTICIPANTS CONTINUALLY ENGAGE IN SIDE CONVERSATIONS

Facilitation actions may include:

- Establishing direct eye contact with the participants involved
- Not embarrassing the participants involved. Try calling on one by name and restating the last opinion expressed in the team, asking the participant for his or her response to the statement. If the behavior persists and is disruptive to the team, remind the team as a whole of the ground rules, which might include: "No side or private conversation."
- If the behavior still persists, having the group take a break and speaking to the participants privately

SITUATION 4: A PARTICIPANT OFFERS AN IDEA THAT IS IGNORED BY THE TEAM

Facilitation actions may include:

- Bringing the team's attention to the fact that someone just offered an idea
- Writing down or otherwise recording the idea
- Asking for further discussion of the idea
- Thanking the participant who offered the idea

SITUATION 5: A PARTICIPANT OFFERS AN IDEA THAT IS RIDICULED OR ATTACKED

Facilitation actions may include:

- Reminding participants as a team of the ground rules, which might include:
  - There are to be no put-downs.
  - Every idea gets fair consideration.
- Writing down or otherwise recording the idea
- Thanking the participant who offered the idea

Keeping the Meeting on Track

Often, no matter how good the intentions to stay on track may be, the meeting digresses and gets off track. How can this be controlled? Again, specific situations will need appropriate actions. However, here we provide two very common situations and facilitation actions to help with keeping on track.

SITUATION 1

One of the following may happen:

- The team gets off the topic.
- Individuals interrupt each other.
- There are constant interruptions (phone calls, beepers, etc.).

Facilitation actions could include:

- Commenting on what has been observed:
  - "I think we are off the topic."
  - "I notice that we are having quite a few interruptions."
- Reminding participants of the ground rules, which might include:
  - Hold all phone calls.
  - Respond to emergency messages only.
  - Leave beepers with a secretary.
  - Do not interrupt the speaker.
- Refocusing the team:
  - Restate the purpose of the meeting or discussion.
  - Summarize progress up to the point of digression. Bring the team back on topic by asking a question or making a statement.

SITUATION 2

The group members seem bored and restless because:

- There is difficulty in resolving an agenda topic.
- Participants are "groping" for ideas.

Facilitation actions could include:

- Using one's voice:
  - Raise the volume
  - Raise the tone
  - Speak faster
- Commenting on what has been observed:
  - For example, "We seem to be getting bogged down."
- Increasing one's movement in front of the team
- Bringing the present agenda topic to closure by
  - Suggesting a possible solution
  - Delegating the solution to someone (e.g., set a firm time for team review)
  - Posting the issue on a "to be discussed" list and coming back to it later
  - Asking the team members if they are ready to move on
  - If necessary, taking a break

Close the meeting with something that makes participants feel like they have accomplished something. Enthusiasm and positive reinforcement are a "catch" for more of the same. Typical things to do:

- Note benchmarks and achievements
- Summarize decisions

- Agree on next steps and follow-up actions
- Thank participants for coming
- Announce the time for the next meeting (if known)

After the closing of the meeting, the leader still has some responsibilities to complete, such as:

- Making sure that minutes are written
- Making sure that minutes are distributed
- Making sure that follow-up actions happen
- Scheduling the next meeting (if needed)
- Debriefing the meeting
- Making sure that there is an evaluation of the meeting

Meeting Minutes

Every meeting must have documentation of its existence. The document should be drafted as soon as possible after the meeting. Its contents should (1) include verification of all dates and name spellings, and (2) be reviewed by one or two members for accuracy and completeness. When the draft has been approved by the members, it should be sent to (1) all members who attended, (2) all members who could not attend, and (3) others who need to be aware of meeting decisions. The final draft should also be marked with a retention stamp for traceability purposes. To help the recorder in the process of taking notes, a typical form like the one in Figure 5.1 may be used.

Meeting notes			
Agenda item	Decision reached	Person responsible for follow-up	Date to check status

Figure 5.1 A typical meeting-notes form.

Summary

In this chapter, we have addressed some of the most common logistical issues of teams. Specifically, we discussed concerns about the meeting, ground rules, and some of the actual handling situations between members. In the next chapter, we will cover the effects of change in healthcare.

Selected Bibliography

Goonan, K., and P. Stoltz. 2004. Leadership and management principles for outcomes-oriented organizations. *Medical Care* 42 (4 Suppl): III31–III38.

Norton, W., and L. Sussman. 2009. Team charters: Theoretical foundations and practical implications for quality performance. *Quality Management Journal* 16 (1): 7–17.

Chapter 6

The Effects of Change in Healthcare

Introduction

So far we have touched on some of the general issues of healthcare and addressed the concerns about change, teams, and the logistical problems that a team may have to encounter in the process of solving quality problems. In this chapter, we will focus specifically on the effects of change in healthcare. As we mentioned in the earlier chapters, change is inevitable and it happens all the time and everywhere. The question is how this change affects healthcare. To answer this question, we must understand at least the following several questions.

What Are We Trying to Accomplish?

In any endeavor of quality improvement, this question is very critical, for it sets the tone of what is about to happen. By asking this question, we focus on the objectives of what is to be accomplished—in other words, on *what it is* that has to be improved. That is, the question asks *what the aim is of this improvement* that we are seeking. The answer should be as specific as possible in terms of time, affected population (patients, in this case), and measurement. When we are in the process of defining our aim for any healthcare improvement, we should consider whether or not the pending improvement is

- *Safe:* Avoid patient injury from the care that is intended to help them.
- *Effective:* Match care to science; avoid overuse of ineffective care and underuse of effective care.
- *Patient centered:* Honor the individual and respect choice.
- *Timely:* Reduce waiting for both patients and those who give care.
- *Efficient:* Reduce waste.
- *Equitable:* Close racial and ethnic gaps in health status.

In a visualization format (Figure 6.1), we may express these six items as the "no-harm" approach or campaign. One can see that each one of these items may be articulated in a direct relationship to the patient by focusing on both internal and external requirements in the organization. Ultimately, the success of this

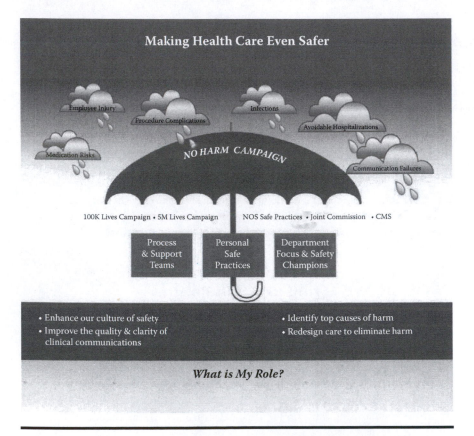

Figure 6.1 No-harm campaign.

approach or campaign depends on each and every individual throughout the organization.

How Do We Know Whether the Change Is Indeed an Improvement?

The answer to this question is measurement. This means that whatever we choose to do, we must be able to measure and track the change quantitatively and report on the results. We must focus on measuring characteristics that will lead us to improvement. If not, remember the words of Daniel Boorstin (1983 p.46) who cautions us that "the greatest obstacle to discovery is not ignorance, but rather the illusion of knowledge." With the wrong measurements that is easy to do. This is very important to recognize because once one has been taught or used erroneous ideas, it is hard to change. Obviously, for improvement to be considered as positive, the results must be better than before the change occurred.

Here we must make the distinction between measurement of research and measurement for learning and process improvement. The first deals with discovering new knowledge and the second with improving efficiency and effectiveness of the learning or process. In this book, we deal with the measurement for learning and process improvement as we try to bring improvement into the daily practice of healthcare, whether that practice is the doctor's office, clinic, urgent care facility, or even hospital. The significance of this approach may be summarized in Table 6.1.

Table 6.1 Measurement for Improvement

Characteristic	Measurement for Learning and Process Improvement
Purpose	To bring new knowledge into the daily practice
Tests	Many sequential, observable tests (reality testing)
Biases	Stabilize the biases from test to test (aim for consistency)
Data	Gather "just enough" data to learn and complete another cycle (cycles must be compatible)
Duration	"Small tests of significant changes" accelerate the rate of improvement (especially if the changes are recognized as assignable root causes)

What Are the Changes That Will Result in Expected Improvement?

All improvement requires making changes, but not all changes result in improvement. Organizations therefore must identify the changes that are most likely to result in improvement. In other words, the improvement must be expected (known to some degree) before the change occurs. That is part of the applicability and appropriateness of planning. One of the simplest and most often used approaches is the plan-do-study-act (PDSA) cycle. It is a model for testing a change in the real work setting by planning it, trying it, observing the results, and acting on what is learned. This is the scientific method used for action-oriented learning. Typical examples of such planning for improvement include:

- Shortened lead time and reduced errors in blood testing
- Developed a time-saving system for managing intravenous pumps
- Reduced errors and lead time for collecting and processing tissue samples
- Increased capacity by reducing room down-times between patients
- Boosted laboratory capacity and reduced errors through improved organization
- Increased physician productivity through standardized work processes
- Streamlined preregistration processes

However, these are but a small sample of the improvements that may be made all across healthcare. The ability to develop, test, and implement changes is essential for any individual, group, or organization that wants to improve continuously. Many kinds of changes will lead to improvement, but these specific changes are developed from a limited number of change concepts.

A change concept is a general notion or approach to change that has been found to be useful in developing specific ideas for changes that lead to improvement. Creatively combining these change concepts with knowledge about specific subjects can help generate ideas for tests of change. After generating ideas, PDSA cycles can be run to test a change or group of changes on a small scale to see whether they result in improvement. If they do, the tests can be expanded and gradually incorporate larger and larger samples until one is confident that the changes should be adopted more widely.

Where do we find these items for change? The basic answer is the reply to the question, "What is a bothersome activity or item that we have to do over again routinely?" Another basic question is, "Is there a better way to do this?" Typical approaches to finding improvement projects may be to use methodologies such as Lean or Six Sigma or the basic problem-solving technique (Stamatis 1996, 2002a, 2002b, 2002c, 2003a, 2003b, 2003c, 2003d). Specifically, items of concern may include:

- *Eliminate waste.* Look for ways of eliminating any activity or resource in the organization that does not add value to an external customer. (Use process or value mapping.)
- *Improve work flow.* Improving the flow of work in processes is an important way to improve the quality of the goods and services produced by those processes. (Use process or value mapping and teams.)
- *Optimize inventory.* Inventory of all types is a possible source of waste in organizations; understanding where inventory is stored in a system is the first step in finding opportunities for improvement. (Use Lean techniques.)
- *Change the work environment.* Changing the work environment can be a high-leverage opportunity for making all other process changes more effective. (Use process mapping and Lean techniques.)
- *Producer and/or customer interface.* To benefit from improvements in quality of products and services, the customer must recognize and appreciate the improvements. (Use the Kano model, quality function deployment [QFD], benchmarking, and Pugh diagram.)
- *Manage time.* An organization can gain a competitive advantage by reducing the time to develop new products, waiting times for services, lead times for orders and deliveries, and cycle times for all functions in the organization. (Use process or value mapping, and project management.)
- *Focus on variation.* Reducing variation improves the predictability of outcomes and helps reduce the frequency of poor results. (Use SPC [statistical process control] as much as possible.)
- *Error proof.* Organizations can reduce errors by redesigning the system to make it less likely that people in the system will make errors. One way to error proof a system is to make the information necessary to perform a task available in the external world, rather than just in one's memory, by writing it down or by making it inherent in the product or process. (Use mistake-proofing methodology and robust designs, and design processes using the design for Six Sigma [DFSS] methodology.)
- *Focus on the product or service.* Although many organizations focus on ways to improve processes, it is also important to address improvement of products and services. (Use benchmarking, Six Sigma, Lean, and teams.)

Table 6.2   The PDCA Model

PDCA Model	Actions	Example[a]
		Problem: planned visits for blood sugar management
Plan	Plan the test or observation, including a plan for collecting data. (1) State the objective of the test (2) Make predictions about what will happen and why (3) Develop a plan to test the change (who? what? when? where?) (4) Document what data need to be collected	Ask one patient if he or she would like more information on how to manage his or her blood sugar
Do	Try out the test on a small scale (1) Carry out the test (2) Document problems and unexpected observations (3) Begin analysis of the data	Dr. S. asked his first patient with diabetes on Tuesday
Check (study)	Set aside time to analyze the data and study the results (1) Complete the analysis of the data (2) Compare the data to predictions (3) Summarize and reflect on what was learned	Patient was interested; Dr. S. was pleased at the positive response
Act	Refine the change, based on what was learned from the test (1) Determine what modifications should be made (2) Prepare a plan for the next test	Dr. S. will continue with the next five patients and set up a planned visit for those who say yes

Notes: *Implementing changes:* After testing a change on a small scale, learning from each test, and refining the change through several PDCA cycles, the team can implement the change on a broader scale—for example, for an entire pilot population or on an entire unit. For example, testing a change: three nurses on different shifts use a new medication reconciliation and order form; implementing a change: all 30 nurses on the pilot unit begin using the new medication reconciliation and order form.

Table 6.2   The PDCA Model (Continued)

Spreading changes: After successful implementation of a change or package of changes for a pilot population or an entire unit, the team can spread the changes to other parts of the organization or in other organizations. For example, if all 30 nurses on a pilot unit successfully implement a new medication reconciliation and order form, then "spread" would be replicating this change in all nursing units in the organization and assisting the units in adopting or adapting to the change.

[a] Depending on their aim, teams choose promising changes and use PDCA cycles to test a change quickly on a small scale, see how it works, and refine the change as necessary before implementing it on a broader scale. This diabetes example shows how a team started with a small-scale test.

Testing Changes

The PDCA cycle is shorthand for testing a change in the real work setting by planning it, trying it, observing the results, and acting on what is learned (see Table 6.2). This is the scientific method used for action-oriented learning and understanding the process. Reasons to test changes abound; some of the most important are:

- To increase the belief that the change will result in improvement
- To decide which of several proposed changes will lead to the desired improvement
- To evaluate how much improvement can be expected from the change
- To decide whether the proposed change will work in the actual environment of interest
- To decide which combinations of changes will have the desired effects on the important measures of quality
- To evaluate costs, social impact, and side effects of a proposed change
- To minimize resistance upon implementation

Summary

This chapter addressed some of the basic issues concerning the effects of change in healthcare. In the next chapter, we will focus on the customer satisfaction process and how we can deal with it in the many phases of healthcare.

References

Boorstin, D. 1983. *The Discoverers: A History of Man's Search to Know His World and Himself.* New York: Random House

Stamatis, D. H. 1996. *Total quality management in healthcare.* New York: McGraw–Hill.

————. 2002a. *Six Sigma and beyond: Design for Six Sigma.* Boca Raton, FL: St. Lucie Press.

————. 2002b. *Six Sigma and beyond: Foundation of excellence performance.* Boca Raton, FL: St. Lucie Press.

————. 2002c. *Six Sigma and beyond: Statistical problem solving and basic math.* Boca Raton, FL: St. Lucie Press.

————. 2003a. *Six Sigma and beyond: Design of experiment.* Boca Raton, FL: St. Lucie Press.

————. 2003b. *Six Sigma and beyond: Statistical process control.* Boca Raton, FL: St. Lucie Press.

————. 2003c. *Six Sigma and beyond: Statistics and probability.* Boca Raton, FL: St. Lucie Press.

————. 2003d. *Six Sigma and beyond: The implementation process.* Boca Raton, FL: St. Lucie Press.

Selected Bibliography

Feinstein, K. 2000. We can't reward what we can't perform: The primacy of learning to change systems. *Health Affairs (Millwood).* July–December (supplement Web exclusives): W118–119.

Frampton, S., L. Gilpin, and P. Charmel. 2003. *Putting patients first: Designing and practicing patient-centered care.* San Francisco, CA: Jossey–Bass.

Neuman, K. 2000. Understanding organizational reengineering in health care: Strategies for social work's survival. *Social Work in Health Care* 31 (1): 19–33.

Pillar, B., and D. Jarjoura. 1999. Assessing the impact of reengineering on nursing. *Journal of Nursing Administration* 29 (5): 57–64.

Thompson, D. N., G. A. Wolf, and S. J. Spear. 2003. Driving improvement in patient care: Lessons from Toyota. *Journal of Nursing Administration* 33 (11): 585–595.

Van Matre, J., and K. Koch. 2009. Understanding healthcare clinical process and outcome measures and their use in the Baldrige award application process. *Quality Management Journal* 16 (1): 18–28.

Chapter 7

Customer Satisfaction

Introduction

So far we have discussed the issues facing healthcare and the concept of change and its effect on healthcare. In addition, we had a cursory view of the logistical concerns about the teams. In this chapter, our focus is customer satisfaction. The issue is very important because, as we have said several times, satisfaction is dependent on whom we recognize as the customer. In healthcare, that is a dynamic definition since many are considered to be customers.

To be successful in 2010 and beyond, organizations must recognize and deal with the convergence of two indisputable forces: the primacy of customer service as a competitive weapon and the pervasive role of information technology in the value chain. These are not independent forces. Although information technology (IT) has the ability to redefine businesses, alter industry structure, and foster entirely new types of enterprise, its greatest unrealized potential is in the area of customer service.

The concept of high-quality customer service is difficult to define, especially in healthcare. Everyone seems to recognize quality service when they experience it. However, defining customer service that is perceived as high quality is complicated because it involves individual perceptions. Healthcare customers typically do not merely regard the finished product or service as the measure of service; they will also take into account the process by which the finished service or product was obtained—the overall experience. This may include the time it takes to obtain the service, the friendliness of the medical staff, and so on. An outstanding performance on one aspect can help overcome a mediocre performance on another.

Another factor that complicates the evaluation of quality customer service is that the only opinion or point of view that matters is that of the customer. Customer service may meet all the criteria for quality, but if, according to the customer, it is lacking some key ingredient, then it fails as quality customer service. Therefore, service quality, as perceived by customers, can be defined as the extent of discrepancy between customers' expectations or desires and their perceptions.

The next key factor is to determine which criteria define the customers' expectations of quality service. The Marketing Science Institute of Cambridge, Massachusetts, identified 10 dimensions of service quality in focus group studies. These dimensions are tangibles, reliability, responsiveness, competence, courtesy, credibility, security, access, communication, and understanding the customer. For a detailed explanation of these items, see Zeithaml, Parasuraman, and Berry (1990). These 10 dimensions, to varying degrees, are consciously or subconsciously used by the customer to assess the quality level or the service received. The customer then compares the assessed level to his or her preconceived expectations. Shortfalls result in customer dissatisfaction.

Almost all organizations compete on service to some degree. Does the Cleveland Clinic sell open heart surgeries or the personal attention, expertise, and overall care that come with and after the surgery? The perceived quality of all processes involved in the purchase and service experience balanced against expectations determines whether the customer will return to the clinic. Several factors contributing to organizations' emphasis on quality customer service will accelerate and become more acute in the years to come.

Much has been written about customer service and customer satisfaction (Stamatis 1996a, 1996b; Butterfield 1987; Sarazen 1987; Blume 1988; Chandler 1989; Goodman 1989; Goizueta 1989; Wells 1989; Vanocur 1989; Graham 1991; Lovelock 1989; Test 1990; Hunt 1990; Tague 1990; Sheridan 1993; Shoemaker 1994; Janson 1994; Wargo 1994; Weiner 1994; Griffin 1994; Powers 1994; Trabue and Jones 1994; Zemke 1994; Pyzdek 1994; London 1994; Berwick 1994; Silverstein 1991, and many others). However, it may be summarized as follows: Know thy customer (Albrecht and Zemke 1985). In order to win on perceived quality, it is necessary to have more refined data than one's competitors do (know more about evolving customer needs by segment and more about changing competitive performance) and to use this information from quality-directed research in a strategic framework (Buzzell and Gale 1987).

To optimize customer service and satisfaction, the service must be understood before asking customers what they want. In order to do that, it is necessary to have data. The data may be qualitative and/or quantitative. Contrary to what most people think, service is not as mushy and touchy-feely as it has been made out to be. To be understood, it requires hard work from management and nonmanagement alike, in addition to measuring what is important. In healthcare, this is of super importance because of the fluent definition of what is or who is the customer. It may be the patient, medical doctor, community, government, etc.

When we talk about customer service and/or satisfaction, we talk about creativity. Creativity allows us to handle or diffuse problems at hand or later on in the process of conducting everyday business. We talk about how, or rather what, the organization has to do to gain not only the sale but also the loyalty of the customer. We want to know the payoff of the transaction both in the short and long term. We want to know what our customers want (Hutchens 1989). We want to know if our customers are satisfied.

Satisfaction, of course, means that what we delivered to a customer met his or her approval. A typical list or a guideline to make sure that we connect with the customer is shown in Table 7.1. The idea here is to find out whether or not the customer is delighted and is willing to come back. Fleiss (1989) and Feldman (1991) have written of precisely that delight in their examples. Fleiss has written about Ben and Jerry's ice cream and Feldman has written about excellence in a cab ride.

As important as delightfulness is, some of us minimize it, if not disregard it altogether. At this point, of course, we fail. Some of the issues that will guarantee failure in sales, satisfaction, and loyalty are:

■ Employees are required to adhere to a rigid chain of command.
■ Employees are closely supervised.
■ Conflict—in whatever form—is not allowed.
■ Rewards are based on "carrot and stick" principles.

On the other hand, we increase our chance for success if we allow employees to take personal responsibility for their actions in the areas of communication, performance, and customer satisfaction. How do we go about sensitizing employees to all these issues? First, we must identify how we define the customer. Second, we must understand the levels of customer expectations about quality. Third, we must understand the strategy for customer service quality. Fourth, we must understand the measurement and feedback cycles of customer satisfaction.

In the case of customer definition, we have defined a customer as the person or unit receiving the output of a process of the system. In fact, in the next chapter, we will emphasize the fact that the customer may be an immediate, an intermediate, or the ultimate customer (supplier-input-process-output-customer [SIPOC] model). It may be a person or a process.

Table 7.1 Opportunities to Connect with Your Customer

Item	Suggested Phrases	Tone/Frame of Mind
Hardship—death in family	• "Sorry for your loss."	• Empathy—lower tone, slow pace
Lost job	• "This must be difficult." • "I'm sorry to hear that." • "Best of luck to you."	• Empathy
Accident claim	• "Is everyone OK?" • "I'm sorry to hear that." • "Is everyone safe or in a safe location?"	• Empathy • Concerns
Life events—adding a spouse	• "Congratulations!" • "That is great; this change will give you a ___ discount."	• Sincere • Positive
Life events—buying a home (moving)	• If appropriate, "Good luck with your move." • "Congratulations on your new home." • "This is going to save you $___."	• Is he or she positive?
Life events—divorce	• "This must be a complicated time for you." • "I'm sorry to hear that." • "This must be a difficult time."	• Empathy • Sincere • Helpful • Simpler is better
Life events—adding a child	• "I'm sure your son/daughter is very excited."	• Positive

Table 7.1   Opportunities to Connect with Your Customer (Continued)

Item	Suggested Phrases	Tone/Frame of Mind
Life events—birthday	• "Happy birthday …" "Happy belated birthday…" "Happy early birthday." • "A lot of good/nice people are born in___ [month]."	• Congratulatory • Sincere • Positive
Deleting lien	• "Congratulations on paying off your loan." • "This must be a great feeling."	• Positive
Special lines	• "You'll have fun with this ___." • "Congratulations on your new ___." • "I saw a picture on the Internet/in a magazine and it's really nice."	• Congratulatory • Positive
Policy renewal	• "Thank you for renewing with us. [If appropriate] You have been with us for a long time." • "We really appreciate your business."	• Positive • Upbeat
Payment	• "Thank you for making your payment." • "We appreciate your business." • "If you have questions, you can call us 24/7."	• Sincere • Helpful
Apology is needed	• "I am so sorry." • "I will take care of this for you."	• Sincere

(Continued)

Table 7.1 Opportunities to Connect with Your Customer (Continued)

Item	Suggested Phrases	Tone/Frame of Mind
Inconveniences caused	• "I apologize for the inconvenience." • "I apologize for the confusion." • "I will follow up and call you back." • "I will make this a priority."	• Sincere
Noisy background/bad connection	• "I would be glad to hold if…" • "Would you like me to call you back?" • "In case we are disconnected, can you give me a number where I can reach you?"	• Helpful
Geographic location	• "That state is beautiful!" • "____ [sports team] has had a good year!" • "Send us some sunshine." • "Hope everyone is safe." (bad weather)	• Upbeat

Customer satisfaction, on the other hand, is when the customer is satisfied with the service and it meets his or her needs, wants, and expectations. To further understand customer satisfaction, we must also look more deeply into the levels of specific satisfaction. To understand the notion of the levels of customer satisfaction, we must also recognize that there are levels of customer satisfaction that, in a sense, define the basic ingredients of quality. There are at least three levels of customer expectations about quality:

Level 1. The expectations are very simple and take the form of assumptions, "must have," or "take it for granted." For example, (a) I expect the airline to take off, fly to my destination, and land safely; (b) I expect to get the correct blood for my blood transfusion; and (c) I expect the bank to deposit my money into my account and to keep a correct balance for me.

Level 2. The expectations are a step higher than in level 1, and they require some form of satisfaction through meeting requirements and/or specifications. For example, (a) I expect to be treated courteously by all healthcare personnel while I am in the hospital; (b) I went to the hospital expecting to have my hernia repaired, to hurt some after it was done, to be out on the same day, and to receive a correct bill; and (c) I went to the bank and the bank teller was very friendly, informative, and helpful with my transactions.

Level 3. The expectations are much higher than in levels 1 or 2, and they require some kind of delightfulness or a service that is so good that it attracts me to it, as in the following examples. (a) They gave all the patients gourmet food unless a patient was on a special diet. (b) Everyone who was involved with me treated me with respect and explained things very carefully to me. But what surprised me was that someone called me at home the next day to find out how I was doing. (c) At my house closing, the bank officer not only treated me with respect and answered all my questions, but also, just before we shook hands to close the deal, he gave me a housewarming gift.

The strategy issue is also a very important element of customer satisfaction, primarily because it sets the tone for the appropriate training, behavior, and delivery of the specific service. The strategy for service quality should address (1) customer service attributes, (2) approach for healthcare service quality improvement, (3) developing feedback systems for customer service quality, and (4) measurement.

Customer Service Attributes

The delivery of the service must by timely, accurate, with concern, and with courtesy. One may ask why these elements are important. The answer is that all services are intangible and are a function of perception. As such, they depend on interpretation. In addition and perhaps more importantly, service by definition is perishable, and, if left unattended, it can backfire on the organization (Stamatis 1996b). In healthcare, this relates directly to *caring, observant, mindful, friendly, obliging, responsible,* and *tactful* (or, used as an acronym, COMFORT). These characteristics are the most basic attributes of customer service; without them, there can be no true service of any kind. They all depend on interpersonal skills, communication, empowerment, knowledge, sensitivity, understanding, and some kind of external behavior.

Caring shows that indeed you are very much interested in what the customer has to say. You may spend time with the customer to find out what his or her real needs, wants, and expectations are. It is not unusual even to tell the customer that you may not be able to help, at the expense of losing him. Furthermore, you may go as far as suggesting someone else or some other organizations.

You must be *observant*. In most cases, when dealing with service-related items—especially in healthcare—observations may contribute to satisfying the customer more than direct communication. Pay attention to body language and mannerisms and, if necessary, read between the lines. Always try to be one step ahead of the customer. Anticipate his or her action. Actively listen to what the customer is communicating as well as—and perhaps more importantly—what he or she is not communicating.

You must be *mindful*. Remember that you and your organization exist to satisfy the customer. Without the customer's need, you do not have a job nor does the organization have a service to provide. The customer has a choice and therefore, if you or the organization does not recognize the urgency, the sensitivity, the uniqueness, the expectations, and the influence that the customer has, you will not be successful in satisfying the customer. In fact, he or she may choose another healthcare facility or even a different provider.

You must be *friendly*. Friendliness does not mean being a pest. Offer guidance and information, and let the customer know you are there to help. If you have to, provide feedback to help the customer make his or her decision. If you do provide feedback, be truthful. For example, someone comes into your office and asks you for a specific medication that he or she has heard in an advertisement. As a physician, rather than fill the expectations of that patient, you should explain that that medication is not for him or her because of potential problems with other medication. Instead, you should suggest something else.

You must be *obliging*. Patience is the key word in customer satisfaction. Sometimes the customer does not know what he or she wants and may be making up his or her mind while talking with you. You are serving as the "guinea pig" for the customer's decision. As such, accommodating the person may make the difference between a satisfied and a dissatisfied customer. It may make the difference between a sale and a walkout. When obliging the customer, do not hesitate to educate him or her as well. Try to provide much self-education, especially for chronic issues.

You must be *responsible*. You are the expert. The customer is looking to you to provide the appropriate information in a clear, concise, and easy-to-understand manner. Do not try to make the sale at all costs. That strategy may backfire. What you are trying to accomplish is to develop a relationship where your expertise can indeed help the customer.

You must be *tactful*. In any service organization and in any service delivery, there are going to be problems between you and the customer. Healthcare is no different. Do not panic. Tactfulness is the process through which the conflict may be resolved. Your focus is to satisfy the customer and thus you should try to identify the problem, analyze it, and then resolve it in the most expedient way. Being tactful does not mean that you have to give in to the customer all the time. What it does mean is that you act in a professional manner, are composed, and communicate to the customer in a way that is not threatening or demeaning. It means that you are willing to listen and exchange information with the intention of resolving the conflict. It means that you have a way of presenting the facts and information in a nice and nonintimidating way. It means listening patiently. It means thinking before speaking. It means listening to the customer without interrupting.

Notice that cost is not an attribute that will make or break either service or satisfaction because, in healthcare service especially, cost is equated with value. This does not suggest that high cost is a prerequisite to good healthcare service or vice versa. It simply suggests that it is necessary to continue to generate more value for the customer without "giving away the store." It is indeed a very delicate balance.

Approach for Healthcare Service Quality Improvement

The basic question one must be able to answer is, "Why bother with healthcare service quality?" The answer is a three-pronged approach. The first is cost, the second is time to implement the program, and the third is the patient service impact. Together, they present a nucleus for understanding and implementing a system that is responsive to both patients and the organization for optimum satisfaction.

Develop Feedback Systems for Customer Service Quality

The feedback system that is chosen will make or break the organization. Make sure not to mix the focus of customer satisfaction and marketing. They are not the same. The focus of customer service and satisfaction is to build loyalty, and the focus of marketing is to meet the needs of the customer profitably. Another way of putting it is that marketing's function is to generate customer value profitably, whereas the purpose of customer service and satisfaction is to generate repeatability, recognition, and overall satisfaction with the transaction.

The concern here is to make sure that a goal exists; a reporting system for measurement is appropriate and useful for the particular service, as is the reward of service quality. The question then becomes how to develop a system that is responsive to the customer's needs, wants, and expectations. To answer these concerns, we must look to the customer. The value of the information must focus on at least the following areas:

- Knowing what customers are thinking about the organization, its service, and its competitors
- Measuring and improving performance
- Turning strongest areas into market differentiators
- Turning weaknesses into developmental opportunities—before someone else does
- Developing internal communication tools to let everyone know how he or she is doing
- Demonstrating commitment to quality and customers—in essence, two distinct kinds of measurement of the feedback:
  - Customer satisfaction, which is dependent upon the transaction
  - Service quality, which is dependent upon the relationship

Implementation

Perhaps the most important strategy is that of implementation. As part of the implementation process, management must define the scope of the service quality as well as the level of patient service as part of the organization's policy. Furthermore, management must also define the plan of implementation. The plan should include the time schedule, task assignment, and reporting cycle.

Measurement

Measurement is by far one of the most important ingredients in customer service. We look for items that crystallize the quality service in such a way that the elements become determinants of all our future expectations. Zeithaml et al. (1990) have defined five commitments, to which "competition" and "management leadership" have been added here:

- *Reliability* is the ability to provide what was promised, dependably and accurately. Never overpromise and always *keep promises.*
- *Responsiveness* is the willingness to help patients and provide prompt service. Always get the definition of *prompt* from the customer.

- *Assurance* is the knowledge and courtesy of employees and their ability to convey trust and confidence. Employees need to be empowered to carry out this assurance of both power and knowledge.
- *Empathy* is the degree of caring and individual attention provided to customers.
- *Tangibles* are the physical facilities and equipment and the appearance of personnel.

Competition

Competition, the ability to assess what the competition is doing, is of paramount importance. When evaluating or researching the competition, we are interested in the service they provide, the cost of that service, their patients, and opportunity for growth.

Perhaps one of the most important aspects of studying the competition is the notion of zone of tolerance (ZOT). A pictorial view of ZOT is shown in Figure 7.1. Competition decreases the zone of tolerance because, as competition increases, the patient is able to find precisely what he or she is looking for, through availability. In essence, through competition analysis, we want to go beyond mere satisfaction of the customer to identify an extremely satisfied customer, a loyal customer, and, of course, a delighted customer.

Management Leadership

A very popular general once said, "The definition of leadership is the art of influencing people to progress with cooperation and enthusiasm towards the accomplishment of a mission." The sole objective of leadership is to accomplish a mission. The objective is not to make everybody happy or to make oneself popular with employees; if that happens, it is a bonus. In fact, it is possible to be a successful leader without happy employees or popularity, provided that that is objective as one transmits and interprets it. The art of obtaining the enthusiastic cooperation of employees is the crux of the leadership problem. The mission objectives as the leader interprets them may not at first seem desirable to employees. It is up to the leader to make these objectives seem desirable. Through the leader's ability, personality, education, and experience, he or she must inspire employees, both individually and collectively, to their best efforts. The leader should inspire rather than demand and lead rather than drive.

Low → Adequate → Zone of tolerance → Desired

Figure 7.1   Zone of tolerance.

Leadership is learned by practice and study. People are not born with the ability to lead; it must be acquired and cultivated, just as the pilot has to learn to fly, the teacher to teach, and the athlete to play a sport. One cannot become a successful leader just by reading about it. A prerequisite for good leadership is a certain amount of ability and risk taking, and a burning desire to become a leader.

Leadership is a position where everything is dynamic. As a consequence, the leader must be able to adjust and improve. In fact, continual improvement is one of the basic essentials of leadership. The leader must develop these abilities until they become natural. To paraphrase Wheatley (1992), leaders who never progress beyond the mechanics are poor at best. Normally, a leader will not be successful if he or she rigidly adheres to rules or tries to imitate a successful leader. A leader must develop techniques that best fit his or her personality.

The fact that leadership is an art should not discourage anyone from taking the call of becoming a leader. However, the leader must recognize that leadership does not provide specific formulas, rules, or methods that will fit every situation. Leadership is intangible; it cannot be seen, felt, or measured except through its results. Moreover, one cannot predict the results with mathematical accuracy. If one has skill as a leader, however, one can predict results within the limits of the objectives.

Since leadership is a form of human relations, it must take into consideration the changeable and complex personality of man himself. Techniques of leading must keep pace with the changing customs, beliefs, and ideals of the society in which we live. Some techniques that were sound in the past century are worthless today (Rhinesmith et al. 1989).

Especially in healthcare service quality, one must not only understand the concept of leadership, but also must practice it. Leadership has become more technical and more in need of measurement because organizations have become more complex. As a consequence, the responsibility and accountability of today's leaders have increased. Perfection in leadership, as in any art, will never be realized. No matter how skillful one becomes as a leader, one can always improve.

One of the strongest common tendencies of all people is a desire for successful achievement. An individual usually prefers success in a given field. If that is not forthcoming, a person will usually shift his or her attention to some other field in which he or she may achieve the desired success. Humans work for many reasons; however, the primary reason is to gain satisfaction of some sort. The nature of this satisfaction may be in any form—advancement, recognition, affection, esteem of others, and so on. If, as a result of his or her work, a person does not approach the desired end, enthusiasm quickly falls, and with it falls the quality of the work being done. This is where a good leader with responsibility, authority, and love of people helps channel the effort and enthusiasm of all concerned toward a specific goal.

Why is leadership an issue of patient satisfaction? Because it is the leader's ability to develop a vision and make decisions about the following:

■ *Attracting new customers.* New patients provide growth and new opportunities for the organization.

■ *Differentiating the organization from competitors.* Differentiation provides for niches in the market and the opportunity to delight the customer because of much more specialization than would otherwise be provided.

■ *Keeping patients for the long term.* Loyalty is much more economical than pursuing new patients. Loyalty also creates good will and serves as advertisement through word of mouth. Long-term patients provide the organization with testimonials. Do not overdo it or become complacent with it. Remember that *there is no such thing as loyalty that two cents off will not cure.*

■ *Improving the organization.* Through the knowledge that the organization may gain from benchmarking, focus groups, surveys, and so on, adjustments can be made in both the delivery of the service and the organizational structure as well as the patient base.

■ *Cost of poor quality.* This is the barometer of improvement. By analyzing internal and external costs, the organization has the opportunity to streamline unnecessary costs and focus on improving the service. Stamatis (1996a) provides a very detailed (but not exhaustive) list of service items that cost of quality may address.

■ *Patient retention.* It is the business of the organization to know how much patient retention programs cost and how effective they are. How much does it take to retain patients? How much of the budget goes to patient acquisition as opposed to patient retention? If the cost is very high, then the relationship needs a different kind of measurement or perhaps a different customer base, a different delivery system, or even a new service.

■ *Lifetime patient cycle.* The organization must know the lifetime patient cycle so that appropriate actions can be taken to secure the vitality of the organization. A typical patient cycle is as follows:
  – Dissatisfaction (problem): The first signs of frustration about the service occur.
  – Anger: A recurring problem is faced by the patient.

- Change: Obviously if the patient is uncomfortable, he is looking for an effective change to make things better. The change provided by the staff (nursing aide or nurse) may indeed provide not only satisfaction to the patient and his family members, but it may also create an organizational change of improvement and a competitive advantage, if the problem of the patient is a systems issue and common to the facility.
- Impact of change: This is where the patient analyzes the impact of the change. It may be financial, personal, organizational, and/or utilitarian.
- Change occurs: At this point, the patient, after a thorough analysis and evaluation, makes the change.

Employee Empowerment

Perhaps one of the most important issues in any conversation about patient satisfaction is the notion of employee empowerment. Much has been written about empowerment; however, in healthcare, it takes an extra dimension because the patient's experience is the focus of satisfaction. However, this experience is delivered by many in the organization, whether it is the doctor's office or hospital or clinic. The empowerment has to be delegated to all, to do all that is necessary at the time that is needed. It is very important here to recognize that the empowerment concept leads the healthcare professional (at any level) to make sure that the patient's experience is the best that it can be. This means that not only the direct medical concerns have to be addressed with sensitivity, but also simple things such as bedside manners and so on. Some typical examples include:

- Take any complaint or problem seriously, doing more than just apologizing. Reassure the patient or family that you will address the issue or get someone who can.
- If you cannot solve the problem yourself, find someone to help you and let the patient know what you have done.
- Remember that the majority of people who deal with you are anxious, stressed, nervous, worried, and quite often depressed. You need to do your best to make them as comfortable as possible.
- Do not forget how important the so-called little things are to people. A warm smile, asking how things are going, and reassuring a patient that he or she is in the best place possible for medical care go a long way.
- Ask patients about themselves and find out what is important to them. Treat people like a friend or a family member.
- Be aware of your nonverbal communication and its power; be sensitive to your gestures, eye contact, voice tone, and body language.

Six Ps and S Model

Patient satisfaction is always important and more often than not it depends on the simplest items that do not cost anything except personal attention. A very simple model to follow for an in-house patient, the Six Ps and S, is shown in Table 7.2. Obviously, this model is not comprehensive, but it does demonstrate the delicate need and desire that the patient recognizes as a minimum interaction and reacts to with satisfaction.

To satisfy these seven characteristics of customer satisfaction in healthcare, team members must have some standards for excellence and willingness to listen for improvements. It is strongly suggested that maybe a poster should be placed in the patient's room and comments should be appropriately posted as the staff make the rounds. It is also highly suggested that visitors be encouraged to add comments. The idea here is to make sure to connect with the customer. A typical guideline for such connectivity is presented in Table 7.3.

For this excellence to be sustained, healthcare providers and all who work in healthcare must foster a culture of service excellence that is solely dependent on the level of commitment and teamwork from everyone. Typical items that may be identified and tracked for satisfaction include:

- Displaying a positive attitude
- Responding in a timely manner
- Offering open and constructive communication
- Maintaining a clean and safe workplace environment
- Taking ownership and being accountable
- Taking pride in personal appearance
- Honoring and respecting diversity
- Respecting and being sensitive to patient privacy
- Fostering and supporting innovation
- Committing to team members
- Being courteous and practicing established etiquette

Considerations in Defining the Customer (Patient) for Healthcare

As we already have discussed, there are several customers in any organization, including healthcare. However, an additional perspective has been introduced by Tucker (2009). He suggests that we should look at the customer in healthcare from two points of view. To make his point, Tucker gives a

Table 7.2   A Simple Model to Satisfaction for an In-House Patient

Item	Reason
Safety: Safety is paramount to all patients and staff. It is imperative that all patients be assured that their safety is going to be secured by all means possible. To ensure this, staff will be rounding on (visiting) you once an hour to see if you need anything and to help keep you safe. During this visit, the staff will introduce themselves and check the rest of the six Ps, and make sure everything is OK. The staff will also tell the patient when they will be back.	*Why?* Perhaps one of the most important anxieties that all patients have is their safety. Therefore, the staff should make sure that patients feel comfortable and are assured that someone will be looking after them. Safety should be emphasized and should not be taken for granted.
Pain: We will ask you if you are experiencing any pain or discomfort. We will ask you to rate your pain on a scale of 1 to 10.	*Why?* It is important that your pain stays at acceptable levels during your stay. We want you to be as comfortable as possible to promote healing. It is important that you alert us to any new pain or other discomfort.
Personal needs: We will check to see if you need to use the toilet or any assistance. If you are wearing a brief, we will ensure that it is clean and dry. We want you to know that we are regularly here to help you with toileting.	*Why?* Patients who fall while trying to get to the bathroom may be seriously injured. We also want your skin to remain clean and dry to prevent any pressure sores. If you are at high risk for a fall, we will remain with you while you use the toilet.
Pulmonary hygiene: We will ask you to do breathing exercises. The goal is to take 10 slow, deep breaths through your incentive spirometer every hour.	*Why?* Breathing exercises can help prevent you from getting a lung infection. Hospitalized patients frequently do not breathe deeply enough to clean their lungs. These exercises will help keep your lungs clean.

Table 7.2 A Simple Model to Satisfaction for an In-House Patient (Continued)

Item	Reason
Position: We will help you change position, which often can help keep you comfortable and prevent positions to make you uncomfortable. We will take actions to reduce pressure on your skin and inspect areas of your skin at risk for a pressure sore.	*Why?* Changing positions often can help keep you comfortable and prevent pressure sores from developing. We may ask you to sit up for a while or ask you to walk or stand with assistance to help prevent your muscle pressure from becoming weak while you are in the hospital. Pressure sores can develop when you stay in the same position for too long, when your skin remains wet too long, or when objects (such as oxygen tubing) touch your skin in the same place for too long. It is important to prevent pressure sores because they can take a long time to heal, they are painful, and they can lead to life-threatening infections. If you are at high risk for developing pressure sores, we will perform other specific activities.
Possessions: We will put items nearby and make sure that you can use your call light.	*Why?* Your personal items (tissue, glasses, call light) should remain within your reach. Patients who get up without assistance may fall and be hurt. It is important that you know how to use your call light to ask for assistance and that it is within your reach.
Place: We will make sure that your room is clean and free from clutter, equipment is safe, and alerts are in place.	*Why?* Your room needs to remain clean and uncluttered to prevent falls. It is important to keep your bed in the lowest position and that all wheels on equipment be locked. We may have special alerts in place to prevent falls (yellow suns, bed alarms). Your table, telephone, and wastebasket need to be within your reach.

Table 7.3 Connecting with Your Customers … Consider Their Points of View

Scenario	Do Not Say	Options	Preferred Options
The organization cannot provide options that the patient is seeking.	"There is nothing I can do about that."	• Use empathetic statements—for example: "I can hear that you are frustrated…" "I understand that this can be upsetting."	When you cannot give customers what they are asking for, look for options that can be offered.
Patient indicates having had a poor experience with the organization.	"It's not our fault."	• Apologize if the customer has the perception that something wrong has been done "May I apologize? I'm sorry that you had that experience…"	Take ownership and focus on offering options that will achieve some resolution. These options will vary depending on the situation.
System limitations	"Our system won't let me…"	If system constraints prevent doing what the patient is requesting, explain the limitations and how the issue can be resolved.	• If you discover a limitation based on current capabilities, proactively challenge the processes. • Use your resources to determine if there is another alternative that the systems do support that may address the customer's need.

Helpful hint: Take "don't" statements and replace them with more acceptable words and phrases.

Payment past due	• "I understand that things happen…" • "What I need is…" • "In order to help you, I need…" • "Let me see what I can do to help you at this point…"	• "It's unfortunate that…" …your policy does not cover the situation. …your payment arrived late. …your premium increased. …you did not receive your mail. • "I understand that things happen. Let me see what options are available for you."
	• "You could have…" • "You should have…" • "You need to…"	
Affirmation with the customer	• "I can do that…" • "I can help you…" • "I understand…" • "Yes," "Certainly," "Sure" • "Sure, certainly, that will be fine"	• "I would be happy to help you!" • "I'd be glad to take care of that for you!" • "It would be my pleasure!"
	• "No problem!" • "OK" • "Yeah" • "All right"	
Customer has not previously received service meeting his or her needs.	Always take ownership for the organization by using "we" and "our."	• "This is what I will do to address your concern." • "I'll confirm that information and follow up with you. May I call you back?"
	"They" statements	

(Continued)

Table 7.3   Connecting with Your Customers … Consider Their Points of View (Continued)

Scenario	Do Not Say	Options	Preferred Options
Potentially escalated call	"A supervisor will tell you the same thing …"—This statement is NEVER acceptable!	"I would be happy to find a supervisor for you." (Be sure not to keep the patient waiting for a long period of time)	"Would it be acceptable for me to review this with my supervisor and call you back?"
Patient is pressing to get his or her point across.	• "If you will let me finish …" • "You are not listening to me."	• Be patient until the patient is finished speaking. • Soften your tone. • "Here is what I can do to help."	• "I would really like to help you with this." • "It sounds like you have additional concerns. Let's talk about the options I have to resolve your situation." • "I understand that this situation is frustrating and I would like to help you fix this as soon as possible."
Hold time	"Just one moment …"	• Set expectations. Tell the patient what you will be doing during any period of silence • "One moment while I …" • "It will just take a moment to …" • Know when hold should be used.	• "I would be happy to check that for you. It will take one moment." • "I would like to review that information on your policy. Thank you for being patient while I do that."

Language barrier	"I don't (or can't) understand you"	If there is a language problem, ask, "Would it be helpful if I contact an interpreter?" If you are having difficulty hearing the patient, offer to hang up and call the customer back to obtain a better connection	• Use active listening. • Be patient and speak clearly. • Match the customer's rate of speech and repeat information as needed.
Patient indicates that he or she may explore other insurance providers.	"I am not authorized to suggest a different insurance carrier."	Focus on retaining the business. Review all applicable discounts. Check to be certain all accidents and violations were reconciled correctly.	• Let patients know that the organization values them as customers and appreciates their business. • Share some of the benefits that the organization provides (24-hour availability, online policy information, exceptional resolution service, etc.).
Patient is dissatisfied with organization's policies or guidelines.	"If you aren't happy, you can file a complaint with the Department of Insurance or the Joint Commission Agency."	Acknowledge the customer's unhappiness and offer an apology if appropriate.	• Focus on what can be done. • Offer options that apply to the situation.

(Continued)

Table 7.3   Connecting with Your Customers … Consider Their Points of View (Continued)

Scenario	Do Not Say	Options	Preferred Options
Misunderstanding with direction provided by health representatives	Do not say any derogatory remarks about other staff.	• Apologize for any miscommunication issues. • Remember that everyone is working for the same organization and that all staff at some level are customers as well.	• Take ownership and focus on what can be done to help. • Offer viable options.
Communicating in a manner patient will understand	• Do not say words with special meaning. • Do not say words that explain the internal steps of your actions. • Do not say words that belittle the patient.	Use terms understood by customers.	Present information in a way that gives customers the ability to understand their issues, whether insurance, admission, billing issues, etc., in layman's terms while not talking down to them.

| Patient is intent on conveying his or her perspective (not actively listening to customer service representatives [CSRs]). | Do not say "Sir" or "Ma'am" as a way to interrupt. | Patiently wait until the patient finishes speaking and then address him or her politely by name. Exercise active listening. Use the patient's name throughout the interaction to personalize the experience. |
| Patient is unsure whether CSR understands his or her perspective. | "Like I said…" | • Use terms that do not make the patient feel inferior—for example:
"Let me recap for you."
"Let's review that information together."
• If you can sense that the patient does not understand your explanation, try restating it in another way.
• Incorporate details that the patient has shared during the conversation when restating the information. |

(Continued)

Table 7.3 Connecting with Your Customers … Consider Their Points of View (Continued)

Scenario	Do Not Say	Options	Preferred Options
Premium increase	"Your rates increased due to a rate revision for your entire state."	Provide the following information to the patient: "Your renewal premium reflects a premium change that affected all organization customers in [state]. Like all health insurers, we periodically review our claims experience to determine if our premiums are adequate to cover our cost of claims. The results of our recent review indicated that it was necessary to increase our premium levels. In some cases we excluded options to make us more competitive."	Offer additional information: "Many factors can influence your health insurance rates and coverage. Recently, rising medical costs are contributing to rising health insurance rates. These increases are not unique to our organization; most companies are reacting to increased costs by raising rates. Again, because a variety of factors specific to your policy are evaluated when determining rates, not all customers will experience rate increases and/or adjustments in coverage."

scenario of a surgeon in a hospital environment and identifies the *purist* and *pragmatic* views.

As a Lean purist, the patient is the customer. He or she receives the benefit of the service—although with multiple other internal–external customer relationships. All activities should be assessed with respect to the value to the patient. Tucker (2009) goes on to say that there is also a pragmatic/realistic view of the situation as a customer does several things:

- "Consumes" the product or service. Clearly, the patient is the "consumer" customer. This would follow the purist view.
- Pays for the service. The insurer (commercial or government) pays for the service. But, from a process perspective, the payer is so far removed from the surgery process as to be irrelevant to any analysis of the current processes in most surgery departments.
- Possesses the right to select the provider. In a situation where surgeons are independent contractors with respect to the hospital, they clearly have the right to select which hospital in which to perform surgery. The typical patient does not even select the surgeon. The access process would be a referral from the patient's primary care physician (PCP) to a particular surgeon with whom he or she is familiar and/or who is on the list (from the insurer) of acceptable surgeons. And, while a patient or insurer may be the payer for a given surgery, the surgeon brings an enormous revenue stream to the hospital over the long run.

Another characteristic of a customer is that he or she "can complain and get a response." Would a hospital administrator be more upset if one patient decided to go to another hospital or if one surgeon decided to take all of his revenue somewhere else? The system drives the hospital to keep the high-revenue surgeons happy, and many will wield this influence to get what they want and need—maybe at the expense of other priorities.

So what are we to make out of Tucker's scenario? First, we must keep the patient in mind as the primary customer. He or she needs a safe, effective, satisfying surgical experience. Many processes can be optimized with this in mind. Many "patient dissatisfiers" could be eliminated by eliminating waste for the nurses. Is the blanket-warmer out of blankets? (It takes 30 minutes for them to get warm if it is loaded right now.) Can the nurse find needed supplies?

Obviously, as important as the patient is in being satisfied, we must also keep a keen eye on the surgeon's perspective. After all, would someone rather work with a hospital where

- He or she can do four cases in 6 hours and leave or is there all day to do two cases because everything is scheduled "to follow" on a "first come–first served" basis?
- Operating room (OR) turnaround is just chaos? Equipment cannot be located or pieces are piled on a shelf in the equipment room and staff has to scavenge through them like a rat at the trash heap?
- Hospital staff cannot tell whether the next patient is even in the building, much less prepped and ready to roll?
- The 9 a.m. patient is still in the waiting room because all of the day surgery beds are filled with patients that are scheduled for the afternoon?
- The patient is "ready," but the fax machine to which the office faxed the appropriate documents yesterday cannot be found?
- He or she waits for an inpatient because transport has been "optimized," but an OR suite and crew wait for 30 minutes during peak transport periods.
- He or she is up to the elbows in somebody's gut and finds out that a needed supply is out of stock or cannot be found?
- Changes get made to preference cards in a timely manner or there are only a couple of scrub techs who know what is needed for a case?

All of these are problems that can be approached with Lean healthcare tools and methodologies. And, ultimately, if these problems are fixed for the surgeon, safer, higher quality care can be provided for more people with the existing resources.

The moral of this scenario as Tucker has presented it is to spend some time observing the process and making sure that the right customer is being addressed. Listen to staff (surgeons, nurses, techs, clerks at the OR desk, or whoever is responsible for the process). Just pick a place and start. The clock is ticking and it is necessary to find the true customer in the process and make sure that "that" customer is satisfied.

Developing a Patient Satisfaction Instrument

Perhaps the easiest and most common instrument for identifying patient satisfaction is the questionnaire. Over the years, questionnaires have been used in many applications in many organizations. Their purpose is to gain a variety of information on anything from demographics to quality, cost, or competition. One of the applications is in the area of patient satisfaction. A questionnaire may be a formal survey, a checklist or outline for a personal interview, or even the script for a phone survey. However, regardless of the specific use or structure of the questionnaire, some crucial points must be always kept in mind:

- Effective survey design is a complex task requiring research, data analysis, and high-level design skills.
- Information from a survey is only as good as the quality of the question asked, the sampling methods used, and the rate of response.
- People will answer surveys only if it is clear to them that there is a benefit to doing so. If the benefit is clear only to the surveying organization, the response rate will generally be very low.
- Audits need to be performed regularly. A company that bases its service strategy on an annual audit is begging to be blind-sided. In a competitive market, audits or surveys should be performed more than once a year.
- With patient audits or surveys, no news is bad news. The organization is a winner with any type of feedback. If the results identify deficiencies or problems anywhere in the organization, management should target a corrective action plan so that the quality focus is reestablished as soon as possible in the specific area or areas affected. If the results of the audit or survey are positive, management continues to focus on continual improvement since whatever is being done is working.

In addition to these points, when a questionnaire is being designed, consideration of the response is also important. For example, is the response to an open-ended question, closed-ended question, attitude scale, etc.? Open-ended questions are easy to construct and allow respondents to articulate their answers based on their own vocabulary and experience. However, they present a problem in length and interpretation—for example:

What do you think of the registration process in the emergency room?
Response: _____

_____

On the other hand, a closed-ended question is very direct and limited—for example:

Was the registration process in the emergency room prompt?
Yes □ No □

There are several types of attitude scales, each with specific advantages and disadvantages. It is beyond the scope of this book to address each type. For further information on attitude scales, see Kerlinger (1967, 1973), Cronbach (1970), Rokeach (1968), Brown (1958), Edwards (1957), Guilford (1954), Nunnally (1967), and Thurstone and Chave (1929), to name a few. Some of the most commonly used scales in this area include:

- Thurstone: Participants are given a checklist and they mark all statements with which they agree.
- Likert type: The participant is asked to circle or check one of the following categories:

  1 (strongly disagree)   2 (disagree)   3 (undecided)
  4 (agree)   5 (strongly agree)
- Guttman (forced choice): The participant is asked to make a forced decision between two choices. For example,

  I would rather speak to someone than fill out forms: Yes □ No □
- Semantic differential: A pair of extreme adjectives is used. For example,

  Circle one: Poor Excellent

Attitude scale construction involves careful selection and editing of items pertaining to the area of interest. Edwards (1957) has developed a series of techniques and criteria for constructing an attitude scale. However, the following criteria are only a summary for editing attitudinal statements:

- Avoid statements that refer to the past rather than the present.
- Avoid statements that are not factual or can be misinterpreted as factual.
- Avoid statements that can be interpreted in more than one way.
- Avoid statements that are irrelevant to the concern under consideration.
- Avoid statements that are likely to be endorsed by almost everyone or almost no one.
- Select statements that are believed to cover the entire range of the affective scale of interest.
- Keep the language of the statements simple, clear, and direct.
- Statements should be short, rarely exceeding 20 words.
- Each statement should contain only one complete thought.
- Statements containing universals, such as *all, always, none,* and *never,* often introduce ambiguity and should be avoided.
- Words such as *only, just, merely,* and others of a similar nature should be used with care and moderation in writing statements.
- Whenever possible, statements should be in the form of a simple sentence rather than in the form of compound or complex sentences.
- Avoid the use of words that may not be understood by those who will be given the complete scale.
- Avoid the use of double negatives.

When the study is designed to generate actionable data, avoid an odd-numbered response scale, if possible. The odd scale, more often than not, does not discriminate the response enough to make a sound decision. In such a scale, most people aim for the average, which is the middle number in this kind of scale.

Preliminary Steps to an Effective Survey

For any organization, it is important to gather information to find out either where the organization is or how to improve to a certain level. The process of finding that information has to be very critical, accurate, and well thought out before even the first question is asked. To develop an effective survey, the following questions should be considered (this list is by no means exhaustive):

- What survey is most effective for the organization: face to face, phone, or mailed?
  - It all depends on the goal, budget, and schedule of the survey.

- What sorts of response rates can be expected from an effective mailed customer audit?
  - A well-designed, well-targeted, and well-implemented mail survey should get about a 60–70% response. If the response rate is lower, it almost always signifies design shortcuts or poor targeting.

- What influences response rates?
  - Many factors influence response rates, including whether or not respondents believe answering the survey will have any social utility. The well-educated tend to respond more readily to surveys. Specialized audiences, if their interests are being surveyed, tend to respond more readily. Length of the survey can influence response. This makes it reasonable to reflect the objective of the survey.

- How can a survey designer encourage response rates?
  - Reward the respondent by
    - Showing positive regard
    - Giving verbal appreciation
    - Using a consulting approach
    - Supporting his or her values
    - Offering tangible rewards
    - Making the questionnaire interesting and useful
  - Reduce costs to the respondent by
    - Making the task appear brief
    - Reducing the physical and mental effort required

- Eliminating chances for embarrassment
- Eliminating any implication of subordination
- Eliminating any direct monetary cost

Some other items of concern may be the issues of

- The order of the questions
- The level of difficulty and jargon usage
- Response rate
- Time constraints
- The option for audit versus mailed versus face-to-face versus phone surveys
- The needs of the respondent or the patient
- Coders for the results—especially if the survey is an open-ended question type

Healthcare Concerns about Customer Satisfaction (CSat)

Many healthcare organizations spend millions of dollars on surveys, yet still lack actionable information. Perhaps for this reason, CSat surveys have acquired a reputation for being unactionable and frustrating. To be sure, healthcare has embraced CSat. In fact, CSat entered the world of healthcare as bright-eyed and aspirational as any discipline; yet at least in some quarters we see cracks of disappointment. What has happened? Where or what are the possible faults? Are we misled? What is the evil—if there is one?

To be sure, never has a market intelligence discipline been so warmly welcomed. After all, the notion that pleasing customers is a good business practice hardly evoked controversy. In healthcare especially, where the focus has been "patient care" and "do no harm," CSat is indeed a very welcome notion. However, we do not track satisfaction to enhance satisfaction; we track satisfaction to enhance productivity and improvement and thereby profits. (Even not-for-profit organizations look for profit. The not-for-profit designation is for tax purposes only. *All* organizations—except local, state, and federal governments—regardless of their tax designation, need profit to survive.)

None of us ever questioned CSat's intentions. However, if the intent for enabling greater customer satisfaction could have extended to the execution of customer satisfaction work, things might be better. The problem seems to be that we indeed have failed the promises and expectations to some extent and we continue to be in a cloud of delusion as time goes on—thinking that we will indeed solve our problems in healthcare if we only satisfy the customer (patient).

Born to replace the "squeaky wheel" approach to solving customer problems, CSat promised a more disciplined process for managing customer issues. Instead,

CSat moved quickly beyond its initial charter into areas and in ways that not only proved ineffective, but also undermined CSat's ability to deliver on its core promise.

The problems began with a small leap: from managing customer issues to enhanced analysis (i.e., understanding what the most common customer problems were). But that leap was made without first thinking all the way through the issues and consequences of that enhanced analysis. Sadly, the evolution of customer satisfaction became devolution through these stages: insubstantial theory, haphazard execution, measurement confiscation, and inappropriate application (Murphy and Goodwin 2009a, 2009b; Murphy and David 2009).

Insubstantial Theory

Good answer seeking the right question? The advent of customer satisfaction as a fresh source of analytic information for organizations happened naturally and logically. Who would not want to explore this new resource? The indications today are, however, that early advocates were not pursuing tough questions about the concept itself. As time has progressed, we have found that the questions are more often than not quite superficial and do not provide avenues for improvement. Scientific process generally poses a question and then gathers data. Customer satisfaction was not born of theory, but rather spawned from a data resource. The moral here is that we should develop hypotheses and then test them—not the other way around of defining results and then moving them to the customer.

Satisfaction is an attitude, rather than a behavior, and therefore a spurious goal in and of itself. Yes, satisfying customers overall is generally a good thing, but it is a means rather than an end. The consequence of forgetting this is that it leads companies to pursue improvements that may be totally inconsequential to the bottom line. After all, if the main purpose of our business is to be popular, we may soon be looking for a new business. We must be aware of the classic trap of thinking that a high score is better than a low one. More often than not, however, that measure is point to point or self-referential (our score this year versus our score last year) and the only thing that matters is generating an annual increase. So consider: the average patient score for last year was a 7; conversely, this year the rating is an 8. This is good, right? Not if our primary competitor advanced from a 6 to a 9! To use this kind of measure, we must have a competitive context for truly assessing customer satisfaction. Unfortunately, it is not a trivial assignment. Because this is difficult, however, does not obviate the fact that it is necessary.

Haphazard Execution

More rigor or rigor mortis? Because customer satisfaction was so readily accepted (its face validity was practically unquestioned), the usual thorough effort of exploring methodological issues often happened after the fact, if at all. Performance is not an absolute measure. If satisfaction does mean something, then acting on that meaning certainly is not about simply increasing our score every year. It demands a competitive context. Some key questions often have been glanced over.

Questionnaire design. How much does the exact wording of the question matter? What is the proper scale? How should that scale be developed? What questions should be added? Does the questionnaire length matter? Does placement in the questionnaire matter?

Driver analysis. How do we determine what the driver is? Is it derived, self-explicated, and/or correlated with variables internal or external to the CSat study?

Comparative analysis. How do we compare responses from choosers of different brands? What do we do about the different types or segments of choosers of other brands?

We must consider how we design CSat questionnaires. Is CSat a serious discipline with a rigorous methodology or just a popular measure whose effectiveness changes with the whim of the question writers and survey designers? We have all seen how subtle wording changes can affect the outcome of a question. Questionnaire placement also matters.

In another case, when we change the polarity of the response scale in our questions, we create a problem in the respondent's mind and the scoring may drop or increase by several points depending on the polarity change. What do these differences in outcomes mean for the ability of customer satisfaction studies to capture the reality of customer satisfaction or dissatisfaction precisely? How much faith should be put in comparisons with other available customer satisfaction scores that could be gathered in even slightly different ways?

Another problem is the tendency to wedge too many questions into CSat studies. CSat proponents believe that nothing is too minor to measure or to matter—a belief eagerly embraced by the client side. "Never miss an opportunity to collect more information" is often the battle cry. "You never know what might turn out to be important." Thus, we typically subject once-agreeable respondents to a disagreeably long list of questions about which they likely have little or no interest. Increasingly, the rational choice for even the most helpful respondent is to decline. Only some kind of remuneration saves the day, but even then a completed survey does not promise a thoughtfully completed survey. Remuneration risks changing the nature of a satisfaction survey and it does not preclude the customer's feeling exhausted and abused.

Our statistical methods are getting better and better, but are still limited to the questions we ask and the dependent variables we have available. Do whatever factors increase CSat scores comprise the criteria for what is important? What if it is unrelated to profits or revenues? Of course, linking survey data to actual customer databases has big implications for confidentiality and how we do surveys. Without the linkage, though, validation is nearly impossible. A good dependent variable—a surrogate for sales—is essential for sound driver analysis.

The integration of competitor information raises new, thorny issues. How do we validly compare CSat scores across healthcare facilities, if we have had the foresight to collect competitive data? Can the loyalists of one facility (say, hospital A with clinic B or mortality rate of hospital A with hospital B) be compared to those of other, similar (but not exactly the same) facilities or is, say, a selection of a surgical procedure choice a de facto segmentation variable rendering line-item comparisons irrelevant? This point can be illustrated by contrasting users of Windows-based PCs with Mac owners. There is no question that the latter product is the "ease of use" winner, but there is substantial evidence that ease of use is less important to Windows choosers, thereby reducing the comparability between CSat scores that are likely driven by different variables.

This de facto segmentation problem derails other analyses. Addressing large negative gaps in satisfaction drivers might be erroneous if our patients have already decided that they like us in spite of a shortcoming or if a shortcoming does not matter to them much.

Measurement Confiscation

Customer satisfaction or self-satisfaction? Over the past decade, the *raison d'être* for CSat has quietly morphed from correcting customer problems to measuring organization performance, especially in the large hospitals. Various reasons can be cited for this transformation—metrics-driven executives, performance-based personnel systems, etc.—and the evidence for this transformation lies in the ubiquitous scorecards and dashboards lining corporate conference rooms and boardrooms. Kudos to the scorecards where forward-looking strategy and research dictated the measures required versus the plethora of scorecards retrofitting whatever data were available. The latter metrics are often as relevant as a map of Greece would be for exploring the moon.

Most researchers are painfully aware that management teams often believe that information grows on trees. They are, sadly, oblivious to such concerns as sample availability, projectability, and *a priori* (design) versus *a posteriori* (solution) issues and concerns in sample and solution interpretation, budget constraints, respondent cooperation, respondent endurance, etc. And when we speak of confidence levels and the statistical limitations of nonparametric statistics, they, like Elvis, have already left the building. As a result of this ignorance or indifference, quite often at the end of the study we expand the scope of the study beyond the original objective without a blink. We have become addicts to net *satisfaction scores* rather than *thoughtful design*. We seem to have forgotten that methodology drives results rather than the other way around.

Customer feedback is a gift, not an obligation. The sad truth is that life is never as much about us as we believe it to be. In the business environment, customers are not product designers; they are product choosers. In healthcare, they are sensitive about their own "best" and they choose their physician, clinic, nursing home, or even the hospital based on other people's interpretation of "good service." They evaluate based on qualitative rather than quantitative data.

This is a troubling trend because, as leaders and top managers focus on cost per bed or cost per patient or accessibility to the facility, they fail to focus in depth on anything other than the profit/loss statements and earnings per share. Thus, when we set targets for this nonparametric statistic without ample samples, we are treading on dangerous ground. It is not uncommon to see net satisfaction score goals set that are within the margin of error for the mean score. In other words, goals are set that can be "achieved" or "not achieved" just due to the effects of random sampling.

Inappropriate Application

Who gave satisfaction a bad name? The politics of customer satisfaction have increased the demand for data reduction. Without easy proof of the relationship between satisfaction and revenue, organizations began seeking other applications. The founding principle of "pleasing the customer" has now been replaced with "pleasing the organization." No longer do we ask how we do in our service; rather, we lobby customers with, "Give us a 10!"—ineffectual, inappropriate, and insulting.

What were once intended to be useful data, employable to aid the customer and thereby better the organization, now largely bypass the customer and pander exclusively to the organization. We see this not only in healthcare but also in all kinds of service-oriented organizations—small and large. In some cases, we have seen where CSat is directly associated with value as a compensation schematic. The pretense, of course, is that CSat is about the customer's dissatisfaction and therefore about the employee's bonus. Again, here we see the focus shifted from customer satisfaction to employee satisfaction. It is unfortunate that as CSat has become more and more of a performance and pay measure, the politics surrounding it have grown as well. The failure of management to grapple with sample integrity leaves truck-size openings for tampering. Examples of obvious misuse are numerous. Here are some:

- Selection of data to project or identify preconceived hypotheses
- Latitude of recoding results
- Rehearsing customers for good scores
- Attaching good scores to bonuses

There are many grounds for questioning CSat measures, but these disputes with executives mostly focus on the execution of CSat studies in an attempt to improve scores; no one ever attacks a CSat study when scores are going up. This role alone has swung the relationship pendulum between market intelligence and management from partner to police. With costs skyrocketing and the information explosion of health services in healthcare, CSat is indeed a major concern and it certainly should be continued. The promise of greater profitability through increased customer satisfaction is clear, and we have all read multiple books that attempt to show these links. But from our experience within some really world-class organizations, we have not seen this link work well in practice. In any particular business, dozens of factors can and do interfere with delivering on the CSat promise.

Despite the somber statements made here, we do not think that customer satisfaction studies should be abandoned. Instead, we will argue that customer satisfaction deserves—or, really, demands—a revised strategy and set of expectations. Once that is done, creative changes in how we execute this strategy can lead to real value.

If market research does not help facilitate and fulfill the task of providing *actionable* solutions, the customer service or quality functions within the organization might execute a similarly integrated analysis and the voice of the customer (VOC) function could be removed from market research along with the accompanying budget. From our experience, most surveys in healthcare have little impact in the real world for the following four reasons:

- Surveys do not measure or report events that people either care about or can influence.
- Surveys are presented in a vacuum so that other data describing the customer experience often contradict them, giving everyone an excuse for inaction.
- Surveys are poorly packaged, so no one can quickly determine what the problem is and what should be done to address it.
- Surveys do not create an economic imperative to take action by showing the cost of inaction.

All four of these can be remedied, but to do so requires market research to go beyond its comfort zone and actually look at data from the operations and service part of the organization. Let us review each of the reasons:

■ *The data are not relevant; they do not tell me what needs to be fixed.* In most cases, this means the survey is either too general or too tactical, missing the *actionable insight.* Most surveys are usually about the *relationship* or about the *transaction.* The *relationship* surveys measure what happened over the past (day, week, month, or year) and focus on ratings over general dimensions of the relationship. Relationship surveys often ask for general comments when a respondent really wants to say, "This one specific thing you do bugs me."

The *transaction* surveys measure the tactical interactions: "How did Stacey, the customer service rep, handle your call after your discharge from your surgery?" In most cases, the transaction survey is conducted right after or within 24 hours of the call because the outcome of the transaction is often not obvious at that point. However, this impedes production of actionable insights that are bigger than the call but smaller than the relationship (i.e., Stacey did fine, but the system never followed through on her promises of action).

■ *The data provided are not telling me what I hear from other reliable sources.* Internal customers are receiving two other ongoing flows of information about the customer experience. The first describes what the company has done for (e.g., on-time delivery) or to (e.g., missed delivery) customers via transactions by units like operations, medical records, and billing. Operational data describe events of commission or omission while survey data reflect attitudinal data.

■ *I cannot easily make sense out of this survey report. I will need to study it later when I have more time.* Most survey reports are poorly packaged, precluding the desire to move quickly to action. Part of this is because most research reports indicate findings with a list of problems or opportunities. These reports do not suggest a specific set of priorities within opportunities or make recommendations for specific actions. Because the internal customer, the strategic business unit (SBU), or the vice president of customer experience cannot make an immediate determination of the problem and the appropriate resulting action, no action takes place. This often occurs because of internal boundaries and lack of effective communication channels between the market research department and the internal user of the data.

■ *I agree that there is a significant problem, but I have other issues right now. I will get to this next quarter.* Most reports do not create an economic imperative to take action from showing the cost of inaction. It is common for reports to highlight satisfaction measures, strengths, and weaknesses; however, what happens to the bottom line if no action is taken?

So, how can survey reports be made more actionable?

- *Ask a direct question about what did not work.* Do not hesitate to show the respondent a predefined list of things that could have gone wrong.
- *Integrate survey data with other sources, including operational data and contact data.* If research data are placed within the context of the contact data and key data that describe what the organization has done to the customers, they instantly become more relevant and less contradictory.
- *Suggest specific actions.* A standard management rule is "Do not give an executive a problem; give him or her a problem with a suggested solution." Talk to a couple of operating people from the SBU for at least the top two issues.
- *Create an economic imperative to act now.* If necessary, reframe the problem to make it more relevant and actionable. Cut it in size!
- *Cut through the clutter.* Internal clients are busy, swamped with information from other sources, and primarily concerned about the bottom line. Unless reports cut through the clutter with immediate, relevant information, they will continue to be ignored. The best course of action is to tell clients what it will cost them not to take action.

Summary

This chapter discussed the customer issue in healthcare. Specifically, it gave the rationale for understanding the CSat and explained some of the measurement characteristics in the process of improvement. The next chapter will discuss the process.

References

Albrecht, K., and R. Zemke. 1985. *Service America: Doing business in the new economy.* New York: Dow Jones-Irwin.

Berwick, D. M. 1994. Kevin speaks: The voice of a customer. *Continuous Journey* April/May: 2.

Blume, E. R. 1988. Customer service: Giving companies the competitive edge. *Training Development Journal* September: 25–27.

Brown, R. 1958. *Words and things.* New York: Free Press.

Butterfield, R. W. 1987. A quality strategy for service organizations. *Quality Progress* December: 23–25.

Buzzell, R., and B. Gale. 1987. *The PIMS principles.* New York: Free Press.

Chandler, C. H. 1989. Beyond customer satisfaction. *Quality Progress* February: 45–47.

Cronbach, L. 1970. *Essentials of psychological testing,* 3rd ed. New York: Harper & Row.

Edwards, A. 1957. *Techniques of attitude scale construction.* New York: Appleton.

Feldman, P. D. August 19, 1991. I searched for excellence and finally found it in a cab. *Marketing News,* p. 6.

Fleiss, R. 1989. Here's the scoop on Ben and Jerry's. *Office Systems 89* February: 49.

Goizueta, R. C. 1989. The business of customer satisfaction. *Quality Progress* February: 52–53.

Goodman, J. 1989. The nature of customer satisfaction. *Quality Progress* February: 46–48.

Graham, J. R. August 19, 1991. Do it right the first time; you may not get a second chance. *Marketing News,* p. 4.

Griffin, P. 1994. Taking the mystery out of customer service. *Continuous Journey* June/July: 6.

Guilford, J. 1954. *Psychometric methods,* 2nd ed. New York: McGraw–Hill.

Hunt, S. March 1990. It's basic but necessary: Listen to the customer. *Marketing News,* p. 6.

Hutchens, S. 1989. What customers want: Results of ASQC/Gallup survey. *Quality Progress* February: 56–58.

Janson, R. 1994. Time to get some satisfaction. *Continuous Journey* June/July: 4–5.

Kerlinger, F. 1967. Social attitudes and their criteria! Referents: A structural theory. *Psychological Review* 74: 68–76.

———. 1973. *Foundations of behavioral research,* 2nd ed. New York: Holt, Rinehart and Winston.

London, M. J. 1994. Betting pay on customer satisfaction. *Continuous Journey* April/May: 4.

Lovelock, C. H. January 30, 1989. Competitive advantage lies in supplementary, not core, services. *Marketing News,* p. 8.

Murphy, D., and P. David. October 2009. By the numbers: Why your customer satisfaction surveys are not actionable. *Quirk's Marketing Research Review* October: 22–44.

Murphy, D., and C. Goodwin. 2009a. Satisfying no longer: Part I: Satisfaction research needs to return to focusing on the customer. *Quirk's Marketing Research Review* July: 62–64.

———. 2009b. Satisfying no longer: Part II: The consequences of bad satisfaction. *Quirk's Marketing Research Review* August: 50–54.

Nunnally, J. 1967. *Psychometric theory.* New York: McGraw–Hill.

Powers, V. 1994. Can you read my mind? *Continuous Journey* June/July: 3

Pyzdek, T. 1994. Toward service systems engineering. *Quality Management Journal* April: 68–75.

Rhinesmith, S. H., J. N. Williamson, D. M. Ehlen, and D. S. Maxwell. 1989. Developing leaders for the global enterprise. *Training and Development Journal* April: 64–66.

Rokeach, M. 1968. *Beliefs, attitudes, and values.* San Francisco, CA: Jossey–Bass.

Sarazen, J. S. 1987. Customer satisfaction is not enough. *Quality Progress* December: 36–38.

Sheridan, B. M. 1993. Changing service quality in America. *Quality Progress* December: 48–50.

Shoemaker, C. June 1994. Higher bank fees don't equal value. *Marketing News,* p. 16.

Silverstein, M. August 1991. World-class customer service builds consumer loyalty. *Marketing News,* p. 4.

Stamatis, D. H. 1996a. *Total quality management in healthcare.* New York: McGraw–Hill.

————. 1996b. *Total quality service: Principles, practices and implementation.* Boca Raton, FL: St. Lucie Press.

Tague, J. P. March 5, 1990. Philosophy lifts Midway to new heights. *Marketing News,* p. 8.

Test, A. March 5, 1990. Would you want yourself as your own customer? *Marketing News,* p. 10.

Thurstone, L., and Chave, E. 1929. *The measurement of attitude.* Chicago, IL: University of Chicago Press.

Trabue, G., and Jones, P. 1994. Exceeding expectations at Eastman Chemical. *Continuous Journey* June/July: 4, 8.

Tucker, R. August 20, 2009. Who is the customer in surgery? http://leanhealthcareexchange.com/?p=524 (retrieved on October 29, 2009).

Vanocur, S. 1989. A conversation with Sander Vanocur. *Quality Progress* February: 45–48.

Wargo, R. A. 1994. How to avoid the traps of benchmarking customer satisfaction. *Continuous Journey* June/July: 2–3.

Weiner, M. B. 1994. S.N.U.B.NET: The crime of unused customer feedback. *Continuous Journey* June/July: 4–5.

Wells, F. 1989. Marketing factors and customer satisfaction. *Quality Progress* February: 32–36.

Wheatley, M. 1992. *Leadership and the new science.* San Francisco, CA: Berrett–Koehler.

Zeithaml, V., A. Parasuraman, and L. Berry. 1990. *Delivering quality service: Balancing customer perceptions and expectations.* New York: Free Press.

Zemke, R. 1994. Q&A with Ron Zemke. *Continuous Journey* June/July: 2.

Selected Bibliography

Baird, K. 2000. *Customer service in health care: A grassroots approach to creating a culture of service excellence.* San Franscisco, CA: Jossey–Bass.

Daniel, A. L. 1992. Overcome the barriers to superior customer service. *Journal of Business Strategy* January/February: 18–24.

Fuller, W. A. 1987. *Measurement error models.* New York: John Wiley & Sons.

Hams, R. M. 1994. Practically perfect presentations. *Training and Development Journal* July: 67–69.

Kahn, A. 1991. Maximize customer service through technology. *Chain Store Age Executive* October: 56.

Katz, S. N. 1991. Power skills for effective meetings. *Training and Development Journal* July: 72–76.

Naisbitt, J. 1989. Megatrends: Ten new directions transforming our lives. In *Total customer service,* ed. W. H. Davidow and B. Uttal. New York: Harper & Row.

Young, W., A. Minnick, and R. Marcantonio. 1996. How wide is the gap in defining quality care? Comparison of patient and nurse perceptions of important aspects of patient care. *Journal of Nursing Administration* 26 (5): 15–20.

Chapter 8

Understanding
the Process

Introduction

In the last chapter, our focus was customer satisfaction (CSat). Specifically, we talked about the principles of CSat and how it affects the customer in the healthcare industry. This chapter will define the process and what we must be aware of so that we may improve it.

The classical definition of a process is a collection of interrelated work tasks initiated in response to an event that achieves a specific result for the customer of the process. However, this simple and straightforward definition may be embellished with more detailed information to be more specific. We can say that a process is something that achieves a specific result that is identifiable and countable. We also may say that a process is the result of an initiated response that creates value. Value-adding activity is any activity that transforms inputs to meet customer requirements for which the customer is willing to pay. On the other hand, non-value-added activities are those activities that take time, resources, or space but do not add to the value of the product or service. These activities should be eliminated, simplified, reduced, or integrated. Some other inclusions of a process may be identified with the following observations:

- The customer of the process:
  - A customer receives the result or is the beneficiary of it.
  - The customer can be a person or an organization.

149

- The customer can be identified and can pass judgment on the result and process.
- The customer point of view helps identify and name the process accurately.

■ Work tasks:
  - A collection of actions, activities, steps, or tasks make up a business process.
  - A step in the initial work flow will probably be divided into more detailed steps later.

■ A collection of interrelated items making a whole:
  - The process steps must relate to each other.
  - Interrelationship is through sequence and flow ... the completion of one step leads to (flows into) the initiation of the next step.
  - Steps are also interrelated by dealing with the same work item.
  - Steps are related by being traceable back to the same initiation event.

Thus, a process depends on some input that is transformed into a value and that value is the outcome. We illustrate that as

Inputs → Process → Output

In a more complicated form, we can represent this as the SIPOC model, which is:

Supplier → Input → Process → Output → Customer

It is quite obvious from either model that everything around us may be defined as a process. We find processes in our everyday life and in manufacturing and nonmanufacturing areas. A typical comparison of manufacturing and healthcare differences is found in Table 8.1. In healthcare, processes are abundantly clear and may be found in a single physician's office or in a very complex hospital. Improvement is the result of changing a process in its entirety or individual components. The way to evaluate the necessity for change is to recognize and address the following:

■ A need for change is in order.
■ Culture change is the challenge.
■ Benchmark, benchmark, benchmark!
■ Form cross-functional dependencies.
■ Focus on quick wins first.

Table 8.1 Differences of Processes in Manufacturing and Healthcare

Manufacturing	Healthcare
Tangible processes (motors)	Technology distribution (tangible/intangible processes)
Data collection abounds	Data collection can be challenging
Processes 100% repeatable	Various types of processes
Required skills and engineering knowledge	Cross-functional business skills

- Start with the function closest to the problem area.
- Use basic statistical and team-based tools.
- Lean tools are a great fit to healthcare processes.
- Avoid a "shotgun" approach to training.
- Recognize that different environments require different approaches.

Once the necessity has been evaluated and resolved, the next step is to evaluate the change. Here the responsibility is twofold: (1) current state—what we are doing now and (2) future state—what we would like to be doing. When we begin the evaluation for the current state, we must focus on making the case for change. In other words: Why is change needed now? What will happen if we do not change?

Part of the discussion will result in mixed interpretations about overall direction and priorities of business. In fact, it is not unusual for the current business model discussion to cause lack of unified direction about which priorities to focus on, because some individuals feel comfortable with the status quo and do not see the need to change. In some cases, owners, management, and leadership are the abstinent force and resist the change because they have been accustomed to "seat of the pants" managing decisions. This kind of action, of course, creates animosity between co-workers but, above all, creates lack of clarity and connection within systems and processes (alignment) for overall improvement. In essence, this kind of behavior does inhibit optimal communication and business success; therefore, it must be avoided.

The second part of the discussion is the future state. What do we want this process to be? What are the benefits of this change? How does this impact our strategic goals? How will we maintain positive gains? Is it possible for us to do it? To answer these questions, we must have clear determination and communication of business strategy that provide vision, mission, and values of business. We must develop and communicate a clear business identity and consistent "model" for success from a sales and marketing point of view. (Yes, indeed, healthcare must at all levels recognize that sales and marketing play an important role in satisfaction, improvement, and profitability.) Stores are managed to focus both on customer and on employee development, providing continued sales and profit growth and a pipeline of future managers as business grows—as are physicians' offices, clinics, urgent care facilities, hospitals, and convalescent (skilled and unskilled) facilities.

It is imperative that all concerned have a clear focus on systems and processes that support the overall identity and direction of the business and bring about behaviors that support them. Development and implementation of organization structure that more evenly distributes key roles and responsibilities to enhance attainment of goals are necessary.

To be successful in the evaluation of a process, the management and leadership must develop a vision through appropriate recognition and articulation of

- Key stakeholders. This means to develop a specific strategy that will identify and define who is active to support and participate. The answer to these two concerns is critical to success. What steps are necessary to achieve the vision?
- Deliverables. What measurable will change and by how much? Are the deliverables clear, mutually understood, and doable, and do they agree with the assigned business strategy?
- Execution of strategy: Is the strategy consistent and focus? Is it aligned across the business at all levels? Is the planned execution effective and will it fend off competitive forces? Is the strategy accounting for long-term viability of the business as a successful, ongoing concern?
- Is growth for both revenue and commensurate profitability appropriate and applicable?
- Is accomplishment of true "esprit de corps" (improvement of the morale of the team) on target?

In the second requirement to be successful in the evaluation of a process, the owner, manager, or leader must provide direction and support for the business. This means:

- Conducting strategic planning sessions for the business (to include communication and/or implementation strategy)
- Determining and communicating the "competitive position" for the business
- Conducting training for managers that focuses on both productivity/profitability and employee development (professional management and leadership roles and responsibilities)

- Conducting audit and develop systems and processes that support the business strategy; creating recommendations planning for both implementing and sustaining the improvement
- Determining and implementing revised organization structure, if necessary

In order for these responsibilities to be understood and carried out in the entire organization, the owner or leader must have a very good understanding of

- Business key leadership individual: the ability to provide direction, set overall business structure, drive change, manage culture, and lead the business (inspire people)
- Business managers: the ability to understand their role (fit) and support successful implementation of the business plan in their location or area of responsibility and communicate the needs of the organization openly and honestly
- Employees: the ability to understand their role (fit) and support for a successful implementation of the business plan in their location or area of responsibility and give an opportunity to communicate the needs of the organization without fear of retaliation in any form
- Suppliers: the ability to understand their role in the business plan and support its success for the organization
- Customers (patients): the ability to understand their needs, satisfaction, and what is really necessary to provide continued growth and long-term business viability

One can use many tools and methodologies to evaluate, measure, optimize, and understand what the process does and how it behaves. It is beyond the scope of this book to identify all of them; however, a good list is shown in Table 8.2. The reader is encouraged to see Munro (2009), Brassard and Ritter (1994), and Stamatis (1997, 2003a, 2003b, 2003c).

In the hospital, urgent care, nursing home facility, and clinic, one may find many processes that are quite obvious. For example, one may think of admitting, or billing, or radiology, or drawing blood, or housekeeping, or so many others as processes. But a process may also be identifiable in a physician practice office.

For example, a physician's internal medicine practice may have several processes that, with the help of a process flow diagram or a value stream map, can focus on the medical filing process or even the patient flow. A physician's OB/GYN office may have several processes that, with the help of a process flow diagram or a value stream map, can focus on the reception/appointment process as well as patient flow. An orthopedic office may have several processes that, with the help of a process flow diagram or a value stream map, can focus on the x-ray process, casting, billing, medical filing, and so many other activities.

Table 8.2 Tool Chart

Basic Tools: Project Charter and Process Map Are the Foundation to a Successful Project	
Manufacturing	**Healthcare**
Statistical tools are in wide and frequent use; important and can be validated with data	Wide and frequent use of basic statistical tools for projects; they are extremely important
Statistical process control Design of experiments Gauge repeatability and reproducibility Taguchi Regression Hypothesis testing	Pareto charts Control charts Some regression and hypothesis *Team tools:* Cause and effect matrix Failure mode and effect analysis Brainstorming Wide and frequent use for projects
Common roles and responsibilities	**Fundamental skills for healthcare**
Executive support Mentoring/coaching Project management Training development/deployment Project status and financial tracking	Leadership Facilitation skills Presentation/training experience Educational background Project management

The idea here is to communicate to the reader that, in all processes, with some simple thinking and planning, we can improve the status quo. However, this basic transformation of the process has to be done in a collaborative manner by all concerned by using a brainstorming of ideas and then graphing, plotting, or diagramming the current process. The results of this little effort will generate standardized work and a pull system for the patient.

Failure Mode and Effect Analysis (FMEA)

Failure mode and effect analysis is a methodology to evaluate a system, a design, or a process for possible ways in which failures can occur. For each bona fide or potential failure, an estimate is made of its effect on the total system and of its seriousness. In addition, a review is made of the action being taken (or planned) to minimize the probability of failure or to minimize the effect of failure.

This simple, straightforward approach can be very technical (quantitative) or very nontechnical (qualitative), utilizing three main factors for the identification of the specific failure:

- *Occurrence:* how often the failure occurs
- *Severity:* how serious the failure is
- *Detection:* how easy or difficult it is to detect the failure

How complicated the approach is always depends on the complexity of the problem as defined by the following (Juran and Gryna 1980):

- *Safety.* Injury is the most serious of all failure effects. In fact, in some cases, it is of unquestionable priority and, of course, at this point it must be handled with a hazard analysis and/or failure mode and critical analysis (FMCA).
- *Effects on downtime.* How are repairs made? Can repairs be made while the machine is off duty or while the machine is operating?
- *Access.* What hardware items must be removed to get at the failed component? This area will be of great importance as environmental laws are changed to reflect world conditions for disassembly.
- *Repair planning.* Repair time, maintainability, repair tools, cost, and recommendations for changes in design specifications should all be considered. Here, the mistake-proofing approach, DOE (design of experiment), or design for manufacturability may be considered.

To carry this methodology to its proper conclusion the following prerequisites in understanding are necessary:

- *Not all problems are important.* This is very fundamental to the entire concept of FMEA because unless this concept is internalized, one will be "chasing fires" in the organization. It is necessary to recognize that some problems have a higher priority than others for whatever the reason. FMEA helps identify this priority.
- *Know the customer.* The customer is usually thought of as the end user. However, a customer may also be defined as a subsequent or downstream operation, as well as a service operation. When the term customer is used from a FMEA perspective, the definition plays a very major role in addressing problems. For example, as a general rule in the design FMEA, one views the customer as the end user, while in the process FMEA, the customer is viewed as the next operation in line. This next operation may indeed be the end user, but it does not have to be. Once the customer (internal, intermediate, or external) is defined, the definition may not be changed—at

least, not for the problem at hand—unless one recognizes that changing it may indeed have changed the problem and/or consequences.

■ *Know the function.* It is imperative to know the function, purpose, and objective of what one is trying to accomplish. Otherwise, time and effort will be wasted in redefining the problem based on interpretations of specific problems or situations. If needed, take extra time to make sure that the function or purpose of what one is trying to accomplish is understood.

■ *Be prevention oriented.* Unless continual improvement is recognized to be in the organization's best interest, the FMEA is going to be a static document to satisfy customer or market requirements. The push for this continual improvement makes the FMEA a dynamic document that changes as the design and/or process changes, always with the intent to make a better design and/or process.

The reader is strongly encouraged to read Stamatis (2003d, 2004) for an exhaustive discussion on FMEA.

Systems Thinking

In healthcare—much more than in any other industry and especially if dealing with design for Six Sigma (DFSS)—we must be able to think in a system approach. A system may be considered to be a nucleus of elements structured to accomplish a function and satisfy an identified need. A system may also vary in form, fit, and function. For example, a world communication network, a group of aircraft accomplishing a mission at a designated geographical location, or a small ship transporting cargo from one location to another are all considered systems. On the other hand, examples of a functional system are a financial system, a quality system, a purchasing system, and a design system. The elements of a system include all equipment, related facilities, material, software, data, services, and personnel required for its operation and support, to the degree that it can be considered a self-sufficient entity in its intended operational environment throughout its planned life cycle.

In healthcare, we may have a system in a general practitioner's office, a laboratory, admissions, medical records, surgery, medical billing, and many other areas. Especially in a DFSS project, systems thinking is imperative for it relates to the support of all components of the system and includes the elements of test and support equipment, supply support, personnel and training, transportation and material handling, special facilities, computer resources, data, and so on necessary for the accomplishment of breakthrough innovations in design of process, product, or service. It is imperative that, when pursuing improvements in healthcare, the experimenter or engineer take a holistic approach so that all interactions and interfaces are accounted for. The more aware the experimenter or engineer is of the parameters, interactions, and interfaces of the undertaken study, the greater the chance of success will be. For more information, see Stamatis (2003e, 2003f, 2004).

Poka-Yoke (Mistake Proofing/Error Proofing)

Shigeo Shingo, considered the father of poka-yoke, is often quoted as saying, "The idea behind poka-yoke is to respect the intelligence of workers by taking over repetitive tasks or actions that depend on the vigilance of memory." This process includes adding features to a design or process to assist the operator in the performance of the task. Poka-yoke, in any of the various spellings, is another name for error proofing or mistake proofing a design or process.

The focus of poka-yoke is on sensitizing us about the differences between prevention and detection and doing something about it. Prevention prevents errors from occurring or prevents those errors from causing defects. Detection identifies a defect and immediately initiates a corrective action to prevent multiple defects from leaving the workstation. Detection devices are used to deal with an error that is difficult to eliminate or is in the process of being located. The main idea of a prevention approach is to keep an error from producing multiple defects. Sometimes the error (or root cause) of the defect is hard to find. In this case, it is often profitable to create solutions that detect and react to an error or a defect instead of preventing an error or a defect. Such devices are detection devices.

Using detection devices in error proofing is different from regular product or process inspection. Error proofing initiates a corrective action once an error or defect has been detected. Regular product or process inspection should not be referred to as error proofing unless the inspection is tied to an immediate corrective measure. An example of inspection that is not tied to an immediate corrective action is SPC (statistical process control) or a continual inspection with a process controller.

A number of criteria should be considered when choosing between a prevention or detection approach. The proposed device must be considered for its ability to

- Prevent an error that causes the defect or initiate a corrective action before multiple defects occur
- Be designed and installed quickly and easily
- Be cost effective to implement and easy to maintain

History shows that no matter how much we train the operator or document the process, human error occurs. Poka-yoke is the methodology of reducing or eliminating human error, which causes defects. The methodology is based on two essential attitudes about human behavior: Mistakes are inevitable and errors can be eliminated. Based on these attitudes, the following corollary assumptions may be made about work processes and workers:

- Few workers make errors intentionally.
- Error is inherent in the nature of humans.
- Human errors are invited to occur by processes that do not use error proofing.

A poka-yoke methodology alters the work environment with a goal of reducing human errors and their defects. In healthcare, major efforts are being made to introduce poka-yoke—especially in surgery. Why this effort? Because errors in healthcare can be the difference between life and death, the more we can do to prevent them the better. Errors (mistakes) also impact financial costs and increase the stress levels of staff. With these major concerns, it is critical to design and continually strive for an error-proof process. In an industry where human life is at stake, 99% quality should never be good enough. In some other environments where the well-being of humans is not at stake, 99% could perhaps be acceptable. Imagine if only 99% of the world's bridges were stable, if our cars only started 99 out of 100 times, or our telephones only connected 99% of our calls. The result would be collapsed bridges, stranded motorists, and many missed conversations.

The ultimate goal in error proofing is to design a system that will detect and prevent errors from happening. Visual inspection is a possible method of removing errors, but it is only 80–90% effective. For instance, how many people go straight through intersections without ever seeing the stop sign? There are many examples of error proofing in our everyday lives. Some examples are the overflow drains on sinks, automatic shutoff on small appliances, and alarms for seat belts in cars. An example of a preventive poka-yoke is that a car will not allow a driver to remove the key unless the gear shift is in the park position. This prevents the car from being able to move while unattended.

While redesigning and standardizing our processes, it is very important that we are mindful of any step where an error can happen and that we design the best possible poka-yoke to prevent it from being able to happen. Inspection is not reliable enough to risk human life. We must integrate strategies to prevent and detect errors before the process is complete.

Every process has variation and most processes are very complex. Our challenge is to remove the variation so that all processes are predictable and consistent. The ultimate goal, as stated before, is to design the processes to ensure that errors will not happen. In most cases, to eliminate or prevent errors, we must develop processes where, because of the error-proofing mechanisms put in the system, humans and equipment are not able to make mistakes and variation is restricted.

Effective error proofing is able to detect and prevent errors reliably and consistently without being affected by emotion or distractions. It does not normally replace the need for human intervention, but it does assist in bringing the concern or problem to the attention of the staff before the problem can interfere with the next step in the process. When used as part of the process in any healthcare environment, it improves product and service quality for both internal and external customers by preventing defects from getting into the product or service.

In some cases, the distinction is made between error proofing and mistake proofing. The first is associated with design and the second with manufacturing or service. Mistake proofing reduces costs primarily by reducing waste and human issues from the workplace. Error proofing improves the design by allowing a greater quantity of good products to reach the final customer without rework. Error proofing also improves the quality of workers' lives by improving worker safety. It is not always necessary to create all designs and processes with error proofing in mind. Trade-offs among quality, price, and delivery must be considered. Sometimes focusing on mistake proofing is just as acceptable. For more information on poka-yoke, see Shingo (1986) and Stamatis (2004). Mistake proofing is one more way to address the relentless war on waste in the process. A typical list is shown in Table 8.3.

Advance Practice Quality Planning (APQP)

Advance quality planning (AQP) is the generic methodology for all quality planning activities in all industries, so APQP is AQP. However, traditional APQP emphasizes the *product* orientation of quality and has been used primarily in the automotive industry. In the last year or so, APQP has been gaining ground in healthcare as well and now stands for advance *practice* quality planning. In this book, the three terms are used interchangeably.

Before we address the "why" of planning, we must assume that things do go wrong. Obviously, many specific answers address the question of why they go wrong. Often the answer falls into one of four categories:

- We do not have enough time, so some things do not get done.
- We have done something in a particular way, so we minimize our effort.

Table 8.3 The Relentless War on Waste

Waste in Process	Possible Opportunities for Poka-yoke
• Waste of overproduction • Waste of transportation • Waste of overprocessing • Waste of inventory • Waste of motion • Waste of making defective products or poor quality • Waste of engineering	• Lab tests • Patient transfers • Charge tickets • Drugs, supplies • Searching for charts • Professional liability • Large centralized machines

Considerations for implementing poka-yoke
1. What are the biggest problems in the healthcare facility? 2. Do most patients go through similar diagnostic and treatment steps? 3. How long does the end-to-end patient journey take—and how long could it take? 4. What is the demand to get into the facility—and how long do patients have to wait? 5. How could most of the waiting time within and between departments be eliminated? 6. What is the demand to get out of the facility—how many patients are ready to go or are in the wrong rooms or beds? 7. How could these activities be managed visually to track progress and delays? 8. Who will take responsibility for transforming the end-to-end patient journeys?

- We assume that we know what has been requested, so we do not listen carefully.
- We assume that, because we finish a project, improvement will automatically follow, so we bypass the improvement steps.

In essence, the customer appears satisfied, but a product, service, or process is not improved at all. This is precisely why it is imperative for organizations to look at quality planning as a totally integrated activity that involves the entire organization (single facility or entire hospital). The organization must expect changes in its operations by employing cross-functional and multidisciplinary teams to exceed customer desires—not just to meet requirements. A quality plan includes but is not limited to

- A team to manage the plan
- Time to monitor progress
- Procedures to define operating policies
- Standards to clarify requirements
- Controls to stay on course
- Data and feedback to verify and to provide direction
- An action plan to initiate change

Advanced quality planning, then, is a methodology that yields a quality plan for the creation of a process, product, or service consistent with customer requirements. It allows for maximum quality in the workplace by planning and documenting the process of improvement. It is the essential discipline that offers both the customer and the supplier a systematic approach to quality planning to detect prevention and to continual improvement. Some specific uses in healthcare are:

- New applications of surgery
- New routing of patients
- New introductions of equipment in a facility
- Introduction of new technology by a medical device company (Especially in the medical device industry, they are expected to demonstrate the ability to participate in early design activities from concept through to prototype and on to production by using APQP.)
- New introduction of vaccination or vaccinations

An effective AQP is one where the planning is initiated as early as possible, well before blueprint release. That, of course, is indicative of the company's management attitude and willingness to establish a policy of prevention, as opposed to detection. Furthermore, it must be willing to

- Provide the resources needed to accomplish the quality improvement task
- Prevent waste (scrap, rework, and repair), identify required engineering changes, improve timing for new product or service introduction, and reduce costs
- Facilitate communication with all individuals involved in a program and ensure that all required steps are completed on time at acceptable cost and quality levels
- Provide a structured tool for management that enforces the inclusion of quality principles in program planning

When we are ready for a process breakthrough approach for satisfying the customer with something better than the status quo, AQP is the vehicle for measuring this breakthrough approach from very early (concept stage) all the way through production. Therefore, we use AQP when we need to meet, or exceed, expectations in the following situations:

- During the development of new processes, services, and products
- Prior to changes in processes and products
- When reacting to processes or products with reported quality concerns
- Before equipment is transferred or changed to new locations
- Prior to process or product changes affecting product safety or compliance to regulations

It follows, then, that the basic requirements for appropriate and complete AQP are

- A team approach
- A systematic development of products or services and processes
- A reduction in variation (this must be done, even before the customer requests improvement of any kind)
- Development of a control plan

As AQP is continuously used, the obvious need for its implementation becomes stronger and stronger. That need may be demonstrated through

- Minimizing the current level of problems and errors
- Yielding a methodology that integrates customer—and supplier—development activities, as well as concerns
- Exceeding current reliability and durability levels to surpass the expectations of the competition and the customer
- Reinforcing the integration of quality tools with the latest management techniques for total improvement
- Exceeding the limits set for cycle time and delivery time
- Developing new, and improving existing, methods of communicating the results of quality processes for a positive impact throughout the organization

To be sure, there are no guarantees for making AQP work. However, three basic characteristics are essential and must be adhered to for AQP to work in any process:

- Activities must be measured based on who, what, where, and when.

- Activities must be tracked based on shared information (how and why), as well as work schedules and objectives.
- Activities must be focused on the goal of quality–cost–delivery, using information and consensus to improve quality.

As long as our focus is on the triad of quality–cost–delivery, AQP can produce positive results. After all, we all need to reduce costs while we increase quality and reduce lead time. This is the focus of an AQP program, and the better we understand this, the more likely we are to have a workable plan in any process. For more information on APQP, see Stamatis (1998, 2004).

Measurement

Any organization interested in understanding its processes must be willing to make an effort in measuring, monitoring, and doing analysis of what it finds. In healthcare, processes and services that are deemed important or critical for improvement—both direct and supportive, including services provided by any contracted service—must be evaluated. The monitoring should include the use of internal reviews (audits) of each department or service at scheduled intervals (not to exceed 1 year) and data related to these processes. Individuals not assigned to the department or service will conduct the internal review (audit).

Measurement, monitoring, and analysis of processes throughout the organization require established measures that have the ability to (1) detect variation, (2) identify problem processes, (3) identify both positive and negative outcomes, and (4) evaluate effectiveness of actions taken to improve performance and/or reduce risks. The organization must define the frequency and detail of the measurement. Some typical functions that National Integrated Accreditation for Health Organizations (NIAHO 2009) recommends be measured at hospital facilities, clinics, nursing homes, or physicians' practices should include the following as appropriate and applicable:

- Threats to patient safety
- Medication therapy/medication use; to include medication reconciliation and the use of dangerous abbreviations
- Operative and invasive procedures; to include wrong site/wrong patient/ wrong procedure surgery
- Anesthesia/moderate sedation
- Blood and blood components
- Restraint use/seclusion
- Effectiveness of pain management system

- Infection control system, including nosocomial infections
- Utilization management system
- Patient flow issues, to include reporting of patients held in the emergency department or the post anesthesia care unit (PACU) in excess of 8 hours
- Customer satisfaction, both clinical and support areas
- Discrepant pathology reports
- Unanticipated deaths, nonsentinel events
- Sentinel event/near miss
- Other adverse events
- Critical and/or pertinent processes, both clinical and supportive
- Medical record delinquency
- Physical environment management systems
- Blood use: AABB transfusion criteria
- Prescribing of medications: prescribing errors and appropriateness of prescribing for drug use evaluations
- Surgical case review: appropriateness and outcomes for selected high-risk procedures
- Specific department indicators that have been defined by the medical staff
- Moderate sedation outcomes
- Appropriateness of care for noninvasive specialties
- Utilization data
- Significant deviations from established standards of practice
- Timely and legible completion of patients' medical records
- Any variant analyzed for statistical significance

The idea here is for the organization to have enough information (data) to evaluate the quality of care provided to patients. It is important to mention that these measurements should reflect items that the organization has defined as important or critical and should have some representation in the standards under which the facility operates.

Project Management

Project management (PM) is the application of knowledge, skills, tools, and techniques in order to meet or exceed stakeholder (customer) requirements from a project. Meeting or exceeding stakeholder requirements means balancing competing demands of

- Scope, time, cost, quality, and other project objectives
- Stakeholders (customers) with differing requirements
- Identified requirements and unidentified requirements (expectations)

Knowledge about project management can be organized in many ways. In fact, the official *A Guide to the Project Management Body of Knowledge* (PMBOK) identifies 12 subsections of project management (Duncan 1994):

- Project management
- Project context
- Process of project management
- Key integrative processes
- Project scope management
- Project time management
- Project cost management
- Project quality management
- Project human resource management
- Project communications management
- Project risk management
- Project procurement management

In the following summary of PM subsections, we identify how quality initiatives management may be implemented efficiently with an undertaking of a project management approach using the PDCA (plan-do-check [study]-act) model. We also discuss some of the basic concepts of project management and how the methodology of project management may be used.

Let us begin our summary discussion by emphasizing that the lifeblood of any PM initiative is the *project*. A project is a task or, quite often, a bundle of tasks performed by people and constrained by limited resources, describable as processes and subprocesses that are planned, executed, and controlled within definite time limits. Above all, they have a beginning and an end. Projects differ from operations primarily in that operations are ongoing and repetitive, while projects are temporary and unique. A project can thus be defined in terms of its distinctive characteristics: It is a temporary endeavor undertaken to create a unique product or service. "Temporary" means that every project has a definite ending point. "Unique" means that the product or service is different in some distinguishing way from all similar products or services.

Projects are undertaken at all levels of the organization. They may involve a single person or many thousands of people. They may require less than 100 hours or over 1,000 hours to complete. Projects may involve a single unit of one organization or may cross organizational boundaries, as in joint ventures and partnering. Examples of projects include:

- Developing a new product or service
- Effecting a change in structure, staffing, or style of an organization

- Designing a new product or service
- Developing a new or modified product or service
- Implementing a new business procedure or process

"Temporary" means that every project has a definite ending point. The ending point is when the project's objectives have been achieved or when it becomes clear that the project objectives will not or cannot be met and the project is terminated. Temporary does not necessarily mean short in duration. It means that the project is not an ongoing task; therefore, it is finite. This point is very important since many undertakings are temporary in the sense that they will end at some point. For example, installation of a new x-ray machine in the radiology department eventually will be complete and the machine will be normally operated as designed. This installation may involve a new facility, new personnel or training of the old personnel, proper maintenance, and so on. All these items are a consideration of appropriate application of PM.

Projects are fundamentally different because the project ceases work when its objectives have been attained, while a nonproject undertaking adopts a new set of objectives and continues to work. The temporary nature of the project may apply to other aspects of the endeavor as well:

- The opportunity or market window is usually temporary since most projects have a limited time frame in which to produce their product or service.
- The project team seldom outlives the project since most projects are performed by a team created for the sole purpose of performing the project, and the team is disbanded and members reassigned when the project is complete.

On the other hand, a project or service is considered unique if it involves doing something that has not been done before and is therefore unique. The presence of repetitive elements does not change the fundamental uniqueness of the overall effort. Because the product of each project is unique, the characteristics that distinguish the product or service must be progressively elaborated. "Progressively" means "proceeding in steps; continuing steadily by increments" and elaborated means "worked out with care and detail; developed thoroughly" (*American Heritage Dictionary* 1992). These distinguishing characteristics will be broadly defined early in the project and will be made more explicit and detailed as the project team develops a better and more complete understanding of the product.

Progressive elaboration of product characteristics must not be confused with proper scope definition, particularly if any portion of the project will be performed under contract. In contrast to a project, there is also a program. A program is a group of projects managed in a coordinated way to obtain benefits not available from managing them individually (Turner 1992). Most programs also include elements of ongoing operations as well as a series of repetitive or cyclical undertakings. (It must be noted, however, that in some applications, program management and project management are treated as one and the same; in others, one is a subset of the other. It is precisely this diversity of meaning that makes it imperative that any discussion of program management versus project management require a clear, consistent, and agreed upon definition of each term.)

Process of Project Management

The process of project management is an integrative one. The interactions may be straightforward and well understood, or they may be subtle and uncertain. These interactions often require trade-offs among project objectives. Therefore, successful project management requires actively managing these interactions so that the appropriate and applicable objectives may be attained within budget, schedule, and constraints.

A process from a project management perspective is the traditional dictionary definition: "a series of actions bringing about a result" (*American Heritage Dictionary* 1992). In the case of a project, there are five basic management processes:

- *Initiating:* recognizing that a project should be begun and committing to do so
- *Planning:* identifying objectives and devising a workable scheme to accomplish them
- *Executing:* coordinating people and other resources to carry out the plan
- *Controlling:* ensuring that the objectives are met by measuring progress and taking corrective action when necessary
- *Closing:* formalizing acceptance of the project and bringing it to an orderly end

Operational management—the management of ongoing operations—also involves planning, executing, and controlling; however, the temporary nature of projects requires the addition of initiating and closing activities. These processes occur at all levels of the enterprise, in many different forms, and under many different names. Even though there are many variations, it is imperative to understand that operational management is an ongoing activity with neither a clear beginning nor an expected end.

Finally, it must be understood that these processes (initiating, planning, executing, controlling, and closing) are not discrete, one-time events. They are overlapping activities that occur at varying levels of intensity throughout each phase of the project. In addition, the processes are linked by the results they produce since the result or outcome of one becomes an input to another. Among the central processes, the links are iterated; planning provides executing with a documented project plan early on and then provides documented updates to the plan as the project progresses. It is imperative that the basic process interactions occur within each phase such that closing one phase provides an input to initiating the next. For example, closing a design phase requires customer acceptance of the design document. Simultaneously, the design document defines the product description for the ensuing implementation phase. For more information on this concept, see Duncan (1994), Kerzner (1995), Stamatis (1996a, 1997), and Frame (1994).

Key Integrative Processes

In project management, the key integrative processes are

- *Project plan development:* taking the results of other planning processes and putting them into a consistent, coherent document
- *Project plan execution:* carrying out the project plan by performing or having performed the activities included therein
- *Overall change control:* coordinating changes across entire project

Although the processes seem to be discrete and different from each other, this is not the case in practice. In fact, they do overlap and interact in ways that are beyond the scope of this book to describe. A typical summary of a key integrative process is shown in Table 8.4.

Project Management and Quality

Project management is a problem-solving methodology. On the other hand, Lean methodology is a "process project" that requires total acceptance for improvement. For that improvement to occur, Lean must be implemented in the entire organization. Both Six Sigma and Lean fit the profile of project management. Every component of project management is designed to facilitate the solving of complex problems. It uses teams of specialists. It makes use of a powerful scheduling method. It tightly tracks costs. It provides a mechanism for management of Lean and Six Sigma. It depends on the integration of several skills and disciplines. It encourages monitoring of processes and depends on feedback for evaluation. It requires leaders with clear vision and doable objectives. It requires knowledge of appropriate and applicable tools, and it plans for success.

Table 8.4   Key Integrative Processes

Project Plan Development	*Project Plan Execution*	*Overall Change Control*
Inputs		
Outputs of other processes Historical information Organizational policies Constraints	Project plan Supporting detail Organizational policies	Project plan Progress report Change request
Tools and techniques		
Project planning methodology Stakeholder skills and knowledge Project management information systems	Technical skills and knowledge Work authorization system Status review meetings Project management information system	Change control system Progress measurement Additional planning Computer software Reserves
Outputs		
Project plan supporting detail	Work results Change requests	Project plan updates Corrective action Lessons learned

In addition, project management makes and at the same time facilitates change. By definition, projects have a start, middle (work accomplished), and a finish. The finish comes when the objectives for the project are satisfied. Project objectives always address changes that will be made in some current situation. If an organization does not want to make a change, then project management is not an appropriate management method for it. This does not imply that changes should not be made there, only that there is no motivation for change. In such an organization, the introduction of project management would have little support and may even be resistance. For a discussion on change and when change actually takes place, see Stamatis (1996a, 1997).

Since the implementation of Lean and Six Sigma is a project (with a beginning, work changes, and an end), project management is indeed a method that can be used in the implementation process. (It is very important to differentiate the concepts of Lean and Six Sigma methodologies as philosophies to improvement and the implementation of both. The implementation of both by definition is a project. Here, we are talking about the physical implementation of both Six Sigma and Lean.) For specific examples of implementation strategies of project management in the implementation of quality initiatives in service industries and healthcare, the reader is encouraged to see Stamatis (1994, 1995a, 1995b, 1996a, 1996b).

Generic Seven-Step Approach to Project Management

Much has been written about how to use project management in a variety of industries and specific situations. Many articles and books have proclaimed specific approaches for the best results in a given situation. Rather than dwell on a particular approach, here is a summary discussion of a generic seven-step approach of using project management in a quality orientation for any organization. The seven steps are based on the four-phase cycle of any project.

Phase 1. Define the Project

1. Describe the project. Describing a project is not as simple as it might seem. In fact, this step may be the most difficult and time consuming. To be successful, the project description should include simple specifications, goals, projected time frame, and responsible individuals as well as constraints and assumptions. Capturing the essence of highly complex projects in a few words is an exercise in focus and delineation; however, we must be vigilant of avoiding becoming too simple and in the process failing to convey the scope of the project, while a detailed, complex description may cloud the big picture. The key is clarity without an excess of volume or jargon.

2. Appoint the planning team. After describing the project, begin to identify the right players. Too many people on a team can stifle the decision-making process and reduce the number of accomplishments. Cross-functional teams are among the most difficult to appoint. Except in the pure project organization, where the team is solely dedicated to completing the project, roles and priorities can cause conflict. In cross-functional teams, the

project leader must seek support from the functional managers and identify team goals.

3. Define the work. Once the planning team is in place, team members must define the work. Since each member hails from a different department, there will be many different concepts of the project's work content. There are many ways to divide the work for convenient use in planning. Two common ways are the process flow diagram and the work breakdown structure (WBS). The method should be chosen to reflect the most useful division and summarization for the situation. After all, the objective of this step is to define the tasks to be done, rather than the order of doing them.

Phase 2. Plan the Project

4. Estimate tasks. Before a project schedule is created, each task must be evaluated and assigned an estimate of duration. There are essentially two ways of looking at this process. The first is to establish the duration of this task by estimating the time it takes to complete the task with given resources. The second way is to estimate the types and amounts of resources needed and the effort in terms of resource hours necessary to complete the task.

5. Calculate the schedule and budgets. The next step is to construct a network logic diagram or a performance evaluation review technique (PERT) and a budget. The focus of the logic diagram and/or the PERT is to develop appropriate scheduling datelines and, more importantly, to define the critical path. The focus of the budget is to estimate the costs of the project based on all activities. The identification of the critical path will identify bottleneck areas as well as opportunities for improvement. Tasks not on the critical path may have a float that can be calculated and may be used to facilitate the efficiency and utilization of resources without affecting the project's final date.

Phase 3. Implement the Plan

6. The start of the project can really make an impact on project team members' attendance, performance, and evaluation. Kick-off meetings should convey the following ideas:
   - This is a new project.
   - Project management is going to be used to manage the project.
   - A plan exists that is open to all, and it is going to be followed.
   - The focus is on the start of activities.
   - A realistic status is needed to allow timely decisions.
   - The focus will always be on forecasting and preventing problems.

Phase 4. Track Progress and Complete the Project

7. The essence of this step is to bring the project to closure. This means that the project must be officially closed and all deliverables must be handed over to the stakeholders (customers). In addition, a review of the lessons learned must take place and a thank-you for the project team is the appropriate etiquette. Key questions of this step include:
   - Where are we?
   - Where should we be?
   - What do we have to do to get there?
   - Did it work?
   - Where are we now?
   - Can the process employees take over?
   - Can the process employees maintain the new system?
   - What have we learned from the successes in this project?
   - What have we learned from the failures in this project?
   - What would we have done differently? Why? Why not?

Process Flowchart

A process flowchart diagram provides an overall process flow definition and a step-by-step description of each operation in a process. In any service, a process flow is a graphic presentation of the flow and sources of variation of machines, materials, methods, personnel, environment, and measurement from the start to the end of the process.

Standard symbols have been developed to show the flow in a graphic form (see Table 8.5). Generally, using these symbols, the detail of the process can be varied based on the needs and goals at hand. There are five types of flowcharts: basic, deployment, opportunity, spaghetti diagram, and process (micro level) flowcharts:

- *Basic flowcharts* (macro level) identify all the major steps in a process—more than six steps. They are mostly used for the 60,000-foot view for management review. A "macro" process flowchart is used to show a very basic process from raw material to finished goods. An example is shown in Figure 8.1.
- *Deployment flowcharts* map out the process in terms of who is doing the steps, and it is conveyed in the form of a matrix showing the various participants and the flow of steps among these participants. These flowcharts are helpful if the *process being mapped crosses departmental boundaries.*

Table 8.5   Standard Symbols Used for a Flowchart

Symbol	Name	Meaning
O	Operations	Object is changed at the workplace
→	Transportation	Object is moved
□	Inspection	Object is examined
D	Delay	Object is waiting for next operation
◊	Decision	If acceptable, continue; if not, repair, scrap, etc.
∇	Storage	Object is retained and protected against unauthorized removal

Supplier	Customer
Patient: information about condition	Physician
Physician: order to test EW secretary	Phlebotomist lab technician
EW secretary: information about patient and test	Dispatcher
Dispatcher: information about...	Phlebotomist
Phlebotomist: blood sample	EW secretary

Figure 8.1   Sample of a descriptive flowchart (macro): lab test in emergency ward (EW).

- *Opportunity flowcharts* list the various activities that comprise the process and list differences between value-added and non-value-added activities.
- *Spaghetti diagram flowcharts* use a continuous line to trace the path of a provided part, document, person, or service through all its phases. Spaghetti diagrams expose inefficient layouts and large distances traveled

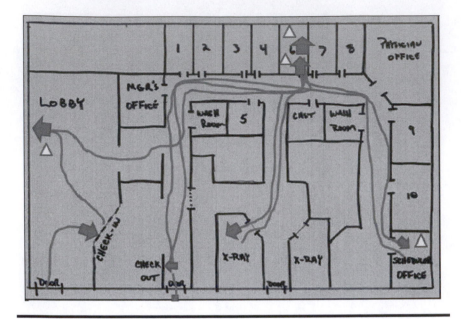

Figure 8.2 A typical spaghetti diagram.

between steps. These diagrams should also display electronic information flow (e-mails, spreadsheets, documents, etc.). A typical spaghetti diagram is shown in Figure 8.2. In this case, we observed that the patient average time was 67 minutes, with a standard deviation of 59 minutes.

■ *Process flowcharts* (micro level) examine the process in detail and indicate all the steps or activities that would include the decision points, waiting periods, tasks that frequently must be redone (rework), and any feedback loops. This is the ground-level listing of the tasks and activities. A "micro" process flowchart is used to show all the details and operations (steps) in a process. An example is shown in Figure 8.3.

Through a flowchart, the operator may be able to identify the points in the process where more information may be collected. As a general generic rule, there are three such points in any process:

■ *Incoming material.* Although this check is more expensive than good supplier and vendor quality, the order should be checked for completeness and quality.

Basic Process	Problems, Complexity, and Waste
Physician orders test	Ordered wrong test Incomplete specification No forms Put order in wrong place
EW secretary calls dispatcher	Physician's handwriting illegible Dispatcher's line busy Gave dispatcher wrong information
Dispatcher sends phlebotomist	Phlebotomist not available Phlebotomist went to wrong patient Elevators slow/unavailable or hall construction Out of supplies
Specimen given to EW secretary	Put vial in wrong place Secretary misplaced paperwork

Figure 8.3   Sample of a flowchart (micro): process for lab tests in emergency ward (EW).

- *In process.* This is the focus of statistical process control. It is important for at least three reasons, which become the impetus for good quality in the process. As a consequence, the process must be checked during operations (working hours) to make sure that it produces acceptable services or products:
  - Expensive operations
  - Irreversible operations
  - Assembly or finishing operations
- *Finished goods or service.* Inspecting only at this point is a waste. The service or goods at this point are very expensive and serve no other reason than to identify what the customer will see when the product or service is delivered. If it is used as a sorting mechanism, then a lot of money is wasted before a solution is found.

People have different ideas about a process based on what they do and how and when they do it in the process. It is imperative, then, to use the process flowchart as a tool to show the relationship between the different process parts.

By using a flowchart, ideal settings of the process, differences between shifts and/or operators, and process streams may be discovered. (A process stream may be a multiple cavity, different fixtures or pallets, several machines producing the same part, or teams using different settings and/or procedures). In general, the team's effort will be improved.

Value Process Mapping

A value process mapping (VPM) diagram is a complete view of the process from 60,000 feet high. It is similar to the traditional process flow; however, it shows the flow of materials and information as well as all value and nonvalue processes. It helps to understand the entire process as it identifies the metrics associated with that particular process, such as cycle time, tack time, process time, pitch time, and other metrics that define the process. In Chapter 10 we will discuss the VPM in more detail. However, here we give a very cursory approach to value process mapping:

- Start with a customer request—typically, patient or physician. This does not need to be the typical factory-looking icon.
- Have both "material" (or patient) flow and information flow. Sometimes the "product" is information (such as a referral request), but treat that as the product (creating an appointment) and then also document the information flows involved in creating that information (phone calls, computer systems etc.).
- Focus on both the actual process steps and the waiting time in between. VPM analysis focuses primarily on the "white space."
- Have some amount of data that come from real *gemba* (direct from the source) observation and information systems. Hospitals are often very lucky in having real data that would be wanted for a VPM.

Summary

In this chapter, we talked about the process. Specifically, we introduced the definition and then proceeded to present some specific methodologies to further understand and improve it. These methodologies were FMEA, APQP, systems thinking, poka-yoke, project management, and process flow. In the next chapter, we discuss the Six Sigma approach to improvement.

References

American Heritage Dictionary of the English Language, 32nd ed. 1992. Boston: Houghton Mifflin Company.

Brassard, M., and D. Ritter. 1994. *The memory jogger II.* Salem, NH: Goal/QPC.

Duncan, W. R. 1994. *A guide to the project management body of knowledge.* Upper Darby, PA: Project Management Institute.

Frame, J. D. 1994. *The new project management.* San Francisco, CA: Jossey–Bass.

Juran, J. M., and F. M. Gryna, Jr. 1980. *Quality planning and analysis.* New York: McGraw–Hill.

Kerzner, H. 1995. *Project management: A systems approach to planning, scheduling and controlling,* 5th ed. New York: Van Nostrand Reinhold.

Munro, R. 2009. *Lean Six Sigma for the healthcare practice.* Milwaukee, WI: Quality Press.

NIAHO. 2009. http://www.dnv.com/industry/healthcare/key_niaho_materials.asp (see NIAHO accreditation process [pdf]; NIAHO standards and interpretive guidelines [pdf]; NIAHO accreditation application [Word]) (retrieved on October 28, 2009).

Shingo, S. 1986. *Zero quality control, source inspection and the poka-yoke system.* New York: Productivity Press.

Stamatis, D. H. 1994. Total quality management and project management. *Project Management Journal* September: 48–54.

———. 1995a. *Understanding ISO 9000 and implementing the basics to quality.* New York: Marcel Dekker.

———. 1995b. *Integrating QS-9000 with your automotive quality system.* Milwaukee, WI: Quality Press.

———. 1996a. *Total quality service.* Boca Raton, FL: St. Lucie Press.

———. 1996b. *Total quality management in health care.* Burr Ridge, IL: Irwin Professionals.

———. 1997. *TQM engineering handbook.* New York: Marcel Dekker.

———. 1998. *Advanced quality planning: A commonsense guide to AQP and APQP.* New York: Quality Resources.

———. 2003a. *Six Sigma and beyond: Statistics and probability.* Boca Raton, FL: St. Lucie Press.

———. 2003b. *Six Sigma and beyond: Statistical process control.* Boca Raton, FL: St. Lucie Press.

———. 2003c. *Six Sigma and beyond: Statistics and probability.* Boca Raton, FL: St. Lucie Press.

———. 2003d. *Failure mode and effect analysis. FMEA from theory to execution,* 2nd ed., revised and expanded. Milwaukee, WI: Quality Press.

———. 2003e. *Six Sigma and beyond: Design for Six Sigma.* Boca Raton, FL: St. Lucie Press.

———. 2003f. *Six Sigma and beyond: The implementation process.* Boca Raton, FL: St. Lucie Press.

———. 2004. *Six Sigma fundamentals: A complete guide to the system, methods and tools.* New York: Productivity Press.

Turner, J. R. 1992. *The handbook of project-based management.* New York: McGraw–Hill.

Selected Bibliography

Berwick, D. M., and M. J. Coye. 2003. Connections between quality measurement and improvement. *Medical Care* 41 (1 Suppl): I30–I38.

Isaacs, L. S., and J. R. Knickman, eds. 2003. *To improve health and health care.* Volume VI. The Robert Wood Johnson Foundation Anthology. San Francisco, CA: Jossey–Bass.

James, B. 2003. Information system concepts for quality measurement. *Medical Care* 41 (1): I71–I79.

Kirk, S. A., S. M. Campbell, S. Kennell-Webb, et al. 2003. Assessing the quality of care of multiple conditions in general practice: Practical and methodological problems. *Quality and Safety in Health Care* 12 (6): 421–427.

Kizer, K. W. 1999. The "new VA": A national laboratory for health care quality management. *American Journal of Medical Quality* 14 (1): 3–20.

Leape, L. L. 2002. Reporting of adverse events. *New England Journal of Medicine* 347 (20): 1633–1638.

Leatherman, S. T., J. H. Hibbard, and E. A. McGlynn. 2003. A research agenda to advance quality measurement and improvement. *Medical Care* 41 (1 Suppl): I80–I86.

McGlynn, E. A. 2003a. An evidence-based national quality measurement and reporting system. *Medical Care* 41 (1 Suppl): I8–I15.

———. 2003b. Introduction and overview of the conceptual framework for a national quality measurement and reporting system. *Medical Care* 41 (1 Suppl): I1–I7.

———. 2003c. Selecting common measures of quality and system performance. *Medical Care* 41 (1 Suppl): I39–I47.

Stamatis, D. H. 1997. *The nuts and bolts of reengineering.* Red Bluff, CA: Paton Press.

Chapter 9

Using Six Sigma Methodology for Improvement

Introduction

In the last chapter, we discussed the process and some of the fundamental methodologies that may help us to understand it better as well as to improve it. In this chapter, we focus on the Six Sigma methodology and how it may be used in healthcare.

All of business and the world have changed at a staggering rate, especially in the last 10 years. And yet, some areas seem to have remained relatively untouched, to the detriment of society. For example, in healthcare, the cost of medical care is increasing at an alarming and unsustainable rate worldwide. Admittedly, a significant percentage of these cost increases can be attributed to an aging population and technological advances. These two factors inevitably are largely beyond control because of the technological and demographic developments of modern society. However, in healthcare, the focus has been on treatment and cost, although, in fact, other issues are just as important for efficiency and optimization of operations whether in the physician's office, clinic, nursing home, or even hospital. This is the area where some control may be realized.

To be sure, healthcare is a very sophisticated and personal business with specialists and high technology. However, inefficiency can be measured and appropriate changes implemented to improve the quality throughout healthcare operations. The efforts to resolve these inefficiencies are more affordable and in fact can contribute to better healthcare for a large percentage of the population. We are indeed in the middle of a very dynamic transition.

The transition is part of a process that is committed to learning how to bring about change in a world of high technology and specialization so that an excellent job of good health—however defined—is delivered. To facilitate this transition, those in healthcare and others who work in the area have devoted much time to thinking of improvements that will be sustainable. Three major ones are the (1) invention of health collaborator teams (nurse, physician, specialist, and so on), (2) focus on key measurements (indicators) based on outcomes, and (3) focus on methodologies such as Six Sigma and Lean.

As the combination of these three components is being utilized in many organizations on a daily basis, we see that operational inefficiencies are associated with the direct medical service delivery process. Of course, others are associated with the administrative, logistical, and operational sides of the healthcare delivery system as well. Both areas can benefit from systematic process innovation activities and, more importantly, from working side by side with design, operations, purchasing, and engineering at the inception of both health and business decisions through the service or product delivery. The transition began some time ago with basic quality initiatives, moved to total quality management, and is presently at the stage where two process-innovation approaches—Six Sigma and Lean Thinking—are popular in the industry (De Koning and De Mast 2006; George 2003; Robinson 1990; Smith 2003; Stamatis 2003a, 2003b, 2003c, 2003d, 2003e; Stalk and Hout 1990). Both provide a systematic approach to facilitate incremental process innovations.

Lean Thinking emerged within the Japanese automobile industry after World War II (Ohno 1988), but can be traced back to the early days of the Ford Motor Company (Ford and Crowther 1926). Similarly, Six Sigma, originally introduced by Motorola, is the culmination and synthesis of a series of century-long developments in quality improvement (QI) (Stamatis 2000, 2003a, 2003b, 2003c, 2003d, 2003e; Box and Bisgaard 1987; Garvin 1988; Snee 2004) building on a number of other approaches—in particular, Juran's trilogy (Juran 1989). Lean Thinking and Six Sigma have gone through parallel developments in recent years. Both approaches are now also used widely in administration and service areas, although they were originally applied to the manufacturing environment (Snee and Hoerl 2004). The latest development is a synthesis of these two approaches (Hoerl 2004).

The proliferation of Lean Thinking was facilitated by the publication of Womack, Jones, and Roos (1990). Lean, as it is often abbreviated, represents a fundamental break with Western manufacturing traditions. Stated somewhat simplistically, the traditional mass manufacturing concept of the West was based on the following assumptions:

- A separation of "thinking" from "doing" is most effective.
- Defects are unavoidable.
- Organizations should be designed as a hierarchical chain of command.
- Inventories are necessary evils used to buffer production from fluctuations in market demand.

Toyota and other Japanese companies developed Lean Thinking as an alternative paradigm. Lean is an integrated system of principles, practices, tools, and techniques focused on reducing waste, synchronizing work flows, and managing variability in production flows. An important distinction in Lean is between value- and non-value-added activities. Value-added activities contribute to what the customer wants from a product or service (Stamatis 2003a, 2003b, 2003c, 2003d, 2003e; George 2003). Everything else is a non-value-added activity, but sometimes it is necessary. The primary analytical tool in Lean is the value stream map, an extended process flowchart with information about speed, continuity of flow, and work in progress. This tool highlights non-value-added steps and bottlenecks and is used to guide QI activities. The value stream map provides a holistic picture of the entire value chain in an organization. For more on Lean, see Chapter 10 and George (2003) and Standard and Davis (1999).

On the other hand, Six Sigma was originally a methodology for company-wide QI introduced by Motorola in 1987. It was further developed by General Electric in the late 1990s (Stamatis 2002a, 2002b, 2003a, 2003b, 2003c, 2003d, 2003e; Breyfogle 1999; De Koning and De Mast 2006; Harry 1997; Pyzdek 2001). The methodology is characterized by its customer-driven approach, emphasis on decision making based on careful analysis of quantitative data, and a priority on cost reduction (Bisgaard and Freiesleben 2004).

Six Sigma is deployed by carrying out improvement projects. Project selection is usually based on a translation of the organization's strategy into operational goals (Pyzdek 2004; Stamatis 2003a, 2003b, 2003c, 2003d, 2003e). Six Sigma provides an organizational structure of project leaders and project owners. Project leaders are called black belts (BBs) and green belts (GBs). Members of upper management play the role of project owners, or champions.

Six Sigma's approach is similar to that of good medical practice used since the time of Hippocrates: Relevant information is assembled followed by careful diagnosis. After a thorough diagnosis is completed, a treatment is proposed and implemented. Finally, checks are applied to see if the treatment was effective. To operationalize this problem-solving strategy, Six Sigma deploys five phases—define, measure, analyze, improve, and control (DMAIC)—that are rigorously followed whenever a problem, large or small, is approached. In some cases for healthcare, we see an extra "I" to denote implementation and the model thereby becomes DMAIIC. This stage, however, is a combination of some of the requirements from the "improve" and the "control" phases. The reason for this combination is to emphasize the importance of elimination of barriers and to track the transition.

In the "define" phase, a charter is drafted that includes a cost-benefit analysis. If this analysis meets the company-established thresholds, the charter will be accepted, and the project will continue through the DMAIC process meaning that the project becomes scheduled for solution and assigned to a team headed by a GB or BB reporting to a champion. The selection of GB or BB depends on the magnitude and the complexity of the problem. Complex problems are usually assigned to BBs or master black belts (MBBs). In the subsequent "measure" phase, baseline data are assembled, and the diagnosis is started in earnest. The problem is translated into quantifiable terms using critical-to-quality (CTQ) characteristics. The "analysis" phase continues the diagnosis and involves an identification of possible causal relationships between inputs and the CTQs.

After the diagnosis is completed, the team proceeds to the "improve" phase and suggests a solution to the problem. The GB or BB designs and implements process changes or adjustments to improve the performance of the CTQ. Finally, in the "control" phase, control systems are developed to ensure that improvements are maintained and the new, improved process can be handed over to the day-to-day operations staff. Each of the five DMAIC phases involves detailed plans that help to guide project leaders through the execution of the QI project (De Koning and De Mast 2006; Stamatis 2003a, 2003b, 2003c, 2003d, 2003e).

To secure a successful launch and deployment of Six Sigma, an organizational infrastructure is created. For example, a deployment plan for strategically relevant projects ensures an alignment of project goals with the long-term organizational objectives. Further, Six Sigma uses a stage-gate approach to project management whereby projects are monitored carefully by champions and appropriate actions are taken if a project does not meet specified completion dates.

One perceived weakness of Six Sigma methods is their complexity. In the case of simple problems with obvious and easy-to-implement solutions, rigorous adherence to the Six Sigma problem-solving process may be considered "overkill" and inefficient (Stamatis 2003a, 2003b, 2003c, 2003d, 2003e; George 2003). Furthermore, Six Sigma typically does not resort to standard solutions to common problems, as does Lean. Finally, the danger of suboptimizing a process, while failing to take into account the entire value chain, is ever present. Nevertheless, Six Sigma offers a structured, analytic, and logically sound approach to problem solving, as well as a strong organizational framework for its deployment. It offers a cooperative approach and flexibility for recognizing small and large problems; more importantly, through its methodology, it allows the use of very simple to highly complex statistical analysis.

Unfortunately, many organizations have yet to embrace the flexibility of this adaptable system. The Six Sigma process is a discipline that strengthens this cooperative approach and, by the nature of its functional model, provides a step-by-step prescription to achieve breakthrough strategies once a project has been selected. The intent of this methodology is shown in Figure 9.1. In its entirety, the classical model consists of define, measure, analyze, improve, and control (DMAIC). Its intent is shown in Figure 9.1 and an overall summary is shown in Table 9.1.

Now that we have a good overview of what the Six Sigma methodology is all about, let us examine the DMAIC model in a little more detail. The reader is encouraged to see Stamatis (2002a, 2002b, 2003a, 2003b, 2003c, 2003d, 2003e) and Breyfogle (2003) for very detailed and descriptive discussions of the Six Sigma approach to solving problems.

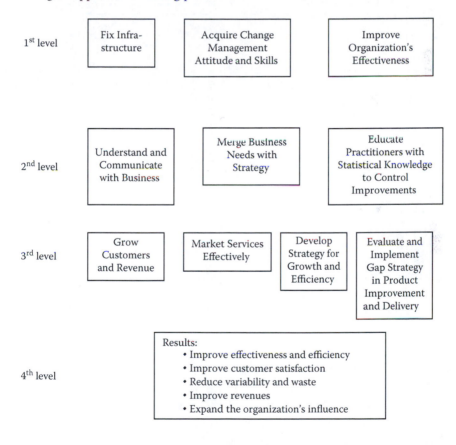

Figure 9.1   The Six Sigma intent.

Table 9.1   Overview of the DMAIC Model

Stage and Definition	Substeps	Typical Tools	Typical Deliverables
Define			
Refine the Six Sigma project's understanding of the problem to be addressed	Define problem Identify customer Identify CTQs Map process Scope/update project	Brainstorming Cause-and-effect diagram Process mapping Cause-and-effect matrix Current FMEA Y/X diagram CT metrics	The "real" customers Data to verify customers' needs collected Team charter (goal, scope, timeline, financial benefits) High-level "as is" process map
Measure			
Establish techniques for collecting data about current performance	Identify measurement and variation Determine data type Develop data collection plan Perform measurement system analysis Conduct data collection Perform graphical analysis Conduct baseline analysis	Process mapping Cause and effect FMEA Gauge R&R Graphical techniques	Key measurements identified Rolled throughput yield Defects identified Data collection plan completed Measurement capability study completed Baseline measures of process capability Defect reduction and goals established

Analyze			
The team narrows its focus on a distinct group of project issues and opportunities by looking more closely at the data	Perform capability analysis Select analysis tools Apply graphical analysis tools Identify sources of variation	Process mapping Graphical techniques Multivariate studies Hypothesis testing Correlation Regression	Detailed "as is" process map The sources of variation and their prioritization SOPs reviewed Vital few factors (KPIVs) with appropriate and applicable data identified Refined problem statement with "new" understanding Estimates of the quantifiable opportunity
Improve			
The team generates ideas, designs, and pilots; implements improvements; and validates them	Generate improvement alternatives Create "should be" process map Conduct FMEA Perform cost/benefit analysis Pilot Validate improvement	Process mapping Design of experiments Simulation Optimization	Alternative improvements Implementation of "best" alternative for improving the process "Should be" process map developed Validation of the improvement Cost/benefit analysis for proposed solution Implementation plan developed Communication plan established for any changes

(Continued)

Table 9.1 Overview of the DMAIC Model (Continued)

Stage and Definition	Substeps	Typical Tools	Typical Deliverables
Control			
To institutionalize the process or product improvement and monitor ongoing performance	Conduct poka-yoke Develop long-term MSA plan Implement control charts Develop reaction plan Update SOP and training plan	Control plans Statistical process control Gauge control plan Mistake proofing Preventive maintenance	Control plan completed Evidence that the process is in control Documentation of the project Translation opportunities identified Systems and structures changed to institutionalize the improvement Audit plan completed

Define

The first stage—define—refines the Six Sigma project team's understanding of the problem to be addressed. This stage also sets the critical groundwork for getting the team organized, determining the roles and responsibilities, establishing goals and milestones, and reviewing the process steps. The key points of this stage can be summarized as

- Voice of the customer
- Project scoping
- Cause-and-effect prioritization and project planning

There are five substeps within this stage; each has its own focus and linkage to the customer:

- *Defining the problem* means that the problem is based on available data, is measurable, and excludes any assumptions about possible causes or solutions. It must be specific and real.
- *Identifying the customer* is a little more demanding. Look for the functionality of the product or service that the organization provides to satisfy a specific need, want, or even an expectation. Depending on market analysis, the Kano model may be a quality function deployment (QFD) or extensive secondary research to identify the customer for which the organization is looking and how it can be successful in satisfying him or her. Therefore, it is necessary to identify "who" is directly impacted by the problem and at what cost. Begin by a random sample analysis to identify the overall impact and then proceed with a detailed analysis of the cost of poor quality (COPQ). The focus of the team is to identify a large base of customers so that the benefits and improvement can be expanded to larger groups of customers.
- *Identifying critical to quality (CTQ)* is the phase in which the project team must determine what is important to the customer from the customer's point of view. Identification of CTQs ascertains how the particular characteristics appear when meeting customer expectations. Typical questions here include: What is good condition? What is on time? and so on.
  - After CTQs are identified, everyone in the team must agree on developing an operational definition for each CTQ. Effective operational definitions accurately describe the critical to quality characteristic (which is specificity in meaning), so that the customer's expectation is captured. CTQs are always written, in order to ensure consistent

interpretation and measurement by multiple people. Typical methods of identifying CTQs include, but are not limited to, focus groups, surveys, and interviews. The outputs are CTQs, operational definitions, and parameters for measuring.

- An organization—any organization—is a collection of processes, which are the natural business activities performed that produce value, serve customers, and generate income. Managing these processes is the key to the success of the organization. Process mapping is a simple yet powerful method of looking beyond functional activities and rediscovering the core processes. Process maps peel away the complexity of the organizational structure and focus on the processes that are truly the heart of the business. Armed with a thorough understanding of the inputs, outputs, and interrelationships of each process, the organization can understand how processes interact in a system, evaluate which activities add value for the customer, and mobilize teams to streamline and improve processes in the realms of *should be* and *could be.*

■ *Mapping the process* is nothing more than a high-level visual representation of the process steps leading up to fulfillment of the identified CTQ. This as-is process map will be useful throughout the process as a method for segmenting complex processes into manageable portions; a way to identify process inputs and outputs; a technique to identify areas of rework; a way to identify bottlenecks, breakdowns, and non-value-added steps; and a benchmark against which future improvements can be compared with the original process.

■ *Scoping the project and updating the project charter (if necessary)* is the last step of the define stage of the project. During this step, the team members will further specify project issues, develop a refined problem statement, and brainstorm suspected sources of variation. The focus of this step is to reduce the scope of the project to a level that ensures the problem is within the team's area of control; data can be collected to show both the current and improved states, and improvements can be made within the project's time frame.

A refined problem statement is a highly defined description of the problem. Beginning with the general problem statement and applying what has been learned through further scoping, the team writes a refined problem statement that describes the problem in narrow terms and indicates the entry point where the team will begin its work. In addition, a considerable amount of time is spent at this step to identify the extent of the problem and how it is measured.

Measure

The second stage—measure—is designed to establish techniques for collecting data about current performance that highlights project opportunities and provides a structure for monitoring subsequent improvements. Upon completing this stage, the team will have a plan for collecting data that specifies the data type and collection technique, a validated measurement system that ensures accuracy and consistency, a sufficient sample of data for analysis, a set of preliminary analysis results that provides project direction, and a baseline measurement of current performance.

The focus of this stage is to develop a sound data collection plan; to identify the key process input variables (KPIVs); to display variation using Pareto charts, histograms, and run charts; and to develop baseline measures of process capability and process sigma level. There are seven substeps of this stage:

- Identify measurement and variation
- Determine data type
- Develop data collection plan
- Perform measurement system analysis
- Conduct data collection
- Perform graphical analysis
- Conduct baseline analysis

The measured substeps establish the requirements of measurement and variation, including the types and sources of variation and the impact of variation on process performance, different types of measures for variance and the criteria for establishing good process measures, and the different types of data that can be collected and the important characteristics of each data type.

As for variation in this subset, one of the requirements is to define the variation based on type, of which there are two:

- *Common causes:* conditions in a process that generate variation through interaction of the 5Ms (machine, material, method, measurement, manpower) and 1E (environment). Common causes affect everyone working in the process and affect all of the outcomes. Common causes are always present and thus are generally predictable. They are generally accepted sources of variation and offer opportunities for process improvement.
- *Special causes:* things in a process that generate variation due to extraordinary circumstances related to one of the 5Ms or 1E. Special causes are not always present, do not affect everyone working in the process, do not affect all of the outcomes, and are not predictable. They are also called assignable causes.

In the "determine data type" substep, the team must be able to answer the question, "What do we want to know?" Reviewing materials developed during the previous stage, the team determines the process or product characteristics about which they need to learn more. A good start is the definition of the data. The data type is determined by what is measured. Two types of data can be collected by measuring:

- *Attribute.* One way to collect data is merely to count the frequency of occurrence for a given process characteristic—for example, the number of times something happens or fails to happen. Data collected in this manner are known as attribute data. Attribute data cannot be meaningfully subdivided into more precise increments and are discrete by nature. Go/no go and pass/fail data are examples of this category.
- *Variable.* A different way to look at data is to describe the process characteristic in terms of its weight, voltage, or size. Data collected in this manner are known as variable data. With these types of data, the measurement scale is continuous—they can be meaningfully divided into finer and finer increments of precision.

In the "develop data collection plan" substep, the team develops and documents its plans for collecting data. Therefore, for optimum results, at least the following should be considered:

- What the team wants to know about the process
- The potential sources of variation in the process (Xs)
- Whether there are cycles in the process and how long data must be collected to obtain a true picture of the process
- Who will collect the data
- Whether operational definitions contain enough detail
- How data will be displayed once collected
- Whether data are currently available and what data collection tools will be used if current data do not provide enough information
- Where errors in data collection might occur and how errors can be avoided or corrected

Remember that a data collection plan is the documentation of

- What data will be collected
- Why the data are needed
- Who is responsible for collecting the data

- How the data will be collected
- When the data will be collected
- Where the data will be collected

In the "perform measurement system analysis" substep, the team needs to verify the data collection plan once it is complete and before the actual data are collected. This is called a measurement system analysis (MSA). A typical MSA will indicate whether the variation measured is from the process or the measurement tool. The MSA should begin with the data collection plan and end when there is a high level of confidence that the data collected will accurately depict the variation in the process. MSA is a quantitative evaluation of the tools and process used in making data observations.

Perhaps the most important concept in any MSA study is the rubric of measurement system failure before collecting all the data. Rather than fixing the measurement system, quite often the organization focuses on fixing the gauge, fixing the measurement system, and training the operators (measurement takers).

In the "develop data collection" substep, the team must make sure that the collected data are appropriate, applicable, and accurate and that they provide enough information to identify the potential root cause of the problem. It is not enough to plan carefully before collecting the data and then assume that everything will go smoothly. It is important to ensure that the data continue to be consistent and stable as they are collected. The number one rule of data collection is "be there." Do not turn over data collection to others. Plan for data collection, design data collection sheets, train data collectors, and then stay involved throughout the data collection process. The outcome of this step must be an adequate data set to carry into the analyze stage.

Analyze

The third stage—analyze—serves as an outcome of the measure stage. The team should narrow its focus on a distinct group of project issues and opportunities. In other words, this stage allows the team to target improvement opportunities further by taking a closer look at the data. Remember that the measure, analyze, and improve stages frequently work hand in hand to target a particular improvement opportunity. For example, the analyze stage might simply serve to confirm opportunities identified by graphical analysis. Conversely, the analyze stage might uncover a gap in the data collection plan that requires the team to collect additional information.

Of paramount importance in this stage are the recognition and utilization of the data. There are two possibilities:

■ *Attribute:* data reflecting one of two conditions, usually in a qualitative format, such as yes/no, good/bad, and so on
■ *Variable:* data reflecting a range of conditions, such as processing time, pressure, temperature, and so on

Another important aspect of this stage is the introduction of hypothesis testing. This is a statistical analysis to validate differences between data groups. For example, for attribute data, use the chi-square or hypothesis testing for one or two proportions at the p value of .05 level of significance. In the case of variable data, use analysis of means (one-sample t-test or two-sample t-test), analysis of variance for means, analysis of variance (F-test, homogeneity of variance), correlation, regression, and so on.

There are four substeps for this stage:

■ *Perform capability analysis.* This is a process for establishing the current performance level of the process being examined. This baseline capability is used to verify process improvements through the improve and control phases. Capability is stated as a short-term sigma value so that comparisons between processes can be made.
■ *Select analysis tools.* This substep allows the team to look at the complete set of graphical analysis tools to determine how each tool might be used to reveal details about process performance and variation.
■ *Apply graphical analysis tools.* Graphical analysis refers to the technique of applying a set of basic graphical analysis tools to a set of data to produce a visual indication of performance.
■ *Identify sources of variation.* This substep continues the process of narrowing and focusing that began with project selection. The team will use the results produced by graphical analysis to target specific sources of variation.

Upon completion of this stage, the team members should be able to answer the following questions:

■ *What* was the improvement opportunity?
■ *What* was the approach to analyzing the data?
■ *What* are the root causes contributing to the improvement opportunity?
■ *How* were the data analyzed to identify sources of variation?
■ Did analysis *result in any changes* to the problem statement or scope?

Improve

As an outcome of the analyze stage, the team should have a strong understanding of the factors impacting their project, including:

■ Key process input variables (the vital few Xs that impact the Y)
■ Sources of variation—where the greatest degree of variation exists

The fourth stage—improve—is to generate ideas; design, pilot, and implement improvements; and validate the improvements. Perhaps the most important items in this stage are the process of brainstorming, the development of the *should be* process map, the review and/or generation of the current failure mode and effect analysis (FMEA), a preliminary cost-benefit analysis, a pilot of the recommended action, and the preliminary implementation process.

Design of experiments (DOE) is an effective methodology that may be used in both the analyze and improve stages. However, DOE can be a difficult tool to use in healthcare (unless it is used in the medical devices industry, pharmaceutical organizations, or laboratory environments). The difficulty arises due to the small adjustments that need to be made to input factors so that output can be monitored in real time. In traditional hospitals, nursing homes, and physicians' offices, other creative methods are frequently required to discover and validate improvements. Typical tools are run charts, 5 Whys, Pareto chart, and others. The substeps of this stage include:

■ *Generate improvement alternatives.* The emphasis here is to generate alternatives to test as product or process improvements. Basic tools used here are brainstorming and DOE. With either tool, a three-step process is followed:
  – Define improvement criteria. Develop criteria to quality characteristics.
  – Generate possible improvements. The best potential improvements are most effectively evaluated based on the criteria matrix.
  – Evaluate improvements and make the best choice. (Some of the criteria items include must criteria; desirable criteria—both the list and the weight are evaluated; score improvements against desirables; and cross-multiply and prioritize.)
■ *Create "should be" process map.* This is a map that represents the best possible improvement the project team is capable of implementing. It is possible that a number of improvements could be made to improve a process. The individual process map steps will serve as the input function of the FMEA.
■ *Conduct FMEA.* The FMEA is meant to be a "before the failure" action, not an "after the fact" reaction. Perhaps the most important factor in any FMEA is the fact that it is a living document and therefore it should be continually updated as changes occur or more information is gained.

■ *Perform cost/benefit analysis.* This analysis is a structured process for determining the trade-off between implementation costs and anticipated benefits of potential improvements.
■ *Pilot.* This step is a test of sorts. It is a trial implementation of a proposed improvement, conducted on a small scale under close observation
■ *Validate improvement.* One way to validate effectiveness of the changes made is to compare the sigma values before and after the changes have been made. (Remember that this means comparing the same defects per million opportunities.)

Control

The fifth stage—control—is to institutionalize process or product improvements and monitor ongoing performance. This stage is the place where the transition from improvement to controlling the process and maintaining the new improvement takes place. Of course, the transition is the transferring of the process from the project team to the original owner.

To facilitate a smooth transition and ensure that the team's work "sticks," a detailed control plan must be developed. The objective of the control plan is to document all pertinent information regarding at least the following:

■ Who is responsible for monitoring and controlling the process?
■ What is being measured?
■ What are the performance parameters?
■ What corrective measures must be taken when problems occur?

To make sure these questions and issues are addressed, the control plan should include at least:

■ Mistake proofing
■ Long-term MSA plan
■ Appropriate and applicable charts (statistical process control)
■ Reaction plan
■ The new and/or revised standard operating procedures (SOPs)

The substeps of this stage include:

■ *Conduct poka-yoke (mistake proofing).* The idea here is to remove the opportunity for error before it happens. At a minimum, mistake proofing is a way to detect and correct an error where it occurred and to avoid passing the error to the next worker or the next operation. This keeps the error from becoming a defect in the process and potentially impacting the customer CTQ.

■ *Develop a long-term MSA plan.* Similar to the original MSA conducted in the measure stage, the long-term MSA looks at all aspects of data collection relating to ongoing measurement of the Xs and high-level monitoring of the Ys. Specifically, the long-term MSA documents how process measurements will be managed over time to maintain desired levels of performance.

■ *Implement control charts.* A control is simply a run chart with upper and lower control-limit lines drawn on either side of the process average. Another way to view the control chart is to see it as a graphical representation of the behavior of a process over time.

■ *Develop a reaction plan.* A reaction plan provides details on actions to be taken if control charts indicate that the revised process is no longer in control. Therefore, having a reaction plan helps ensure that control issues are addressed quickly and that corrective actions are taken.

■ *Update the standard operating procedures (SOPs) and training plan.* Updating SOPs and training plans is the practice of revising existing process documentation to reflect the process improvements.

Upon completion of the control stage, the process owner will understand performance expectations, how to measure and monitor Xs to ensure performance of the Ys, and what corrective actions should be executed if measurements drop below the desired and anticipated levels. Finally, at the completion of the control stage, the team is disbanded while the black belt begins the next project with a new team.

A pictorial view of the entire Six Sigma model as used in healthcare is shown in Figure 9.2. Please notice that the inclusion of the implementation (I) stage is included in this model. However, upon examination, it can be seen that, in fact, the requirements of the "I" stage are indeed incorporated in the improvement and control stages.

Design for Six Sigma

To understand the philosophy of designing for Six Sigma, let us look at two different quotes from Confucius:

A man who commits a mistake and doesn't correct it is committing another mistake.

To know what you know and know what you don't know is the characteristic of one who knows.

. A pictorial view of the DMAIIC model

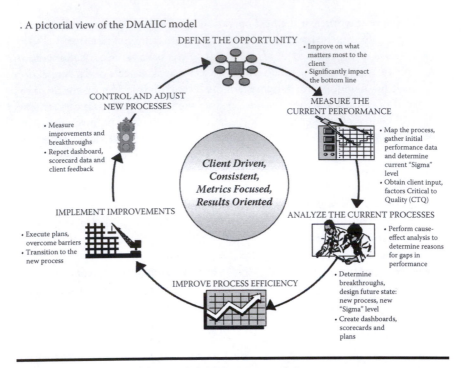

Figure 9.2   A pictorial view of the DMAIIC model.

Obviously, the first quote requires us to fix problems, and that is the essence of the DMAIC model. However, the second quote is a little more complicated because it forces us to think outside of our own thinking box, realizing that there might be another answer to the things that we do not know. At this juncture, Albert Einstein provides us with an insight to our predicament: "You can't solve problems with the same level of knowledge that created them." In other words, we have to look elsewhere for our answers. We cannot always depend on history. We have to look beyond our current status and capability if we are indeed committed to continual improvement.

Indeed, Einstein hit a home run with this statement because design for Six Sigma (DFSS) goes beyond the fixing of the problem. It goes beyond the current knowledge. It forces one to think of future designs. Design for Six Sigma is a proactive approach to eliminating problems from occurring. That is a design issue. This is why, when I am asked what I think is the minimum that should be done to investigate a problem, my first question is, *"Do you really want to solve the problem?"* Why ask this? Because some problems are not worth solving. Some problems are not even problems. A problem may be part of the way one has chosen to do business and one may not want to change. Or the problem may be part of everyday variability. Trying to solve it is like trying to stop the tides. Trying to fix it wastes effort and misguided efforts might make things worse.

Some problems are not worth solving because their consequences are too small to worry about. Perhaps they can be trended and attacks made on the ones that cumulatively cause enough loss to worry about. And some problems are blessings in disguise—problems that, when solved, allow an even bigger problem to cause a real disaster. But for problems that really need fixing, design for Six Sigma is the only way. The question now is, "What are the minimum efforts required?" Minimum efforts include:

- Completely understand what happened.
- Identify the causal factors that led to the problem.
- Systematically find the root causes of each causal factor.
- Develop and implement fixes to eliminate the root causes.

Some people suggest using less effort than these four steps suggest. They insist that all that is needed is a *checklist* or a quick *5 Whys* or even the rigor of the *DMAIC* model. They are being penny wise and pound foolish in trying to save time. In reality, instead of saving time, they are really wasting time. They get unreliable, inaccurate answers that lead to fixes that waste even more time. Guessing at answers will not improve performance. Look at some of the organizations that have claimed to use Six Sigma—the DMAIC version. In the short term, they appeared to be making money. But, as time went by, many of these companies lost money and some laid off thousands of workers. It is imperative to understand that the traditional Six Sigma—the program that most people discuss—is focused on eliminating defects in products, manufacturing, and/or service processes, including healthcare, by completing specific, short-term projects with an associated cost benefit. The DFSS process, however, through the DCOV (design-characterize-optimize-verify) model prevents defects by completing projects in the design process aimed at improving functional performance over time with quantified reduction in product and/or service process variability.

Design for Six Sigma is very demanding, and yet, the opportunity for true improvement and real customer satisfaction lies only with a systematic study up front, in the design. The goal is to improve customer functionality through customer satisfaction and customer loyalty. The process of improvement, then, is to establish a functional relationship between customer satisfaction drivers (dependent variables) and specific design parameters, CTQs (independent variables). By reducing the sensitivity of the associated system to noise factors and then manufacturing the independent variables at a Six Sigma level, the performance that drives customer satisfaction and, ultimately, loyalty will be more consistently achieved over time.

Although the DCOV process steps are presented in a sequential flow, process execution is not necessarily sequential. For example, capturing the voice of the customer, system design, and functional mapping are typically iterative processes. However, design for robustness and for producibility and/or serviceability is both simultaneous and iterative. The DCOV process may become generic and can also be applied during any of the following phases—that is, advanced project and forward product, as well as ongoing. To apply these principles to a successful design, the following must occur:

- Understand the fundamental ideas underlying the notion of manufacturability or serviceability.
- Understand how statistically designed experiments can be used to identify leverage variables, establish sensitivities, and define tolerances.
- Understand how product and process complexity impacts design performance.
- Explain the concept of error propagation (both linear and nonlinear) and what role product or process complexity plays.
- Describe how reverse error propagation can be employed during system design.
- Explain why process shift and drift must be considered in the analysis of a design and how it can be factored into design optimization.
- Describe how Six Sigma tools and methods can be applied to the design process in and of itself.
- Discuss the pros and cons of the classical approach to product or process design relative to that of the Six Sigma approach.

When the organization is faced with too much to do and too few reserves, it must not shortcut the investigation process for important problems. Some problems just should not be investigated. For the ones that should be investigated, a rigorous approach is recommended: the DCOV model of define, characterize, optimize, and verify. Table 9.2 provides an overview summary of this model.

To understand the concept of the DFSS, it is necessary to understand the key items that permit use of this methodology. Table 9.3 presents some of the most important elements in understanding the DFSS process.

Now that we have a good overview of what the DFSS methodology is all about, let us examine the DCOV model in a little more detail. The reader is encouraged to see Stamatis (2001, 2003a, 2003b, 2003c, 2003d, 2003e) and

Table 9.2   An Overview of the DCOV

Stage	Task	Tools	Deliverables
Define			
Selection of the appropriate CTSs	**Inputs:** quality/customer satisfaction history; warranty data; benchmarking; functional, serviceability, corporate and regulatory requirements; evaluation of process in integrating targets; surveys; audit of current design/process; brand profiler; Kano analysis; quality function deployment (QFD); design specifications **Action:** definition of customer and/or product requirements; relating requirements to customer satisfaction; peer review **Output:** projected targets and preliminary model of understanding	Kano model Quality function deployment Regression Conjoint analysis	Kano diagram CTS scorecard Y relationship to customer satisfaction Benchmarked CTSs Target and ranges for CTS Ys
Characterize			
System design and functional mapping	**Inputs:** functional boundaries interface matrices as applicable; function trees $(Y \rightarrow y)$; P-diagram; robustness and/or reliability checklist; functional boundaries and interfaces of system	Functional structures Axiomatic designs TRIZ P-diagram	Function diagram(s) Mapping of $Y \rightarrow$ critical function $\rightarrow y$'s P-diagram, including critical

(Continued)

Table 9.2   An Overview of the DCOV (Continued)

Stage	Task	Tools	Deliverables
	Design specification (SDS); functional tree ($y \rightarrow x$); P-diagrams; robustness and/or reliability checklist	R&R checklist DOE	Technical metrics, y's Control factors, x's Noise factors, n's Transfer function Scorecard with target and range for y's and x's Plan for optimization and verification R&R checklist
	Action: activities that actually help the decomposition of Y into contributing elements, y_i; relate independent y's to x's (modeling) or relate correlated y's to x's (modeling, axiomatic design); choose robustness strategy; *innovate:* (1) structured inventive thinking (SIT), or (2) theory of inventive problem solving (TRIZ); understand operations capability; peer review		
	Output: Pareto diagrams; benchmarked CTSs, and target range of y; results of screening experiments, prior engineering knowledge; preliminary target and/or range estimates of x_i; internal and/or external benchmark of manufacturing capability of x's		

Optimize

Design for robustness and design for producibility and/or serviceability	**Inputs:** P-diagram (important y_1's), what to measure, control factors (x's), noise factors, error states; experimental plan (two-step optimization with confirmation run); robustness and reliability checklist; design FMEA (including noise factor analysis); process capability; present process capability; historical process data (model, surrogate); assembly and/or operating process flow diagrams (process mapping); reference gauge R&R capability studies; process FMEA, including noise factor analysis **Action:** reduce sensitivity to noise (parameter design, robustness assessment, reliability, and robustness); determine tolerances (tolerance design, statistical tolerancing, reliability, and robustness); eliminate specific failure modes using strategies such as beef up (redundancy), eliminate noise, compensate; activities that actually help the optimization process to produce x_1's nominal with Six Sigma capability by applying robustness methods to process (using two-step	Design FMEA Process FMEA Experimental design—response surface Parameter design—two-step optimization Tolerance design Simulation tools Error prevention—compensation, estimate noise, mistake proofing Gauge R&R Control plan	Transfer function Scorecard with estimate of sigma Target nominal values identified for x's Variability metric for CTS Y or related function (e.g., range, standard deviation, S/N ratio improvement) Tolerances specified for important characteristics Short-term capability, z-score Long-term capability Updated verification plans: robustness and reliability checklist (if available) Updated control plan

(Continued)

Table 9.2   An Overview of the DCOV (Continued)

Stage	Task	Tools	Deliverables
	optimization: (1) reduce variability; (2) shift to target; use appropriate error proofing such as DFA, DFM, assembly, and/or operation sequence, poka-yoke, and so on; update control plan; peer review **Output:** short-term capability; long-term capability; updated control plan. Also, veriability metric for CTS or related function (i.e., range, standard deviation, S/N ratio improvement); target and tolerances specified for specific characteristics		
Verify			
Verify that the capability and product integrity over time is as designed and as the customer expects	**Inputs:** data from previous steps. Also, reliability and/or robustness plan; design verification plan with key noises **Action:** four predominant activities are conducted here: 1. CTS/CTQ characteristic/measure and a comparison between the $Z_{estimate}$ and Z_{actual}	Reliability testing Specific testing Design reviews	

2. Subassessments (as needed)

3. Test/simulation and comparison between the $Z_{estimate}$ and Z_{actual}

4. Variability over time for product, service, and process. Also, correlate tests to customer usage; improve ability of tests to discriminate good/bad parts, subsystems, systems; peer review

Output: overall review of assessments for previous steps with champion or appropriate management. Also, test results such as key life testing; accelerated tests; long-term process capabilities; product performance over time (Weibull, survival plot, kappa statistic, etc.); reliability/robustness demonstration matrix

Table 9.3 Key Elements in Understanding DFSS

Dimension	Key Concept	Behaviors and/or Expectations
Customer	Operational definition	Must know and satisfy needs, wants, and expectations
Quality	Value added	Must be able to relate the value with which the customer is willing to associate the product and/or service with what he or she is paying
Statistical	Risk and/or benefit	Use and/or develop appropriate and applicable statistical, reliability, and mathematical models to explain situations and forecast specific outcomes
Relationships	Trust	Sharing and/or reflecting on inputs and outputs in addition to the actual process; understanding and accepting the holistic approach to process
Informative	Advice	Learning facts about plans/progress; commenting on use of information; providing custom/accurate and sufficient knowledge
Facilitative	Alternatives	Exploring interests, abilities, ideas; revealing other views without any fear of retaliation; questioning the feasibility and applicability as well as the attainability of objectives; discussing own decisions about career expectations, training, and education
Confrontation	Challenge	Respecting decisions as well as actions; providing insight into unproductive strategies or behaviors; being willing to evaluate need as well as the capacity to change

Table 9.3   Key Elements in Understanding DFSS (Continued)

Dimension	Key Concept	Behaviors and/or Expectations
Mentoring	Motivation	Disclose experiences and be willing to be a role model; take risks; enriching experiences and relationship throughout the organization
Employee vision	Initiative	Thinking critically about own process as well as own career; realizing own personal potential as part of the team of improvement; initiating change and being part of the negotiating transition for the outcome suggested

Breyfogle (2003) for very detailed and descriptive discussions of the Six Sigma approach to solving problems.

Define

In the first phase of the DCOV model, the define stage is first explored. This means that the appropriate CTSs are selected. The purpose of this stage is twofold: (1) identify the critical to satisfaction (CTS) drivers, Y, and (2) establish operating window for chosen Ys for new and aged conditions ($a \leq Y_i \leq b$). The process for exploring the define stage is divided into three areas:

- *Inputs.* These are the activities that are the initiators for further evaluation. Typical activities are quality/customer satisfaction history; warranty data; benchmarking; functional, serviceability, corporate, and regulatory requirements; evaluation of process in integrating targets; surveys; audit of current design/process; brand profiler; Kano analysis; QFD; and design specifications.
- *Action.* These activities help in the selection of the Ys. Typical activities are definition of customer and/or product requirements and relating requirements to customer satisfaction, and peer review.
- *Output.* This is the result of the action. Typical results are projected targets and the preliminary model of understanding.

Characterize

In the second phase of the DCOV model, the characterize stage is explored. This stage is generally completed through a two-step approach. The first is the system design and the second is the functional mapping. In both cases, the goal is to characterize the robustness of the design. Therefore, the purpose of the first step is to flow CTS Ys down to lower y's ($Y = f(y_1, y_2, y_3,\ldots y_n)$) and to characterize robustness opportunities ($Y = f(x, n)$). The purpose of the second step is to relate CTS y's to CTQ design parameters (x's) and to optimize the strategy to deliver this robustness.

The process for exploring the first step of the characterize stage is divided into three areas:

- *Inputs.* These are the activities that will generate the activity of this step. Typical activities are functional boundaries and interface matrices as applicable, function trees ($Y \rightarrow y$), P-diagrams; robustness and/or reliability checklist, and so on.
- *Action.* These activities actually help the decomposition of Y into contributing elements, y_i; Obtain $Y = f(y_1, y_2, y_3,\ldots y_n)$ through modeling such as DOE using computer aided engineering (CAE) or hardware (if applicable), experience and/or prior knowledge, and peer review.
- *Output.* This is the result of the action. Typical results are Pareto diagrams, benchmarked CTSs, and target range of y.

The process for exploring the second step of the characterize stage is divided into three areas:

- *Inputs.* These are the activities that will generate the activity of this step. Typical activities are functional boundaries and interfaces of system design specification (SDS); functional trees ($y \rightarrow x$); P-diagrams, robustness, and/or reliability checklist.
- *Action.* This comprises activities that actually help the decomposition of y into contributing elements x_i. Typical activities are relate independent y's to x's (modeling) or relate correlated y's to x's (modeling, axiomatic design), choose robustness strategy, innovate structured inventive thinking (SIT) or theory of inventive problem solving (TRIZ), and understand operation capability, peer review.
- *Output.* This is the result of the action. Typical results are results of screening experiments, prior engineering knowledge; Pareto diagram, preliminary target, and/or range estimates of x_i; and internal and/or external benchmark of manufacturing capability of x's.

Optimize

In the third phase of the DCOV model, the optimize stage is explored. This stage is generally completed through a two-step approach. The first is the design for robust performance and the second is the design for producibility. In both cases, the goal is to improve robustness. Therefore, the purpose of the first step is to characterize the present long time in service robustness for the product and to improve robustness by further minimizing product or service sensitivity to operations and usage conditions—as required. The purpose of the second step is to characterize capability and stability of the present process. This step is performed simultaneously with the first step. A further goal in this second step is to minimize process sensitivity to product or service and operation variations—again, as required. The process for exploring the first step of the optimize stage is divided into three areas:

- *Inputs.* These are the activities that will generate the activity of this step. Typical activities are P-diagram (important y_i's , what to measure, control factors (x's), noise factors, error states; experimental plan (two-step optimization with confirmation run); robustness and reliability checklist; design FMEA (including noise factor analysis); and process capability.
- *Action.* This is the activities that actually help find nominals for x's that minimize variability. In other words, they specify tolerances. Typical activities are reduce sensitivity to noise (parameter design, robustness assessment, reliability, and robustness); determine tolerances (tolerance design, statistical tolerancing, reliability, and robustness); eliminate specific failure modes, using strategies such as beef up (redundancy), eliminate noise, compensate, and so on.
- *Output.* This is the result of the action. Typical results are the variability metric for CTS or related function range, standard deviation, signal-to-noise (S/N) ratio improvement, target and tolerances specified for specific characteristics.

The process for exploring the second step of the optimize stage is divided into three areas:

- *Inputs.* These are the activities that will generate the activity of this step. Typical activities are present process capability, historical process data (model, surrogate), assembly/operation process flow diagrams (process mapping), reference gauge repeatability and reproducibility study, capability studies, and process FMEA, including noise factor analysis.

■ *Action.* These activities actually help the optimization process to produce x_is nominal with Six Sigma capability by applying robustness methods to process (using two-step optimization to reduce variability and shift to target); using appropriate error proofing such as design for assembly (DFA), design for manufacturing (DFM), design for service (DFS), service/assembly sequence, poka-yoke, and so on; update control plan; and peer review.

■ *Output.* This is the result of the action. Typical results are short-term capability, long-term capability, and updated control plan.

Verify

In the fourth phase of the DCOV model, the verify stage is explored. This stage is generally completed through a two-step approach. The first is the overall DFSS assessment and the second is the test and verify stage. In both cases, the goal is to verify that the capability and product integrity over time are as designed and as the customer is expecting them. Therefore, the purpose of the first step is to estimate sigma for process capability and product or service function over time.

The second step is to assess actual performance, reliability, and operation capability, as well as to demonstrate customer-correlated (real-world) performance over time. It is imperative to understand that if the results of design for robust performance, design for producibility or serviceability, assessment, and testing are not satisfactory, the model may revert back to the previous stage or even further back in the functional mapping stage. Furthermore, in every one of these just mentioned stages, a trade-off analysis should be performed to ensure that all CTSs are met.

The process for exploring the first step of the verify stage is divided into three areas:

■ *Inputs.* These are the activities that will generate the activity of this step. Typical activity is data from previous steps

■ *Action.* These activities actually help the DFSS overall assessment. Four predominant activities are conducted here:
  –CTS/CTQ characteristic/measure and a comparison between the $Z_{estimate}$ and Z_{actual}
  –Subassessments—as needed
  –Test/simulation and comparison between the $Z_{estimate}$ and Z_{actual}
  –Variability over time for both product and process

■ *Output.* This is the result of the action. Typical results are overall review of assessments for previous steps with champion or appropriate management.

The process for exploring the second step of the verify stage is divided into three areas:

- *Inputs.* These are activities that will generate the activity of this step. Typical activities are reliability and/or robustness plan and design verification plan with key noises.
- *Action.* These activities actually help to conduct physical and analytical performance tests enhanced with appropriate noise factors. Typical activities are correlate tests to customer usage; improve ability of tests to discriminate good and bad service, subsystems, systems; and peer review.
- *Output.* This is the result of the action. Typical results are test results such as key life testing, accelerated tests, long-term process capabilities, product performance over time (Weibull, survival plot, kappa values, and so on), and reliability/robustness demonstration matrix.

Special Note

One may wonder why a discussion on a prevention methodology with a Six Sigma flavor is necessary. The answer is that unless there is a focus on preventing the problems from happening to begin with, the organization will repeat the same problems and fight the same fires. A good example of this result is the statistics that Cooper (1986–2000; see note at end of chapter) presents over a 14-year time span—a period in which industries had supposedly learned the value of customer satisfaction, profitability, quality, and efficiency. The statistics presented by Cooper show the causes of new product or service failures in all industries. They also illustrate that there is inadequate understanding of the market and that nonrobust products or services are the key factors in new product or service failures. Some of the statistics are eye-opening (the percentages are measured as multiple responses and therefore do not equal 100%):

- Inadequate market analysis: 45%
- Product or service problems or defects: 29%
- Lack of effective marketing effort: 25%
- Higher costs than anticipated: 19%
- Competitive strength or reaction: 17%
- Poor timing of introduction: 14%
- Technical or operation problems: 12%
- All other causes: 24%

One can see that designing the right product or service is in the best interest of the organization. Items to consider include:

- *In the identification (preliminary) stage:* Develop and validate model(s) and transfer functions using DOE, regression, and physical properties; use transfer functions to optimize the process.
- *In the design (for the fully characterized process) stage:* Determine DPU (defects per unit) long term (LT), DPMO (defects per million opportunities) LT, and Z_{est} for Xs and Ys.
- *In the optimize stage:* Determine ability to control to optimum (target) value using Minitab, Excel, contour plots, transfer functions, and Monte Carlo simulation—as appropriate and applicable.
- *In the validate stage:* Examine normality assumption: transformation, alternate distribution, or mixture of distributions? What are the Xs? Determine relevant Ys (CTQs). Determine relevant Xs.

Synthesis of Lean Thinking and Six Sigma

Lean provides a total system approach but is short on details, organizational structures, and analytic tools for diagnosis. Six Sigma, on the other hand, offers fewer standard solutions but provides a general analytic framework for problem solving and an organizational infrastructure. The ideal solution is to combine the two approaches. Many practitioners have done so tacitly for quite some time. At the very minimum, an integrated healthcare framework for Lean Six Sigma consists of the following five elements:

- *A structured approach.* The deployment infrastructure is based on Six Sigma organizational mechanisms consisting of a task force deployment strategy using BBs, GBs, and champions.
- *Project-based deployment.* A project is a chronic problem scheduled for solution (Juran 1989). Nonstandard problems are solved only with a project-by-project approach (Juran). Projects are classified as either "quick wins" (Lean) or "advanced" (Six Sigma). Lean projects apply best practices and focus on implementing standard solutions. Such projects typically involve speed, reduction of lead time, inventory, and processing time. Six Sigma projects apply to more general and complex problems and involve solid, data-based analytic methods and statistics, including quality improvement (QI) and control methods. The problem-solving algorithm of DMAIC is always used, and projects are monitored after each phase is completed. Typical Six Sigma projects involve increasing quality, decreasing defects,

reducing variation, and increasing yield, although they more generally involve systematic process innovation (Stamatis 2003a, 2003b, 2003c, 2003d, 2003e; Bisgaard and De Mast 2006).

- *Organizational competency development.* A dedicated workforce of Lean Six Sigma project leaders (champions, GBs, and BBs) is trained in a curriculum that resembles that of Six Sigma with additional Lean components.

- *Organizational anchoring of solutions.* To secure the implementation of solutions and guard against backsliding, tasks and responsibilities are clearly defined, procedures are standardized, and process controls are imposed as part of an improvement project.

- *Linking strategy with project selection.* Strategic objectives are translated into performance indicators and tactical goals. These are then used as a basis for project selection and help secure an alignment of projects with the overall organizational strategy.

Lean Six Sigma Healthcare

Lean Six Sigma has recently also been applied in the healthcare sector. For example, the Lehigh Valley Health Network system has reported a 4.4% increase in inpatient bed use and market increase relative to competitors, treated more outpatients, and reduced patient services net margin by 11% below budget (Hardner 2009). George (2003) describes pioneering work on Lean Six Sigma at Stanford Hospital and Clinics.

Van den Heuvel, Does, and Vermaat (2004) describe their own experience with Lean Six Sigma at the Red Cross Hospital in the Netherlands. Of course, as is often the case, elements of Lean Six Sigma were applied at the hospital years before the term itself was used. The Red Cross Hospital in Beverwijk is a 384-bed, medium-sized general hospital employing a staff of 966 with a yearly budget of $72.1 million (USD). In addition to being a general healthcare provider, the Red Cross Hospital also houses a national burn care center with 25 beds that provides specialized services to all of the Netherlands. In 2004, the Red Cross Hospital had 12,669 admissions, performed 11,064 outpatient treatments, and received 198,591 visits to its outpatient units, of which 78,832 were first contacts.

The Red Cross Hospital began to use Six Sigma in 2002. However, the hospital management had already introduced a basic quality assurance system and obtained an International Organization for Standardization 9002 certification in 2000. Prior to the implementation of Six Sigma, management also deployed a number of teams to work on specific QI projects. At the time, management believed that these pre-Six Sigma projects worked well. Indeed, a number of the projects were completed with good results. However, over time, management discovered that an organizational framework and programs for project management, coordination, tracking, and support were necessary. Specifically, upper management identified the following problems:

- Projects were not necessarily of strategic relevance.
- Projects did not always have a significant business case.
- A systematic project-tracking system was missing.
- There was no uniform method for project management and control.
- Too many projects were not completed.

At the end of 2001, the hospital management was introduced to Six Sigma and found that this methodology provided solutions to many of these problems. The initial implementation of Six Sigma at the Red Cross Hospital is described in the literature (Van den Heuvel, Does, and Bisgaard 2005; Van den Heuvel, Does, and Verver 2006). In addition to outlining Six Sigma's management framework and lessons learned relevant to healthcare, these articles also describe selected examples of projects. A sampling will provide an impression of the range of problems tackled:

- Shortening the length of stay in chronic obstructive pulmonary disease patients
- Reducing errors in invoices received from temporary agencies
- Revising the terms of payment
- Allowing parents to room in with their children
- Reducing the number of patients requiring intravenous antibiotics
- Shortening the preparation time of intravenous medication
- Reducing the number of mistakes in invoices

This list illustrates the important point that Six Sigma projects in healthcare typically include both medical and administrative problems. Indeed, some healthcare professionals think QI methods should address only defects, such as medication errors. Our experience is that significant gains can be made by widening the field of applications to all processes and all operational inefficiency and waste.

The preceding list also shows that several of the Six Sigma projects could just as well be characterized as Lean projects. For example, reducing the length of stay and shortening the preparation time for medication would be typical Lean objectives. On the other hand, the Lean approach would come up short in projects involving reducing errors in invoices received from temporary agencies, revising payment terms, and correcting the number of mistakes in invoices. The distinction between Lean and Six Sigma is artificial and often not helpful.

An integration of the two approaches and a general focus on process innovation, regardless of the origin of the tools and approaches, would be more productive.

Conclusions

Unless healthcare leaders deal with spiraling healthcare costs, a decreasing proportion of the citizens of industrialized societies will be able to afford high-quality healthcare. If healthcare services are inefficient, they cost more and fewer can benefit from the technical advances of modern medicine. A persistence of traditional service practices will drain our economy. Continuous and relentless pursuits of innovations in the service delivery process are necessary. The industrialization of healthcare offers a viable alternative that can provide better economy, greater efficiency, and better service.

Industrializing healthcare does not mean that healthcare becomes less personal and that quality standards are compromised. For example, a modern car, objectively speaking, is far cheaper and of significantly higher quality than a handcrafted car manufactured 100 years ago. Prepackaged vacations typically offer better deals with higher levels of service than individually planned tours. Industrialization of services typically improves quality while making those services much more cost efficient.

The industrialization of healthcare service will require a large number of innovations, especially pertaining to the delivery of services. The popular perception is that innovation, like artistic expression, is the product of genius. However, in today's competitive economic environment, this process must not remain a mystery. Indeed, it need not be. Pianists and painters attend conservatories and art schools to receive intensive training in their professions. Innovation, like artistic performance, can be learned. The combination of Six Sigma and Lean—with their tools, road maps, and management processes—is essentially a carefully managed process for systematically scheduling and carrying out innovation projects that can be taught, learned, and performed with a high degree of success.

Lean and Six Sigma have strongly complementary strengths that are particularly useful for systematically developing healthcare service innovations. Synthesizing these approaches leads to an integrated program combining the best of both programs. Lean Six Sigma incorporates the organizational infrastructure and the thorough diagnosis and analysis tools of Six Sigma with Lean analysis tools and best-practice solutions for problems dealing with waste and unnecessary time consumption. The net result is a process for institutionalized systematic innovation that consistently delivers the intended end results (Drucker 1985).

Summary

This chapter discussed the Six Sigma methodology. It gave an overview of both DMAIC and DCOV. Specifically, it addressed the components of each phase and also made a link between the two and the Lean methodology. In the next chapter, we will discuss the Lean approach to improvement.

Note

R. G. Cooper: *Winning at New Products,* New York: Holt, Rinehart, Winston, 1986; "The Winning Formula," *Engineering World* 7 (2): 28–35, 1997; "Benchmarking New Product Performance: Results of the Best Practices Study," *European Management Journal* 16 (1): 1–7, 1998; "Best Practices for Managing R&D Portfolios," *Research-Technology Management* 41 (4): 20–33, 1998; "The Invisible Success Factors in Product Innovation," *Journal of Product Innovation Management* 16 (2): 115–133, 1999; "New Product Portfolio Management: Practices and Performance," *Journal of Product Innovation Management* 16 (4): 333–351, 1999; "Product Innovation and Technology Strategy," in the "Succeeding in Technological Innovation" series, *Research-Technology Management* 43 (1): 28–44, 2000; "Doing It Right—Winning with New Products," *Ivey Business Journal* July–August: 54–60, 2000; "New Problems, New Solutions: Making Portfolio Management More Effective," *Research-Technology Management* 43 (2): 18–33, 2000; "New Product Performance: What Distinguishes the Star Products," *Australian Journal of Management* 25 (1): 17–45, 2000.

References

Bisgaard, S., and J. De Mast. 2006. After Six Sigma—What's next? *Quality Progress* 39(1) 30–36.

Bisgaard, S., and J. Freiesleben. 2004. Six Sigma and the bottom line. *Quality Progress* September: 37, 57–62.

Box, G. E. P., and S. Bisgaard. 1987. The scientific context of quality improvement. *Quality Progress* June: 20, 54–61.

Breyfogle, F. W. 1999. *Implementing Six Sigma: Smarter solution using statistical methods.* New York: John Wiley & Sons.

———. 2003. *Implementing Six Sigma—Smarter solutions using statistical methods,* 2nd ed. New York: John Wiley & Sons.

De Koning, H., and J. De Mast. 2006. A rational reconstruction of Six Sigma's breakthrough cookbook. *International Journal of Quality and Reliability Management* 23 (5) 766–787.

Drucker, P. F. 1985. *Innovation and entrepreneurship: Practice and principles.* New York: Harper and Row.

Ford, H., and S. Crowther. 1926. Today and tomorrow. Cambridge, MA: Productivity Press.

Garvin, D. A. 1988. *Managing quality: The strategic and competitive edge.* New York: Free Press.

George, M. L. 2003. *Lean Six Sigma for services.* New York: McGraw–Hill.

Hardner, K. November 2009. Your transformer handbook. *CheckUp.* Lehigh Valley Health Network Publication, p. 7.

Harry, M. J. 1997. *The vision of Six Sigma,* 5th ed. Phoenix, AZ: Tri Star.

Hoerl, R. W. 2004. One perspective on the future of Six Sigma. *International Journal of Six Sigma and Competitive Advantage* 1 (1): 112–119.

Juran, J. M. 1989. *Juran on leadership for quality.* New York: Free Press.

Ohno, T. 1988. *Toyota production system.* New York: Productivity Press.

Pyzdek, T. 2001. *The Six Sigma handbook—A complete guide for greenbelts, blackbelts, and managers at all levels.* New York: McGraw–Hill.

———. 2004. Strategy deployment using balanced scorecards. *International Journal of Six Sigma and Competitive Advantage* 1 (1): 21–28.

Robinson, A. 1990. *Modern approaches to manufacturing improvement: The Shingo system.* Cambridge, MA: Productivity Press.

Smith, B. 2003. Lean and Six Sigma—A one–two punch. *Quality Progress* April: 36–41.

Snee, R. D. 2004. Six Sigma: The evolution of 100 years of business improvement methodology. *International Journal of Six Sigma and Competitive Advantage* 1(1): 4–20.

Snee, R. D., and R. W. Hoerl. 2004. *Six Sigma beyond the factory floor.* Upper Saddle River, NJ: Pearson Education.

Stalk, G., and T. M. Hout. 1990. *Competing against time.* New York: Free Press.

Stamatis, D. H. May 2000. Who needs Six Sigma anyway? *Quality Digest.* pp. 29–32.

———. 2002a. *Six Sigma and beyond: Foundation of excellence performance.* Boca Raton, FL: St. Lucie Press.

———. 2002b. *Six Sigma and beyond: Problem solving and basic math.* Boca Raton, FL: St. Lucie Press.

———. 2003a. *Six Sigma and beyond: Statistics and probability.* Boca Raton, FL: St. Lucie Press.

———. 2003b. *Six Sigma and beyond: Statistical process control.* Boca Raton, FL: St. Lucie Press.

———. 2003c. *Six Sigma and beyond: Design of experiments.* Boca Raton, FL: St. Lucie Press.

———. 2003d. *Six Sigma and beyond: Design for Six Sigma.* Boca Raton, FL: St. Lucie Press.

———. 2003e. *Six Sigma and beyond: The implementation process.* Boca Raton, FL: St. Lucie Press.

Standard, C., and D. Davis. 1999. *Running today's factory: A proven strategy for Lean manufacturing.* Cincinnati, OH: Hanser Gardner.

Van den Heuvel, J., R. J. M. M. Does, and S. Bisgaard. 2005. Dutch hospital implements Six Sigma. *Six Sigma Forum Magazine* 4 (2): 11–14.

Van den Heuvel, J., R. J. M. M. Does, and M. B. Vermaat. 2004. Six Sigma in a Dutch hospital: Does it work in the nursing department? *Quality and Reliability Engineering International* 20: 419–426.

Van den Heuvel, J., R. J. M. M. Does, and J. P. S. Verver. 2006. Six Sigma in healthcare: Lessons learned from a hospital. *International Journal of Six Sigma and Competitive Advantage* 1 (4).

Womack, J. P., D. T. Jones, and D. Roos. 1990. *The machine that changed the world: The story of Lean production.* New York: Rawson Associates. pp. 377–388

Selected Bibliography

Allen, I. E., and T. H. Davenport. 2009. Tune up to compose a business solution, sharpen your Six Sigma approach, complement it with other methods. *Quality Progress* September: 16–29.

Bailey, S. P. 1992. How to deal with the process capability catch-22. *ASQ AQC Transactions.* Milwaukee, WI.

Benedetto, A. R. n.d. Adapting manufacturing-based Six Sigma methodology to the service environment of a radiology film library. American College of Healthcare Executives. Fellowship case reports. Available at http://www.ache.org/mbership/AdvtoFellow/CASERPTS/benedetto01.cfm (accessed October 8, 2004).

Benneyan, J. C., R. C. Lloyd, and P. E. Plsek. December 2003. Statistical process control as a tool for research and healthcare improvement. *Quality and Safety in Health Care* 12 (6): 458–464.

Bertels, T., M. Williams, and H. Dershin. 2001. Six Sigma: A powerful strategy for healthcare providers. *Aon Healthcare Alliance Health Line* special edition: 1–5.

Bierly, R., and A. Chakrabarti. 1996. Technological learning, strategic flexibility and new product development in the pharmaceutical industry. *IEEE Transactions on Engineering Management* 43 (4): 368–380.

Box, G., and G. Jenkins. 1976. *Time series analysis, forecasting and control,* 2nd ed. San Francisco, CA: Holden–Day.

Box, G., W. Hunter, and J. S. Hunter. 1978.*Statistics for experimenters: An introduction to design, data analysis, and model building.* New York: John Wiley & Sons.

Breyfogle F. W., M. J. Cupello, and B. Meadows. 2001. *Managing Six Sigma: A practical guide to understanding, assessing and implementing the strategy that yields bottom line success.* New York: John Wiley & Sons.

Casella, G., and R. Berger. 1990. *Statistical inference.* Belmont, CA: Duxbury Press.

Chassin, M. R. 1998. Is health care ready for Six Sigma quality? *Milbank Quarterly* 76 (4): 510, 565–591.

Cooper, R. G. 2001. *Winning at new products: Accelerating the process from idea to launch,* 3rd ed. Reading, MA: Perseus Books.

Dusharme, D. 2004. Quality conversation with Mikel Harry: The foremost expert on Six Sigma talks about its past, present and future [online article]. *Quality Digest* 24 (2). http://www.qualitydigest.com/feb04/articles/06_article.shtml

Dutta, S., and A. Weiss. 1997. The relationship between a firm's level of technological innovativeness and its pattern of partnership agreements. *Management Science* 43 (4): 343–356.

Ettinger, W., and M. Van Kooy. 2003. The art and science of winning physician support for Six Sigma change. *Physician Executive* 29 (5): 34–38.

Franko, L. 1989. Global corporate competition: Who's winning, who's losing, and the R&D factor as one reason why. *Strategic Management Journal* 10 (5): 449–474.

Harry, M. 1994. *The vision of Six Sigma: A roadmap for breakthrough,* 4th ed. Phoenix, AZ: Sigma Publishing Company.

Harry, M., and R. Schroeder. 2000. *Six Sigma, the breakthrough management strategy revolutionizing the world's top corporations.* New York: Doubleday.

Heskett, J. L., W. E. Sasser, Jr., and L. A. Schlesinger. 1997. *The service profit chain.* New York: Free Press.

Johnstone, P. A., J. A. Hendrickson, A. J. Dernbach, et al. 2003. Ancillary services in the health care industry: Is Six Sigma reasonable? *Quality Management in Health Care* 12 (1): 53–63.

Lanham, B., and P. Maxson-Cooper. 2003. Is Six Sigma the answer for nursing to reduce medical errors and enhance patient safety? *Nursing Economics* 21 (1): 38–41.

Levitt, T. 1976. The industrialization of service. *Harvard Business Review* September–October: 54, 63–74.

Rosenberg, N. 1982. *Inside the black box: Technology and economics.* New York: Cambridge University Press.

Rozgus, A. 2003. Using the sixth sense: By implementing the Six Sigma approach, companies can move ahead of the pack. *Concrete Producer* August: 1.

Scalise, D. 2001. Six Sigma: The quest for quality. *Hospitals & Health Networks* 75 (12): 2, 41–46.

———. 2003. Six Sigma in action: Case studies in quality put theory into practice. *Hospitals & Health Networks* 77 (5): 2, 57–62.

Seecof, D. 2000. Applying the Six Sigma approach to patient care [online article]. *Healthcare Solutions Insights* 1:2(5). GE Medical Systems Healthcare Solutions.

Shingo, S. 1989. *A study of the Toyota production system.* New York: Productivity Press.

Stamatis, D. H. 2004. *Six Sigma fundamentals.* New York: Productivity Press.

Womack, J. P., and D. T. Jones. 2003. *Lean thinking,* 2nd ed. New York: Free Press.

Chapter 10

Using Lean Methodology for Improvement

Introduction

In the last chapter, we discussed a specific improvement methodology called Six Sigma. In this chapter, we focus on Lean. Even though Lean was originally thought of as a methodology of improvement in manufacturing, when applied to healthcare, Lean principles can eliminate many obstacles to excellence, such as cumbersome information technology systems, worker frustration, and inadvertent errors and oversights that can increase patient safety risks. Surprisingly few improvements require costly or sweeping high-tech "fixes." Most often, simple, well designed interactions based on scientific observations and experiments bring nearly unimaginable improvement ... fast. The idea of Lean in any environment is to increase efficiency and effectiveness in the organization and/ or process and to improve value to the customer.

A *Lean enterprise* views itself as part of an extended value chain, focusing on the elimination of waste between the organization and its suppliers, and the organization and its customers—the entire SIPOC (suppliers, inputs, process, outputs, customers) model. However, in most cases in healthcare, Lean is used on individual processes—*Lean organization*. In both cases, Lean has it origins in the teaching and writings of total quality management (TQM) and just in time (JIT), which espouse the idea of "delighting the customer through a continuous stream of value-adding activities." One may go as far as to say that *Lean* is an extension of the phrase "world class," implying high standards and high performance to satisfy the customer. In other words, value is always defined from the customer's perspective. That is why understanding the customer's needs is a prerequisite for driving Lean principles and methodologies in any organization. The primary objectives of the Lean organization or enterprise are to

- Identify and specify "value to the ultimate customer and/or consumer" correctly in all its products and services. This means that, from the time a customer need is recognized until it is satisfied, the process and all its elements must add value for the "value stream" to be meaningful. The basic components of this Lean system are waste elimination, continuous flow, and customer pull.
- Analyze and focus the value stream so that it does everything from product development and production to sales and service in a way that activities that do not create value are removed and actions that do create value proceed in a continuous flow as pulled by the customer.

Essentially, Lean is a three-pronged approach incorporating:

- A quality belief (philosophy)
- Waste elimination
- Employee involvement supported by a structured management system

Lean thinking begins with driving out waste so that all work adds value and serves the customer's needs. Identifying value-added (things that the customer is willing to pay for) and non-value-added steps (things that the customer is not willing to pay for) in every process is the beginning of the journey toward Lean operations. The classical wastes in all processes include:

- *Overproduction:* producing more, sooner, and faster than required by the next process
- *Excess transportation:* any transport that adds cost but no value to the product
- *Excess inventory:* not only a waste, but also creates waste
- *Excess processing:* doing more work than necessary
- *Waiting:* operator or machine idle time
- *Correction:* repairs to products
- *Motion:* walking or wasted motion to pick up or store parts

In order for Lean principles to take root, leaders must first work to create an organizational culture that is receptive to Lean thinking. The commitment to Lean must start at the very top of the organization, and all staff should be involved in helping to redesign processes to improve flow and reduce waste.

Although healthcare differs in many ways from manufacturing, there are also surprising similarities: Whether building a car or providing healthcare for a patient, workers must rely on multiple, complex processes to accomplish their tasks and provide value to the customer or patient. Waste—of money, time, supplies, or goodwill—decreases value. Therefore, just as in any other enterprise, successful healthcare Lean depends on five initiatives:

- *Defining the value of a product or service:* Specify all activities that add value to a product or service. All other activities are waste and should be removed. Eliminating waste is a significant source of improvement in corporate performance and customer service.
- *Identifying the value stream:* Identify business and transformation processes to deliver a product or service to the customer. Begin to manage the value stream as a whole instead of as independent steps or processes. Practice system thinking.
- *Creating flow:* Arrange value-adding steps and eliminate waste to remove obstacles that prohibit continuous material or information flow.
- *Produce to the pull of the customer:* Change the method of production from large-batch production to producing only what is demanded by the customer. This involves not only finished products but also work in process throughout the entire value stream.
- *Pursuing perfection:* Every asset and every action adds value to the product or service for the customer. Lean thinking represents a path of sustained performance improvement instead of individual process steps.

Lean, then, is about value in a process. Lean is about doing more with less: less time, less inventory, less space, fewer people, and less money. This means that the ultimate goal of Lean is zero waiting time; zero inventories; scheduling—internal customer pull instead of push system; batch to flow— cut batch sizes; line balancing; and cutting actual process times. Therefore, for all intents and purposes Lean is about *value, speed,* and *getting it right the first time.*

This is a very important concept and must not be confused with the Six Sigma methodology. While the Lean methodology concentrates on creating more value with less work, the Six Sigma system strives to identify and eliminate defects in product development and in solving existing problems in existing processes. Thus, Lean Six Sigma provides a method to accelerate a company's decision-making processes, while reducing production inefficiencies as well as increasing product quality.

In this day and age, where everyone talks about reform in healthcare, most of the discussions are falling short of understanding the *principles* of this "reform" that is supposed to revolutionize healthcare. When we talk about principles, we mean the use of rigorous, systematic, and objective methodologies to obtain reliable and valid knowledge. Specifically, we are looking for a process that requires the following:

- Development of a logical, evidence-based chain of reasoning
- Methods appropriate to the questions posed
- Observational or experimental designs and instruments that provide reliable and generalizable findings
- Data and analysis adequate to support the findings
- Explication of procedures and results clearly as well as detail, including specifications of the population to which the findings can be generalized
- Adherence to professional norms of peer review
- Dissemination of findings to appropriate departments and organization
- Having the data available for further analysis (if necessary) or for replication of the findings and the opportunity to build on the findings

Unfortunately, to our knowledge, there is no magic wand or algorithm that will determine the best approach or tool or methodology to solve a particular problem. For that matter, there is no easy way to determine what is common (acceptable) and what is genuinely different (not acceptable). Indeed, historically, in all walks of life, commonality and differences have themselves been conditioned and shifting based on cultural trends, demographics, and so many other variables.

In healthcare in particular, we believe that *success,* however defined, is based on three fundamental principles that, when understood and applied, will show very positive results:

- The environment under consideration for improvement must be willing to create a Lean improvement culture—minimum or no waste—by engaging the workforce in daily improvement activity.
- Management must be willing to tap improvement opportunities that are hidden or difficult for managers to spot. More often than not, these opportunities are found in processes that are overlooked for many reasons.
- Leadership and management must promote rapid organizational learning. (Leadership and management are very different and require different responsibilities and abilities and certainly have different expectations. Leadership focuses on the long-term vision, goals, and viability of the organization. Managers focus on execution plans that will put the vision and goals into the organization effectively and efficiently.)

To start the application of Lean, most organizations follow the classic choices described by Liker and Meier (2005) in *The Toyota Way Fieldbook:*

- *Philosophy:* Work with top team on how to think Lean; how to ask the right questions, be welcoming of problems, be visible and near the work, instill intrinsic motivation to improve, but not for sake of targets.
- *Process:* Define the organization as a set of value streams; start on optimizing one.
- *People:* Start to introduce this new way of working to all staff.
- *Problem solve:* Take Lean's relentless curiosity about errors and defects, combine with the tool set around root causing and putting right and implement via small projects under banner of "right first time" or "error free."

One must decide which blend to choose locally by examining the levels, support, problems, culture, politics, and timescale present. In any case, just get started on something. Many organizations start with value stream mapping (VSM), others with training everyone in the concept of change, and yet others with general training on improvement methods. The VSM is the most practical because Lean is about starting with the customer and delivering what the customer needs with no waste. This is the value stream or why the organization exists; it does not exist to run an outpatient department or any other particular process. Looking across departments with a VSM approach starts to generate new ways of doing things.

Lean Enterprise versus Lean Organization

Lean enterprise is the entire supply chain, which is known as the SIPOC model. It includes individuals, functions, process, and customers, which are sometimes separate but operationally synchronized organizations. A typical overview is shown in Figure 10.1. The objectives and principles of the Lean enterprise as defined by Womack and Jones (1996) include:

- Correctly specify value for the customer.
- Identify all the action required to bring a product from concept to launch, from order to delivery, and from raw material into the hands of the customer and on through its useful life.
- Remove any actions that do not create value or make those actions that do not create value proceed in continuous flow as pulled by the customer.
- Analyze the results and start the evaluation process over again.

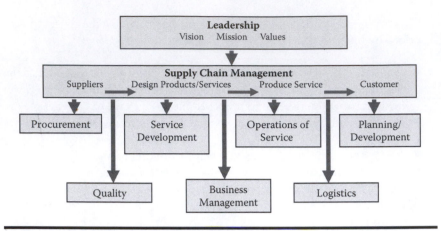

Figure 10.1   A typical Lean enterprise view.

On the other hand, the principles of the Lean organization include:

■ Clear communication
■ "No blame" culture
■ Waste reduction
■ Continuous improvement
■ Employee involvement
■ Cross-functional teams
■ Top management involvement

The Lean organization is one component of the Lean enterprise. Therefore, the responsibilities are different. Key differences are in the way management and leadership view the organization and understanding a business management system designed to achieve world-class excellence in customer satisfaction. Beginning with the voice of the customer, the system continuously strives to improve quality, delivery, and cost. The system provides the necessary tools to achieve specific business objectives with the involvement of all employees.

The ability to lead and make sound business decisions requires a complexity of knowledge and skills. *This knowledge and skill is epitomized in the leader.* The role of the leader in any Lean or Six Sigma methodology implementation process is very important and critical. The leader should, at a minimum, be able to

■ Understand the human dimension
    – Creating long-term employee motivation
    – Managing and defusing dysfunctional behavior

- Assume the helm
  - Managing the transition to a new work team
  - Developing and maintaining the support of the work team
  - Initiating a simple vision and strategy effective in improving work team performance (it may be introduced in phases)

- Shape corporate culture
  - Understanding the critical components of corporate culture
  - Forming productive organizational norms
  - Establishing a high-performance work environment

- Facilitate strategic decisions
  - Making critical distinctions between problems, decisions, and polarities
  - Knowing how to frame a decision properly
  - Selecting the decision makers
  - Knowing when the decision has been made
  - Anticipating the impact of adaptive responses

- Lead the strategic change
  - Planning a change initiative
  - Anticipating and plan and deal with resistance
  - Addressing culture as a barrier to change

- Be politically conscious
  - Gaining credibility in executive circles
  - Building networks and relationships
  - Learning how to avoid getting derailed

- Create organizations that work
  - Creating an organizational charter
  - Selecting an effective management team
  - Thinking systemically
  - Learning to manage image and expectations
  - Creating meaningful performance indicators
  - Eliminating turf battles and duplication
  - Recognizing the limitations on the application of common systems

In the Lean organization, it is also very important to initiate a policy deployment that may be captured in its conceptual form as in Figure 10.2. This deployment is called the hoshin kanri methodology ("hoshin" means shining metal, compass, or pointing the direction and "kanri" means management or control)

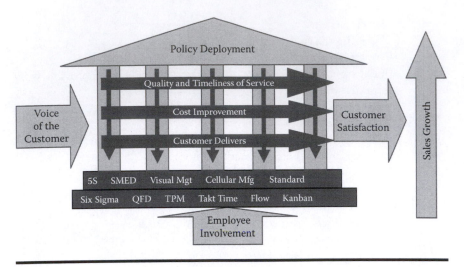

Figure 10.2   A conceptual view of policy deployment.

and is designed to capture strategic goals and integrate these goals with the entire organization's daily activities. In essence, it involves both planning and deployment. Specifically, it focuses on

- Development of targets
- Development of action plans to achieve the targets
- Deployment of both

Hoshin kanri began in Japan in 1960–1965 as statistical process control (SPC) and later became total quality control (TQC). In the Lean methodology, hoshin kanri is most commonly referred to as policy deployment (PD). In its core purpose, it is a systems approach to management of change in critical business processes. Another way of saying it is that the hoshin kanri methodology is to improve the performance of critical business processes in the organization.

Improvement, however, must be thought of in terms of (1) management or strategic planning, and (2) daily management. This is an important distinction because the decisions made by the management will affect the goals of the entire organization. In addition, these decisions will have a direct effect on promoting

- Breakthrough thinking
- Process-oriented rather than task-oriented issues
- The notion that there are no bad people—just bad processes

Above all, the Lean organization must value its employees. It is in fact the foundation upon which the entire principle is founded. Without the involvement and ownership of the employees, Lean will not work. Because this is such an important matter, management must understand some of the key issues with which all employees are faced and take appropriate action. The classical needs of all employees are on Maslow's hierarchy of needs. The idea of recognizing Maslow's hierarchy is that employees do have needs and, unless those needs are satisfied, the initiatives that management will try to deploy will not be successful. The needs are

- Physiological: air, water, food, shelter
- Safety: to/from/at work
- Benefits: social security, job security, etc.
- Love: affection with friends, family, co-workers, etc.
- Esteem: reputation, prestige, and recognition
- Fulfillment: "be all that you can be"

If this PD is so important, is there a way to optimize it? In fact, there is. The process of conducting a PD is identified in the following phases:

- Phase 0: target focus alone
- Phase 1: process management
- Phase 2: self-diagnosis
- Phase 3: alignment
- Phase 4: one core vision

To complete these phases, there are five distinct steps with specific requirements:

1. Measure the system performance:
   a. Develop a plan to manage the strategic change objectives.
   b. Initial direction must be adaptable.
   c. The planning process must be adaptive to respond to business changes.
   d. Regular assessments of planning and implementation must be made.

2. Set core business objectives:
   a. Apply "catchball" to incorporate group dialog.
   b. Toss an idea around.
   c. Provide the optimal objectives for the overall business system.

3. Evaluate the business environment:
   a. Understand the needs of management's customers:
      (1) Stockholders
      (2) Employees
      (3) External customers
      (4) Others
   b. Environmental analysis includes the technical, economic, social, and political aspects of the business.
   c. How does the business perform relative to its competitors?

4. Provide resources:
   a. There are two levels:
      (1) Strategic objectives
      (2) Daily management
   b. Hoshin aligns the system to strategic change initiatives.

5. Define system processes:
   a. Hoshin enables consensus planning and execution between senior management (vision), middle management (strategy), and teams (action) (see Figure 10.3).

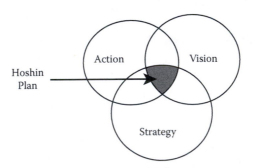

Figure 10.3 Consensus planning and execution between senior management, middle management, and teams.

Applying the Hoshin Method

When the hoshin method is applied, there are four items of concern:

- The *hoshin plan summary* details the core objectives and identifies the key performance indicators of improvement (safety, quality, delivery, and cost [SQDC]). The information may be collected in a form like the one shown in Table 10.1.
- The *hoshin action plan* is a summary of the actions to be taken in order to link the core objectives to implementation strategies. This information may be collected or summarized in a form like the one shown in Table 10.2
- The *hoshin implementation plan* (typically a Gantt chart format) captures pertinent information, such as
  - Recording progress
  - Listing the implementation activities
  - Comparing the current status of milestones to initial projections

The information may be collected in a form such as the one shown in Table 10.3.

- The *hoshin implementation review* examines items such as
  - Performance measure progress
  - Company performance relative to industry performance
  - Highest priority implementation issues

This information may be collected in a form such as the one shown in Table 10.4. In this table, we have identified the performance status on the right of the form and the implementation issues to the left so that we emphasize the performance. It is our focus and the main discussion point. Although the implementation is also important, it has been discussed as part of the implementation plan before, so it is old news here.

The policy deployment is one of the key pillars to any quality initiative, including total quality management, Lean, and Six Sigma. It is based on the plan-do-check-act (PDCA) cycle (see Figure 10.4). However, the process for hoshin begins with the "check" cycle. It must be noted here that many hospitals already are using this model approach and therefore the model is Check-Act-Plan-DO (CAPD). The reason for this is that the current status must be understood before anything else happens. Of course, once the current process is understood, the hoshin methodology is propelled to the other CAPD cycles. In addition to understanding the current process, the organization must be committed to cross-functional management because it enables the continual checking of targets and means throughout the product or service development and/or operation processes.

Table 10.1 Hoshin Plan Summary

Core Objectives	Management Owner	Goals		Implementation Strategies	Target		Improvement Focus			
		Short Term	Long Term		Short Term	Long Term	Safety	Quality	Delivery	Cost

Table 10.2 Typical Action Plan

Hoshin Objective: Department: Team:		Management Owner: Date: Next Review:
Situation Summary		
Core Objectives	*Strategy*	*Targets and Milestones*
Goals		
Short term:		
Long term:		

Table 10.3 Hoshin Implementation Plan

Hoshin Objective: Strategy Owner: Date Updated:
Performance status implementation issues
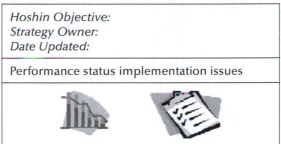

A second requirement of policy deployment is the notion of continual communication horizontally and vertically. Two-way communication is important to ensure understanding and "buy-in." A technique known as *catchball* is very useful to achieve this wide-scale open communication deployment. In terms of definition, *catchball* has been defined in several ways, including:

- It is a participative approach to decision making used in policy deployment to communicate across management levels when setting annual business objectives. It is a process like tossing a ball back and forth emphasizing the interactive nature of policy deployment (from http://www.velaction.com/catchball/).
- *Catchball* is a give-and-take dialogue within the organization. The ideas are generated from the top management, however as long as those ideas are viable and worth discussing by three quarters of the subordinates in the

Table 10.4 Typical Hoshin Implementation Review

Hoshin Objective Title:
Strategy Owner: Date Updated:

Strategy	Implementation Activities	Activity Owner	Schedule and Milestones												Performance	
			J	F	M	A	M	J	J	A	S	O	N	D	Target	Actual

Act

Plan

Check

Do

Figure 10.4   The PDCA cycle.

meeting, the discussion continuous until everyone understands the desired focus of the organization. Each level of the organization should, in turn, develop goals, objectives, and action plans to support the overall goals. It will also be necessary to have functional plans while monitoring and tracking processes and product and service indicators to ensure that quality consistently meets customer requirements and performance goals (from a U.S. Air Force Web site at http://www.laafb.af.mil/SMC/MQ/qi/mqq.htm).

The *catchball* approach not only helps on the two-way communication process, but also enhances the entire process because of its intrinsic value in the areas of bringing all employees together and allowing them to understand their role in the continual improvement process. Furthermore, doable targets and action plans as well as feedback systems can be created to allow bottom-up, top-down, horizontal, and multidirectional communication without fear of management.

The reader must not confuse the hoshin kanri with other strategic models. They are different. Three key factors differentiate hoshin kanri from strategic planning models ("management by objectives," for example) typically used by many organizations:

■ Focus on means or processes used to achieve the goals
■ The concept of *catchball*
■ Vertical integration

Lean Is Not a Toolbox. It Is a Way of Thinking about Work

A Lean transformation cuts across organizational boundaries of department and job description:

- The aim is to create smooth-flowing consumption streams (patients with needs) matched up with smooth-flowing provision streams (healthcare services) so that patients get what they need, where they need it, and when they need it, without waiting.
- Consumption and provision streams run across organizational departments.
- Most improvement efforts have been aimed at particularly deficient single points within discrete departments along the stream rather than viewing the whole stream.

In any endeavor, including healthcare, no one tool will help; it may be necessary to invent one's own. However, just start doing something; even if it is wrong, learn and start again. Because Lean naturally looks at the whole stream or process, it requires a chief process officer (CPO). This person does not have to be managerially locked into the pathway. He or she must report to the chief executive officer (CEO) because the CPO's plans will require major organizational change. Above all, the strategy developed *should not* be formulated around the processes and structure currently in place. One is looking for improvement with a change in the process. So, the old has to be sidetracked and new ways of approaching the process must be thought of. There is another way of viewing this:

- The strategy of a Lean transformation is to create smooth-flowing consumption streams matched up with smooth-flowing provision streams.
- The processes must be reorganized to achieve this.

Organizational structure must change to support the new processes supporting the new strategy. It is a misconception that Lean is a tool or a toolbox. Rather, it is a methodology that provides a way of thinking about work via six principles:

- *Philosophy as the foundation.* Base management decisions on the long-term goal of adding customer value. This is easier said than done when working in regulatory or target cultures, but the audit commission has an interest in Lean and has accepted this principle in other sectors, such as social housing, and allowed councils to "underperform" against target in the understanding that they are embarking on Lean turnarounds

(Steve Mason, Audit Commission, Cranfield Round Table). Maybe the Department of Health (DH) will also change its view? Practical things to do include:

- Change the focus of all board meetings to look at key value streams. All other considerations are secondary, including national performance targets.
- Board members must ask for new-style board reports that inform them on the performance of the whole process from the customer's perspective.
- Board members must devise and promulgate a simple, clear message or mission statement that encapsulates the aims of the Lean transformation that all staff locally understand.
- This is usually intrinsic (i.e., not "we must meet national targets," but rather, "patients will experience no unnecessary waits or errors while in our hospital").

■ *Level out workloads.* Have stability in all work processes so that problems are easily seen and so that continuous improvement is possible. Understand deeply the nature of the demand placed on the process and the capacity it has to meet that demand. Seek to match the two as a basis for all other improvement efforts. Practical things to do include:

- Perform capacity and demand analysis by day or hour or whatever is appropriate, using run charts. Feedback should be given to all relevant managers and reasons for variation discussed.
- Analyze actual versus planned capacity and root-cause reasons for any difference.
- Analyze demand: source, type, urgency, and appropriateness.

■ *Work on flowing work faster and without batching or delays.* Processes should work at the rate of demand placed on them. Queues or waiting lists are signals from a process that this is not happening. Process steps should quickly and automatically signal to each other along the value stream; they should act and think in a coordinated, customer-centric way. Practical things to do include:

- Map the process, adding timings to each step and waiting list counts.
- Involve everyone touching that process and ask why queues develop.
- Look to where demand is coming from and seek to smooth that; eliminate inappropriate demand.
- Foster ownership of a value stream, rather than just process steps, with a value stream group, patient group, chief process owner, and value-stream-oriented reports rather than specialty- or department-oriented reports (i.e., total journey time measurement, demand versus overall capacity reports). For example, anesthetists want patients revived as soon as possible, so they are likely to be motivated to help in flow projects involving improvement in both cycle time and flow.

- *Get quality right the first time.* Stop and fix problems right now. Do not ignore them or invent work-arounds. Management must invite alerts to problems and be prepared to solve them as quickly as possible. Foster a culture of designing-out problems from occurring in the workplace with visual clues, for example. Practical things to do include:
  - Never blame the person; blame the process.
  - Encourage staff to fix the problem and learn and disseminate the information.
  - Have a method agreed to by all staff to report problems easily and quickly.
  - Have an agreed upon escalation protocol so that everyone knows who is responsible for diagnosing and fixing.
  - Enable quick "off-line" testing and remedying.
  - Keep a local problems log and have regular reports on errors and fixes.
  - Advertise successes.
- *Standardize tasks.* This is not to be confused with rigidity. Use standardized procedures simply as the commonly understood base point to improve the process from now on and to ensure sustainability as people move on. Practical things to do include:
  - Standard work does not start with writing, laminating, and hanging up standard work charts. That comes last.
  - Start discussion on what the repeatable, standard elements of work are.
  - Establish a lead person in charge of identifying these, measuring the variation, and investigating why. Do all this from the standpoint of wishing to improve and help the staff have dependable processes.
  - Investigate the relationship between the variation in demand coming in and work processes. Is variation due to the complexity of patients or poor processes (i.e., missing materials, lack of space, etc.)?
- *Grow Lean leaders and managers.* Leaders instill the intrinsic motivation for this new way of thinking. Managers are doing it every day. Managers must be highly visible and near the value-adding work. Managers are there simply to improve the value stream. They should make improvement decisions through consensus and implement swiftly. Practical things to do include:
  - Make other site visits; provide short-term Lean consultant support to management.
  - Encourage study, training, and education in this area.
  - Create a succession plan; aim to keep promising leaders.
  - Improve the management selection process and learn from others doing it well.
  - Encourage experimentation, allow mistakes, and see who takes up that challenge.

A key tenet in Lean thinking is that no matter how many times a process is improved, it can be further enhanced. The idea of perfection rests on the notion of "continual improvement through incremental change based on outcomes" (Tsasis and Bruce-Barrett 2008). Use of the plan-do-study-act cycle helps in pursuing the idea of perfection. In any process improvement initiative using Lean thinking, a small incremental change is recommended based on study of the process. The recommendation is put into place and then studied to determine its impact. If the impact is positive, the change is incorporated in the process, and the cycle begins anew.

Tools Used in Lean

So far we have been talking about the general concepts associated with Lean thinking. In what follows, the discussion will identify the major types of waste that can be found in healthcare processes and describe some of the tools that may be used in process improvement.

Several tools may be used to implement and sustain gains through Lean principles. The reader is encouraged to see Stamatis (1996), Brassard and Ritter (1994), and Tague (2005). Here, we will address six of the most common and most useful. Also, in Appendix B (found on the accompanying CD), we address some additional advanced tools.

5S

Perhaps one of the fundamental issues in Lean is the understanding and application of the 5S philosophy. Anyone who has been involved with quality at any level in the last 15–20 years has at least heard something about the 5S program. Many people refer to it as *the good housekeeping* program, but in reality it is much more than a cleaning program. It is a system of creating and sustaining an organized workplace for the purpose of improving efficiency, productivity, and employee morale (Harkins 2009). Another way of explaining it is to think of it as the first steps to standardization.

To be sure, the methodology and rationale started with manufacturing organizations, but as time has demonstrated, it may be used in all kinds of environments. In healthcare, it is very appropriate to be used in the overall quality initiatives of clinics, labs, hospitals, and physicians' practices because they are susceptible to the accumulations of clutter and inefficiencies that 5S is designed to eliminate.

By integrating the 5S methodology into the healthcare culture, one will see much improvement in the performance of those who work there, while setting an example of excellence for the entire organization to follow. So what is the 5S methodology? Simply put, it is the identification and implementation of five words in the workplace.

Sort (seiri). The rationale for this first word is that clutter is the enemy of any process and clear thinking. If any item is not essential to the day-to-day quality function, it should be removed from the process. Simply put: throw that junk out! To do that, obviously, one must know the process and must be committed to a thorough sorting. Sorting implies separation. This separation must be in two categories: keep or discard. This separation is very critical to an effective 5S program.

In healthcare, much information, material, equipment, and so one are obsolete and yet are kept around just in case they may be needed sometime in the future. In medical labs, it is not unusual to keep obsolete check gauges, documents, mating parts, and prototypes. In physicians' practices, it is not uncommon to find closets and cabinets that house broken gizmos and binders full of dead quality standards, old sample medicine, and other unused items.

Straighten (seiton). The rationale for the second word is an old adage that proclaims: a place for everything, and everything in its place. So, in this phase, the focus is on the lowest level of tasks, which, more often than not, are found on the floor plan. What is done here? All the remaining articles, parts, and so on from the sorting are arranged in a logical and accessible manner.

As a result of removing the nonessentials from the process, many practitioners find that they no longer need many of the racks and cabinets that were used to store these items. This step offers the ideal opportunity to rearrange the flow of the process as well as optimize the flow of people and information.

The idea of this "straighten" is to reinvent a basis for an effective and practical layout of the process and add the tools and visual aids to organize the process contents. This will also facilitate grouping the tools and procedures near where they are most commonly used. Part of this rearrangement includes, but is not limited to, clearly labeling drawers, cabinet doors, and binders and unknotting the nest of cables behind the desks. A good idea for straightening the office, lab, or process is to design a bulletin board visible to all for displaying current and relevant information.

Shine (seiso). The rational for the third word is to make sure that practices become part of an ongoing pattern of cleanliness—in other words, to make sure that this is not a one-time deal. Each person who works in the process, office, or organization should be assigned an area and should keep it neat and organized. As medical staff, nurses, physicians, and other employees maintain their areas, they will develop a sense of ownership and satisfaction. This step is as simple as it sounds. However, it needs commitment from the leadership and management to be successful.

In practice, "straighten" and "shine" largely overlap. Emptying filing cabinets and rearranging furniture provide a convenient time to wash and wax under and behind them. Clean the shelves and countertops. Repaint the walls. Replace the stained and broken ceiling tiles. Strip and wax the floors. Repair the broken handles and hinges. Make the work environment and test area look professional and well groomed. As company executives and/or prospective patients tour the facility, they will see the same precision and consistency employed in the quality of the facility built into every service provided.

Standardize (seiketsu). The rationale for the fourth word is that standardization brings order and consistency. Whereas the first three steps are corrective in nature, the last two are preventive. The step of standardization moves the cleanliness effort upstream by preventing the disorder from occurring in the first place. There are several situations in which this could prove useful by

- Establishing and following procedures for retrieving and returning forms, binders, hand tools, medical records, and so on so that the items get misplaced far less often
- Standardizing best practices for conducting medical tests and issuing first-piece approvals so that tools and equipment are used in a consistent manner that prevents damage and minimizes loss
- Implementing calibration and preventive maintenance programs so that measurement systems remain in a state of readiness.

Standardization builds order into quality-related processes.

Sustain (shitsuke). The rationale for the final word is repeatability and excellence. "Sustain" comes from the Japanese *shitsuke,* which means "a commitment that flows naturally from within." It implies that, by now, the system is in place and everyone has made a commitment to excellence. It also implies that each individual has accountability and responsibility for certain events in the process or organization. Therefore, one can see that even though *sustain* is the last step in the 5S methodology, in reality it is the beginning of the accomplishment of the true goal of continual improvement, in which efficiency, integrity, and diligence are integral to the people who are part of the team. As people committed to these virtues develop quality systems and inspect material and measurement tools, the natural outcome of their work is excellence.

Recently, Munro (2009) and others have added two more "Ss" in the traditional list: safety and oversight.

Safety is the process of avoiding injuries to patients from the care that is intended to help them. This sixth S focuses on eliminating hazards and creating a safe environment in which to work. Once the workplace has been organized and cleaned, potential dangers become easier to recognize. A separate "safety sweep" should be performed to identify, label, and deal with hazards; however, safety measures can also be implemented in conjunction with strategies in the other 5Ss (for example, yellow [safety] tagging can be done at the same time at which red tagging takes place).

Oversight is the process of reviewing care that is provided to patients, to ensure their safety. In the simplest form, oversight is a policy to establish a standard by which direct medical oversight originates and how to access the appropriate source. Oversight programs are designed to identify problems early on so that medical treatment issues can be addressed at the right level and at the right time to make a positive difference. The idea is simple: *Get the patient to the right doctor for the right treatment right away.* Most commonly called utilization management (UM), the actual process is anything but simple and requires the dedicated efforts of many professionals working closely with the same set of marching orders.

As a general rule, treatment plans, specialist referrals, special diagnostic tests, and surgeries are coordinated by case managers or adjusters and approved by key physicians. When questions about the methods or direction of a patient's medical treatment arise, it is the responsibility of the oversight physician to review the file and work with the treating physician or physicians to confirm or redirect the plan of care. This process speaks to the essence of utilization management in a direct and efficient manner, without pitting nurse case managers against doctors in decisions regarding efficacy of care. Oversight emphasizes the use of collaborative teams to address the issue of the patient. Of course, nothing can replace the necessary confidence that each patient must have in his or her doctor's opinions and methods of care. However, nurse case managers can be invaluable and highly cost effective in smoothing the treatment process, solving routine problems, and educating patients in the large and small points regarding their rehabilitation and care.

A very good example of an oversight approach is the countermeasures approach that the Lehigh Valley Health Network system has implemented. The process emphasizes trialing solutions that eventually become very efficient approaches to operations. Good results have been reported in storing and tracking the components on all units at the hospital (Koch 2009).

Value Stream Mapping

The second integral tool used in any Lean approach to improvement is value stream mapping (VSM). It is a technique used to analyze the flow of materials and information currently required to bring a product or service to a customer. The technique was originated at Toyota, and it is known as "material and information flow mapping" (Rother and Shook 1998). Value stream mapping is a helpful method that can be used in Lean environments to identify opportunities for improvement in lead time. Although VSM is often associated with manufacturing, it is also used in logistics, supply chain, service-related industries, healthcare (Graban 2008), software development, and product development.

In a build-to-the-standard form, Shingo (1985, p. 5) suggests that the value-adding steps be drawn across the center of the map and the non-value-adding steps be represented in vertical lines at right angles to the value stream. Thus, the activities become easily separated into the value stream, which is the focus of one type of attention and the "waste" steps of another type. He calls the value stream the process and the non-value streams the operations. The thinking here is that the non-value-adding steps are often preparatory or tidying up to the value-adding step and are closely associated with the person or machine or workstation that executes that value-adding step. Therefore, each vertical line is the "story" of a person or workstation, while the horizontal line represents the "story" of the product or service being created. Typical help for the construction includes:

- Always walk the process while drawing the map. The drawing may be helped with the use of symbols (free download of symbols used in VSM may be found in http://www.ambor.com/public/vsm/vsmfont.html).
- Draw in pencil to allow changes to be made more easily.
- Consult the current process-step owner to understand how the process step is being performed.
- Listen to what the map says and believe it!
- The current state map is just the way we do things today; anything can be changed if the need is strong enough.
- Someone in the business field will figure out how to provide customers with the value they require.

Construction of a VSM

As we already have mentioned, VSM (sometimes called value stream process [VSP]) is a tool commonly used in Lean continual improvement programs to help understand and improve the material and information flow within organizations. VSM is born out of Lean ideology and it captures and presents the whole process from end to end in a method that is easy to understand by those working the process; it captures the current issues and presents a realistic picture.

Through a graphical format that is simple to understand, future state (a diagram showing an improved and altered process) can be formulated and defined. The method encourages a team approach and, through the capture of performance measurement data, provides a mechanism to critique activity constructively. Participants in the activity are encouraged to suggest improvements and contribute toward and implement an action plan.

As with any Lean management tool set, the principal aim of VSM is to improve processes. This is achieved by highlighting areas of waste within a process and therefore enables businesses to eliminate these activities. VSM also has the benefit of categorizing process activity into three main areas:

■ Value add
■ Non-value add (but necessary)
■ Waste

While value stream mapping is not overtly complicated, it does benefit from some preplanning. For example, it is important that a house style is developed using common graphics for use in the diagrams so that everyone participating does so in a common language. This language is usually in the form of symbols that may be found and downloaded from the Web site http://www.ambor.com/public/vsm/vsmfont.html. Table 10.5 has a list of the most common symbols. For a more focused list, see Appendix F. It must be noted here that, specifically for healthcare, although the symbols and concepts are the same, two unique shapes may be substituted: an ambulance instead of a truck and a gurney instead of a push cart.

Furthermore, one needs to ensure that the following are considered and taken into account:

■ Material flow
■ Inventory
■ Buffer stock
■ Suppliers and customers
■ Material transport
■ IT system
■ Information flow

Once these preparations are made, the team is ready for the construction. Typical steps include:

■ *Step 1: Select a sponsor and set expectations.* As with any project, it is important that a sponsor or champion is appointed. This needs to be someone who can make decisions, arbitrate solutions, and plan the project. The sponsor will usually select the processes that will be mapped and will usually have a firm grasp of what achievement is being targeted.
■ *Step 2: Select the team.* The makeup of the VSM team is crucial and it is imperative to adopt a team approach. Each area or stakeholder of the

process should be represented (e.g., medical billing, reception, RNs, PA-Cs, NPs, physicians, radiology, lab, and so on).

■ *Step 3: Select the process to be mapped.* Value stream mapping is suitable for most businesses and can be used in manufacturing, logistics, supply chain, and some service-orientated organizations.

■ *Step 4: Collect data and produce current-state map.* One of the key foundations of VSM is that it utilizes and analyzes business data; this includes process times, inventory or materials information, and customer (or demand) requirements. Do not underestimate the time required to capture reliable data; remember that future-state maps will be developed using information captured here, so it is imperative to have a correct understanding of

Table 10.5   Value Stream Mapping Symbols

VSM process symbols	
Customer/supplier	This icon represents the *supplier* when in the upper left, the usual starting point for material flow. The *customer* is represented when the symbol is placed in the upper right, the usual end point for material flow.
Process Dedicated process	This icon is a process, operation, machine, or department through which material flows. Typically, to avoid unwieldy mapping of every single processing step, it represents one department with a continuous, internal fixed flow path. In the case of assembly with several connected workstations, even if some WIP inventory accumulates between machines (or stations), the entire line would show as a single box. If there are separate operations where one is disconnected from the next, inventory between, and batch transfers, then use multiple boxes.
Process Shared process	This is a process operation, department, or work center that other value stream families share. Estimate the number of operators required for the value stream being mapped, rather than the number of operators required for processing all products.

(Continued)

Table 10.5   Value Stream Mapping Symbols (Continued)

Data box	This icon goes under other icons that have significant information or data requirements for analyzing and observing the system. Typical information placed in a data box underneath factory icons includes the frequency of shipping during any shift, material handling information, transfer batch size, demand quantity per period, etc. Typical information in a data box underneath manufacturing process icons includes: C/T (cycle time)—time (in seconds) that elapses between one part coming off the process to the next part coming off; C/O (changeover time)—time to switch from producing one product on the process to another; uptime—percentage time that the machine is available for processing EPE (a measure of production rates; the acronym stands for "every part, every___"); number of operators—use operator icon inside process boxes; number of product variations available capacity scrap rate transfer batch size (based on process batch size and material transfer rate). In healthcare, more often than not, data boxes will include primarily cycle time, demand, uptime percentage, time between patients, number of personnel (RNs, practical nurses, medical staff, physicians, technologists, and so on), and TAKT time.
Work cell	This symbol indicates that multiple processes are integrated in a particular work cell. Such cells usually process a limited family of similar products or a single product. Product moves from process step to process step in small batches or single pieces.
VSM material symbols	
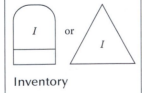Inventory	These icons show inventory between two processes. While mapping the current state, the amount of inventory can be approximated by a quick count, and that amount is noted beneath the triangle. If there is more than one inventory accumulation, use an icon for each. This icon also represents storage for raw materials and finished goods.

Table 10.5 Value Stream Mapping Symbols (Continued)

Shipments	This icon represents movement of raw materials from suppliers to the receiving docks of the facility or the movement of finished goods from the shipping docks of the supplier to customers.
Push arrow	This icon represents the "pushing" of material from one process to the next process. "Push" means that a process produces something regardless of the immediate needs of the downstream process. In healthcare, sometimes this may be shown as a gurney or a push cart.
Supermarket	This is an inventory "supermarket" (kanban stock point). As in a supermarket, a small inventory is available and one or more downstream customers come to the supermarket to pick out what they need. The upstream work center then replenishes stock as required. When continuous flow is impractical and the upstream process must operate in batch mode, a supermarket reduces overproduction and limits total inventory.
Material pull	Supermarkets connect to downstream processes with this "pull" icon that indicates physical removal.
MAX=XX **FIFO lane**	First-in-first-out inventory. Use this icon when processes are connected with a FIFO system that limits input. An accumulating roller conveyor is an example. Record the maximum possible inventory.

(Continued)

Table 10.5 Value Stream Mapping Symbols (Continued)

Safety stock	This icon represents an inventory "hedge" (or safety stock), against problems such as downtime, to protect the system against sudden fluctuations in customer orders or system failures. Notice that the icon is closed on all sides. It is intended as a temporary, rather than a permanent, storage of stock; thus, there should be a clearly stated management policy on when such inventory should be used.
External shipment	Shipments from suppliers or to customers using external transport. In healthcare, this is often replaced with an emergency vehicle.
VSM information symbols	
Production Control Production control	This box represents a central production scheduling or control department, person, or operation.
Daily Manual information	A straight, thin arrow shows general flow of information from memos, reports, or conversation. Frequency and other notes may be relevant.
Monthly Electronic information	This wiggle arrow represents electronic flow such as electronic data interchange (EDI), the Internet, intranets, LANs (local area networks), and WANs (wide area networks). The frequency of information or data interchange, the types of media used (e.g., fax, phone, etc.), and the types of data exchanged may be indicated.
P Production kanban	This icon triggers production of a predefined number of parts. It signals a supplying process to provide parts to a downstream process.

Table 10.5 Value Stream Mapping Symbols (Continued)

Withdrawal kanban	This icon represents a card or device that instructs a material handler to transfer parts from a supermarket to the receiving process. The material handler (or operator) goes to the supermarket and withdraws the necessary items.
Signal kanban	This icon is used whenever the on-hand inventory levels in the supermarket between two processes drop to a trigger or minimum point. When a triangle kanban arrives at a supplying process, it signals a changeover and production of a predetermined batch size of the part noted on the kanban. It is also referred to as "one-per-batch" kanban.
Kanban post	A location where kanban signals reside for pickup; often used with two-card systems to exchange withdrawal and production kanban.
Sequenced pull	This icon represents a pull system that gives instruction to subassembly processes to produce a predetermined type and quantity of product— typically one unit—without using a supermarket.
XOXO Load leveling	This icon is a tool to batch kanbans in order to level the production volume and mix over a period of time.
MRP/ERP	Scheduling using material resources planning (MRP)/enterprise resources planning (ERP) or other centralized systems.

(Continued)

Table 10.5   Value Stream Mapping Symbols (Continued)

Go see	Gathering of information through visual means.
Verbal information	This icon represents verbal or personal information flow.
VSM general symbols	
Kaizen burst	These icons are used to highlight improvement needs and plan kaizen workshops at specific processes that are critical to achieving the future state map of the value stream.
Operator	This icon represents an operator. It shows the number of operators required to process the VSM family at a particular workstation. Sometimes this will be shown as a "stick" figure.
Other Information **Other**	Other useful or potentially useful information.
VA *VA* *NVA* *NVA* *NVA* **Timeline**	The time line shows value-added (cycle) times and non-value-added (wait) times. Use this to calculate lead time and total cycle time.

the business. When the current state is mapped, use icons or graphics to represent each step—the material flow, the information flow, the supplier, and the customer. As part of the map, calculate the total time taken, including both waiting and processing times.

■ *Step 5: Critique current state.* Go mad! Work with the rule that no idea is a bad idea. Use post-it notes or labels to place ideas and possible solutions over the current-state map; encourage everyone to play a part; analyze the data and encourage the team to make suggestions as to how the process could be improved; challenge the current thinking. Comments will usually take the form of suggested improvements, risks, or fixed elements that cannot be altered (e.g., for legal reasons). Above all, look for areas of waste.

■ *Step 6: Map future state.* Taking both the current-state map and the critiques that have been obtained from the previous stages, compile a future-state map. This should incorporate
  – Aligning output and demand at each stage
  – Adequate review of process criticisms from step 3
  – Deployment of key performance indicators (KPIs)

  When the future state is designed, pay close attention to ensure that the process considers the customer requirements. The future-state map should aim for a steady-state production. That is, it should ensure that there are no surplus materials and maximum productivity. Ensure that the map takes the following into account: customer, supplier, material flow, information flow, and so on. The future-state map will normally fall into either a push situation, where goods are produced irrespective of demand, or a pull situation, where goods are produced specifically to demand patterns. Key performance indicators are an important part of the future state, and if they are not already in place, it is necessary to consider what measures are applicable. Remember that mapping the future state does not change the existing process; it is merely a method of graphically representing changes that could be made.

■ *Step 7: Create action plan and deploy.* When the future-state map is being evaluated, consider an action plan that could be implemented to change the current process to the future state. This could be done in a number of ways (e.g., it could be staged in that elements are introduced sequentially, which works well if there is a series of easy-to-introduce changes that can leverage immediate benefits). Another method is a "big bang" approach; for example, the production plant (or the entire practice or the department) could close down on a Friday and all the changes required to implement the future state could be implemented over the weekend and the production team start up the new process in its entirety on Monday morning. There are various options and one should consider one's business to get the best method.

■ *Step 8: Measure benefits.* After the future state has been deployed, after a period of time, a review should be undertaken to ensure that the benefits expected have been obtained. Each change made should be reviewed and the benefits analyzed. Utilize the KPIs deployed at step 4 to provide insight.

Hines and Rich (1997) have identified seven VSM tools. All of them, however, may be used depending on the situation and need to

■ Integrate the data for useful application and results
■ Highlight different issues from the use of different tools
■ Focus on key priorities as the items for improvement

If supply chain response was used individually, its supplier lead time would be identified. However, when data from quality filter mapping are added, on-time delivery would be identified and the appropriate action for improvement may be more optimal.

The Seven VSM Tools

■ *Process activity mapping* is the study of the flow of the processes in a particular patient journey or a process. It is the well known process flowchart; the origins are, of course, in work study and industrial engineering.
■ *Supply chain responsive matrix* is a business term used to describe a tool that is used to analyze inventory and lead time within an organization. The matrix is one of a number of VSM tools. The matrix is represented by showing lead time—the period of time between the initiation of any process and the completion of that process—along the x-axis and inventory along the y-axis. The result shows where slow moving stock resides.
■ *Product variety funnel* is an illustrative tool that shows how the company or supply chain operates:
  – Complexity to be managed
  – Where to target inventory reduction
  – Making changes to processing of products and/or service
  – Gain overview of company or supply chain
■ *Quality filter mapping* is used to analyze processes and functions with respect to quality. The results of a quality filter map show how much waste is being generated within an organization at each stage of the process. The

idea of the filter is to measure in some form (usually as a ratio of parts per million) the three types of quality:

- Product quality—defective item provided to customer
- Defect quality—defective item found prior to receipt by customer
- Service quality—defect that affects the ability of the supplier to provide the service or product to the customer

Results of quality filter mapping are commonly used to feed into continual improvement plans. A revised map is then generated after implementation of improvement plans to measure the result of improvements.

■ *Forrester effect mapping* is a business technique used to analyze the disturbance on the supply chain of reorder activity. The tool is one of the seven VSM tools as defined by Hines and Rich (1997). Forrester's (1961) research showed that demand could be erratic, with peaks and troughs commonplace within most organizations. These variations in requirements and supply are amplified within the supply chain when reorders are made.

■ *Decision point analysis* includes many procedures, methods, and tools for identifying, clearly representing, and formally assessing the important aspects of a decision situation; for prescribing the recommended course of action by applying the maximum expected utility to a well-formed representation of the decision; and for translating the formal representation of a decision and its corresponding recommendation into insight for the decision maker and other stakeholders. Graphical representations of decision analysis problems commonly use influence diagrams and decision trees. Both of these tools represent the alternatives available to the decision maker, the uncertainty they face, and evaluation measures representing how well they achieve their objectives in the final outcome. The decision point is

- The point where actual demand pull gives way to forecast-driven push. We need to know where this point is for two reasons:
  - By knowing where this is, it is possible to assess processes operating downstream and upstream from this point. This will assure a balanced overall operation using the push/pull philosophy.
  - On the other hand, we can also use this knowledge for long-term evaluation of the system. By adjusting or changing the actual demand pull, we can measure various scenarios and see the effects on the value stream.
- The point where products stop being made according to actual demand and are made against forecast only.

■ *Overall structure maps* show supply chain industry level and help to
- Understand how the industry (office or facility) operates

- Bring attention to areas that may not receive sufficient developmental attention, focusing on various tiers both in supplier and distribution area, with assembler as middle point
- Depict number of organizations (departments) involved—area of each part is proportional to how many organizations (departments) are in it (This is similar to volume structure. That is, area of diagram is directly linked to value-adding process [cost-adding process] and makes it possible to analyze value adding required in the final product as it is sold or serviced.)

A classical, simple VSM is shown in Figure 10.5 (current state) and Figure 10.6 (future state). Obviously, some processes can be much more complicated.

The details of these sample maps are less important than the ideas they represent. The format of a value stream map can vary according to the mapmakers' preferences. The important thing about a value stream map is that it is explicit about the flow and value of the process.

Using the future-state value stream map, the group reorganizes staff if necessary to match the requirements of the process. Notice that most processes flow horizontally, while most organizations are organized vertically. This is a fundamental challenge because the process must flow across organizational impediments and boundaries. A patient's journey from a diagnostic center to a treatment facility would be an example of this.

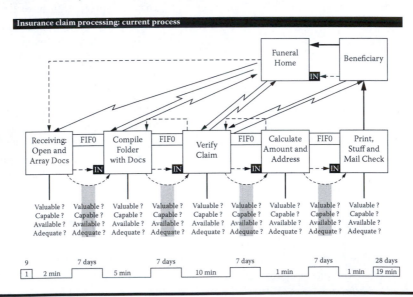

Figure 10.5   Current VSM of an insurance claim process.

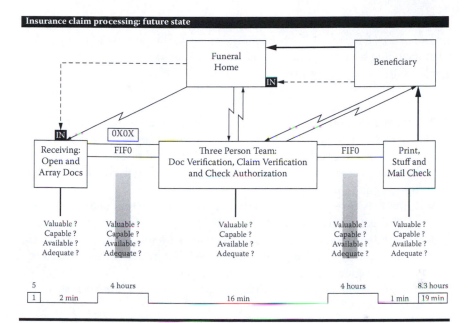

Figure 10.6   Example of a future-state VSM of an insurance claim process.

In the insurance claim case shown, we see that even though the cycle time remained the same (19 minutes), the total process time was reduced from 28 days to 8.3 hours. This is a tremendous improvement (337%), especially for the beneficiary waiting for a payment.

Quick Changeover—SMED Setup Reduction

Single minute exchange of die (SMED) is one of the many Lean production methods for reducing waste in a manufacturing process. It provides a rapid and efficient way of converting a manufacturing process from running the current product to running the next product. This rapid changeover is key to reducing production lot sizes and thereby improving flow (*mura*—the Japanese term, as opposed to *muda,* which is waste). In his classic book, Shingo ([1981] translated into English in 1989), defined the phrase "single minute" as a concept rather than a hard point timing a measurable characteristic. It other words, single minute does not mean that all changeovers and startups should take only 1 minute, but rather that they should take less than 10 minutes (in other words, "single digit minute").

To be sure, the SMED was originally thought of as a manufacturing tool; over the years, however, it has been proved to be very applicable in many industries, including healthcare. In all situations, the original seven steps that Shingo identified to reduce changeover time are applicable:

- Observe the current methodology.
- Separate the internal and external activities. Internal activities are those that can only be performed when the process is stopped; external activities can be done while the last batch is being produced or once the next batch has started. For example, go and get the required tools for the job before the machine stops.
- Convert (where possible) internal activities into external ones (preheating of tools is a good example of this).
- Streamline the remaining internal activities by simplifying them. Focus on fixings: Shigeo Shingo rightly observed that it is only the last turn of a bolt that tightens it; the rest is just movement.
- Streamline the external activities so that they are of a similar scale to the internal ones.
- Document the new procedure and actions that are yet to be completed.
- Do it all again. For each iteration of this process, a 45% improvement in setup times should be expected, so it may take several iterations to cross the 10-minute line.

In addition to the steps, Shingo (1989, p. 47) recognizes eight techniques that should be considered in implementing SMED:

- Separating internal from external setup operations
- Converting internal to external setup
- Standardizing function, not shape
- Using functional clamps or eliminate fasteners altogether
- Using intermediate jigs
- Adopting parallel operations
- Eliminating adjustments
- Mechanizing

Specifically in healthcare, applications are everywhere. A good possible list for using SMED would include:

- Shortages, mistakes, inadequate verification of equipment causing delays that can be avoided by check tables, especially visual ones, and setup on an intermediary jig

- Inadequate or incomplete repairs to equipment causing rework and delays
- Optimization for least work as opposed to least delay
- Unheated tools, which require several wasted "tests" before they will be at the temperature to work
- Using slow, precise adjustment equipment for the large, coarse part of adjustment
- Lack of visual lines or benchmarks for part placement on the equipment
- Forcing a changeover between different raw materials when a continuous feed, or near equivalent, is possible
- Lack of functional standardization—that is, standardization of only the parts necessary for setup (e.g., all bolts use same size spanner, die grip points are in the same place on all dies)
- Much operator movement around the equipment during setup
- More attachment points than are actually required for the forces to be constrained
- Attachment points that take more than one turn to fasten
- Any adjustments after initial setup
- Any use of experts during setup
- Any adjustments of assisting tools such as guides or switches

The standard work combination sheet is the ideal Lean tool for setup reduction. The goal again is to minimize cycle time by

- reducing total setup time
- moving any tasks
  - *from* "internal setup time" (happening during the normal process cycle)
  - *to* "external setup time" (happening before or after the normal process cycle)

SMED Example

A doctor's office visit might take a lot longer if the healthcare provider was wasting time changing out bed sheets and restocking supplies after the patient arrived—rather than arranging for all of that to be done before the patient ever walked into the exam room. Table 10.6 shows a typical form that may be used to track the work.

Office Examples

Setup reduction is needed for every industry, including healthcare and administration—not just manufacturing. Obvious and very simple examples of office changeovers might include but not be limited to

Table 10.6 Typical Standard Work Form

Logo of Physician's Practice

Process: Patient Visit		Version:			Comments	New Operator Cycle Time
Author: Caitlyn Stamatis		Date:				
Sequence	Work Steps	Time				
		Walk	Work	Wait		
1	Replace exam table sheet	2	0.5		X	
2	Empty trash		0.5		X	
3	Set up tubes		1		X	
4	Sterilize equipment		1		X	
5	Calibrate monitors		2		X	
6	Position monitors		0.5		X	
7	Interview patient		5			
8	Examine patient		5			
9	Load x-ray machine	0.5	1			

10	Take x-rays		2			
11	Wait for x-ray processing			2		
12	Interpret x-rays		1			
13	Answer patient questions		2			
14	Write prescription		1			
15	Document chart		2			
16	Handle billing	2	8		X	
17	Schedule next appointment		3		X	
Totals		4.5	35.5	2		

(Continued)

Table 10.6   Typical Standard Work Form (Continued)

	Logo of Physician's Practice		Comments	New Operator Cycle Time
Process: Patient Visit		*Version:*		
Author: Caitlyn Stamatis		*Date:*		
Sequence	*Work Steps*	*Time*		
	Working time available per shift (8 h × 60 min) − (30 min lunch + 30 min breaks)	420	Minutes	
	Demand per shift	14	Minutes	
	TAKT time (420/14)	30	Minutes	
	Cycle time (items 35.5 − 6.5)	29	Minutes	
	Long cycle time means: fewer patients and therefore less money			
	Items 1–6 and 16 and 17 have the potential of improvement by doing the tasks externally			
	New operator cycle time : Recalculate (remeasure) to see what happened after the change			

- The time it takes to change printer paper (or envelopes)
- The time it takes to start up a computer or to open a computer application and get to the needed screen

In any healthcare and administrative situation office, changeover time can also be hidden within more subtle tasks, such as

- The time it takes to change from one computer screen to another
- The reacclimation time it takes to change an office worker's focus from one task to another (just ask any "thinking" worker about the quality and productivity effects of frequent interruptions)

Theory of Constraints

Goldratt's (1990) theory of constraints (TOC) has been seen as having a conflicting approach to Lean. However, we believe that TOC can work in conjunction with Lean to provide focus and improvement. For example, working together, TOC will identify potential improvements that will make a big difference. On the other hand, Lean can then target them for waste reduction. TOC provides focus for improvement. When TOC and Lean work together, they provide useful tools and techniques that enable clear understanding of the system and its dependencies. Again, TOC helps to identify and quantify the opportunities for improvement and together with Lean encourages a pull rather than a push system.

Kanban

Ohno (1988) and Shingo (1989) emphasize that in order to be effective, kanban must follow strict rules of use. But rules alone are not good enough. That these rules must be closely monitored for improvement is indeed a never-ending problem to ensure that kanban does what is required. Toyota's six rules are

- Do not send defective products to the subsequent process.
- The subsequent process comes to withdraw only what is needed.
- Produce only the exact quantity withdrawn by the subsequent process.
- Equalize production.
- Kanban is a means to fine tuning.
- Stabilize and rationalize the process.

Push versus Pull

Pull has been described as "performing work as it is requested or needed by a step in a value stream" (Bushell, Mobley, and Shelest 2002). This is the opposite of push technology, where a product can be created when there is little or no demand. Push processes can lead to large inventories and related costs to maintain them.

Push leads to steps in a service being performed out of order if a next step in the process is not ready. For example, during the transfer of a baby from a surgical suite to a neonatal intensive care unit (NICU), if the baby arrives at the NICU and the respirator and the respiratory therapist are not waiting for the patient, there is a problem. The baby has been pushed to the NICU without the appropriate services and staff on hand to provide appropriate care.

Pull works to ensure that the respirator, respiratory therapist, and charge nurse are ready and waiting when the baby arrives in the NICU. The pull system is based on a concrete order for the customer requirements. It is a central planning approach that determines and disseminates operation schedules to all processes simultaneously (see Figure 10.7). In addition, a pull system offers the following:

- Operation control that is visible and disciplined—typically with the use of kanbans
- Material that is also controlled with the use of kanbans to replenish the system and determine proper inventory levels
- Systems to control inventory and make the operator's indirect work manageable
- Lead time that is based on the customer's rather than the process's need
- Predictable lead time to the customer

Things to consider with such a system include:

- How much to order
- When to order
- Where to keep the stock

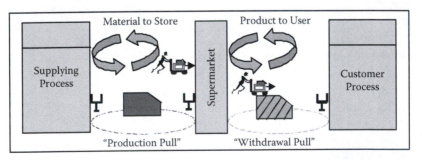

Figure 10.7   A typical pull system.

- How much stock to have
- How much service to offer
- When the service should be offered
- At what point in the process the schedule should be sent

Characteristics include:

- Product delivered when needed
- Low levels of waste

Push, on the other hand, is an approach where one goes to the preceding process to withdraw the necessary units in the necessary quantity at the necessary time. The preceding process produces only enough units to replace those that have been withdrawn. The operation schedule is determined by one process (the pacemaker). Key characteristics include:

- Product delivered late
- High levels of waste
- Low productivity

In relation to Lean, the following Japanese terms are also used:

- *Chaku chaku:* a single-piece process in which a worker takes the piece from one workstation to the next and sets up and operates each machine from beginning to end of the cycle
- *Hanedashi:* auto-eject devices that unload the part from the machine once the cycle is complete. This allows the operators to go from one machine to the next, picking up and loading. This is a key component of chaku-chaku lines.
- *Jidoka:* as practiced at Toyota, this has several meanings. It may mean "automation with human intelligence" (autonomation). Jidoka also refers to the practice of stopping a manual line or process when something goes amiss. The purpose is to free equipment from the necessity of constant human attention, separate people from machines, and allow workers to staff multiple operations.
- *Heijunka:* operation leveling: the overall leveling of the operation schedule in terms of the item produced over time. What is required is a pacing system to establish rhythm—something like AABBCCAA. The reasons for leveling are that it
  - Allows effective use of people, equipment, material
  - Reduces variation between processes

- Reduces lead time and inventory
- Offers quicker response to the changes in customer requirements

Kaizen

This is Toyota's famous tool for continual improvement. The idea is all employees in the organization reexamine their work and improve it in small ways within their control (Imai 1986). The Toyota production system (TPS) is known for kaizen, where all line personnel are expected to stop their moving production line in case of any abnormality and, along with their supervisor, suggest an improvement to resolve the abnormality, which may initiate a kaizen. There are five main elements of kaizen:

- Teamwork
- Personal discipline
- Improved morale
- Quality circles
- Suggestions for improvement

The cycle of the kaizen is to

- Standardize an operation
- Measure the standardized operation (find cycle time and amount of in-process inventory)
- Gauge measurements against requirements
- Innovate to meet requirements and increase productivity
- Standardize the new, improved operations
- Continue the cycle *ad infinitum*

This cycle, of course, is also known as the Shewhart cycle (PDCA) or Deming cycle (PDSA). Minikaizens are like raindrops that add up to make a flood. This Lean concept is quite useful and easy for management to implement, primarily because it may be used in very small steps.

A Final Note for the Lean Discussion

We have emphasized the importance of knowing the process. However, to know that process, we must make a conscious effort to go to the source—going to the *gemba* ("the actual place"—sometimes spelled *gamba*). Furthermore, it means:

- The actual work center
- The actual thing (gembutsu)
- The actual facts (gemjitsu)
- The actual people
- Getting out there to see what is going on
- Analysis utilizing the gemba principle
- Go to the gemba: speak with the data and the processes

The reader will notice that by going to the gemba, the information will be accurate and without a filter. In essence, the person (or team) in charge for the investigation will be able to

- Collect the data based on the six fundamental principles of any investigation:
  - What
  - Why
  - When
  - Who
  - Where
  - How
- Draw a map
- Evaluate data: evaluation means some kind of measurement and resolution (action) based on what was found. Typical measurements are process time, cycle time, and TAKT time:
  - Process time = the total time to complete a task (including both value- and non-value-added functions)
  - Cycle time = the total time to complete the task (including *only* value-added functions)
  - TAKT time = the time that defines how frequently a product must be finished in order to meet customer requirements; it is calculated as TAKT time = available time/customer demand, where available time = 24 hours minus all scheduled delays and customer demand is determined based on statistical analysis and/or historical data for a period of time and specific function.

The reader should not be confused with the different spelling of TACT versus TAKT. In both cases, the calculations are the same. However, TACT is used to identify the original or calculated time based on some historical or theoretical basis. On the other hand, TAKT is the actual calculation of time based on the process under study.

Summary

In this chapter, we discussed in detail the concept of Lean and we provided some specific tools for the application in a given process. We focused on the 5S, SMED, VSM, kanban, kaizen, TOC, and pull-and-push approaches to improvement. In the next chapter, we focus on measurement.

References

Brassard, M., and D. Ritter. 1994. *The memory jogger II*. Salem, NH: GOAL/QPC.

Bushell, S., J. Mobley, and B. Shelest. 2002. Discovering Lean thinking at Progressive Healthcare. *Journal for Quality and Participation* 25 (2): 21.

Forrester, J. 1961. *Industrial dynamics*. Waltham, MA: Pegasus Communications.

Goldratt, E. 1990. *Theory of constraints*. Great Barrington, MA: North River Press.

Graban, M. 2008. *Lean hospitals*. New York: Productivity Press.

Harkins, R. 2009. Count on the 5S improvement method in the lab. *Quality Progress* August: 72.

Hines, P., and N. Rich 1997. The seven value stream mapping tools. *International Journal of Production and Operations Management* 17 (1): 44–62.

Imai, M. 1986. *Kaizen: The key to Japan's competitive success*. New York: Random House.

Koch, A. November 2009. Countermeasure = "experiments." *CheckUP.* A Lehigh Valley Health Network Publication, p. 4.

Liker, J. and D. Meier. 2005. *The Toyota Way Fieldbook*. New York: McGraw-Hill.

Munro, R. 2009. *Lean Six Sigma for the healthcare practice*. Milwaukee, WI: Quality Press.

Ohno, T. June 1988. *Toyota production system—Beyond large-scale production*. New York: Productivity Press.

Rother, M., and J. Shook 1998. *Learning to see: Value-stream mapping to create value and eliminate muda*. Brookline, MA: The Lean Enterprise Institute.

Shingo, S. 1985. *A revolution in manufacturing: The SMED system*. New York: Productivity Press.

———. 1981. *A study of the Toyota production system from an industrial engineering viewpoint*. Translated in 1989. Portland OR: Productivity Press.

Stamatis, D. H. 1996. *Total quality service*. Boca Raton, FL: St. Lucie Press.

Tague, N. 2005. *The quality tool box*. Milwaukee, WI: Quality Press.

Tsasis, P., and C. Bruce-Barrett. 2008. Organizational change through Lean thinking. *Health Services Management Research* 21 (2): 192.

Womack, J. P., and D. T. Jones. 1996. *Lean thinking: Banish waste and create wealth in your corporation*. New York: Simon & Schuster.

Selected Bibliography

Amberg, M. April 1996. The benefits of business process modeling for specifying workflow-oriented application systems. *Business Information Systems*. Bamberg, Germany: University of Bamberg, pp. 1–6.

Barry-Walker, J. 2002. The impact of systems redesign on staff, patient, and financial outcomes. *Journal of Nursing Administration* 30: 77–89.

Burns, L. R., and Wharton School colleagues. 2002. *The health care value chain: Producers, purchasers and providers.* San Francisco, CA: Jossey–Bass.

Chyna, J. T. 2001. Reengineering your medical staff organization: Care, efficiency and relationships. *Healthcare Executive* 16 (4): 20–25.

Drescher, N. I. 2000. Redesign of medication and supply distribution in a day surgery center. *AORN Journal* 72: 854–861.

Fraser, S. W. 2002. *The patient's journey: Mapping, analyzing and improving healthcare processes.* Chichester, England: Kingsham Press.

Gaucher, E. J., and R. J. Coffey. 2002. *Breakthrough performance: Accelerating the transformation of health care organizations.* San Francisco, CA: Jossey–Bass.

Guarisco, S., E. Oddone, and D. Simel. 1994. Time analysis of a general medicine service. *Journal of General Internal Medicine* 9: 272–277.

Hyatt, J. 2009. Keen to be Lean. *CFO* December: 44–46.

Institute for Healthcare Improvement. 2003. *Optimizing patient flow: Moving patients smoothly through acute care settings* (Innovation Series white paper). Boston, MA: Institute for Healthcare Improvement.

Kelly, K., M. Mass, and J. Sona. 1995. *Health care work redesign.* Thousand Oaks, CA: Sage Publications.

Kenagy, J. W. 2004. *Delivering on the promise: An adaptive approach to information technology in healthcare.* Cambridge, MA: Kenagy & Associates.

Lillrank, P., and J. Kujal. 2003. Patient in process—A new approach to managing patient processes in healthcare. *3rd International Conference on the Management of Healthcare and Medical Technology.* Warwick, United Kingdom, September 7–9.

Litvak E., M. Long, and A. Cooper. 2001. Emergency department diversion: Causes and solutions. *Academic Emergency Medicine* 8 (11): 1108–1110.

Long, J. C. 2003. Healthcare Lean. *Michigan Health and Hospitals* 39 (4): 54–55.

Mangum, S., and K. Cutler. 2002. Increased efficiency through OR redesign and process simplification. *AORN Journal* 76 (6): 1041–1046.

Martin, L., F. Gertsen, and J. Johansen. 2003. Applying Lean thinking in hospitals—Exploring implementation difficulties. *3rd International Conference on the Management of Healthcare and Medical Technology,* Warwick, United Kingdom, September 7–9.

Minichiello, T., A. Auerbach, and R. Wachter. 2001. Caregiver perceptions of the reasons for delayed hospital discharge. *Effective Clinical Practice* 4 (6): 250–255.

O'Sullivan, K. 2009. All eyes on reform. *CFO* December: 38–43.

Panchak, P. November 1, 2003. Lean health care? It works! *Industry Week,* 1–5.

Quintero, J. R. 2002. Achieve cost benefits with innovative care management. *Nursing Management* 33 (4): 35–42.

Reid, W. 2004. Developing and implementing organizational practice that delivers better, safer care. *Quality and Safety in Health Care* 13 (4): 247–248.

Rich, N., A. Esain, N. Bateman, L. Massey, and D. Samuel. 2006. *Lean evolution: Lessons from the workplace.* Cambridge, England: Cambridge University Press.

Rozich, J., and R. Resar. 2002. Using a unit assessment tool to optimize patient flow and staffing in a community hospital. *Joint Commission Journal on Quality Improvement* 28 (1): 31–41.

Siegel, E., and B. Reiner. 2002. Work flow redesign: The key to success when using PACS. *American Journal of Roentgenology* 178: 563–566.

Spaite, D., F. Bartholomeaux, J. Guisto, et al. 2002. Rapid process redesign in a university-based emergency department: Decreasing waiting tine intervals and improving patient satisfaction. *Annals of Emergency Medicine* 39 (2): 168–177.

Steckler, A., and L. Linnan. 2002. *Process evaluation for public health interventions and research.* San Francisco, CA: Jossey–Bass.

Stryer, D., and C. Clancy. 2003. Boosting performance measure for measure. *British Medical Journal* 326 (7402): 1278–1279.

Thomson American Health Consultants. 2003. Make these changes to cut delays, diversion hours. *ED Management* 15: 64–65.

Walley, P. 2003. Cellular operation design in healthcare. *3rd International Conference on the Management of Healthcare and Medical Technology,* Warwick, United Kingdom, September 7–9.

Ying, A. n.d. *Impact of hospital computer systems on resident work hours.* Boston, MA: Medical Records Institute.

Chapter 11

Understanding Measurement

Introduction

In the last chapter, we discussed the concept of Lean and provided some specific tools for improvement. In this chapter, we focus on measurement. Specifically, we will explain why measurement is important and how it can be used in the healthcare industry. Standard and Davis (1999) have suggested:

> Performance measurements are much more than a way to monitor work efficiency and departmental output. They actually influence the way an organization operates and the way people do their jobs. Performance measures affect what kind of culture the organization develops, what attitudes people have, what approach is used to solve problems, what behaviors are encouraged and rewarded, and what decisions are made from the actual job function to boardroom. Essentially, what you measure is what you get.

There are many measures that a given organization may have. However, the measures that are selected must link to the business and objectives of the organization. Traditional measures that are used by most organizations fall in categories that

- Focus on financial reporting
- Focus on minimizing variance

- Focus on short-term cost reduction
- Do not necessarily tie in with the needs of the customer
- Do not relate to most employees
- May not align with strategic goals

The hoshin approach is one of the good ways to identify and define measurable indicators based on three priorities. The first priority helps to

- Focus on the vital few strategic gaps
- Create a link between the organizational goals, key objectives, and improvement activities
- Create measurements that are developed from the policy deployment process
- Focus on meeting the daily operation target with the expected level of quality (first priority)
- Identify the consequences of not meeting these targets and amplify them throughout the process
- Focus on the root causes—a *must*

Unless these six items have been thought out and defined with a common "operational definition," all other measurements are meaningless. If they have and everyone agrees, now we can move to the second priority, which focuses on lead times. This will help us to

- Focus on lead time reduction
- Deliver a response that is a competitive weapon

We can do this by focusing on

- Reducing waste
- Eliminating inventory
- Having one-piece flow
- Reducing changeovers
- Having cellular operations (minimizing flow)

Now that we have an alignment with the organizational objectives (first priority) and have agreed on waste reduction (second priority), we are ready to tackle the third priority, which is reducing variation. The idea of reducing variation is the cornerstone of improvement because it (1) is the root of many problems, and (2) focuses on reducing variability in all forms of the process. The significance of this is that being able to reduce variation will lead to more robust systems and therefore better efficiency and, ultimately, better profitability.

In healthcare, just as in any other organization, to identify measurements seems a Herculean task. To make it easy, let us split the organization into levels and identify within each of the levels some measurements that may benefit each one.

Level I (System or Hospital)

A healthcare system has multiple facilities that report their overall numbers in common categories, such as financial (e.g., total admits, total outpatient visits, cost per case, cost per visit, operating margin, net revenue, case mix index), quality (such as methicillin-resistant *Staphylococcus aureus* [MRSA] patients, adverse effects, falls, medication errors, decubitus, postsurgical infection rate, number of codes), service (such as cycle times, registration errors, inappropriate patient transfers, ED patients "left without being seen" or "left against medical advice"), and satisfaction (for customers, staff, and physicians).

The system (or corporate) level measures are usually characterized as "output" measures. For example, a financial output measure might be "growth." A quality output measure might be "on-time starts for OR." All organizations are unique and should design the appropriate measurement levels to serve their needs. If three levels are not enough, add one. If three levels are too many, take one away.

Level II (Departments)

Each department's staff must consider the level I balanced scorecard when developing their departmental measurements. This "departmental scorecard" can be identical to the level I main categories with subcategories or, more likely, will include some department-specific items. For example, in the ED, the following measurements may be identified: door to doc (from when the patient arrives at the ED to when he or she is first seen by the doctor), doc to dispo (from when the patient is first seen by the doctor to when the patient's disposition has been determined), and dispo to depart (from when the disposition has been determined until treatment has been completed in the ED or the patient is admitted for continued care) cycle times; ED volume; ED admits; return visits for same complaint; etc. Operating room level II measurements may include the following: on-time first case starts, on-time subsequent case starts, close to cut for room turnover, on-time case completions, overtime for anesthesia staff, overtime for nurse staff, etc.

Some additional measures for either level I or level II include:

- *Financial:* overall net revenue growth, cost of care experience (across continuum), operating margin, cost per case for inpatients, revenue per case, cost per encounter for outpatients, case mix index, percent paid overtime, length of stay, uncompensated care, bad debt, reimbursement percent, Medicare percent
- *Quality:* percent adherence to practice guidelines (or clinical bundles), use of dangerous abbreviations, medication errors
- *Service:* appointment timeliness, missed appointments, on-time appointments for outpatient visits, community sponsored activities per quarter
- *Customer satisfaction:* patient satisfaction, patient satisfaction mean score, complaints
- *Associate satisfaction:* work environment survey (WES), WES mean score, voluntary turnover, vacancy rate, physician satisfaction, physician satisfaction mean score
- *Leadership development:* internal promotion rate, leadership class attendance, 360 survey mean score, percent top performance evaluation score, employee involvement in Lean events, percentage of staff trained in Lean healthcare

If it is necessary to drill down even further, we may go to level III or more as appropriate.

Level III (Operational Issues)

Operational measurements can become a team's measure for a Lean project, with specifically defined targets. For example:

- Surgical services
  - *Financial:* cost per case (total, labor, supplies, and equipment), revenue per case, revenue per physician, overtime by job title, contribution margin, instrument loss rate
  - *Quality:* surgical site verification and time-outs, postsurgical infection rates, surgical complications, percent unplanned postsurgical admissions, adverse event log
  - *Service:* first case on-time starts, case turnaround time, ED-to-OR time for surgical consult cases, average time to board, percent boarding discrepancies, percent emergency boarding requests
  - *Customer satisfaction:* same as level II, at department level

- *Associate satisfaction:* same as level II, at department level
- *Leadership:* same as level II, at department level

■ ED
  - *Financial:* cost per case, revenue per case, overtime by job title, physician billables, time to close chart, rate of admission, percent payment of deductibles or co-pays on site
  - *Quality:* abandoned rate (seen by doctor, left before being discharged), ED referrals to network physicians, ED repeat visits for same complaint
  - *Service:* left without being seen, average time door to doc, average time doc to dispo, average time dispo to depart, average time dispo to admit
  - *Customer satisfaction:* same as level II, at department level
  - *Associate satisfaction:* same as level II, at department level
  - *Leadership:* same as level II, at department level

■ Billing and coding
  - *Financial:* average bill per case by DRG (diagnosis-related group), average time to code chart, potential lost revenue (incorrect or incomplete documentation), cash balances, charges, accounts receivable, collection ratios
  - *Quality:* rejection rate by reason, compliance percent reimbursement, clean claim rate
  - *Service:* average time to code chart
  - *Customer satisfaction:* same as level II, at department level
  - *Associate satisfaction:* same as level II, at department level
  - *Leadership:* same as level II, at department level

■ Facility management
  - *Financial:* cost per square foot (labor and other), utility costs, facility costs as a percent of operating cost
  - *Quality:* problem log, equipment failure reports, improper processing reports, facility condition index
  - *Service:* average time to respond to requests, average time to request completion, complaints, work orders overdue, inventory levels for specific items
  - *Customer satisfaction:* same as level II, at department level
  - *Associate satisfaction:* same as level II, at department level
  - *Leadership:* same as level II, at department level

Once we have identified what to measure, we then have to understand variation, how to measure, and what we should know about measurement in general.

In measuring any process, there are two common reasons why measurements are made: an ongoing monitoring measurement or a more specific, investigative one.

Monitoring Measurements

Monitoring measurements act as indicators of the general health of the process, much as temperature gives an overall indication of the health of the human body. The measurement is made over a long period so that trends and variation can be understood and points where specification limits or target values are exceeded may be identified. Several considerations should be taken into account when identifying monitoring measurements:

- The measurement should identify the presence of problems, but not necessarily the cause. Breadth is thus more important than depth.
- The measurement should not be intrusive or upset the process in any way because objective decisions can only be made through independent observation.
- Each measurement should be repeatable and made under similar conditions so that each may be compared on an equal footing.
- It should be possible for measurements to be made on a regular basis. This is easy when the process repeats frequently and difficult when it does not. Because it is made frequently, the measurement should be relatively inexpensive and easy to perform.

Investigative Measurements

Investigative measurements are made specifically to find out more about known problems or causes. This may be likened to specific medical tests such as measuring blood pressure. The limited nature of an investigative measurement means that it may differ from monitoring measurement in several ways:

- The measurement may be intrusive.
- The cost of measurement is not particularly important.
- Many different measurements may be made in which each measurement covers a specific area in more detail.

Information gathered may be of two broad types: quantitative or qualitative. Each has its value and they may be gathered and treated quite separately. Quantitative information, the easiest type of information to measure and use, is a numeric quantity. Numbers are precise and help in making clear decisions.

Tools that use quantitative data often work by using a combination of mathematical calculation and comparison of numbers against one another or against a fixed and critical value. Quantitative data are not always available and not always sufficient.

Qualitative information, on the other hand, is non-numeric and typically appears as written text. This often comes in "chunks" in which a phrase or sentence describes a single, independent piece of information (good, bad, etc.). Tools that use qualitative data typically organize and structure these chunks relative to one another, thus revealing further information. Often, a situation is best described by a combination of numeric and non-numeric information, where the qualitative text helps to put the quantitative numbers into context—for example, describing who was using a machine, where, under what conditions, etc.

When what to measure is being identified, two main types of data should be taken into consideration because each has applications for which it is more useful:

- *Attributes*. One of the simplest measurements that can be made in many situations is to count the number of items in a particular classification, such as the number of patients admitted through the emergency room. This attribute measurement answers the question "how many" and its simplicity often makes it a good starting point, with variable measurement being used when the problem area has been more narrowly identified. Attributes are a good way of turning qualitative data into quantitative data—for example, by counting employees who think they are significantly underpaid.
- *Variables*. Beyond attribute measurement is variable measurement, where the question "how much" is asked. Variable measurements have units, such as centimeters and kilograms and also usually require more effort to collect than attributes. The actual measurement usually requires the use of some form of measuring instrument.

In any measurement, several components must be taken into account when deciding what to measure. In healthcare, one of the critical measurement components is the *unit*. It is critical because just about everything from a simple dosage of medication to the size of incision will be made in some kind of unit. These should reflect the range of possible values; for example, it is probably better to measure the length of an incision in millimeters rather than centimeters. Clearly stating the units to be used prevents situations where different people use different units and cause confusion in calculations and displays.

Scale is another issue of measurement. Many measurements are made in the form of numbers because this is an absolute and flexible format, and the scale is simply the possible range of measured values. In some situations, however, numbers are not so useful—for example, when identifying the possible actions of a customer upon finding a defective product. In this case, the measurement scale is typically made up of a defined and discrete set of values. This can be useful when numbers are unclear, and it is easier to describe satisfaction as "high" or "low" rather than as "1" or "5."

Target is also an issue of measurement. There is often a target or goal value for the measurement. This may be a center value about which the measurement varies or a distant target that is to be achieved. The measurement can thus be usefully expressed as a difference from this ideal, rather than as an absolute value. We call this difference "variance."

Limits are yet another component of measurement. As well as a target value, there is often some kind of action limit, beyond which the measurement should not go. If the measured value falls outside such specification limits (customer dependent), then some kind of action may be defined, such as rejection of the measured item or an investigation into the cause of failure. On the other hand, it is desirable to beat target values.

Tool is the item that facilitates measurement. After all, the measurement may be made using some kind of measuring device. It is essential that this tool be accurate and reliable because an uncertain measuring tool will result in worthless measurement values. Measurement tools include all methods of gathering data, from voltmeters to surveys. Each has constraints in use and the data given must be of a known accuracy to enable confident decisions to be made. Calibration and verification as well as validation are also part of this "tool" environment.

If the measurement *process* is clear and well defined, then each measurement can be made in a consistent way, enabling successive values to be compared. Detailing the process also puts into perspective the actual work that has to be done to collect the data and enables the requisite time and resource to be scheduled. Details of the measurement process may include:

■ Who is doing the measuring and how to be sure that person knows what to do
■ When the measurement is done, including times, events, and frequencies
■ What is to be measured, including items and sampling rules
■ What tools are to be used, including calibration details
■ How the measurements are recorded, including design of check sheets
■ What is to be done with the completed data, including storage and actions

When measures are taken, several approaches can help to ensure that the correct data are selected and collected in a way that helps with the subsequent analysis. When a problem is investigated, a single general measurement is often insufficient and can cloak useful information. By measuring the situation in a number of different ways (stratifying or segmenting it), one or more "cuts" may reveal new information that will allow specific corrective action to be identified, as in Figure 11.1. Common measurements used in stratifying data include:

- Raw materials and completed products
- Machines and tools
- People
- Processes and the actions within them
- Time
- External factors, such as temperature and season

For example, a customer support organization counts the number of calls about each discharged patient for his or her satisfaction and finds that more calls are made from the neurology department than anywhere else. They have identified a problem, but cannot find out why without more measurements. They therefore stratify the calls by taking intrusive measures, asking customers questions about suspected causes, such as the type of problem (stroke, headache, epileptic seizures, etc.), customer information (age, occupation, etc.), whether or not they are following the rules of discharge, and so on.

In order to know exactly how a set of measured items behaves, they must all be measured, such as when determining the distribution of the values of a batch of a blood pressure drug study. However, this is seldom possible, for several possible reasons: (1) There is a significant cost in measurement—for example, when there are a large number of items or when it takes a long time to measure each;

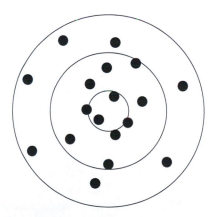

Figure 11.1   Variation in targeted results.

(2) not all items may be available for measurement; (3) there may always be more items (an infinite population); or (4) measuring the item effectively destroys it.

In such cases, a limited *sample* from which the characteristics of all other items (the population) are deduced may be measured. In order to be able to do this reliably, two factors must be taken into account:

- The sample must be large enough to contain a representative set of items from the population, to enable an accurate extrapolation for all other items.
- The sample must be selected entirely at random, to ensure that no biases (intended or not) result in an incorrect picture of the rest of the population.

Most tool descriptions identify the sizes of samples that need to be taken to ensure a representative sample, so knowledge of statistics is not essential, although a deeper understanding in this area (or access to someone with this knowledge) can be very useful. (For more information on sampling calculations, see the Selected Bibliography at the end of this chapter.)

When data are measured, it is important that the accuracy of the data be maintained through careful measurement and accurate instruments. This is best achieved through the use of a clearly defined data *collection process.* It is usually useful to collect not only the data to be used, but also information about the situation in which the data were collected. This may include: (1) the name of the person collecting the data, (2) the date and time of collection, (3) the method or process used for collecting data, (4) identification of any instruments used during data collection, and (5) when the data are to be collected by hand, designing a *check sheet* to ease both the recording and interpretation of data.

A variable often overlooked when recording data is the person doing the job. The best way of reducing any potential variation from this source is through training. This need not be complex or long, but it should be sufficient for the person to understand how to use any instruments, operate any machines, and reliably record all requisite data. It can help if the person knows how the information is likely to be used afterward; fear that the information may be used to his or her disadvantage can tempt someone to tamper with it.

Understanding Variation

The continuously variable nature of the universe is at the heart of the science of statistics and, at first glance, can look very complex, particularly if approached from a mathematical viewpoint. This can lead to its being ignored; this is a pity because even a simple appreciation of it can result in a reduction in haphazard attempts to control it, with a consequent savings in wasted time and degraded performance.

When a process is executed repeatedly, its outputs are seldom identical. For example, when a gun is successively fired at a target, as in Figure 11.1, the bullets will not all pass through the same hole. This lack of repeatability is caused by the variation or variability in the process. If these causes are understood, then this can lead to the development of solutions to reduce the variation in the process and result in more consistent products that require less inspection and testing, have less rejection and failure, cost less to build, have more satisfied customers, and are more profitable.

Variation in process output is caused by variations within the process. These may be one or more of

- Differing actions within the process
- Differing effects within the process
- Differing inputs to the process

As an example for each of these conditions, the variation in the placement of the bullet holes in the target may be affected by (1) the gun being held or used differently, (2) wear in the hammer mechanism causing the shell to be struck differently, or (3) bullets of slightly differing shape or weight. Thus, even if the first point is eliminated by putting the gun in a clamp and firing it remotely, the bullets will still not all hit the target in the identical position.

The reasons why variation occurs can be divided into two important classes, known as *common* and *special* causes of variation. These are discussed further next.

Within any process there are many variable factors, as indicated before, each of which may vary a small amount and in a predictable way. However, when taken together, they result in a degree of randomness in the output, as indicated in Figure 11.2. These seemingly uncontrollable factors are called common causes of variation and they can seldom be eliminated by "tampering" with the process. For example, consider the effect of simple adjustments to the clamped gun, as in Figure 11.2.

The first hole is to the left of center, so the clamp is rotated a little to the right. If the clamp had been left alone, the second bullet would have gone a little to the right of center, but because it has been moved right, the bullet now goes further to the right. As a reaction to this, the clamp is rotated somewhat more to the left. The third bullet tends toward the left anyway, so the result is a hole even further to the left. It can be seen from this that it would have been better not to tinker with the clamp and that the score would be more likely to improve if the whole system were understood first and then fundamental improvements made, such as building a better gun or making better bullets.

Special causes of variation, on the other hand, are unusual occurrences that come from outside the normal common causes. For example, a shot goes outside

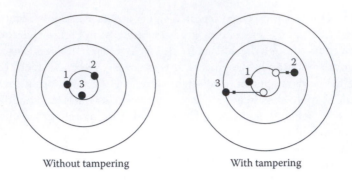

Figure 11.2   Tampering.

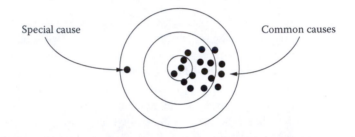

Figure 11.3   Special and common causes of variation.

the main grouping because someone tripped over the gunner as the gun was fired, as in Figure 11.3.

Special causes can thus be addressed as individual cases finding the cause for each occurrence outside the normal grouping and preventing it from recurring. This may be contrasted with the way that common causes must be addressed through the overall process. The way that causes are addressed in a process improvement project is usually first to recognize and eliminate special causes and then to find ways of improving the overall process in order to reduce common causes of variation.

The reader will have noticed that in the short discussion so far we have taken no account of time or sequence because it was not important which measurement came first or last. This is *static* variation. If the order in which measurements are made is known, then significant trends may be detected; this may be useful for catching a problem before it becomes serious. This is *dynamic* variation. For example, if the gunner is initially accurate, but becomes less so as his or her arm tires, then this may not be detected from the final positioning of holes on the target; it could only be seen by plotting the positioning of the holes across time. Dynamic variation is commonly measured using control charts.

Finally, to close the discussion on measurement we also must address the tendency to discard unusual data points. Discarding an outlier would be reasonable if we had reason to suppose it is erroneous data. For example, a blood pressure reading of 1200/80 seems impossible (it probably was supposed to be 120/80). Perhaps the lab technician was distracted by a conversation while marking down the reading. An outrageous observation is almost certainly invalid. But how do we guard against self-deception? More than one scientist has been convinced to disregard data that did not fit the pattern, when in fact the weird observation was trying to say something important.

For our discussion, it suffices to recognize unusual data points and outliers and their potential impact and to know that entire books cover the topic of outliers. Outliers force the distribution of data in two specific ways:

- Skewness is the amount of shift (left or right) that the distribution is displaying in relation to the mean. Rules of thumb regarding the skewness in numerical terms are that skewed left is less than 0, normal is 0, and skewed right is greater than 0.
- Kurtosis is the amount of spread that the distribution is displaying in relation to the normal distribution. Rules of thumb regarding the kurtosis in numerical terms are that platykurtic (flatter tails) kurtosis is less than 0, mesokurtic (normal peak) kurtosis is 0, and leptokurtic (sharper peak) kurtosis is greater than 0.

Summary

In this chapter, we discussed measurement and how it relates to healthcare as well as the importance it bears on making the link of the objectives to the strategy of the organization. In the next chapter, we address primary care and the opportunities that exist for improvement.

Reference

Standard C., and D. Davis. 1999. *Running today's factory: A proven strategy for Lean manufacturing.* Cincinnati, OH: Hanser Gardner.

Selected Bibliography

Cohen, J., and P. Cohen. 1983. *Applied multiple regression/correlation analysis for the behavioral sciences,* 2nd ed. Hillsdale, NJ: Lawrence Erlbaum Associates.

Freund, J. E., and F. J. Williams. 1972. *Elementary business statistics: The modern approach,* 2nd ed. Englewood Cliffs, NJ: Prentice Hall.

Gibbons, J. D. 1985. *Nonparametric statistical inference,* 2nd ed., revised and expanded. New York: Marcel Dekker.

Hammer, M., and J. Champy. 1993. *Reengineering the corporation.* New York: Harper Business.

Manganelli, R. L., and M. M. Klein. 1994. *The reengineering handbook.* New York: AMA–COM.

Rousseeuw, P. J., and A. M. Leroy. 1987. *Robust regression and outlier detection.* New York: John Wiley & Sons.

Stamatis, D. H. 1996. *Creating the future: The nuts and bolts of reengineering.* Red Bluff, CA: Paton Press.

Winkler, R. L., and W. L. Hays. 1975. *Statistics: Probability, inference and decision,* 2nd ed. New York: Holt, Reinhart and Winston.

Chapter 12

Primary Care

Introduction

So far we have emphasized hospitals, nursing homes (skilled and unskilled facilities), clinics, and urgent care facilities. We have mentioned the need for improvement in the physician's practice (Chapter 2), but we have not made it a strong point. In this chapter, we are going to discuss a typical physician's practice and a patient-centered medical home. Our discussion is going to focus on the initiatives that may be taken for improvements. We are also going to give a very detailed example of how a primary care practice should start to focus on its processes.

Healthcare is about partners, people, process, and service. It is the combination of these four items that demands some form of quality healthcare management based on Lean processes, effective performance management, efficient service delivery, and the reduction of waste and inefficiency. This demand is not dependent on the size of the organization or whether the facility is a hospital, nursing home, or physician's practice.

Just like in the hospital and large health facilities, in the primary care area the changes required to implement the patient-centered environment fully require (1) significant knowledge of the process itself, and (2) practice redesign to achieve alignment with payer, corporate, or other consultants, and/or resources to foster the desired improvement. Specifically, it turns out that the same principles hold for primary care improvement as for the big hospitals, nursing homes, and so on. This means that we can still use the traditional approaches to quality as well as methodologies such as

- Lean
- Six Sigma
- Kaizen

Indeed, we can integrate Lean concepts such as workplace organization and 5S, problem solving, and value stream mapping into the physician's organization to maximize efficiency and reduce waste by operational assessment of departments including but not limited to billing, laboratory, radiology, central supply, and so on. Of course, this demands some type of culture change and creating a customer-centered focus through development of physician leadership.

Understanding the Process

Any improvement at any level must start with understanding *the* process. Primary care is no different. Therefore, let us examine what is really primary care and how we can focus on this process for improvement. Primary care is a complex clinical practice that is more than a single physician. It takes a series of well executed processes to care for the patient, and each one of those processes is critical to the ultimate family practice. (See Note 1 in the "Special Note on Measurement" section.)

Who is involved in this practice? It depends on the size of the practice and the specialty that is being offered. Generally, this includes:

- Primary care
    - Family practice physicians
    - Internal medicine physicians
    - Pediatricians

- Primary caregivers could include:
    - MDs (doctors of human medicine, allopathic)
    - DOs (doctors of osteopathic medicine)
    - NPs (nurse practitioners, working in collaboration with a doctor)
    - PA-C (physician assistant-certified), who must work directly under the supervision of the physician

Of course, In addition to the primary caregivers, each office (practice) has a number of unique positions, each contributing a skill necessary for quality patient care. Table 12.1 summarizes some positions and their responsibilities.

Table 12.1 Associates in a Typical Practice

Type	Responsibilities
Physician assistant (PA-C) Bachelors or master's degree with a state license to practice; formally trained to provide diagnostic, therapeutic, and preventive healthcare services, as delegated by a physician	Take medical histories, examine and treat patients, order and interpret laboratory tests and x-rays, and make diagnoses; can also treat minor injuries by suturing, splinting, and casting
Nurse practitioner (NP-C) Master's degree with a state license to practice	Treat both acute and chronic conditions through comprehensive history taking, physical exams, physical therapy, and ordering tests and therapies for patients, within the scope of practice; can serve as a patient's "point of entry" healthcare provider and see patients of all ages depending on the designated scope of practice
RN (registered nurse) Has a minimum of an associate's degree in nursing with a state license to practice professional nursing	In office setting, often takes supervisory or care management role; training in holistic care of patients
LPN (licensed practical nurse) Diploma and state license to practice practical nursing Often functions similarly to clinical medical assistant	Works in a variety of healthcare settings; often found working under the supervision of physicians in clinics and hospitals, or in private home healthcare; in long-term care facilities, sometimes supervise nursing assistants and orderlies
Medical assistant (MA) Special training or a diploma from a junior college	Performs administrative and clinical tasks to keep the offices of physicians and other health practitioners running smoothly Tasks vary from office to office; at small practices, may do both clinical and administrative tasks; may be more specialized at a larger practice

(*Continued*)

Table 12.1 Associates in a Typical Practice (Continued)

Type	Responsibilities
	Should not be confused with physician assistants, who examine, diagnose, and treat patients under the direct supervision of a physician
Medical clerk Special training from a trade school or on-the-job training	Primary duties are to perform clerical work in support of the care and treatment given to patients in a medical facility, including functions such as serving as a receptionist, performing record-keeping duties, performing clerical duties relating to patient care and treatment, and providing miscellaneous support to the medical staff of the unit Work requires a practical knowledge of the medical facility's organization and services, the basic rules and regulations governing patient treatment, and of the standard procedures, medical records, and a medical terminology of the unit supported
Medical biller Special training from a trade school or on-the-job training	To be successful, will know medical terminology, anatomy, how to complete forms properly, and required coding. Will also need to know basic computer information and have a typing speed of at least 35 words per minute Works with patients, other offices' staff, medical staff, and other office personnel Customer service is very important because the people contacted are either colleagues or patients who could be at stressful points in their lives

Table 12.1 Associates in a Typical Practice (Continued)

Type	Responsibilities
Medical scheduler Special training from a trade school or on-the-job training	Must have knowledge of medical terminology, typing, insurance verification, coding, customer service, use of multiline phone system, and use of computerized scheduling system. *Customer service is key: Scheduling will make or break the flow of the day*
X-ray technician Special training in radiology; experience and/or a junior college degree; needs certification	X-ray, ultrasound, and other subspecialty technicians could also be employed in a physician practice. Often, the roles filled by these techs fall under the role of medical assistant in small practices
Phlebotomist Special training in drawing blood; needs certification	Some practices may have a laboratory as a part of the practice or in the same office to serve patients better
Receptionist Special training from a trade school or on-the-job training	Greets patients and monitors sign-in sheet; copies insurance card when indicated; enters any new demographic/insurance information Collects co-pays and balances; puts chart up for clinical staff; files; routes all calls not going through the voice mail system; confirms insurance on same-day-appointment patients
Cashier Special training in office	Verifies that level of evaluation and management (E&M) is properly documented; verifies that all services are marked off on the appropriate encounter form; enters all services with appropriate documented diagnosis; verifies that all patient encounters have been billed
Referral clerk Special training in office	Obtains preauthorizations when required by insurance company; writes referrals to specialists when required by insurance company

(Continued)

Table 12.1 Associates in a Typical Practice (Continued)

Type	Responsibilities
Patient service clerk Special training in office	Takes messages for physicians from patients; faxes test results to specialty offices as necessary; retrieves messages for prescription refills; communicates with specialty offices to schedule testing for patients
Practice administrator Typically has an advanced education (RN, BS, MBA or MHA, etc.) It is a plus, but not entirely necessary, to have a medical background of some type	Provides the "glue" that holds the practice together. Each practice has someone who oversees the total management of a practice; larger practices may also have supervisors in each area (clinical, reception, etc.). Smaller practices may have one manager/administrator for the entire practice Role includes: reporting directly to the board; overseeing daily operations; financial management (accounts payable, establishing, implementing, and maintaining budget, preparing monthly reports for board and CPA firm); human resources (interviewing candidates, hiring/discipline/termination, staff training, compliance, payroll, yearly review of all employee benefits, yearly review of employee pay/performance, yearly review of employee manual); accounts receivable (monitoring daily receipts versus billed charges, benchmarking AR to national standards, identifying deviations and correcting them, negotiating insurance contracts and reviewing them annually, regularly auditing charts for compliance, and preparing monthly reports for board and CPA firm); ensuring compliance with various regulatory agencies

A practice exists to facilitate and provide healthcare to patients. Because there is an interaction between several individuals and the patient, by definition, we have a process. So what is this process? Typically, it is a 13-step process:

■ Step 1: Patient visit is scheduled.
  - Scheduler is responsible for this and other tasks
  - Schedules appointments per appointment guidelines
  - Screens for insurance (physician might not be participating)
  - Takes updated insurance information if appropriate
  - Addresses balance on account (directly or transfers to biller)
  - For a *new patient,* takes preliminary information
  - Confirms all appointments 24–48 hours before appointment time
  - Reschedules as necessary
  - Sorts and delivers mail
  - Writes up checks
  - Prepares new charts
■ Step 2: Insurance verification takes place.
  - Verifies the insurance of appointments 24–48 hours in advance of appointment time
  - Calls patient if insurance is not active
  - Verifies level of benefits (preventive services available, etc.)
■ Step 3: Patient arrives for scheduled appointment.
  - Signs in and provides proof of insurance
  - Waits in lobby and/or fills out necessary papers (if initial visit, it is required that a patient's history and other information be taken)
■ Step 4: Co-pay is collected prior to visit to improve efficiency.
■ Step 5: Patient's medical jacket placed in back office to alert medical assistant (MA) that the patient is ready.
■ Step 6: Medical assistant escorts patient back to clinical area. In addition, a medical assistant may do the following:
  - Prepares patient for physician
  - Verifies that all test results are in chart for the visit
  - Performs testing as ordered (EKG, venapuncture, injection, etc.)
  - Calls patients with test results and relays information from physician
  - Calls in prescription refills
  - Mails cholesterol cards and pap cards
  - Maintains supplies in rooms
  - Monitors expiration date of medications
  - Takes calls from patients with medical questions
■ Step 7: Medical assistant takes vital signs (weight, height, blood pressure, temperature, pulse) and asks about the purpose of the visit. A final

task is to put the chart up for the doctor or the PA or NP. If the patient is diabetic, then a diabetic sticker is placed on the visit sheet to alert the caregiver to perform associated necessary clinical tasks. Also, if there are tests to be performed prior to seeing the caregiver, they are completed here. This step is very important because it allows for the interaction of the patient and practice team in a formal setting. The requirements for this interaction are (1) informed, activated patient, and (2) prepared practice team.

- Step 8: PA or NP completes initial exam. When it is complete, the chart is placed in the rack for the MA to check orders as necessary.
- Step 9: MA checks chart for orders.
- Step 10: MA completes the tests he or she is capable of performing, such as EKG and so on. Then, if necessary, MA sends the patient to a lab or for x-ray. The handoff is recorded appropriately.
- Step 11: PA or NP reviews the test results and discharges the patient. If there is a need for a medical doctor to review the tests or consult the patient, this is where it takes place. If everything is complete, the patient goes to cashier, who reviews the chart appropriately.
- Step 12: A follow-up appointment is scheduled.
- Step 13: Patient leaves happy! Even though the office visit is complete, this does not mean that the patient's visit is totally finished. In some cases, the visit continues long after the patient leaves. If a referral is made to a specialist or other facility, the referral clerk gets involved; the biller is involved after the patient's visit is complete, and the patient services clerk may be involved as well. The biller's responsibilities at this stage are to
  - Send claims (electronic or hard copy) on a daily basis
  - Correct front-end edits and resubmits
  - Retrieve claims acknowledgment report
  - Post insurance payments and bills to a second insurance company, if necessary
  - Monitor month-end reports for rebilling or checking status of claims
  - Talk to patients regarding statements, insurance questions, or balances on account
  - Prepare accounts for small claims or collections

Practice Redesign

To take advantage of the improvement tools, we must first separate the process into new patients and existing patients. The reason for this separation and understanding is that we want the practice to increase the consistency of reporting by physicians in different specialties and accurately record the level of service provided to a patient based on the defining criteria. By knowing and identifying the different patients and services needed, the cashier and billers must follow defined criteria for evaluation and management services. This impacts the reimbursement for services and thus the bottom line of the practice. Typical categories of evaluation management include:

- History
  - Problem focused
  - Expanded problem focused
  - Detailed
  - Comprehensive

- Examination
  - Problem focused
  - Expanded problem focused
  - Detailed
  - Comprehensive

- Medical decision making
  - Number of diagnoses or management options
  - Amount and/or complexity of data to be reviewed
  - Risk of complications and/or morbidity or mortality

- Counseling and/or coordination of care
  - If 50% of encounter involves counseling or coordination of care, then time is used to determine service.

Now that we have a good idea of the typical categories, let us examine the process of the new and existing patients. For the new patients, there are five primary categories:

- Office or other outpatient visit for the evaluation and management of a new patient, which requires three components:
  - A problem-focused history
  - A problem-focused examination
  - Straightforward medical decision making

This means that counseling and/or coordination of care with other providers or agencies is provided consistent with the nature of the problems and the patient's and/or family's needs. Furthermore, usually the presenting problems are self-limited or minor. Physicians typically spend 10 minutes face to face with the patient and/or family.

■ Office or other outpatient visit for the evaluation and management of a new patient, which requires these three key components:
- An expanded problem-focused history
- An expanded problem-focused examination
- Straightforward medical decision making

This means that counseling and/or coordination of care with other providers or agencies is provided consistent with the nature of the problem and the patient's and/or family's needs. Furthermore, usually the presenting problems are low to moderate in severity. Physicians typically spend 20 minutes face to face with the patient and/or family.

■ Office or other outpatient visit for the evaluation and management of a new patient, which requires these three key components:
- A detailed history
- A detailed examination
- Medical decision making of low complexity

This means that counseling and/or coordination of care with other providers or agencies is provided consistent with the nature of the problem and the patient's and/or family's needs. Furthermore, usually the presenting problems are of moderate complexity. Physicians typically spend 30 minutes face to face with the patient and/or family.

■ Office or other outpatient visit for the evaluation and management of a new patient, which requires these three key components:
- A comprehensive history
- A comprehensive examination
- Medical decision making of moderate complexity

This means that counseling and/or coordination of care with other providers or agencies is provided consistent with the nature of the problem and the patient's and/or family's needs. Furthermore, usually the presenting problems are of moderate to high severity. Physicians typically spend 45 minutes face to face with the patient and/or family.

■ Office or other outpatient visit for the evaluation and management of a new patient, which requires these three key components:
- A comprehensive history
- A comprehensive examination
- Medical decision making of high complexity

This means that counseling and/or coordination of care with other providers or agencies is provided consistent with the nature of the problem and the patient's and/or family's needs. Furthermore, usually the presenting problems are of moderate to high severity. Physicians typically spend 60 minutes face to face with the patient and/or family.

For the existing patients, there are also five primary categories:

■ Office or other outpatient visit for the evaluation and management of an established patient that may not require the presence of a physician. Usually the presented problems are minimal. Typically, 5 minutes are spent performing or supervising these services.

■ Office or other outpatient visit for the evaluation and management of an established patient, which requires at least two of these three key components:
  - A problem-focused history
  - A problem-focused examination
  - Straightforward medical decision making

This means that counseling and/or coordination of care with other providers or agencies is provided consistent with the nature of the problem and the patient's and/or family's needs. Furthermore, usually the presenting problems are self-limited or minor. Physicians typically spend 10 minutes face to face with the patient and/or family.

■ Office or other outpatient visit for the evaluation and management of an established patient, which requires at least two of these three key components:
  - An expanded problem-focused history
  - An expanded problem-focused examination
  - Medical decision making of low complexity

This means that counseling and/or coordination of care with other providers or agencies is provided consistent with the nature of the problem and the patient's and/or family's needs. Furthermore, usually the presenting problems are self-limited or minor. Physicians typically spend 15 minutes face to face with the patient and/or family.

■ Office or other outpatient visit for the evaluation and management of an established patient, which requires at least two of these three key components:
  - A detailed history
  - A detailed examination
  - Medical decision making of moderate complexity

This means that counseling and/or coordination of care with other providers or agencies is provided consistent with the nature of the problem and the patient's and/or family's needs. Furthermore, usually the presenting problems are self-limited or minor. Physicians typically spend 25 minutes face to face with the patient and/or family.

■ Office or other outpatient visit for the evaluation and management of an established patient, which requires at least two of these three key components:
  - A comprehensive history
  - A comprehensive examination
  - Medical decision making of high complexity

This means that counseling and/or coordination of care with other providers or agencies is provided consistent with the nature of the problem and the patient's and/or family's needs. Furthermore, usually the presenting problems are self-limited or minor. Physicians typically spend 25 minutes face to face with the patient and/or family.

This separation and understanding of *new* versus *existing* patients is very important because the determination dictates which code to use for payment. The codes for the new patient have more strict criteria. They must meet all three components on new patients versus only two on established ones. Reimbursement for new patients will be more due to the extra time needed to care for them.

Now that we have identified the two categories of patients, we can proceed to identify the specific process and then proceed with improvements. In order to know the process, we must understand its components and the expectations of the specific process. For example, in the Michigan IPIP (improving performance in practice) model, we begin with the outcomes and then define the drivers; only then do we intervene with any particular changes. This is shown in Table 12.2. These high leverage changes were adapted from the chronic care model (see Note 2 in the "Special Note on Measurement" section) and placed in a simple sequence for rapid implementation.

The approach shown in Table 12.2 is a way to focus efforts on high-leverage changes within a practice to ensure that the planned process of care gets done with every patient every time. The key emphasis is on redesign of the care delivery in practices. Clinical experience and research evidence demonstrate that such redesign is more effective for care delivery, is easier for physicians and staff, takes less time, and is more satisfying for patients. The changes fall into four steps:

1. Use registry to identify asthmatics/diabetics prior to visit (this requires the work of implementing a registry or "fixing" the electronic health record [EHR]).
2. Use a template for planned care (e.g., visit planner).
3. Use protocols to standardize the care process:
   - Standard protocols
   - Nursing standing orders to increase reliable execution
   - Defined care team roles: who does what in the protocol
4. Use self-management support strategies with patients.

Implementing these changes only works if they are implemented reliably so that they are used for every patient every time. As such, we emphasize the importance of sustainable, executable plans that are monitored to ensure that

Table 12.2   Overall Health System Diagram

Outcomes	Drivers	Changes through Interventions
Improvements in clinical outcomes— for example, asthma and diabetic patients Identify specific metrics: 1. 2. 3....N	**Use registry to manage population** Identify each affected patient at every visit Identify needed services for each patient Recall patients for follow-up	**Implement registry** Determine staff work flow to support registry Populate registry with patient data Routinely maintain registry data Use registry to manage patient care and support population management
	Planned care Care team members are aware of patient needs and work together to ensure all needed services are completed	**Use templates for planned care** Select template tool from registry or create a flow sheet Determine staff work flow to support template Use template with all patients Ensure registry is updated each time template is used Monitor use of template
	Standardized care processes Practice-wide guidelines implemented per condition (asthma, diabetes)	**Employ protocols** Select and customize evidence-based protocols for asthma and diabetes Determine staff work flow to support protocol, including standing orders Use protocols with all patients Monitor use of protocols

(Continued)

Table 12.2 Overall Health System Diagram (Continued)

Outcomes	Drivers	Changes through Interventions
	Self-management support	**Provide self-management support**
	Realized patient and care team partnership	Obtain patient education materials
		Determine staff work flow to support SMS
		Provide training to staff in SMS
		Set patient goals collaboratively
		Document and monitor patient progress toward goals
		Link with community resources

tools and processes are used consistently. So, let us examine each of the steps more closely.

Step 1: Select a Registry

A system that records relevant patient care information for a specific subpopulation is called a "registry." The care team can use the registry to record critical elements of the care plan, produce care summaries at the time of a visit, and enter data to alter the care plan as needed. A registry is essential to assessing both how care is delivered and how well care is delivered. Identifying the population of patients with asthma or diabetes and understanding their needs for care are at the core of a population-based care delivery system.

Choose a registry in which the application makes it easy to get patient information into and out of the system. Ideally, it should also be easy to transfer information to and from other systems (e.g., billing, lab, appointments) or even to have a direct interface with these systems. Practices can also accomplish the registry function using a paper-based approach. Such an approach is not likely to be a viable long-term tool, but it can get a practice started in understanding how to integrate a registry into its daily process.

Populate the registry. Once a registry has been identified and installed in a practice, the next step is to populate the registry with patient data.

The goal is to have all patients with the condition of interest entered into the registry, enabling the practice to move to a planned care approach by using pertinent data to plan patient care. Set a deadline for completion of this task. Much of the practice redesign depends on it. Give the practice 1 month to accomplish this task.

Common challenges to implementation include:

- Entire population is not in the registry.
  - Use a billing system or some method of identifying all patients with the condition. Then, make sure that these patients get entered into the system.
  - Do not worry about perfection. A registry is a living system; maintenance of population is part of population management.

- Ongoing data entry is not reliable.
  - Revisit roles and responsibilities.
  - Create a clear protocol.
  - Identify barriers in the system that are preventing 90% completion.

Step 2: Identify a Template

Often called "decision support," a template can mean a lot of things. In this context, the idea for this level of decision support is to identify all needed services that have not been completed and make a recommendation to the clinic staff. Many registries, such as CDEMS, DocSite, and RMD, have "visit planners" built into the system. These planners are decision support tools or "templates" for care.

A visit planner or template is a paper or electronic interface used by the staff and clinician to evaluate needed services and to document the completed services for each patient. This is analogous to the flow sheet that many practices use in a paper chart.

The visit planner should be organized by who needs to complete the task so that all staff is involved in using the visit planner (front desk, nurse, physician, etc.). Make sure that the template is used for every patient and at every opportunity for care. A series of implementation PDSA (plan-do-study-act) processes can get a practice to 100% reliable use of the template within a couple of weeks. For example, a planner for a diabetic patient, at the end of the day, may be used to review all diabetes charts to measure:

■ The number of patients for whom a visit planner was used
■ How many of the nurse opportunities were available and how many completed
■ How many of the physician opportunities were available and how many completed
■ Whether all data were entered into the registry within the protocol planned time for the clinic

A common challenge to implementing a template is

■ Cannot get nurses, doctors, or others to complete all tasks on their part of the visit planner:
  – Ensure that all know their roles and responsibilities.
  – Identify barriers to completion (this requires discussion and often reassessing how the process flows).

Step 3: Protocols (Standardize the System of Care)

The use of protocols and standing orders, coupled with clear care team roles, is the critical step for seeing results. To accomplish standardization of care, the practice needs to understand the flow of the patient through the clinic and the key contacts during the visit. This step is intimately tied to step 2: using a planned care template. Protocols require that responsibilities be delegated across the staff. Each staff member makes a contribution to the care of the patient with chronic illness. In fact, nonphysician staff members can effectively perform many steps in high-quality chronic illness care. For example, referrals for eye exams and foot exams, orders for required blood tests, and immunizations are steps appropriate for nonphysician staff. The clinic needs to agree upon nursing standing orders, a standard protocol for what needs to happen for the patient, and specific care team roles in carrying out the protocol. Often, the standing orders can be the same as a protocol.

To implement the appropriate and applicable protocols, the entire staff needs to accept this process and understand their roles and responsibilities for patients with chronic ailments. Just creating the protocols will not be enough. The front desk, the rooming staff, the nurses, and the physicians all need to participate and brainstorm the barriers to completing this every time the patient comes in. All need to accept that this is part of the job—not optional—and that a good system will get this done every time.

Consider the process of recording blood pressure. In most practices, blood pressure recording is close to 100%. We should expect the same for all other processes.

Common challenges to implementing protocols include:

■ Difference of opinion among clinical staff about which protocol to use
  – Conduct PDSA cycles on several protocols to determine which version best matches the process in the office

■ Lack of agreement that a protocol is needed
  – Use guidelines as basis for discussion and share data that demonstrate the gap in care as compared to the goals

Step 4: Self-Management Support (Using Diabetes as a Model)

Educating patients in self-management is necessary to improve patient outcomes when chronic illnesses such as diabetes are treated. Successful self-management education relies on educational tools that are evidence based, incorporate demographic and cultural variables, and emphasize patient collaboration and empowerment. All members of the practice team can help patients set goals for self-management. These goals must be clearly documented and reviewed with patients frequently. Success relies on active collaboration of the healthcare team and patients to improve outcomes.

At least for diabetes self-management, many tools are available in print, video, and computer-based formats. Most practices use some sort of printed materials because they are usually less expensive and easier to obtain. Materials should be patient oriented and include information on what the patient *needs to know and needs to do.* Materials should foster conversation and plans for action. However, in providing these self-management tools, keep in mind the following:

■ Assessing the patients' skill and understanding
■ Setting up plans and goals with patients
■ Following up with patients to determine whether goals are achieved
■ Problem solving when the patient has been unable to meet goals and revising goals when necessary
■ Documenting the goals and plans as well as the results

Because this process of health education is new to the physician and/ or nursing staff, some element of staff training is needed to have successful implementation. All staff that will help with this process should be part of a training session. The doctor does not need to do all of this. Many successful self-management support programs rely upon nursing staff, medical assistants, or others to help patients learn to set goals and provide systematic follow-up. A specific member of the healthcare team needs to be designated to encourage patients to set goals. After goals are set, a follow-up system must be in place. One option would be to assign a staff member to call patients at a designated follow-up interval (for example, 1 week after the goals are set). Alternatively, if telephone follow-up is not feasible, staff can review goals with patients at each and every appointment.

Once a support system is created, it is important to set clear expectations of the staff for implementation, as with any process improvement. While testing the implementation, monitor whether the medical staff are documenting goal setting and follow-up with patients.

Documentation is an essential component of self-management. It is necessary to document the initial goals of the patient. A copy of these goals should be placed in the chart and given to the patient. During follow-up, it is necessary to document (1) progress toward achieving goals, (2) barriers to reaching goals, and (3) modification of existing goals or a new set of goals. Having all of this information in the chart will allow multiple members of the clinical staff to participate in supporting self-management of an individual patient. It is also important to measure whether or not self-management support is occurring. Examples of measures are

- Percent of patients with diabetes who have a documented set of goals in chart or registry
- Percent of patients who receive follow-up after goal setting

Standardized documentation using the registry and/or electronic medical record could be used. In an electronic medical record, a field documenting goals reviewed at each visit could be added. In practices that regularly perform goal setting with their patients, the patients learn to expect it and the process becomes a natural part of care.

Common challenges to implementation of self-management support include:

- Do not know what to teach the patient
  - Review the American College of Physicians (ACP) Foundation Diabetes Guide. Most of what patients need to know and need to do does not require intimate knowledge of diabetes or physiology. Helping to motivate patients is the key issue here. Establish ties with community-based diabetes educators for more detailed teaching. Focus primary care efforts on behavioral modification.

■ Do not have time
- Time is always a problem. Patients can be overwhelmed by too much information at one visit. Keep goal setting brief. Delegate responsibilities throughout the office and share responsibilities for roles among multiple staff when possible.

■ Do not have resources for follow-up
- Develop protocols that can keep this brief. Consider developing peer support groups that can do this for each other.

When this redesign takes place, the practice will have resource savings, but it will also take time, effort, and resolve from everyone in the practice, especially the leaders of the practice. Needless to say, enhanced payment must be adequate to cover more than just the costs of practice redesign and enhancement. This means that it must also return professional joy, security, and fulfillment to primary care practitioners.

To appreciate this redesign effort, let us see the traditional and the new approach roles (see Table 12.3) that are being talked about with the chronic model (see Note 2 in the "Special Note on Measurement" section). Notice that the new approach is much more patient centered and more responsive to the patient's needs. In fact, the new approach focuses on the items that will result in the most satisfaction for the patient:

■ Open-access scheduling
■ Online appointments
■ Electronic health records
■ Group visits
■ Electronic visits
■ Chronic disease management

These specific six items will result in a 26% increase in payment or 12% decrease in effort (Spann 2004). What makes these such powerful incentives is the idea that it will be possible to communicate information electronically, efficiently, and with a minimum chance for errors.

Patient-Centered Medical Home (PCMH)

PCMH is a system of care based on the relationship between a patient and his or her personal primary care physician. The primary care physicians (pediatricians,

Table 12.3 Traditional Care and Chronic Care Models

Traditional Model	New Model
Systems often disrupt the patient–physician relationship	Systems support continuous healing relationships
Physician is center stage	Patient is center stage
Unnecessary barriers to access by patients	Open access by patients
Care is mostly reactive	Care is both responsive and prospective
Care is often fragmented	Care is integrated
Paper medical record	Electronic health record
Unpredictable package of services is offered	Commitment to providing directly and/or coordinating a defined basket of services
Oriented to individual patient	Oriented to individual and community
Communication with practice is synchronous (in person or by telephone)	Communication with the practice is both synchronous and asynchronous (e-mail, Web portal, voice mail)
Quality and safety of care are assumed	Processes are in place for ongoing measurement and improvement of quality and safety
Physician is the main source of care	Multidisciplinary team is the source of care
Physician–patient visits	Individual and group visits involving several patients and members of the healthcare team generates new knowledge through practice-based research
Consumes knowledge	
Experience based	
Haphazard chronic disease management	
Struggles financially; undercapitalized	Evidence based
	Purposeful, organized chronic-disease management
	Positive financial margin; adequately capitalized

internists, family practice doctors) lead a proactive healthcare team to provide long-term coordination and management of their patients' healthcare across all settings. Patients receive the right care in the right setting, and physicians are compensated for the additional time and effort required to manage their patients' care. (See Note 3 in the "Special Note on Measurement" section.)

The idea of PCMH is based on the holistic approach to healthcare. Specifically, at the least, it encourages and participates in the following:

- Combination of place, process, and people
- Improvement of overall outcomes
- Improvement of quality of life for patients and family
- Encouragement and respect of diverse ideas, customs, and beliefs
- Coordination of care
- Encouragement of sharing information across specialties
- Involvement in the transitions of care
- Improvement in the experience of providing care

The desire and encouragement to participate will result in

- Revitalizing the patient–physician relationship and placing the patient and his or her family at the center of care
- Stimulating practice-level innovation to provide enhanced quality, effectiveness, safety, efficiency, and value because practices will be able to invest in systems-based care and measurement of that care
- Enhancing coordination of care across all domains of the healthcare system (hospitals, home health agencies, nursing homes, consultants, and other components of our complex healthcare network)
- Recognizing that care provided by a personal physician, operating in accord with the advanced medical home model, is a highly valuable service
- Leading to the macrosystem changes required to support this enriched healthcare model (financing, coverage, reimbursement, physician education and training, and workforce distribution)

The idea of the PCMH is so prevalent within medical circles that even Blue Cross and Blue Shield (BCBS 2009) has shown interest in implementing the concept. In fact, BCBS of Michigan has already identified specific registries and tracking indicators. For example, for preventive service initiatives, the following have been identified from a physician organization and practice unit perspective. Notice that the focus is on delivery of preventive services by

- Routine application of evidence-based measures and revised office processes
- Using IT to assist the practice in addressing preventive services from a population management perspective
- Accurately assessing patient risk for developing disease

- Developing interventions that encourage individuals to avoid the onset of disease
- Identifying individuals who would benefit from treatment for a condition of which they are unaware

Blue Cross Blue Shield also has initiatives for performance, individual care management initiatives, test tracking, specialist referral, community resources, self-management resources, patient provider agreement, and PCMH and coordination of care initiatives (BCBS 2009). In the case of the coordination, it is important to know that physician organizations and practice units will provide patients with fully coordinated care that is

- *Comprehensive:* Healthcare will be tracked, monitored, and organized in a timely manner.
- *Clear:* Results and outcomes of the patient care will be communicated to all involved parties.
- *Cost effective:* Reduced incidence of duplicate tests, medical errors, and polypharmacy will result in lower healthcare costs.
- *Prioritized:* Available resources will be matched to patient needs by prioritizing appropriately.

Whereas this is the skeleton of the PCMH concept, the question is how we can bring about this change for improvement. The answer lies in three distinct areas:

- Technology and tools
  - Point of care registry
  - Personal health record
  - ER point-of-care data and event satisfaction
  - Electronic prescribing
  - Physician dashboard

- Care coordination management and support
  - Medical home care advocate
  - Educational materials
  - Patient activation tools
  - Practice redesign support

- Case access
  - 24-Hour nurse line
  - Group visits
  - Electronic consultations

Now that we have an overview of what the PCMH is and what the goals are, we must have measurements that will demonstrate improvement. Typical metrics for asthma and diabetes are found in Table 12.4. These metrics are based on the chronic model.

As we can see, there are many areas where primary care may improve its services. Physicians or owners of the practice may focus on

- Capabilities to report practice- and physician-level patient outcomes, efficiency of service, and patient satisfaction
- Clear discussion with the patient as to the roles and responsibilities of the doctor and patient, and documenting this discussion
- Offering 24-hour patient access to a clinical decision maker, with a multilingual approach to care. Access may include extended office hours, telephone access, linkage to urgent care, or a combination

Table 12.4   Typical Metrics for a PCMH

Asthma	Diabetes
Patients 5–40 Y/O	Patients 18–75 Y/O
Symptom assessment (0–90%)	HbAlc test
Action plan (90%)	HbAlc > 9% (<5%)
Appropriate pharmaceutical therapy (90%)	HbAlc < 7% (75%)
	BP < 140/90 (90%)
All three components (75%)	BP < 130/80 (70%)
Patients with more than one ED/UC visit	LDL-C test (90%)
	LDL-C < 130 (90%)
Patients with more than one hospitalization	LDL-C < 100 (70%)
Tobacco use query	Retinal exam referral
Tobacco cessation advice (90%)	Retinal exam (80%)
	Foot exam (90%)
Current flu vaccination	Medical attention for nephropathy (90%)
	Current flu vaccine (75%)
	Self-management goal (90%)
	Smoking status query
	Smoking cessation advice (90%)
	ASA use (ages 40–75 Y/O) (85%)
	Statin use

■ Working with each patient to set individualized health goals and using a team-focused, systematic approach to track appointments and ensure follow-up on needed services

■ Providing effective and timely follow-up with patients on their test results

■ Coordinating patients' care across the health system through a process of active collaboration and communication between providers, caregivers, and patients

■ Providing patients with active counseling, screening, and education on preventive care

■ Coordinating referrals to specialists and providing specialists with patient information needed for proper care, such as lab work and test results

■ Offering patients connections to community services, in coordination with the health system, community service agencies, family, caregivers, and the patient

■ Providing self-management education and support to patients with chronic conditions

■ Developing patient registries to track and monitor patients' care over the long term

■ Providing an online patient portal system that allows for electronic communication and provides patients with greater access to medical information and technical tools

Lean Strategy for Primary Care

To be sure, just as in the hospital environment, in the primary care it is not required to use all the tools available for improvement. It is important, however, that we use the appropriate and applicable ones, always focusing on the following hierarchy of events:

1. Establish the project for improvement
2. "Lean" the practice
3. Solve the problem or problems
4. Guide the implementation process

Facilitate the Project Using Leadership Skills

In order to improve, we must change something. That something becomes the project and, for it to be completed, the leadership of the practice must be on board by

- Discussing the needs of the practice
- Discussing and determining the areas in which the practice feels weak to see whether improvements would foster more time or resources to be applied to the chronic activities and metrics

Based on these discussions, everyone has to agree on a set of mutual goals:

- Create the "aim" statement: a written statement of the accomplishments expected from team's improvement effort. Key components are a general description of aim (e.g., consistently meet patients' informational needs). It may be desirable to add identification of specific patient population (e.g., all diabetic patients from 18 to 75 years of age) or some guidance for carrying out the work (e.g., can start with one physician/nurse team and spread to others). Provide a rationale and point of shared vision for the team's efforts via the acronym SMART:
  - **S**pecific
  - **M**easurable
  - **A**ction oriented
  - **R**elevant
  - **T**imely
- Agree on the practice improvement goals. Goals define the way in which the improved system is expected to work. They establish specific numeric targets for the work as well as describing the magnitude of change expected. However, above all, goals should be challenging, but attainable—stretch goals encourage creativity and innovation.
- Create a mutual plan:
  - Team building
  - Timing
  - Staff considerations
- Conduct training.
  - Determine areas in which the practice will require training

"Lean" the Practice

- Determine value-added from non-value-added activities
- Observe the actual workings of the practice
  - Value stream, process mapping, spaghetti mapping, etc.
- Look for areas of waste
  - Seven wastes (overproduction including conveyance, correction, inventory, waiting, overprocessing, and motion)
  - Waste of money, time, supplies, or services decrease value

- Look for areas with issues around organization and standardization
  - 5S: sort, simplify, sweep (systematic cleaning), standardize, self-discipline (sustain)
- Reassess, readjust, train, and assign practice tasks
  - Compare what you see to practice members' perspectives of themselves

Using Lean Six Sigma

Now that we have identified the process and its problems, we are ready for problem solving and ultimately monitoring the effect of the improvement. One of the tools is Six Sigma using the define, measure, analyze, improve, implement, control (DMAIIC) model:

- *Define:* define areas that need to be improved
  - Areas that require more root cause analysis and problem solving
    - Apply Lean strategies to Lean issues
    - Apply problem strategies to larger issues
  - Develop a plan of attack around simple improvements and more complex requirements
    - Apply 5S to the appropriate areas
    - Apply current state/future state to the areas of waste
    - Root cause analysis for the more difficult areas
    - PDSA
  - Define areas that will require a cross-functional kaizen
  - Discuss findings with practice leadership team
  - Reassess, readjust, train, and assign practice tasks

- *Measure:* what is "measured" will influence behavior
  - Define the outputs that need to be achieved
  - Use tree strategy and/or the $Y = f(x)$ thought process to identify the inputs
  - Define and create measurement systems where more data are required for the outputs and the inputs
    - Define the items that require measurement over time
    - Measure the process—NOT the people
    - Plan with the practice a method to collect that information (e.g., wait times, time to acquire testing results, number of people required to perform a task, survey results, etc.)
  - Discuss findings with practice leadership team
  - Reassess, readjust, train, and assign practice tasks
    - Ensure a robust measurement system for data collection

- *Analyze:* analyze data and findings toward improvement
  - Compare the outputs versus inputs
  - Data analysis
  - Apply metrics to maps
  - Benchmarking
  - Root cause analysis/5 Whys
  - Fishbone/cause and effect
  - Analysis-of-failure modes
  - Review and apply standard quality analytic tools (some of these tools may be found on the IHI.org Extranet and in Appendix C on the accompanying CD)
  - Discuss findings with practice leadership team
  - Reassess, readjust, train, and assign practice tasks

- *Improve:* create a plan of improvement for inefficiencies
  - Apply Lean strategies to Lean issues
  - Create a pull system
  - Clean up areas using 5S
  - Map out future states and agree on the proposals
  - Create a quick changeover process to improve timing
  - Create a kanban process to facilitate the pull system
  - Define areas that require standardized work
  - Implement error proofing to prevent issues from happening
  - Discuss findings with practice leadership team
  - Reassess, readjust, train, and assign practice tasks

- *Implement:* create a plan of improvement for issues or problems
  - Apply problem-solving strategies to larger issues
  - Use analysis to help define improvements
  - Design pilot or pilots and implement
  - Design permanent improvements and plans to implement
  - Collect data and prove out the pilot or improvement
  - Create appropriate ongoing measurement systems
  - Prove out new measurement systems
  - Discuss findings with practice leadership team
  - Reassess, readjust, train, and assign practice tasks

- *Control:* set up and agree upon control plans and future actions
  - Set up a plan to revisit, monitor, and assess
  - Discuss findings with practice leadership team
  - Reassess, readjust, train, and assign practice tasks
  - *Congratulate the team* and *celebrate!* Help guide the implementation of new requirements

Special Note on Measurement

We have repeatedly emphasized the importance of measurement. In primary care, it is also important for practices to measure clinical improvement with data obtained from their registry or EHR (electronic health record). It is therefore critical that the metrics chosen be significant, be measurable, and will indicate improvement. In other words, how one will collect the information and what kind of information are of paramount importance. Appendix E shows an example of how to go about collecting basic information about depression.

Note 1: Understanding the Customer and the Process

To help the practice understand the concerns in defining the customer and process, Table 12.5 identifies the issues of the SIPOC (suppliers, inputs, process, outputs, customers) model in a physician's office. On the other hand, Table 12.6 shows the value proposition template. This template helps in identifying and evaluating the information from Table 12.5 in much more detail.

Note 2: Chronic Model

The chronic care model was developed by Ed Wagner, MD, MPH, director of the MacColl Institute for Healthcare Innovation, Group Health Cooperative of Puget Sound, and colleagues of the Improving Chronic Illness Care Program with support from the Robert Wood Johnson Foundation. It promotes effective change in provider groups to support evidence-based clinical and quality improvement across a wide variety of healthcare settings. For more information on the chronic model, see http://www.improvingchroniccare.org/index. php?p=The_Chronic_Care_Model&s=2.

There are many definitions of *chronic condition*—some more expansive than others (Robert Wood Johnson Foundation 2004). The model characterizes it as any condition that requires ongoing adjustments by the affected person and interactions with the healthcare system. Almost half of all Americans (133 million people) live with a chronic condition. That number is projected to increase by more than 1% per year by 2030, resulting in an estimated chronically ill population of 171 million. Almost half of all people with chronic illness have multiple conditions. As a result, many managed care and integrated delivery systems have taken a great interest in correcting the many deficiencies in current management of diseases such as diabetes, heart disease, depression, asthma, and others (Stockwell et al. 1994; Kenny 1993; Perrin et al. n.d.). Those deficiencies include:

■ Rushed practitioners not following established practice guidelines
■ Lack of care coordination

Table 12.5   SIPOC Model Structure

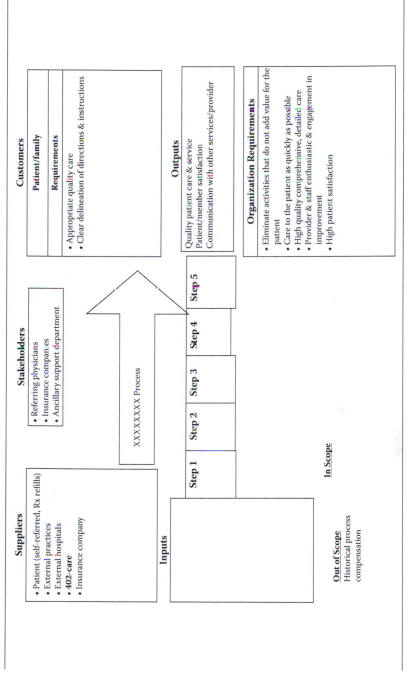

Table 12.6 Value Proposition Template

Project Name:		Project Sponsor:		Date:
VS Manager		Project Owner		
Objectives: What is to be achieved?		Goals: Customer experience, grow the topline, process excellence?		
	Start		End	
Suppliers:	Current State: Value stream map (high level) or list of process steps			Customers:
Inputs:				Outputs:
Current Metrics:				IT Systems:
In Scope				Out of Scope
Issues and Problems		Benefits		
Workshop Logistics:	Workshop Participants	Decision Panel		Next Steps
Date:				
Time:				
Location:				

- Lack of active follow-up to ensure the best outcomes
- Patients inadequately trained to manage their illnesses

Overcoming these deficiencies will require nothing less than a transformation of healthcare: from a system that is essentially reactive—responding mainly when a person is sick—to one that is proactive and focused on keeping a person as healthy as possible (Wagner et al. 1996a, 1996b). To speed the transition, Improving Chronic Illness Care created the chronic care model, which summarizes the basic elements for improving care in health systems at the community, organization, decision support, delivery system design, practice, and patient levels.

The differences between acute and chronic health problems include:

- Acute health problems (e.g., appendicitis, pharyngitis, etc.)
  - Begin suddenly and often have a single diagnosable cause
  - Are of short duration
  - Are self-limited or respond to a specific treatment

- Chronic health problems (e.g., diabetes, asthma, high blood pressure, etc.)
  - Begin slowly and proceed slowly
  - Can rarely be cured
  - Require that the patient take on more self-management
  - Have multiple causes (heredity, environment, social, lifestyle)
  - Often have acute complications

Obviously, all these present challenges, some of which include:

- Dealing with symptoms
- Physical impairment
- Emotional impacts
- Complex medication regiments
- Difficult lifestyle adjustments
- Obtaining helpful medical care

Historically, healthcare has been organized to respond rapidly and efficiently to acute illness or injury. It has been focused on the immediate problem and treated the patient as a passive recipient of a service; it did not consider self-management as a necessary option to deliver healthcare. All these items have caused and continue to cause inefficiencies and high cost in healthcare. This is where reform needs to focus and change in both delivery and understanding the consequences of chronic illness and its effect on the total health system.

So, how can we use the chronic model to our advantage? We can (1) recognize that we do have a problem with the chronic illness, and (2) consider each of the six categories of the model as a challenge and focusing on specific solutions. By doing so, we will have healthier patients; certainly, satisfied providers; and, ultimately, cost savings. Typical considerations include:

■ Community
  – The challenge is that many practices cannot provide all of the services and support that patients and families need for optimal chronic illness care.
  – The solution is community resources that can supplement and support efforts to improve the care of patients with chronic illnesses, mobilize community resources to meet the needs of patients, encourage patients to participate in effective community programs, and form partnerships with community organizations to support and develop interventions that fill gaps in needed services.

■ Health system
  – The challenge is that system change must begin at the top.
  – The solution is a supportive healthcare organization. Strong senior leadership plays an instrumental role in providing motivation; securing resources and removing barriers; creating a culture, an organization, and mechanisms that promote safe, high-quality care; visibly supporting quality improvement at all levels of the organization, beginning with the senior leader; and encouraging open and systematic handling of errors and quality problems to improve care.

■ Self-management support
  – The challenge is that patients need to "own" their health conditions and have the skills and confidence to make the decisions and changes that lead to better outcomes.
  – The solution involves individual and group interventions and teaching that promote patient empowerment and acquisition of self-management skills, empower and prepare patients to manage their health and healthcare, emphasize the patient's and family's central roles in managing their health, and organize internal and community resources to provide ongoing self-management support to patients.

■ Delivery system design
  – The challenge is that relying on 15-minute, acute care visits initiated by patients with problems does not lend itself to effective chronic disease management.

- – The solution is planned visits and active follow-up, individually or in groups, including self-management and prevention education; defining roles and distributing tasks among team members; using planned interactions and education to support evidence-based care; and giving care that patients understand and that fits with their cultural background.

- ■ Decision support
  - – The challenge is that the practice team must have the information needed to make appropriate clinical decisions at the time when those decisions are made.
  - – The solution involves practice guidelines woven into the fabric of patient care through effective professional education, reminders, and ongoing feedback and reinforcement; promoting clinical care that is consistent with scientific evidence and patient preferences; embedding evidence-based guidelines into daily clinical practice; and integrating specialist expertise with primary care.

- ■ Clinical information system
  - – The challenge is that timely access to critical clinical information about individual patients or the population of chronically ill patients makes it possible to deliver high-quality chronic illness care.
  - – The solution involves a registry of key information on all patients with a chronic condition that is the glue that holds an effective chronic care system together, organizing patient and population data to facilitate efficient and effective care, providing timely reminders for providers and patients, identifying relevant subpopulations for proactive care, and monitoring performance of the practice team and care system.

Note 3: Medical Home

The concept of a "medical home" was initially introduced by the American Academy of Pediatrics (AAP) in 1967. In March 2007, the AAP, the ACP, the American Academy of Family Physicians (AAFP), and the American Osteopathic Association (AOA) issued the "Joint Principles of the Patient-Centered Medical Home" in response to several large national employers seeking to create a more effective and efficient model of healthcare delivery.

Primary Care Example

In the following example, we have identified a practice and have broken that practice into specific tasks, see Figures 12.1–12.19. Furthermore, in Figure 12.20

Primary Care Practice

Inputs: What is needed to start?	What Tools/Equipment are needed?	Outputs: What is created (results) ?
Patient name. Reason for appointment.	Phone, Computer-Schedule, Patient file.	Patient appointment is scheduled.

How is the task done (the steps) ?

1. Schedule appointment on computer: Verify phone #, address, Insurance Co, reason for appointment.

Process Name:

Step 1A, Schedule Appointment, Existing patient call in.

Starting Event: Phone call.	Finish Event: Appointment scheduled.

Who does the work?
The medical receptionist performs this task.

Metrics: How is improvement seen?
Patient is scheduled quickly during the phone call.

Most Common Obstacles?

1. Patient wants to be seen by a specific doctor at a time when the doctor is not in office.
2. Patient is requesting an appointment for an issue that the front desk needs feedback from the doctor on.
3. Re-scheduling within the same day.
4. Patient doesn't show up at appointment time but wants to be seen the same day.

Improvement Ideas

1. N/A

Authors:_____

Figure 12.1   Schedule appointment, existing patient calls in.

Primary Care Practice

Inputs: What is needed to start?

- Doctor decides a follow up visit is required after current exam, or testing, etc.
- Patient completes billing process.

What Tools/Equipment are needed?

Phone, Computer-Schedule.

Outputs: What is created (results)?

- Patient appointment is scheduled.
- Billing has the opportunity to verify dollars owed.

How is the task done (the steps)?

1. Schedule appointment on computer. Verify reason for appointment.

Process Name:
Step 1B, Schedule Appointment, Outgoing patient, follow up appointment.

Starting Event:	Finish Event:
Patient stops at main desk before leaving.	Appointment scheduled.

Who does the work?
The medical receptionist performs this task.

Metrics: How is improvement seen?
Patient is scheduled quickly before leaving the office.

Most Common Obstacles?

1. No regular issues.

Improvement Ideas

1. N/A

Authors:_____

Figure 12.2   Schedule appointment, outgoing patient, follow-up appointment.

Primary Care Practice

Inputs: What is needed to start?

- Doctor decides patient needs to see an external specialist or requires external testing, or both.
- Patient completes billing process.

What Tools/Equipment are needed?

Phone, Computer-Schedule

Outputs: What is created (results)?

- Appointment is made for patient.
- Billing has the opportunity to verify dollars owed.

How is the task done (the steps)?

1. Patient completes billing process.
2. Patient requests receptionist to make an external appointment for them.
3. Medical receptionist makes appointment.
4. Directions or instructions are given to patient.

Process Name:
Step 1C, Schedule an appointment for patient with a external specialist or for external testing.

Starting Event:	Finish Event:
Patient stops at main desk before leaving.	Patient file cataloged.

Who does the work?
The medical receptionist performs this task.

Metrics: How is improvement seen?
An appointment is made quickly for patient before leaving the office.

Most Common Obstacles?

1. Information is missing on order form.

Improvement Ideas

1. Doctor/M.A. Standardized work instruction or process.

Authors:_____

Figure 12.3   Schedule an appointment for patient with an external specialist or for external testing.

Primary Care Practice

Inputs: What is needed to start?

Patient Name.
Reason for appointment.

What Tools/Equipment are needed?

Phone, Computer-Schedule.

Outputs: What is created (results) ?

- Patient appointment is scheduled.
- New patient listed in computer.
- New patient file created.

How is the task done (the steps) ?

1. Verify/update new patient on computer.
2. If other family members are listed, create new record with existing data, as available.
3. Complete new patient questionnaire, input in computer.
4. Reason for appointment.
5. Schedule appointment on computer.
6. Have a new patient file folder made and put in file.

Process Name:

Step 1D, Schedule Appointment, New patient.

Starting Event:	Finish Event:
Phone call.	Appointment scheduled.

Who does the work?
The medical receptionist performs this task.

Metrics: How is improvement seen?
Patient is scheduled quickly during the phone call.

Most Common Obstacles?

1. Patient does not know relevant information.
2. Phone interruptions or temporary backlog of patients checking in or out.

Improvement Ideas

1. Consider sending a questionnaire to patient, to be completed and sent back before appointment.
2. Consider using a web site for patient to use to document history before appointment. Develop some incentive for this to be used.

Authors:_____

Figure 12.4   Schedule appointment, new patient.

Primary Care Practice

Inputs: What is needed to start?

Prescription request is made.

What Tools/Equipment are needed?

- Patient file.

Outputs: What is created (results) ?

- Patient file is placed in file cabinet.

How is the task done (the steps) ?

1. A request for a prescription comes in, by phone, fax or computer.
2. File Clerk obtains patient file.
3. MA, verifies request prescription request with doctor.
4. If prescription is non generic, prescription requires prior authorization.
5. MA calls in prescription or orders it on computer.
6. File Clerk picks up Patient file and puts it away in file system.

Process Name
(Step 1E) Prescription Request Filled.

Starting Event: Prescription request is made.	Finish Event: Patient file placed in file cabinet.

Who does the work?
- File Clerk
- MA
- Doctor

Metrics: How is improvement seen?
- There is no undue delays in the prescription authorization process.

Most Common Obstacles?

1. Some non generic medications need a referral authorization before submitting prescription.
2. Patient file gets shuffled from one person to the next.

Improvement Idea

- Computerized database would eliminate or greatly reduce the paperwork shuffling required.

Authors:_____

Figure 12.5   Prescription request filled.

Primary Care Practice

Inputs: What is needed to start?

Printed schedule.

What Tools/Equipment are needed?

Printed schedule.
Patient file.

Outputs: What is created (results) ?

- Patient file placed in 2 day out box.

How is the task done (the steps) ?

1. Medical receptionist prints out schedule.
2. File clerk finds patient file or orange file.
3. Patient file denoted with day, AM or PM and placed in box in alphabetical order.

Process Name:
(Step 2A) Pull patient file –
Two days out.

Starting Event:	Finish Event:
2 days before appointment.	Patient file placed in box.

Who does the work?

- File Clerk for that day.

Metrics: How is improvement seen?

All patient files quickly found.

Most Common Obstacles?

1. Files are in Diagnostic Lab or on Dr. Desk (not where they belong).

Improvement Ideas

1. Computerized database for patient files.

Authors:_____

Figure 12.6   Pull patient file—two days out.

Primary Care Practice

Inputs: What is needed to start?
Printed schedule.
Patient file.

What Tools/Equipment are needed?
Printed schedule.
Patient file.

Outputs: What is created (results) ?
- Patient file reviewed and ready for patient visit.

How is the task done (the steps) ?
1. Medical receptionist prints out schedule.
2. File clerk finds patient file or orange file.
3. Patient file denoted with day, AM or PM and placed in box in alphabetical order.
4. Medical Receptionist checks if balance is due. – File sent to billing if balance due.
5. Verify medical insurance.
6. Highlight patient file.
7. Install attention folder when required.
8. Physical – insert form.

Process Name:
(Step 2B) Review patient file –
One day out or day of appt.

Starting Event:	Finish Event:
1 day before appointment.	Patient file placed in box.

Who does the work?
- File clerk for that day.
- Medical receptionist.

Metrics: How is improvement seen?
All patient files quickly reviewed and prepared.

Most Common Obstacles?
1. Phone call distractions.
2. Lunch time staff shortage.
3. Other interruptions.

Improvement Ideas
1. Computerized database for patient files would reduce the patient file movement.

Authors:_____

Figure 12.7   Review patient file—one day out or day of appointment.

Primary Care Practice

Inputs: What is needed to start?	What Tools/Equipment are needed?	Outputs: What is created (results)?
- Patient sign in.	- Computer. - Patient files.	- File is fully checked and placed on cabinet ready for Medical Assistant. - Red light turned on.

How is the task done (the steps)?

1. Patient signs in.
2. Patient file pulled.
3. Medical Receptionist verifies file is ready, no balance due, insurance, address, phone.
4. Patient asked to confirm information in file.
5. Scan Insurance Card.
6. Medical receptionist verifies insurance is current.
7. Record/re-schedule events in file.
8. Computer file updated if necessary.
9. Verify different doctor – as primary.
10. Late arrivals – get 30 minutes leeway before being called.

Process Name:
(Step 3) Check In / Registration.

Starting Event:	Finish Event:
Patient sign in.	Patient file placed on cabinet.

Who does the work?
Medical Receptionist.

Metrics: How is improvement seen?
- Check in and info verification is quick.

Most Common Obstacles?

1. Patient is slow (elderly).
2. Checking insurance.
3. Lost file.
4. Multiple patients arriving at the same time – Especially Tuesday & Thursday AM, senior bus.
5. Phone call interruptions.

Improvement Ideas

1. Verify insurance is current in advance.

Authors:_____

Figure 12.8   Check in/registration.

Primary Care Practice

Inputs: What is needed to start?

- Red light turns on.
- File is ready to be picked up.

What Tools/Equipment are needed?

BP Test tools, scale, thermometer, EKG, X Ray, etc based on patient issue.

Outputs: What is created (results)?

- Prepared file is placed in diagnostic lab.

How is the task done (the steps)?

1. M.A. obtains the patient file.
2. Current records are placed on top of the file.
3. New info summarized on purple cards.
4. Patient brought to room.
5. M.A. checks vitals, temp, BP, weight, recheck BP if required.
6. M.A. verifies reason for visit.
7. Verify current medications, re-fills and allergies.
8. MA performs initial in house test if feasible.
9. Encounter/billing form is updated with DR name, MA name & room number.
10. Place patient file in diagnostic lab.

Process Name:
(Step 4A) M.A. performs patient prep – current patient with issue.

| Starting Event: M.A. picks up patient file. | Finish Event: M.A. places patient file in diagnostic lab. |

Who does the work?

Medical Assistant (MA)

Metrics: How is improvement seen?
- Process moves quickly with no undue delays.

Most Common Obstacles?

1. Some insurance companies will not cover some test. (Doctor needs to order first).
2. New insurance required additional verification step, through billing.
3. Lack of MA knowledge for preliminary test to be performed.
4. Doctor orders vary on what tests are required.
5. Multiple family members to be seen during one visit.
6. Potential overbooking – depending upon extent of paperwork required.

Improvement Ideas

1. New insurance standard payment practices could be investigated before appointment (if known).
2. Lack of standardized procedure/ work instruction for test to be performed.
3. Multiple patient appointments may be identified before the appointment, so additional time block could be scheduled.

Authors:_____

Figure 12.9 M.A. performs patient prep—current patient with issue.

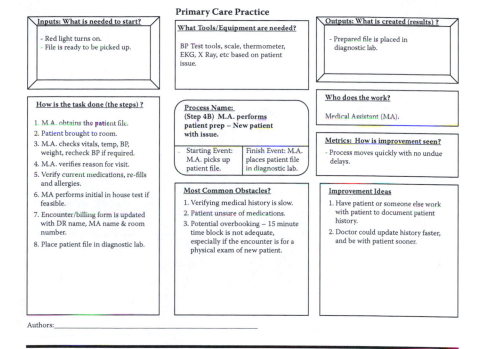

Primary Care Practice

Inputs: What is needed to start?

- Red light turns on.
- File is ready to be picked up.

What Tools/Equipment are needed?

BP Test tools, scale, thermometer, EKG, X Ray, etc based on patient issue.

Outputs: What is created (results)?

- Prepared file is placed in diagnostic lab.

How is the task done (the steps)?

1. M.A. obtains the patient file.
2. Patient brought to room.
3. M.A. checks vitals, temp, BP, weight, recheck BP if required.
4. M.A. verifies reason for visit.
5. Verify current medications, re-fills and allergies.
6. MA performs initial in house test if feasible.
7. Encounter/billing form is updated with DR name, MA name & room number.
8. Place patient file in diagnostic lab.

Process Name:
(Step 4B) M.A. performs patient prep – New patient with issue.

Starting Event: M.A. picks up patient file.	Finish Event: M.A. places patient file in diagnostic lab.

Most Common Obstacles?

1. Verifying medical history is slow.
2. Patient unsure of medications.
3. Potential overbooking – 15 minute time block is not adequate, especially if the encounter is for a physical exam of new patient.

Who does the work?

Medical Assistant (MA).

Metrics: How is improvement seen?
- Process moves quickly with no undue delays.

Improvement Ideas

1. Have patient or someone else work with patient to document patient history.
2. Doctor could update history faster, and be with patient sooner.

Authors:_____

Figure 12.10   M.A. performs patient prep—new patient with issue.

Primary Care Practice

Inputs: What is needed to start?

- Red light turns on.
- File is ready to be picked up.

What Tools/Equipment are needed?

BP Test tools, scale, thermometer, EKG, X Ray, etc based on patient issue.

Outputs: What is created (results) ?

- Prepared file is placed in diagnostic lab.

How is the task done (the steps) ?

1. M.A. obtains the patient file.
2. Place new/current records on top.
3. Patient brought to room.
4. M.A. checks vitals, temp, BP, weight, recheck BP if required.
5. M.A. verifies reason for visit.
6. MA verifies/updates current medications, re-fills and allergies.
7. MA perform initial in house test if feasible.
8. Encounter/billing form is updated with DR name, MA name & room number.
9. Place patient file in diagnostic lab.

Process Name:
(Step 4C) M.A. performs patient prep – Normal Physical Exam.

| Starting Event: M.A. picks up patient file. | Finish Event: M.A. places patient file in diagnostic lab. |

Who does the work?

Medical Assistant (MA).

Metrics: How is improvement seen?

- Process moves quickly with no undue delays.

Most Common Obstacles?

1. If medical/allergic history form is full, MA creates a new form, time consuming.
2. Variation is doctor policy – ex. no physical exams back to back.
3. Potential overbooking – 30 minute time block is not adequate, especially if the encounter is for a physical exam of new patient.

Improvement Ideas

1. Have patient or someone else work with patient to document patient history.
2. Doctor could update history faster, and be with patient sooner.

Authors:_____

Figure 12.11   M.A. performs patient prep—normal physical exam.

Primary Care Practice

Inputs: What is needed to start?
- Patient file.

What Tools/Equipment are needed?

Outputs: What is created (results) ?
- Updated patient file.

How is the task done (the steps) ?
1. No analysis performed.

Process Name
(Step 5) Doctor sees patient.

Starting Event: Obtain patient record.	Finish Event: Place patient file in diagnostic lab.

Who does the work?
Doctor or Physician Assistant.

Metrics: How is improvement seen?

Most Common Obstacles?
1. N/A

Improvement Ideas
1. N/A

Authors:_____

Figure 12.12   Doctor sees patient.

Primary Care Practice

Inputs: What is needed to start?	What Tools/Equipment are needed?	Outputs: What is created (results) ?
- Doctor updated patient file.	- Patient file. - Office test equipment.	Completed patient file given to billing.

How is the task done (the steps) ?
1. MA obtains file from Diagnostic Lab.
2. Update test required on purple card.
3. MA fills out in office form for in office test required.
4. MA performs in office test (EKG, PF, X Rays, injections).
5. MA fills out referral forms for each out office test.
6. MA fills out.
7. (Doctor reviews in office test results, with patient, writes additional orders, if required).
8. MA reviews and documents additional test referrals.
9. MA updates encounter/billing form.
10. MA dismisses patient and takes patient file to billing/check out. Billing relays follow up to scheduling.

Process Name
(Step 6) MA completes testing/paperwork.

Starting Event: Obtain patient record.	Finish Event: MA gives file to billing.

Who does the work?
Medical Assistant.

Metrics: How is improvement seen?
Process is performed with no undue delays.

Most Common Obstacles?
1. MA does not always reprioritize order of in office test to be performed if in office test are busy.
2. Doctor does not always fill out patient encounter form completely.
3. Doctor's diagnosis and orders are not always legible.
4. MA repeats paperwork, due to patient refusing required immunizations.
5. Need to improve communication between doctor and MA.

Improvement Ideas
1. Develop a visual or pull system to quickly reveal what test are backed up
2 & 3. Use computer database and set required fields on form.
4. Eliminate use of recommended immunization refusal form.

Authors:_____

Figure 12.13   M.A. completes testing/paperwork.

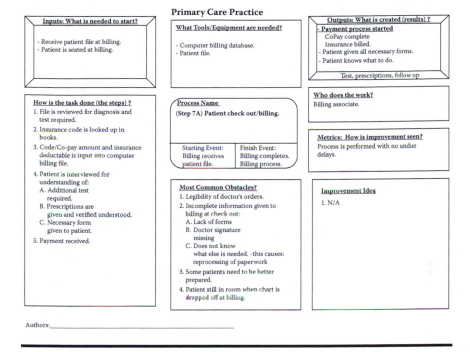

Primary Care Practice

Inputs: What is needed to start?

- Receive patient file at billing.
- Patient is seated at billing.

What Tools/Equipment are needed?

- Computer billing database.
- Patient file.

Outputs: What is created (results) ?
- **Payment process started**
     CoPay complete
     Insurance billed.
- Patient given all necessary forms.
- Patient knows what to do.

Test, prescriptions, follow up

How is the task done (the steps) ?
1. File is reviewed for diagnosis and test required.
2. Insurance code is looked up in books.
3. Code/Co-pay amount and insurance deductable is input into computer billing file.
4. Patient is interviewed for understanding of:
   A. Additional test required.
   B. Prescriptions are given and verified understood.
   C. Necessary form given to patient.
5. Payment received.

Process Name

(Step 7A) Patient check out/billing.

Starting Event:	Finish Event:
Billing receives patient file.	Billing completes. Billing process.

Most Common Obstacles?
1. Legibility of doctor's orders.
2. Incomplete information given to billing at check out:
   A. Lack of forms
   B. Doctor signature missing
   C. Does not know what else is needed. -this causes: reprocessing of paperwork
3. Some patients need to be better prepared.
4. Patient still in room when chart is dropped off at billing.

Who does the work?
Billing associate.

Metrics: How is improvement seen?
Process is performed with no undue delays.

Improvement Idea

1. N/A

Authors:_____

Figure 12.14   Patient check out/billing.

Primary Care Practice

Inputs: What is needed to start?
- Patient file.
- Billing database.
- Computer files.

What Tools/Equipment are needed?
- Computer billing database.
- Patient file.

Outputs: What is created (results)?
- Approved or denied insurance coverage.
- Patient notified of status of test approval.

How is the task done (the steps)?

1. Check insurance type
   - BCN Online–
     Immediate response.
   - Call and notify
     patient.
2. Non Blue Care Network
   - Call Insurance
     company.
   - Present case verbally.
   - Esc level 1, submit
     data.
   - Esc level 2, submit
     data for nurse review.
   - Esc level 3, Engage
     doctor and Insurance
     in a discussion.
   - Insurance gives
     decision to approve or decline.

Process Name
(Step 7B) Patient check out/billing
–Insurance Referral.

Starting Event:	Finish Event:
Billing receives patient file.	Billing completes. Billing process.

Who does the work?
- Insurance Referral Specialist.

Metrics: How is improvement seen?
- Percent first time through.
- No undue delays in process.

Most Common Obstacles?

1. Not knowing insurance companies
   rules.
2. Inadequate documentation from
   doctor to meet insurance companies
   criteria (ex: ordering test).

Improvement Idea

1. Improved documentation from doctor,
   that matches insurance company criteria.
2. Gather criteria from Top 3 Insurance
   companies.

Authors:_____

Figure 12.15   Patient check out/billing—insurance referral.

Primary Care Practice

Inputs: What is needed to start?

- File clerk picks up patient file in billing.

What Tools/Equipment are needed?

- Patient file.

Outputs: What is created (results) ?

- Approved or denied insurance coverage.
- Patient notified of status of test approval.

How is the task done (the steps) ?

1. Obtain file from billing.
2. If test is required within two weeks.
3. File given to scheduler to make an appointment for external test.
4. Referral Specialist contacts HMO and verifies test to run.
5. Completed patient file is picked up by file clerk and if required, test results are faxed to other doctors, pharmacies, etc.
   - Document fax record on file.
   - Patient file is placed in file system.

Process Name

(Step 7C) Patient check out/billing –HMO Insurance Referral.

Starting Event:	Finish Event:
Billing receives patient file.	Billing completes. Billing process.

Most Common Obstacles?

1. Some tests take longer to get authorization.

Who does the work?
- File Clerk.
- Insurance Referral Specialist.

Metrics: How is improvement seen?
- Percent first time through rate.
- No undue delays in process.

Improvement Idea

- N/A

Authors:_____

Figure 12.16   Patient check out/billing—HMO insurance referral.

Primary Care Practice

Inputs: What is needed to start?	What Tools/Equipment are needed?	Outputs: What is created (results) ?
- Monthly report of past due patient accounts. - Cash only report.	- Computer billing database. - Patient file.	- Thorough analysis and attempted communication with patient documented. - Documented record of no action from patient.

Who does the work?
Insurance referral specialist.

How is the task done (the steps) ?

1. Monthly report flags post balance patient accounts.
2. Code A >/ 20 account list prioritized by amount due.
3. Review list of previous communications (patient contact list).
   - Multiple phone calls due to no response.
   - Minimum of two letters – no response also.
4. Transfer patient file to Dr X or Dr Z financial decision.

Process Name
(Step 8) Other Bill Collection Efforts – Post Patient Balance Collection.

Starting Event: Monthly report.	Finish Event: Send file to Bad box.

Metrics: How is improvement seen?
Increased number of post balance issues collected.

Most Common Obstacles?

- No reply from patient.

Improvement Idea

1. Bad Box turn-over on decisions.

Authors:_____

Figure 12.17 Other bill collection efforts—post patient balance collection.

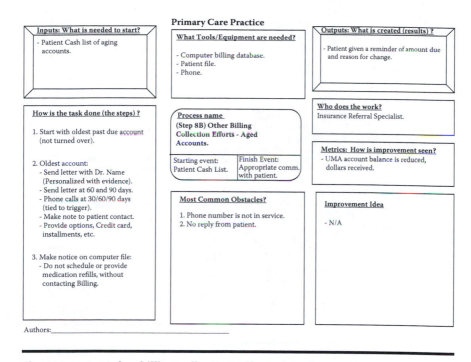

Primary Care Practice

Inputs: What is needed to start?
- Patient Cash list of aging accounts.

What Tools/Equipment are needed?
- Computer billing database.
- Patient file.
- Phone.

Outputs: What is created (results) ?
- Patient given a reminder of amount due and reason for change.

How is the task done (the steps) ?

1. Start with oldest past due account (not turned over).

2. Oldest account:
   - Send letter with Dr. Name (Personalized with evidence).
   - Send letter at 60 and 90 days.
   - Phone calls at 30/60/90 days (tied to trigger).
   - Make note to patient contact.
   - Provide options, Credit card, installments, etc.

3. Make notice on computer file:
   - Do not schedule or provide medication refills, without contacting Billing.

Process name
(Step 8B) Other Billing Collection Efforts - Aged Accounts.

Starting event:	Finish Event:
Patient Cash List.	Appropriate comm. with patient.

Most Common Obstacles?

1. Phone number is not in service.
2. No reply from patient.

Who does the work?
Insurance Referral Specialist.

Metrics: How is improvement seen?
- UMA account balance is reduced, dollars received.

Improvement Idea

- N/A

Authors:_____

Figure 12.18 Other billing collection efforts—aged accounts.

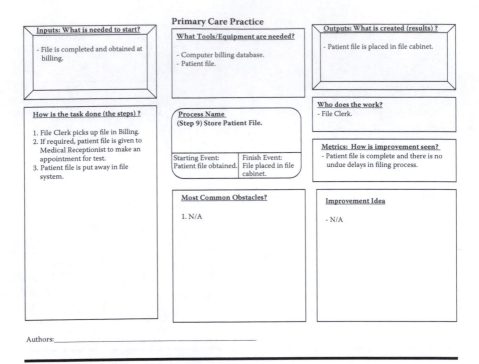

Primary Care Practice

Inputs: What is needed to start?

- File is completed and obtained at billing.

What Tools/Equipment are needed?

- Computer billing database.
- Patient file.

Outputs: What is created (results) ?

- Patient file is placed in file cabinet.

How is the task done (the steps) ?

1. File Clerk picks up file in Billing.
2. If required, patient file is given to Medical Receptionist to make an appointment for test.
3. Patient file is put away in file system.

Process Name
(Step 9) Store Patient File.

Starting Event: Patient file obtained. | Finish Event: File placed in file cabinet.

Who does the work?
- File Clerk.

Metrics: How is improvement seen?
- Patient file is complete and there is no undue delays in filing process.

Most Common Obstacles?

1. N/A

Improvement Idea

- N/A

Authors:_____

Figure 12.19   Store patient file.

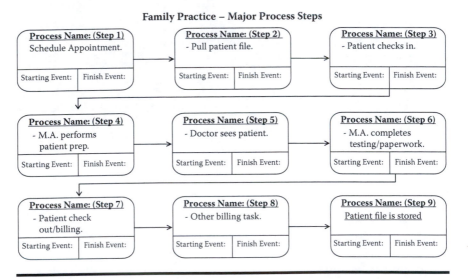

Family Practice – Major Process Steps

Process Name: (Step 1)
Schedule Appointment.

Starting Event: | Finish Event:

Process Name: (Step 2)
- Pull patient file.

Starting Event: | Finish Event:

Process Name: (Step 3)
- Patient checks in.

Starting Event: | Finish Event:

Process Name: (Step 4)
- M.A. performs patient prep.

Starting Event: | Finish Event:

Process Name: (Step 5)
- Doctor sees patient.

Starting Event: | Finish Event:

Process Name: (Step 6)
- M.A. completes testing/paperwork.

Starting Event: | Finish Event:

Process Name: (Step 7)
- Patient check out/billing.

Starting Event: | Finish Event:

Process Name: (Step 8)
- Other billing task.

Starting Event: | Finish Event:

Process Name: (Step 9)
Patient file is stored

Starting Event: | Finish Event:

Figure 12.20   Family practice—major process steps.

we have identified the major process steps for this particular practice. The reader will notice that, after the tasks have been identified, then and only then the focus of improvement can begin. In this example, we provide an approach of evaluating the practice starting with primary concerns and following up with secondary concerns.

Concerns and Comments

Evaluating the process from this flow, the following may be generalized as potential issues or opportunities to improve. Obviously, in some cases, we need more information and more analysis. However, this is an excellent way to start the process:

1. Scheduling time block is not tuned to patient requirements.
   - Physical exams need additional time
   - New patients
   - Special-issue patients
2. Necessary patient data are located on multiple systems.
   - Scheduling database
   - Billing database
   - Patient medical file (paper)
3. Patient file movement is slow and cumbersome.
   - Misplaced or damaged files
4. Variation in standard office procedures and doctor-specific instructions leads to confusion for medical assistants.
   - For example, cholesterol test requirement—fasting versus not fasting
   - For example, some doctors see all patients, even if schedule is full, which increases wait time for other patients
5. Filling out a new paper medical record form is time wasted for MA.
6. Legibility of doctor diagnosis or test required and forms not completed lead to confusion, rework, and errors by MAs and billing personnel.
7. Workload on MA may be excessive.
   - Consider shifting medical history updates to another portion of process

Secondary Concerns

8. To gain an understanding of the entire process, it may be necessary to analyze standard practices of each doctor and the process flow (PF).
9. Variation in insurance company policy's and test criteria leads to confusion and additional work.

- Consider performing an analysis of the various companies to determine how many from each is seen at this particular family practice. Perhaps the smaller volume insurance companies could be eliminated.

Summary

In this chapter, we discussed the issues of primary care and how we can define the process as well as how we can redesign it for improvement. We also gave an extensive example of how to start the process of understanding a physician's practice by using a process map. In the next chapter, we will discuss information technology in healthcare.

References

BCBS. June 5, 2009. Physician's group incentive program fact sheet.

Kenny, S. 1993. Survey of physician practice behaviors related to diabetes mellitus in the U.S.: Physician adherence to consensus recommendations. *Diabetes Care* 16: 1507–1510.

Perrin, J., C. Homer, D. Berwick, A. Woolf, J. Freeman, and J. Wennberg. n.d. Variations in rates of hospitalization of children in three urban communities. *New England Journal of Medicine* 320: 1183–1187.

Robert Wood Johnson Foundation. September 2004 (update). *Chronic conditions: Making the case for ongoing care. Partnership for solutions.* Baltimore, MD: Johns Hopkins University.

Spann, S. 2004. Report on financing the new model of family medicine. Task force report 6. *Annals of Family Medicine* 2 (suppl. 3). S1–S21.

Stockwell, D., S. Madhavan, H. Cohen, G. Gibson, and M. Alderman. 1994. The determinants of hypertension awareness, treatment, and control in an insured population. *American Journal of Public Health* 84: 1768–1774.

Wagner, E., B. Austin, and M. Von Korff. 1996a. Improving outcomes in chronic illness. *Managed Care Quarterly* 4 (2): 12–25.

———. 1996b. Organizing care for patients with chronic illness. *Milbank Quarterly* 74: 511–544.

Selected Bibliography

Backer, L. 2009. Building the case for the patient-centered medical home. *Family Practice Management* 16: 414–418.

Barr, M. 2008. The need to test the patient-centered medical home. *Journal of American Medical Association* 300 (7): 834–835.

Burnette, P. 2009. Think big, start small. *CFO* December: 46–47.

Calkins, E., C. Boult, E. Wagner, and J. Pacala. 1999. *New ways to care for older people: Building systems based on evidence.* New York: Springer.

Fisher, E. 2008. Building a medical neighborhood for the medical home. *New England Journal of Medicine* 359 (12): 1202–1205.

Glendinning, D. 2008. Higher Medicare pay earmarked for practices in medical home trial. *American Medical News* 51 (21) http://www.ama-assn.org/amednews/2008/05/26/gvl10526.htm. Retrieved on December 5, 2009.

Hadfield, D., and S. Holmes. 2006. *The Lean healthcare pocket guide: Tools for the elimination of waste in hospitals, clinics and other healthcare facilities.* New York: MCS Media.

Iglehart, K. 2008. No place like home—Testing a new model of care delivery. *New England Journal of Medicine* 359 (12): 1200–1202.

Institute of Medicine. 2001. *Crossing the quality chasm.* Washington, DC: Institute of Medicine, National Academy Press.

Kellerman, R., and L. Kirk. 2007. Principles of the patient-centered medical home. *American Family Physician* 76 (6): 774–775.

Lewis, M. August 15, 2008. Medical home model improves efficiency, docs say. *Medical Economics.*

McCulloch, D., M. Price, M. Hindmarsh, and E. Wagner. 1998. A population-based approach to diabetes management in a primary care setting: Early results and lessons learned. *Effective Clinical Practice* August–September: 12–22.

Narayan, K., J. Boyle, L. Geiss, J. Saaddine, and T. Thompson. 2006. Impact of recent increase in incidence on future diabetes burden, U.S., 2005–2050. *Diabetes Care* 29 (9): 2114–2116.

Patient-Centered Primary Care Collaborative (PCPCC). Joint principles of the patient centered medical home. http://www.pcpcc.net/node/14 (accessed January 16, 2009).

Sia, C., T. Tonniges, E. Osterhus, and S. Taba. 2004. History of the medical home concept. *Pediatrics* 113 (5): 1473–1478.

Von Korff, M., J. Gruman, J. Schaefer, S. Curry, and E. Wagner. 1997. Collaborative management of chronic illness. *Annals of Internal Medicine* 127: 1097–1102.

Wagner, E., C. Davis, J. Schaefer, M. Von Korff, and B. Austin. 1999. A survey of leading chronic disease management programs: Are they consistent with the literature? *Managed Care Quarterly* 7 (3): 56–66.

Zidel, T. 2007. *A Lean guide to transforming healthcare.* Milwaukee, WI: Quality Press.

Chapter 13

Immediate Applications for Information Technology (IT) in Healthcare

Introduction

In the last chapter, we discussed the process of primary care and patient centered health care (PCHC). In this chapter, we discuss the applications of information technology (IT) as it applies to healthcare in general. By all accounts, the IT intervention in healthcare has the most probability for success in primary care. However, practitioners are not 100% convinced that this infusion of the new technology will be as successful as predicted. Thus, we see the following as we move toward health IT adoption:

- Industry leaders are pushing for health IT as the solution to quality and cost issues, but successful examples are few and inconsistent.
- Many clinicians are strongly drawn to health IT as a mechanism for improving quality of care, but they cannot fully articulate what they need and therefore are left to sort through the varying and often contradictory statements of industry leaders, experienced colleagues, and vendors.

■ Unfortunately, many clinicians assume that existing health IT systems will include the improvement tools they need, but discover that, in fact, important tools are not available or are awkward and sometimes very expensive to use.

Many who advocate the expanded use of health IT appear to believe that it will catalyze improvements in care. While this may be the case in a few narrow instances, we believe that most current health IT systems have a long way to go before they encompass the functionality that would support robust ongoing improvement of care. Additionally, the success of health IT-enabled improvement depends critically on the skills of clinical and administrative staff in primary care settings to understand and use solid improvement methods—methods that need not rely solely on health IT to be effective. The following sections discuss typical areas where IT may be effective in hospitals, convalescent homes, clinics, or primary care facilities.

Billing and Administration

These domain functions are likely to be the most mature for several reasons: the underlying processes have been quite defined prior to automation, healthcare business processes resemble similar processes in other industries that are well understood, the efficiency benefits are relatively easy to document, and healthcare payers and suppliers to healthcare organizations are providing encouragement to move toward electronically managed processes.

Our observation as an IPIP (improving performance in practice) coach has been that most primary care practices started their use of information technology in this area. In addition, we have noticed that truly improving the process of patient care would be impossible without first improving the billing and administrative functions of the practice. The quandary of the primary care clinician working at top speed in a broken system just to keep from falling behind has been eloquently expressed by many.

Electronic Documentation

This domain is less mature and is the predominant focus of many current health IT efforts. Enabling the development of effective electronic medical records (EMRs) is the familiarity of paper records, as well as widely shared traditions of creating, using, saving, and retrieving paper records. These provide at least a scaffold for defining a set of enhanced functions made available through electronic technology. From our experience, many have identified this area as their primary focus currently, and we have heard a number of success stories about implementation of EMRs, especially among networks of clinics or independent physician organizations.

Patient Care

This area is much less able to use IT technology designed to improve the overall system of care continuously, as contrasted to operational or documentation improvements that might reduce certain kinds of errors and waste. From our experience, those who described established practices for using health IT to improve the system of care often cited registries as being critical tools and, in some cases, were skeptical of EMRs or would prefer that EMRs follow and build upon registries, rather than the reverse.

Through learning from and observing private clinics and physicians' practices as well as some hospitals, we have noticed that primary care practices (primarily) are generally addressing two distinct types of improvement: one attainable directly through applying technology to improve operational processes and documentation and the other attainable only through systems that permit continual, ongoing improvement of a system of care. We have summarized the two main ideas of improvement in Table 13.1.

While direct benefits of technology may be more familiar to clinicians and industry leaders and may be the logical place to start for most practices, we believe that, once implemented, the benefits will soon plateau. Technology-enabled improvements *in the system of care,* however, offer recurring benefits and the potential for long-term, continual gains in efficiency and quality of patient care.

It must be emphasized here that, in practical terms, achieving initial efficiency benefits from the technology may be a crucial step for primary care practices. For many primary care professionals, improving the efficiency of their practices may be the only way that they can relieve the pressure of daily demands so that they are able to turn their attention to broader scale systemic improvements in care.

Health IT Focused on Improving Patient Care

The idea of using IT in improving patient care is to support fundamental improvements in care beyond those that would accrue if currently understood errors and waste could be removed. To do this, it is imperative that knowledgeable individuals participate in expert meetings within the practice or facility to formulate ideas and practical practices that add greatly to its robustness.

Table 13.1 Types of Improvements

Direct benefit of the technology	1. Operational efficiency: Scheduling Billing 2. Safety through reduction of administrative or clinical error: CPOE Drug interactions or allergies Missing information
Use of technology to bring improvements to the system of care	1. Proactive planning for population care: Queries and follow-up with subpopulations 2. Whole-patient view for planned care: All pertinent information in one place (all providers and conditions, over time)

Perhaps a good starting point for implementing health IT is to support *ongoing improvements to the quality of patient care as a fundamental property of the healthcare system.* Many efforts to harness health IT to healthcare improvement focus on promoting safety, reducing errors, providing clinical decision support, and improving continuity of care. All of these clearly contribute to the quality of patient care. Yet, they fail to describe the full scope of the opportunity to use health IT to advance healthcare quality.

If we imagined a system of care where no known safety lapses ever occurred, where there were no errors, where relevant clinical decision support was reliably and conveniently available, and where patient data were accessible seamlessly throughout the system, we could still identify major opportunities for improvement. Some examples might include:

■ Providing care and information specifically tailored to the needs, preferences, and medical challenges of each individual
■ Applying prevention strategies for individuals and populations
■ Providing care in ways that are easier to access
■ Proactively reaching out to patients whose conditions may not be responding to standard approaches

- Eliminating wasted effort and material from the healthcare system
- Partnering fully with patients and families or caregivers

One way of encapsulating this vision of a healthcare system is the so-called "care model" developed by the team at the MacColl Institute for Healthcare Innovation (http://www.centerforhealthstudies.org/research/maccoll.html) and its well-known program, Improving Chronic Illness Care (http://www.improvingchroniccare.org/). Originally developed to provide a framework for chronic care, it has been broadened and generalized to look at the overall framework of care and is especially helpful when considering the design of primary care.

The purpose of the model is not to provide a detailed explication of the care model, but rather to suggest that a thoughtfully described model of care can be very helpful as a starting point for thinking about using health IT for improvement (more information can be found at the preceding links and at http://www.ihi.org/IHI/Topics/PatientCenteredCare/SelfManagementSupport/EmergingContent/System+ChangeModelChronicCareModel.htm).

Recognizing that there are many kinds of improvements in any environment, including healthcare, the use of technology to bring about improvements to the system of care is only a single contribution to improvement that allows reliably delivered quality services as defined by the Institute of Medicine (2001). Here, we must remind the reader that (1) improvement is viewed as an ongoing, never ending process, and (2) functionality for improving the quality of patient care must start with the needs of patients—both individual patients and populations or groups of patients. Therefore, there are two priorities:

- Proactive planning for population care
- Planned care for the individual patient as a "whole"

A useful health IT system would provide comprehensive support to clinicians addressing an individual patient's current health status or health concerns, as well as their entire span of healthcare needs today and over time. Similarly, health IT can help clinicians improve the care they provide to whole groups of patients by providing an expanded view of health management of more than one patient at a time. This concept and the methodology to support its activation are less familiar to many clinicians because it is practically impossible to accomplish in a paper-based system. However, just having an electronic system does not ensure that population management functionality will be available. Ideally, health IT will support the work of primary care providers related to individual patients and to groups of patients at a single point in time and over the course of time.

Population (Proactive) Care

To provide effective care for populations, data must be used to answer questions and provide insights into the health status of groups of patients so that their care can be improved consistent with evidence-based recommendations. Key functionality focuses on having flexible, powerful, and easy-to-use tools for querying databases. A "query" is a question asked of the database that results in a list of patients who meet the criteria. A "filter" denotes specific criteria for a data field or item that is defined in the query. In other words, if the user wants to run a query on the database that lists all patients who have diabetes and red hair, the query would contain two filters: one for the diagnosis of diabetes and one for the color of hair.

Two major types of queries are important to focusing on population-related issues. The first defines a subpopulation of interest. This may be a whole panel of patients or, more broadly, all patients served by an organization or a group of organizations. Typically, the initial query will be aimed at a specific subpopulation, such as all patients with a certain condition (e.g., diabetes) or all female patients aged 21 or greater.

The second type of query is used to ask questions about the healthcare status of patients in the chosen subpopulation. For example, if an initial query is used to identify patients with diabetes, then the second type of query can be used to ask questions such as "Which of our diabetic patients have not had an eye exam in the last year?" or "Which of our diabetic patients are out of control based on their last HbA1c result?"

It is critical that the lists of patients include not only useful demographic data for each patient in the lists, but also the associated data that help to understand why the listed patients are on the list. Queries help care teams take action toward proactive population care. The appropriate actions can range from doing nothing (just learning and measuring) to assigning a team of people to contact everyone on the list today (as in the case of a serious medication recall). Usually, the appropriate action falls between these two extremes—for example, creating a mailing or call list for the patients on the list to remind them to come in for a specific type of treatment, test, or screening. Support for direct outreach to patients can be provided through a variety of mechanisms, including automatic or customized e-mails, phone calls, and postal mail.

An information system that supports quality improvement should be able to tie the outreach to a patient's specific data with a rationale for why this is an important issue to resolve and the benefits of doing so—for instance, the rationale for having a particular lab test done promptly. Another benefit of queries is to identify changes that are needed to the system of care—for instance, if a large number of patients are not showing the health results that would be expected based on their care. Using queries to explore *why* patients may not be responding to their care may uncover other opportunities for improving the system of care.

Health IT systems that support improvement of proactive population-based care will need several quality characteristics related to queries and follow-up:

- *The ability to query the database should be open to everyone who is involved in improvement activities.* Anyone on a care team should be able to ask any questions about his or her patient group (panel). Primary care practices will need to determine who in their practice can query the database in support of proactive care for populations. Practice currently ranges from only a few select people to anyone in the practice. A good answer will address issues about who should see data from which patients.

- *The health IT system should support instant access to query results.* Instant availability of results is essential to supporting improvement. Any time a query has to be passed to someone else to run or has to be put in a queue for overnight processing (or worse, days and weeks), the energy for the effort necessary to drive improvement is diminished. When a query is generated from an experience with a patient or a conversation with another provider, while the idea (question) is fresh, an answer has the biggest impact. For example, recently a doctor relayed an experience in which she was examining a diabetic patient who had recently become pregnant. Immediately after the patient encounter, the doctor asked, "How many of my diabetic patients are of child-bearing age? Of those, how many are on birth control? How many of them have had any kind of pregnancy counseling?" Because her health IT system allowed her to ask these questions immediately, she knew within minutes how many patients she had for each question and who they were.

- *The querying system should allow the user to ask any question.* This means that any data in the database should be accessible to being queried. Using terminology already defined, if a data item exists in the database, a filter can be constructed and built into a query. Furthermore, any set of multiple filters on multiple data items can be combined into a query.

- *The everyday user of the health IT system should be able to construct and run queries without technical assistance.* Because database querying is a fairly technical process, the user must be shielded from this technical complexity by a "wizard" that is extremely easy to use. This means that the interface to the query system should contain defaults that will capture the most common questions, as well as provide the option to override the defaults easily. Building needed queries should not require technical assistance except in rare cases.

■ *The user should be able to specify the inclusion of any data items in the reports generated by queries.* The simplest form of report from a query is a list of patient names. This, however, is rarely enough information; contact and demographic information are a must. However, to support quality improvement, the query system needs to allow the user to specify that the resulting list or report can include any desired patient data. This aspect of the query feature promotes investigation, which is a critical component of improvement.

■ *The health IT system should support the ability to "drill down" into data.* Drilling down into the data can take two forms: (1) by changing the query slightly—for instance, by adding another filter or by editing the value criteria in one or more existing filters—the list of resulting patients is refined (drilling down into the query), or (2) by linking from the query result to the individual patient records, the user can click on any given patient name and see that patient's data to better understand why that patient is in the resulting query list (drilling down into patient-specific data).

■ *The users should be able to save queries for reuse or refinement.* Although there are a number of ways to accomplish this storage of queries, the most successful seems to be saving the query logic in a file.

■ *The health IT system should support the sharing of queries.* If a certain query is found to be useful, the person or team that created it should be able to share it with others who may want to pursue the same opportunity for improvement of care. This sharing must be easy to do, such as simply clicking a button that e-mails that query to the other interested parties or uploading it to a shared Web site for collaborative improvement. Note that what is being shared is not the list of patients that resulted from the query, but rather the query logic, which can then be applied to other panels of patients. To be able to share queries across databases requires certain standardization: query structure, database structure and fields, and the process for sharing the queries themselves.

■ *The types of action taken on the lists of patients in a query need to be flexible.* The system should support a complete list of possible actions that can be taken on the list of patients (e.g., automatic e-mails or phone calls, creation of call lists, notifications to specific members on the care team or even providers outside the care team, creation of reports that summarize findings from the list, or the placement of a reminder into the patient's record so that the issue is addressed at his or her next encounter).

■ *The action taken on the list should incorporate and use patient data to further segment the action.* The system should be able to utilize other pertinent patient-specific data to adjust which patient gets which action. For example, if the query results in a list of diabetic patients who have not had an HbA1c in the last 6 months, the action could be different for those diabetic patients whose last HbA1c was above 10 (possibly direct phone call) and those whose last HbA1c was in control (an automatic letter reminder to come in at their convenience). Also, including the actual patient data in the contact (by letter, e-mail, or phone) can help the patient become more involved and understand the need for action.

■ *The system needs to automate the actions whenever possible.* This is an area where an electronic system can improve efficiencies. When appropriate, automated contact can save resources and provide completeness in a way that individual manual contact cannot. Of course, care must be taken that automated contact is appropriate. Whereas an e-mail or letter reminder of the need for an eye exam would seem very appropriate, an e-mail notification of the results of an HIV/AIDS test would not.

Whole-Patient (Planned) Care

Most patients' health needs are a mixture of acute episodes like a strep throat, treatment of chronic conditions like asthma or hypertension, and recommended preventive and health promotion activities such as routine screenings, vaccinations, or smoking cessation support. For a health IT system to support the "whole" patient, it must be able to present a coherent view of all aspects of the health status of the patient. Several types of functionality will contribute to improvement of care for the "whole patient."

A summary of all pertinent patient data should be available in one place to support the planning of care. At a minimum, the whole-patient view should include demographics, vital signs, a problem list (including current and past conditions), a medication list, past labs and other diagnostic tests for the patient, vaccinations and immunizations, risk factors, other relevant measures (such as personal health questionnaire [PHQ] score for depression or number of cigarette packs smoked per day), consults and education, referrals, notes, and reminders.

These data items need to be displayed densely so that they fit into one screen (without the need to scroll) or onto one piece of paper. (See Tufte 1983, pp. 167–168, for an overview of why and how dense data displays result in better use of information and do not result in information overload or confusing the user.) The display should also include data items that are clinically related to existing patient data. Evidence-based reminders can be unobtrusively indicated by using differentiation or affordances (visual clues to the function of an object), as opposed to using attention-distracting and time-consuming pop-ups that require separate clicking.

The ability to view data over time is fundamental to understanding and coordinating improvement efforts. At a minimum, time-ordered display of numeric data (run charts) should be available at the click of a button. Ideally, the run charts should include annotations of pertinent changes in therapies. Another type of display is the traditional flow sheet. An electronic version of a flow sheet provides much more flexibility than the traditional paper-based flow sheet. With the latter, the user is limited in the number of data items being tracked and the number of encounter columns to display. With an electronic flow sheet, these limitations go away.

A well-designed health IT system will use existing patient data (such as diagnoses and lab values) to produce materials for the patient. The provider should see a choice of recommended materials and select the ones that are clinically appropriate for the patient. Clearly, the materials should include the patient's data to help make the educational interaction more meaningful. Quality characteristics of a system for planned care for individual patients include:

- *Data for the whole patient should be displayed in one place.* Even those health IT systems that capture most of the pertinent data for great care often do not have mechanisms for pulling the data into a single location. A single, comprehensive display will require sophisticated design allowing a dense display of data that is easily readable and reflects the unique situation of each patient.
- *The whole-patient display of patient data should be dynamic in order to match the dynamic nature of each patient.* Each patient is a dynamic entity or system; therefore, the data needed to guide care are also dynamic in nature. This means that template-based displays of patient data will fall short of displaying a comprehensive summary of all of the pertinent data. Each patient is different and each patient's health-related data change over time.
- *The whole-patient display of data should be used for planning, conducting, and following up after the patient encounter.* To plan for the care of the 15–30 patients to be seen by the care team on a given day (or the following day), using the paper chart is an exercise in futility. Many important aspects of care for most of the patients will be missed, including important interactions between conditions and the treatments for those conditions. Few teams can afford the 5, 10, or even 20 minutes it might take to collect all the necessary information from the chart. Even with most electronic medical records, the important data are scattered in many places and reviewing all those data in all those places requires too much time. If all the necessary data, along with the evidence-based prompts and reminders, are on one page or one screen, it is possible to review the planning for 15–30 patients in less than 30 minutes. The same rationale holds for

conducting the encounter (face to face or virtual) as well as follow-up to the encounter.

■ *The whole-patient display of patient data should support care across all conditions and health issues, rather than just the complaint that brings the patient to a particular encounter.* For patients with multiple conditions, the interactions between these conditions are often overlooked. Even if the patient has come in for a sore throat, the provider can quickly assess and address the patient's diabetes or asthma care.

■ *The whole-patient display of patient data should act as a central location for other views of patient data, such as run charts of lab results and vitals.* Critical to the idea of a central location for viewing the whole patient is the concept that these other views (run charts, electronic flow sheets, etc.) should be only one click away and that the whole-patient view remain on the screen and be on the main screen again when the run chart or flow sheet is closed.

■ *The whole-patient display of patient data should incorporate evidence-based prompts and reminders in a useful and nonintrusive way.* In most health IT systems, prompts and reminders are in their own location (not in a single, whole-patient view) or are scattered about in various templates. When the evidence-based prompts and reminders are displayed (perhaps using color coding to represent priority or severity) within the single, whole-patient view, the provider (and the rest of the care team) can see and react to the reminder, and also see the context for the reminder.

■ *The health IT system should provide a portal for the patient for both input and viewing data, giving the patient some control over his or her record.* Although there is controversy over the issue of ownership of the data, almost everyone agrees that patients should have access to their clinical data and even ability to input data (e.g., weight or blood pressure readings from home). These are important steps to involving patients in their own care. The portal should also provide an additional channel of communication between the patient and the provider that allows the patient to ask questions or divulge information that he or she forgot or was too embarrassed to tell the provider at the last visit.

Measurement

The health IT system must be able to provide feedback to the care team, organization, and patient about the quality of care actually delivered. Measurement is a key tool for knowing whether changes to the healthcare system are resulting in improvement. The reporting of key measures of quality of care is one critical area of functionality. Measurement needs to be automated to produce summary statistics on a regular basis. However, the system also needs to support the ability to ask the system manually, at any time, to produce a key measures report.

Tracking process and outcome over time (months) will allow the care team to determine whether they are progressing and at what rate. Trends that can be subdivided by demographic measures (sex, ethnicity, age, etc.) can be used to investigate the impact of demographic factors on the improvement effort.

Standard measures can be used to compare one group with another (providers, clinics, organizations, etc.), but there is a danger that, over time, standard measures can be "gamed." If the stakes are high, the stakeholders may resort to improving the measures instead of the care. For example, a clinic may not accept certain high-risk patients if they would adversely affect performance measures.

Allowing the care team to modify or add additional measures without requiring supplier or IT resources allows the care team quickly to test new ideas that may result in an improvement. This ability will encourage the provider team to innovate and facilitate the healthcare improvement process buy-in. Health IT systems should facilitate a patient-oriented view of the quality of care. Bundled measures or indexes (Nolan and Berwick 2006) allow easy tracking of how often all recommended care is being delivered. These measures reflect patient expectations regarding clinical quality (i.e., that all recommended tests and treatments appropriate for a patient's condition are performed and that the outcomes are acceptable). Bundled indexes are harder to "game" than standard indexes. Typical quality characteristics of a health IT measurement system include:

- *The measurement module allows the user to customize any report by adding or changing a filter.* To help the care team explore why a particular measure or set of measures is not showing improvement, it is often useful to run the "standard" report with a modifying filter to drill down into specific subsets of patient data. It is often very useful to run reports by provider, by site, or by some patient designator.
- *The query and filter structures for measurement and reporting features are identical to those used for the proactive population-based care tool and for reminders and prompts.* Many current health IT systems utilize two or more separate sets of criteria for bringing evidence-based guidelines to bear. For example, a number of systems have a set of criteria for generating prompts and reminders for a specific patient and a different set of criteria for running population queries about whether patients have received care that is evidence based. Using a single system of querying and filtering for both measurement and reminders has important benefits. First, a consistent set of evidence-based guidelines will also help identify patients in need of care (proactive population-based care). Second, this design results in a simpler system, allowing clinicians to

maintain and utilize fully the prompts and reminders, the reporting system, and the tools for proactive population-based care, without the need to depend on information technology specialists (except in rare, extremely complex situations).

■ *Ability to customize the data presented, as well as the "look and feel" of the data, at the user level.* A critical aspect of ongoing improvement of care is the cycle of investigation and learning. To keep that cycle vital, the methods and tools for investigation and learning must adapt as knowledge grows and spawns more questions. For example, if certain cycles of learning point toward pain management as an important potential source of improvement, then the health IT system has to allow the users to add and track pain management issues that may not have been present in the system before.

■ *Ease of use.* Our experience has shown that organizations and teams that are successful at ongoing improvement of care feel that they should not be reliant on information systems specialists to use the health IT system effectively. This means that the system has to be sophisticated enough to track any data and to ask any question, and that the user must feel that he or she can do all of that without technical guidance (or at least without much and not often). Health IT has not yet experienced leaps in user-friendliness similar to the advent of the first Apple Macintosh computer or the broad availability of desktop publishing software that allows a nondesigner to produce polished publications.

■ *Interoperability.* Within discussions of IT, the term "interoperability" can be used to include a wide array of concepts. For our purposes, we use the Institute of Electrical and Electronics Engineers (IEEE) definition: the ability of two or more systems or components to exchange information and to use the information that has been exchanged (IEEE 1990). From the user's perspective, all electronic data systems should appear as if they get their data from one database. Assuming that lab results are produced in a separate database, the lab results should flow electronically into the clinical database at regular intervals, behind the scenes. The same principle applies to the practice management system and any other data system in use. If data have to be entered manually into one database, they should never have to be entered again.

■ *Data available across the entire continuum of care (all settings and providers).* This quality characteristic is related to interoperability. If all or most health IT systems were interoperable, then connecting primary care to specialty care, emergency room, general hospital, urgent care clinics, dental offices, etc., would be achievable. There is a clear need for having data from the continuum of care available for improvement efforts.

■ *Appropriate data structures to support improvement.* If the purpose of the health IT system is to support ongoing improvement of care, then data need to be stored and displayed in a way that is actionable. For instance, the results of a Pap smear often contain verbose descriptions of findings in no specific order. However, for improvement activities, the kernel of knowledge that would make the Pap smear actionable is the Bethesda scale and the date. Similarly, data that are constrained to billing codes may make it very difficult to track the progress of a chronic diagnosis over time.

■ *Automation.* For both proactive population-based and individual patient care, automation can play a significant role in improving care. For example, for population-based proactive care, the system should automate contacting the appropriate patients. An example of automation to support better individual patient care would be the automatic generation of patient education handouts (including and utilizing patient-specific data and information). Once an action is determined to be appropriate for better care, the health IT system should produce the action based on patient data—in many cases, without even requiring provider interaction. An example would be the production of a mailing list for all diabetic patients who have not had an eye exam in the last year.

Change Concepts

Change concepts are general notions or approaches that are useful in developing specific, actionable ideas for change that can be tested and that will lead to improvement. A useful change concept will stimulate many testable change ideas that can be pursued in practice and helps to widen the field of testable ideas that can be considered. "A change concept is a general notion or approach that has been found to be useful in developing specific ideas for change that result in improvement. … Using change concepts will provoke new ways of thinking about the problem at hand" (Langley et al. 1996). Being able to generate specific change ideas from broad change concepts is a key improvement activity. Fundamentally, there are three broad change concepts.

Use of Models, Including Models of the Desired Care System and Models of Improvement

Two kinds of models can be especially useful in implementing health information technology to support improvement: a model of the desired system of care and a model for generating improvements in that system. Having a model to describe the system of care is critical for successful adoption of technology for several reasons. A model allows the organization to articulate the desired performance of the system and to understand how close the current system is to the intended one. It helps in identifying those areas where technology can help move the system to its intended state. It allows informed choice about what kinds of technologies are needed to support improvement and how those technologies should be adapted and implemented. Because the adoption of technology will bring unforeseen issues, having a model provides guidance for dealing with the unexpected without losing sight of the aims of the whole system.

A model provides a mechanism for maintaining and expanding technological tools over time. A care model, on the other hand, can be understood as a current best approximation for what perfect care would be. Models describe an optimal system that, although it may never be fully attained, is worthy of continuing pursuit. On the other hand, a model of care is not fixed and final; it can be enhanced by learning gleaned through the improvement process.

The second type of model, a model for how to improve the system, provides the means to move closer to the idealized model of care. Deming and others have described the basis for a robust model for improvement that is grounded in "profound knowledge." Profound knowledge, in Deming's formulation, includes systems theory, a theory of knowledge, understanding variation, and psychology of people. Therefore, a useful model for improvement will incorporate an understanding of people, how people learn, an appreciation for complexity of systems, and dynamics of "inherent" and "special" variation in systems. Deming left a rich legacy of writings and these should be fundamental source material for the organization intending to improve.

Most models for improvement make use of a plan-do-study-act (PDSA) cycle that is based on how people learn and are motivated for improvement. Using PDSA cycles allows teams to clarify the aim for improvement, measure impact of improvement, and develop, adapt, and implement changes. (Some sources for learning about improvement methods are provided in Appendix D on the CD that accompanies this book.)

In organizations that are skilled at improvement, the care system model and the model for improvement are integrally connected. The model for improvement is the vehicle for closing the gap between the current state and the intended model of care. Use of the model for improvement allows the care model to be extended and improved and the vision of care to be expanded. The care model points to a vision of the future; the model for improvement allows practical action today in pursuit of that vision.

Focus on a Practical, Patient-Oriented View of Functionality and What It Should Be Able to Accomplish

Much of the current discussion of health IT focuses on the reduction of waste in administrative processes or the avoidance of certain kinds of dangerous errors, such as medication errors, lost lab results, etc. In Chapter 11 and earlier in this chapter, we proposed certain patient-oriented functionality as the starting point for assessing, adapting, and implementing health information technology.

These kinds of improvements will clearly bring positive results to patients and are consistent with quality concepts of mistake-proofing processes. As important as these improvements are, however, once accomplished, they have limited potential to generate significant, continuing improvements over time. Using technology to improve the system of care will offer large and ongoing opportunities for improvement, including optimizing the care team and involving patients and families as partners in care.

Some technologies can offer benefits in both areas. Reminder systems can help to prevent errors, and they can also be used to support implementation of a robust model of care. A reminder system could alert a provider to a drug allergy, thereby avoiding an error; it could also remind a provider to perform certain screening or preventive care, thus increasing the overall value of an encounter to the patient.

Report writing is another function that has relevance in both areas. Reports can support reduction in errors by focusing on compliance with currently expected practice; reports can also be used more flexibly as a tool for learning that is available to all.

Use of Learning Strategies to Accelerate Progress in Testing and Applying Change Ideas

Improvement is a participatory activity, highly reliant on active testing via PDSA cycles and open sharing of what has been learned that will support additional testing and implementation. Learning communities can be a helpful way to accelerate change. They can support growth in understanding the health IT functionality that supports improvement in care, help larger numbers of users evaluate and adapt existing tools and systems, and provide guidance on how to test a promising idea in a variety of settings. Given the challenges of health IT interoperability, local learning communities can make interoperability, at least on a local level, more feasible by sharing technological links.

Communities can be constructed in many ways, from highly informal to more structured. The span of their focus may be on

- Clinically related areas of improvement, such as chronic care or how best to apply the available evidence to patients with multiple complex conditions
- Operational improvements that affect quality of care, such as flow and access
- How technology can best be used to support effective care processes, such as how to empower patients using technology or the best ways to design reminder and alert systems

Many types of learning relationships can be built, whether they bring together multidisciplinary learning groups within a single organization, use listservs to link individuals across organizations, encourage opportunities for observation of the work of peers in other organizations, or are formal collaborative learning methods.

Specific Change Ideas

To translate a broad change concept into specific actions requires identifying specific change ideas that are consistent with that concept. Change ideas are dynamic: As experience grows, new ideas come to light. Appendix D (see accompanying CD) presents some suggested change ideas and some potential ways of testing them based on the work of Langley and Beasley (2007) in the Institute for Healthcare Improvement. Each practice will need to determine what would be the most helpful tests to aid learning and continuous improvement.

Implications for Spread

One of the goals of undertaking this book was to identify a number of successful practices ready for spread to large numbers of healthcare entities, including primary care organizations. In actuality, while we found many organizations and primary care practices that were highly committed to using health IT and extremely resourceful in applying it to improving the quality of care, we found few examples of changes ready for spread. This should not be highly surprising because health information technology that supports robust quality improvement is at a relatively immature stage of development. However, if we compare the progress that has been made since my last book on healthcare in 1996, it is possible to notice an exponential progress with more to come.

Whereas the improvement is steady, one cannot say that all across healthcare everyone is embracing the principles of improvement. In fact, the work of Rogers (1995)—even though it is somewhat dated—is still appropriate and suggests some typical attributes of "spreadable" ideas, such as

- *Relative advantage:* the degree to which innovation is seen as superior to the idea that it supersedes
- *Compatibility:* the degree to which an innovation is perceived as being consistent with existing values, past experiences, and needs of adopters
- *Complexity:* the degree of difficulty to adopt and use
- *Trialability:* the degree to which an innovation can be introduced on a limited basis
- *Observability:* the degree to which results are visible to those testing and to others

It is important here to recognize that, even for Rogers, these spreadable ideas are dependent on commitment of both leadership and management, on at least a weekly basis, if success is to be achieved. It also must be recognized that these ideas will exhibit some typical attributes (see Table 13.2) that must be overcome.

Furthermore, the traditional view of adopter categories may oversimplify the differences in need between the innovative and early adopter groups versus those of the early majority. Some suggest that early majority users are highly intolerant of technology that is unreliable, complicated to use, and nonstandardized (Moore 2002).

Nonetheless, there is significant outside pressure on primary care clinicians to adopt health IT from regulators, health plans, health networks, and, increasingly, patients. Therefore, an appropriate strategy may be to foster additional testing and learning related to the proposed health IT functionality for improvement and to establish spread-based mechanisms to disseminate that learning. We do believe that sharing, as well as inviting testing and input, would accelerate the field's readiness to adopt health IT for quality improvement when it becomes more robust. Langley and Beasley (2007) have identified typical improvements, which are summarized in the following sections.

Table 13.2 Typical Attributes for Spreadable Ideas in an Improvement Environment

Current Situation in Health Insurance Technology for Improvement
Relative advantage → mixed reaction—front line
Compatibility → disruptive to current work
Complexity → generally high
Trialability → difficult
Observability → not easy, takes effort

Data Structures to Support Improvement

Many of the data collected in healthcare are complex. For purposes of documenting the medical record, this level of complexity can often be justified (for reasons of totality and legality). However, in many situations, the level of detail appropriate for medical documentation can get in the way of using the data for the improvement of care. This is especially obvious when the data are used to guide action across a population of patients.

To support improvement of care based on data, especially for groups of patients, data need to be available to the provider (care team) in a form that supports quick and concise interpretation. For example, the full documentation of a Pap smear is often highlighted by commentary from the analyst. This commentary may bring some depth to the interpretation of the Pap smear that should be documented when further inquiry is warranted. However, to support proactive care for patients (especially groups of patients), the Pap smear result stated in the *Bethesda scale* is all that is needed. Further, since the Bethesda scale is a fixed finite set of results, the computer can apply evidence-based guidelines to these results very easily. Attempting to design a computer program to respond appropriately to the general Pap smear report is a monumental (and probably futile) task. The result delivered in a Bethesda scale is actionable with strong support from an electronic system, whereas the full textual report is problematic.

Another aspect of data structures that continues to restrict improvement activities is the billing and reimbursement coding mind-set that permeates much of healthcare data. For example, in many health IT systems, patients with asthma do not have a diagnosis of asthma; they have a data history of billed visits with a billing diagnosis code of asthma. For visits to the clinic that did not involve their asthma (and hence no billing code of asthma was issued), there is no way to relate that visit to their chronic condition of asthma. Additionally, an asthma billing code is often used for a patient who arrives wheezing (whether the patient has a diagnosis of asthma or not). This may not look like a data problem on the surface, but if the health IT system is queried as to how many asthmatics are in a panel, the numbers may be far from reality. While we are trapped in the reimbursement code mind-set, it will be hard to come up with data structures that allow clinicians to understand truly the whole clinical picture of their patients.

Research and innovation are needed to define data structures that are actionable and to build a consistent approach to defining these actionable data structures operationally from the complex medical data that make up much of the medical record today. Computer systems should be designed to take advantage of actionable data structures (e.g., set all the default settings to the simpler actionable data structures and allow the complexity to be accessed only when it is vital through data-query wizards that are easy to use).

Dense Display of Data

Humans are complex and dynamic systems and therefore the data that might provide a representation of that complex and dynamic nature will require clever new methods of being displayed. To facilitate the interpretation of complex and dynamic displays of data and the use of the gleaned knowledge in a busy practice, all the pertinent data need to be in one location (see Chapter 12 Primary Care Example for the discussion about the functionality needed to support the improvement of care for individual patients). However, if the electronic system is going to put all the pertinent data on one screen, the science of dense displays of data will need to be exploited.

The standard design of a health IT system today is template based. Every screen is the same for all patients (except, of course, for the patient-specific data entered). This design makes sense for a system whose main purpose is documentation. However, if the purpose of the system is to support improvement of care, then the template design falls short in its ability to track and display the diversity in patients. Dynamic systems (people) require dynamic displays. It is fundamental for ongoing improvement of care that providers see the information in the data quickly and without missing the interactions (conditions, meds, labs, patient goals, etc.).

Human brains are designed for complex pattern recognition processing; therefore, the more data, correctly arranged, the better. Some useful work in this area has been explored by Tufte (1983, pp. 167–168) and others, but the specific application to the design of a whole-patient view is in its infancy.

Transferability of Data

Most experts agree that we are a long way from having a health IT system that can handle all aspects of the continuum of care (scheduling, billing, inpatient, primary care, specialty care, laboratory results, etc.). This means that the sharing of data across various health IT systems is a critical issue for any providers who want to adopt health IT. Although much talk and activity have been centered on standards for data transferability, the overall effort has been haphazard and piecemeal. There does not appear to be an emerging common structure for healthcare data. In other words, we are nowhere near the standards-setting stage. In addition to this nonstandard approach, there are issues with privacy. Therefore, innovation and research are needed into how best to share data without the fear of having them misused by unscrupulous individuals (in and out of healthcare).

Data structures for billing and documentation are often very different from the data structures that best support improvement. This is best illustrated by the experiences of those who have built interfaces between different types of health IT systems. Several health IT experts in our experience spoke of the effort to build interfaces between EMRs and chronic disease registries. The assumption was that EMRs would have many data elements that would not have a home in the registries and that the EMRs would have a data home for all the data from the registries. In fact, both systems had data that did not have homes in the other system.

Simply put, the systems relied on different types of data. For example, the registries were being used to track data on the number of times a patient exercised or the number of cigarettes smoked per day or the last PHQ score, but the EMR had no specific places to store these types of data. The lack of the designation of a diagnosis in most practice management systems (essentially billing systems) has already been discussed. Some related areas in need of innovation and research include:

- Design of sharing systems (one warehouse with many feeds or many feeds that all share interfacing structures)
- Ownership of the data (including responsibility for accuracy)
- Measures of accuracy of the data
- The issue of data structures (already mentioned), specifically for interfacing health IT systems that serve different purposes

Customization

Ongoing improvement of quality requires the ability of the care team to ask new questions or, at least, slightly different questions. There is a natural progression of learning that is used to support changes and more learning. Poor ability to customize a health IT system will stifle this type of learning and, therefore, improvement efforts. Some specific areas where customization is useful for improvement include:

- Querying the system (ability to create custom reports by adding or editing queries and altering the list of data items displayed)
- Adding new data fields
- Adding practice-specific (or even patient-specific) reminders
- Building relationships between data items (e.g., when X shows up, I want Y to show up with X)

On the other hand, evidence-based guidelines should be protected from being adjusted (in the name of customization), except when the evidence changes. In other words, fixed standards are best set by an agreement of the larger body of clinicians and scientists, and customization should be at the discretion of the individual provider (with the ability, of course, to share the customization ideas with others). We are faced with a tension between standard, static features and the ability to customize to support improvement. Currently, almost all systems err on the side of inflexibility, which results in stifling improvement. Research and innovation into how to optimize around this tension are needed.

Optimal Design of Alerts and Reminders

With most health IT systems, users find ways to turn off or circumvent portions (or, in some cases, all) of the alert and reminder systems. Typically, alert systems are designed such that a response is required, or they display an alert while the provider is in the middle of an important interaction with the patient and health IT system. After several days or weeks of this, providers learn to bypass the alert. Human factors design, along with mistake proofing combined with medical understanding and prioritization, could go a long way toward creating a much better system of alerts, avoidance of errors, and reminders.

Designs That Are Patient-Centric (Patient-Controlled) Personal Health Records (PHRs), Communications, Home as Hub

Despite the positive coverage of the idea of patient centeredness, the patient is typically nowhere near the center in the functioning of health IT systems. Again, this is due to the history of health IT being focused on billing and documentation, from which patients are traditionally kept away. Opportunities for innovation abound:

- Patient portals with direct access to data for comments and additions
- Secure electronic communication between patient and care team
- Computerized physician order entry (CPOE) where the "P" may also stand for patient or at least patient and provider (CP2OE)
- Home as hub
- Patient-controlled record
- Patient seeing the costs associated with medications and labs before they are ordered

Summary

This chapter focused on IT as it is and should be applied in healthcare at large. Specifically, we addressed issues concerning (1) billing and administration, (2) electronic documentation, and (3) patient care. We also discussed some elements of the change concepts and addressed the issues concerning these specific change ideas and their spread. In the next chapter, we will discuss the process of project selection.

References

Institute of Electrical and Electronics Engineers. 1990. *IEEE standard computer dictionary: A compilation of IEEE standard computer glossaries.* New York: Institute of Electrical and Electronics Engineers.

Institute of Medicine. 2001. *Crossing the quality chasm: A new health system for the 21st century.* Washington, DC: Committee on Quality of Health Care in America, Institute of Medicine, National Academies Press.

Langley, G. J., K. M. Nolan, T. W. Nolan, C. L. Norman, and L. P. Provost. 1996. *The improvement guide: A practical approach to enhancing organizational performance.* San Francisco, CA: Jossey–Bass.

Langley, J., and C. Beasley. July 2007. *Health information technology for improving quality of care in primary care settings.* Prepared by the Institute for Healthcare Improvement for the National Opinion Research Center under prime contract number: 290-04-0016, NORC subcontract number: 6275-IHI-01. AHRQ publication no. 07-0079-EF. Agency for Healthcare Research and Quality. U.S. Department of Health and Human Services. Rockville, MD. http://healthit.ahrq.gov/portal/server.pt/gateway/PTARGS_0_1248_661809_0_0_18/AHR HIT_Primary_Care_July07.pdf (retrieved on August 31, 2009).

Moore, G. A. 2002. *Crossing the chasm.* New York: Harper Collins Publishers.

Nolan, T., and D. M. Berwick. 2006. All-or-none measurement raises the bar on performance. *Journal of the American Medical Association* 295 (10): 1168–1170.

Rogers, E. M. 1995. *Diffusion of innovations,* 4th ed. New York: Free Press.

Stamatis, D. H. (1996). *Total quality service.* Boca Raton, FL: St. Lucie Press.

Tufte, E. R. 1983. *The visual display of quantitative information.* Cheshire, CT: Graphics Press.

Selected Bibliography

Committee on Quality of Health Care in America, Institute of Medicine. 2001. *Crossing the quality chasm: A new health system for the 21st century.* Washington, DC: Committee on Quality of Health Care in America, Institute of Medicine, National Academies Press.

Graban, M. 2009. *Lean hospitals: Improving quality, patient safety and employee satisfaction.* Boca Raton, FL: CRC Press.

Chapter 14

Project Selection

Introduction

In the last several chapters, we discussed the significance of understanding the process, the requirements of change, the development of teams, what improvement is, and how this improvement relates to healthcare. In this chapter, we will address the selection of projects for improvement and discuss the deliverables for each stage of the DMAIC model.

When we discussed the methodology of Lean, we introduced the hoshin kanri deployment and suggested that the macro value stream map be based on this policy. When we talk about selection of projects for either Lean or Six Sigma, we also recommend that we start with reviewing the policy deployment and then integrate the hoshin methodology into our projects. Recall that the hoshin approach was used

- To develop long-term strategic objectives
- To identify areas of improvement to achieve strategic goals
- For process improvement (SMED, 5S, standard work, etc.)
- To determine where the organization is going—vision
- To identify key processes
- To perform a gap analysis between the current state and the vision
- To develop a strategic approach to continuous improvement

Now we can use the same hoshin approach to focus on projects that link the organizational goals with improvement in specific areas and specific projects.

The selection is very critical and it must be well thought out. The selected project must not be too large because it will cause valuable time to be lost in determining the operational definitions in the entire DMAIC (define, measure, analyze, improve, and control) model and not too small because the value added will not be commeasurable with the effort given to the project. Therefore, to maximize the success of the selected project, consider the following:

■ The problem must be of a recurring nature.
■ The problem must have a narrow scope.
■ Metrics or measurements must be available that can be developed quickly.
■ The process under consideration must be in control.
■ There must be a direct correlation with customer satisfaction.
■ There must be an objective, tangible cost reduction amount.

If any of these items is present, then the organization should pursue either Six Sigma or Lean methodology. Specifically, in healthcare, the priority hierarchy that is suggested is to address issues and problems in the following order:

1. Customer related: fix external customer satisfaction issues (patients, regulatory agencies, governmental agencies, community, etc.)
2. Company related: fix or improve items regarding cost reduction, efficiency, bottleneck operations, process capability, etc.
3. Internal process improvement: improve operational metrics (see Chapter 11 for specific level I, II, and III improvements)

The lifeblood of both Lean and Six Sigma is the project. Therefore, for either one of these methodologies to survive, quality needs and overall strategic plans must exist in the organization. That is, a system must be established in the organization to address the items detailed in the following sections.

Link between Quality Function Needs and Overall Strategic Plan

This is the most important issue not only in Six Sigma, but also in any Lean endeavor that tries to address improvement of any kind. The focus here is on the quality function needs and the plan to support these needs, both now and in the future. Of course, these needs have to be in line with organizational aims, policies, and plans. Some key considerations are competition, cost, differentiation of product, and usage of appropriate tools.

Link between Strategic Plan and Quality Plan

The second most important issue in Six Sigma methodology and Lean is to correlate the strategic plans with an actual quality plan. This means that the organization has or is willing to develop programs that deal with feedback, corrective action, data collection, processing and analysis, and process and product development. In addition, it means that the organization has or is willing to develop an infrastructure to address such issues as organization, administrative support, control processes, internal audits, processes that identify customer needs, and policies for inspection and testing.

Theory of Variation (Common and Special Causes)

It is beyond the scope of this book to have a lengthy discussion on variation. However, it is imperative that common (inherent) variation and special (assignable) variation are clearly understood. We associate common variation with random, material, prevalent, or normal variation; stable process; predictability; and process improvement through management intervention. On the other hand, we associate special variation with abnormal activity, unpredictability, and specific knowable causes. To understand variation, we must also understand the components of variation: total variation = variation due to factor A + variation due to factor B + variation due to interaction AB + variation due to sampling error.

Typical examples of common variation include:

- Slight variation in raw material
- Slight machine vibration
- Lack of human perfection
- Variation in gauge readings
- Variation in tooling
- Variation in operator skills

Special cause variations include:

- Difference in machines or processes
- Batch of defective raw material
- Faulty machine setup
- Test equipment out of calibration
- Unqualified operator
- Part-time seasonal help
- Variable workforce

Sometimes, it is possible to have variation due to a combination of both types—for example:

- Equipment failure
- Price roll-back
- Employee downsizing

Some typical problems that the Six Sigma and Lean methodology may tackle that confirm Deming's intuitive knowledge about variation and system thinking include:

- Poor design of product and/or service
- Poor instruction and poor supervision
- Failure to measure the effects of common causes and to reduce them
- Failure to provide production workers with information in a statistical form
- Procedures not suited to requirements
- Machines not suited to requirements
- Settings of the machines chronically inaccurate
- Poor lighting
- Vibration
- Mixing product from streams of production (especially in pharmacies in hospitals)
- Uncomfortable working conditions
- Shift of management's emphasis from quality to quantity
- Management's failure to face the problem of inherited defective material

Quality Function Mission Is Very Important in Strategic Planning

The focus here is to make sure that the mission is aligned with the business strategy of the organization. In other words, the goal should be to establish an organizational mission statement in clear and simple language so that (1) it is understood by everyone in the organization (and by others), and (2) the key driving forces to achieve customer satisfaction are identified in such a way that improvement must begin with

- Establishing priorities
- Defining organizational policies

- Analyzing trade-offs to resolve conflict with cost, delivery dates, and other parameters
- Maintaining continual improvement activity

To appreciate even further the power and influence of the mission, let us look at its hierarchy:

- The *mission* is the broad policy of why the organization exists. The focus is on defining the quality mission and policy and providing quality awareness in the organization. It also involves setting goals to meet the mission, training and team concepts, measuring mission accomplishments, and determining the mission's relationship with vision, values, and goals.
- The *vision* is made up of the key processes that assist in fulfilling this mission.
- The *values* are the key indicators to affirm the vision and the mission.

In the context of the Six Sigma methodology, it is imperative to recognize that no organization can function without some (written or unwritten) quality principles and policies. Therefore, management must champion the key principles and policies for the entire organization. Typical issues include:

- The need for quality principles and the right policies (creed, beliefs, truths, rules, and moral and ethical standards as they relate to the uniqueness of the organization's history, management, and state of development)
- Appropriate approval from executive management (practiced by everyone)
- Participation by key managers
- Understanding the need for customer relations (internal and external)
- Understanding the need for continual improvement
- Understanding that everyone should be involved and concerned
- Understanding the importance of quality
- Understanding the importance of planning and organization

Metrics and Goals That Drive Organizational Performance

We cannot talk about performance in the abstract. Performance is always the result of a function. Therefore, for performance to be of value, the organization must have metrics and goals. The goals should be attainable, realistic, measurable, and related to customer usage. The metrics, on the other hand, must be identified as real measures for these goals. One should not be afraid to take a risk if the risk is commensurable with the anticipated benefit. Fundamental requirements used as metrics may be the following items:

- Customer satisfaction
- The voice of the customer
- Economic ramifications
- Environmental and legal impact
- Worthiness
- Applicability

A visual representation of the link between metrics and goals may be seen in Table 14.1.

Table 14.1   Links of Metrics and Goals

Customer-driven master plan	Hoshin planning	Work teams
	Daily control	Standardization
	Cross-functional management	Continual improvement
	Quality dynamic control plan	Vertical trends
		Seven management tools
		Seven basic tools
		Quality assurance
		Kano model (inputs)
		Quality function deployment
		Customer and supplier awareness
		Audit tools
		Information system
		Statistical methods

←――――――――――――――――――――――――――――→

Resource Requirements to Manage the Quality Function

The last item in strategic planning is resources. It must be recognized and understood that a typical organization embracing the Six Sigma and Lean philosophies requires everyone directly involved to be appropriately trained, especially at managerial levels. Thus, the issues associated with resource requirements are quite important for the organization. Typical items of concern include:

- Appropriate and applicable training
- Knowledgeable personnel
- Adequate leadership commitment
- Inspection and testing availability
- Work performance personnel
- Verification capability

How Is Robustness Incorporated into Six Sigma and Lean Methodologies?

Robustness is an issue of both design and process. The aim is to identify factors that are important enough in the presence of noise so that satisfaction is the result. A typical strategy for robustness is to

- Change the technology to be robust
- Make basic current design assumptions insensitive to noise
- Reduce or remove the noise factors
- Insert a compensation device
- Send the error state or noise somewhere else where it will be less harmful—in other words, disguise the effect

What Is the Significance of the Project?

The aim of the Six Sigma and Lean methodologies is improvement in specific projects, authorized by management, which black belts or green belts attack with the intention to remove the specific problem. The project has to be worth pursuing with regard to return on investment (ROI) (business case), as well as customer satisfaction. The project is the lifeblood of both methodologies, and it requires very rigorous investigation, analysis, implementation, and follow-up to make sure that the gains claimed become gains realized. It usually follows the following pattern:

- Develop the problem statement.
- Determine the problem objective.
- Determine the COPQ (cost of poor quality) parameters.
- Identify CTQ (critical to quality) and operational definitions.
- Determine which tools should be used to measure the current status and to prioritize the input variables that contribute to the problem as defined.
- Validate improvement to determine the relationship of $Y = f(x...)$.
- Institutionalize the results in such a way that the gains are sustained.

A suitable project may be identified in various ways. However, the main factors that make a project a suitable candidate for Six Sigma and Lean are that it has

- Recurring events
- Narrow scope
- Available metrics or measurements that can be developed quickly
- Control of the process
- Customer satisfaction
- An annual cost savings target of over $50,000; the classic goal is $250,000

For the project to be effective, there are two issues of concern: the project objective and the problem statement. The project objective provides a clear macrostatement of the problem. This allows the process owner and team members to focus on what needs to be improved (Y variables). Team members should be specific about the defect, but not include possible solutions. A useful problem statement must have the condition, the criteria, and the measurement (e.g., "missing medications will be reduced by 20%, resulting in a profit impact of $100,000 and customer satisfaction of 15% increase in the next 12 months").

The problem statement states the goal or goals of the project. It also links to the business objectives through expected output variable performance, impact on ROI, and project timing. It is important to use enough detail to define success.

What Is the Cost of Poor Quality?

The COPQ is the items that drive the project's ROI improvement. Typical examples may be the cost of scrap, the cost differential of reduced quality material, headcount reduction, and transportation costs to receive defective products as well as to send new ones.

What Is Customer and CTQ Identification?

The customer is typically the one who dictates the output specifications (Ys in the statement $Y = f(x)$). That is why it is very important to specify project customers (and to prioritize for more than one). In other words, the more that is known about the customer's needs, wants, and expectations, the more precise and accurate the project requirements will be to satisfy them. Customers may be internal or external.

In conjunction with the appropriate customer, it is imperative also to specify and define the project operationally in terms of CTQ and variable measurements. This means that the more that is known about the customer's needs, wants, and expectations, the more the project can be aligned to satisfy the CTQ requirements as well as focus on variable measurements for evaluating success.

What Is the Significance of a Data Collection Plan?

Data are the driving force for any analysis. Therefore, it is important to know and identify a data plan, explaining what data must be collected and how they will be collected. Without appropriate and applicable data, project results may be questionable.

Measurement for Projects

As we have mentioned many times, measurement is very important in the pursuit of improvement. Therefore, measurement

- Has an improvement-oriented measure (metrics)
- Provides no data without a rationale and purpose
- Ensures that employees (i.e., the process workers) know why things are being measured
- Ensures that employees know what to do about the measures if a negative trend occurs

There are many different types of measurements. Many times they will be part of a "balance scorecard" or "quality dashboard"—a broad set of categories on which the organization is measured. Traditional scorecards are based on safety, quality, cost, and environmental items. These measurements have goals (based on four elements: focus, validity, connectivity, and integration); when a certain category is not meeting its goal, resources (such as a PDCA [plan-do-check-act] kaizen event) are planned. Performance measurements are of three types:

1. Strategic measures (outcome measures): market segmentation (industry structure, growth, ROI, concentration, innovation, customer loyalty, logistical complexity) and competitive strength (relative market share, quality, intellectual property, customer coverage, etc.), to name a few
2. Organizational measures: leanness, culture, incentives, training and development, etc., to name a few
3. Process measures: customer satisfaction, product or service excellence, capacity utilization, capital intensity, productivity, cycle time, lead time, throughput, etc., to name a few

The approach to measurement for projects is to describe the need for this performance measurement in relation to the Lean or Six Sigma project. This means

- Describing the interim containment actions and/or permanent countermeasures that are planned to address the problem
- Collecting data daily (if appropriate) for each item listed in item (1) in the preceding list (If one measurement will suffice for a group of activities, then note each activity.)
- Creating the appropriate visuals denoting the targets and anticipated results, if applicable
- Monitoring data and making appropriate changes, if needed
- Continuing with the PDCA and/or kaizen event methodology

What Are Some of the Common Formulas Used in Six Sigma?

In addition to the statistical formulas, everyone should be familiar with some basic formulas:

Proportion defective = [number of defectives]/[number of units]

Final yield (noted as Y_{final}) = 1 − proportion defective

Defects per unit (DPU) = [number of defects]/[number of units]

Defects per opportunity (DPO) = [number of defects]/[number of units × number of opportunities]

Defects per million opportunities (DPMO) = DPO × 1,000,000

First pass yield = 1 − [number of units reworked]/[number of units input]

Specific Project Expectations of the DMAIC Model for Each Phase

Proper project selection is one of the most critical success factors influencing the outcome of all projects in both Lean and Six Sigma. One should be prepared to answer these specific questions as one moves more deeply into the project:

- What was the improvement opportunity?
- Was the sample of data sufficient for analysis?
- Are the preliminary analyses results providing project direction?
- Is the baseline measurement of current performance accurate and appropriate?
- What are the root causes contributing to the improvement opportunity?
- How were the data analyzed to identify sources of variation?
- Did analysis result in any changes to the problem statement or scope?
- *Define* phase:
  - Overview
    - The purpose of the define phase is to further refine the Six Sigma project team's understanding of the problem to be addressed. In addition, the project team will use the define phase to get organized, determine roles and responsibilities, establish goals and milestones, and review process steps.
  - Key concepts
    - Voice of customer
    - Project scoping
    - Cause and effect prioritization
  - Project planning
    - Note: Because subsequent Six Sigma process steps build upon work completed during the define phase, project team members should ensure that the customer and CTQs have been accurately identified. Likewise, the project team should ensure that the current process has been accurately mapped, the project has been narrowly scoped, and a descriptive problem statement has been written before proceeding to the measure phase.
  - Outcomes: at the completion of the define phase, the project team will have
    - Defined the problem with a problem statement
    - Specifically identified the process's or product's customer
    - Defined CTQ characteristics from the customer's viewpoint
    - Scoped the project
    - Produced a refined problem statement

- *Measure* phase
  - Overview
    - The purpose of the measure phase is to establish techniques for collecting data about current performance that highlight project opportunities and provide a structure for monitoring subsequent improvements.
  - Key concepts
    - Sound data collection plan
    - Identification of key process input variables (KPIVs)
    - Variation displayed using Pareto charts, histograms, and run charts
    - Baseline measures of process capability, and process sigma level
  - Outcomes: upon completing the measure phase, project teams will have a
    - Plan for collecting data that specifies the data type and collection technique
    - Validated measurement system that ensures accuracy and consistency
    - Sufficient sample of data for analysis
    - Set of preliminary analysis results that provides project direction
    - Baseline measurement of current performance

- *Analyze* phase
  - Overview
    - As an outcome of the measure phase, the project team should be narrowing its focus on a distinct group of project issues and opportunities. The analyze phase allows the project team to further target improvement opportunities by taking a closer look at the data.
    - Note: The measure, analyze, and improve phases frequently work hand in hand to target a particular improvement opportunity. For example, the analyze phase might simply serve to confirm opportunities identified by graphical analysis. Conversely, the analyze phase might uncover a gap in the data collection plan that requires the project team to collect additional information.
  - Key concepts
    - Attribute versus variable data:
      - Attribute data reflect one of two conditions, such as yes/no, defect/no defect, or accurate/inaccurate.
      - Variable data reflect a range of conditions, such as processing time, items processed, or number of defects.

- Hypothesis testing
  - Statistical analysis used in Six Sigma to validate differences between data groups
- Outcomes: upon completion of the analyze phase, project team members should be able to answer the following questions:
  - What was the approach to analyzing the data?
  - What are the root causes contributing to the improvement opportunity?
  - How were the data analyzed to identify sources of variation?
  - Did analysis result in any changes to the problem statement or scope?

■ *Improve* phase
  - Overview: as an outcome of the analyze phase, project team members should have a strong understanding of the factors impacting their project, including:
    - Key process input variables—the vital few Xs that impact the Y
    - Sources of variation—where the greatest degree of variation exists
    - The purpose of the improve phase is to
      - ■ Generate ideas
      - ■ Design, pilot, and implement improvements
      - ■ Validate improvements
  - Key concepts
    - Brainstorming
    - "Should be" process map
    - FMEA
    - Cost/benefit
    - Pilot
  - Implementation
    - Note: Design of experiments (DOE) is an effective tool that can be used in both the analyze and improve phases of the DMAIC process. However, DOE can be a difficult tool to use outside a manufacturing environment, where small adjustments can be made to input factors and output can be monitored in real time. In non-manufacturing, other creative methods are frequently required to discover and validate improvements. For further details regarding DOE, see Stamatis (2003a, 2003b).
  - Outcomes: at the conclusion of the improve phase, the project team will have
    - Identified alternative improvement
    - Implemented the best alternative for improving the process

- Validated the improvement
- Prepared for transition to the control phase

■ *Control* phase
 - Overview
 - The purpose of the control phase is to institutionalize process or product improvements and monitor ongoing performance. Following the improve phase, the project team needs to transition control of the process back to the process owner.
 - Key concepts
 - To facilitate a smooth transition and ensure the project team's work "sticks," a detailed control plan will be developed. The objective of the control plan is to document all pertinent information regarding:
 ■ Who is responsible for monitoring and controlling the process
 ■ What is being measured
 ■ Performance parameters
 ■ Corrective measures
 - Key components of the control plan include:
 ■ Mistake proofing
 ■ Long-term MSA plan
 ■ Control chart— statistical process control (SPC)
 ■ Reaction plan
 ■ Updating standard operating procedures (SOPs)
 - Outcomes
 - Upon completion of the control phase, the process owner will understand performance expectations, how to measure and monitor Xs to ensure performance of Y, and what corrective actions should be executed if measurements drop below desired levels.

Likewise, after completion of the control phase, the project team members disband while the black belt begins the next project with a new team.

Summary

This chapter discussed the importance of identifying, defining, selecting, and evaluating a project in a typical Six Sigma or Lean methodology. Furthermore, a summary of each phase outcome of the DMAIC model was highlighted. In the next chapter, we address the ISO 9000 standards.

References

Stamatis, D. H. 2003a. *Six Sigma and beyond: Design of experiments.* Boca Raton, FL: St. Lucie Press.

———. 2003b. *Six Sigma and beyond: Design for Six Sigma.* Boca Raton, FL: St. Lucie Press.

Selected Bibliography

Eckes, G. 2001. *Making Six Sigma last.* New York: John Wiley & Sons.

Kloppenborg, T., and J. Petrick. 2004. Managing project quality. *Quality Progress* September: 63–68.

Pande, P. S., L. Holp, and P. Pande. 2001. *What is Six Sigma?* New York: McGraw–Hill.

Stamatis, D. H. 1996. *Total quality service.* Boca Raton, FL: St. Lucie Press.

———. 2002. *Six Sigma and beyond: Foundations of excellent performance.* Boca Raton, FL: St. Lucie Press.

———. 2003. *Six Sigma for financial professionals.* New York: John Wiley & Sons.

———. 2004. *Six Sigma fundamentals.* New York: Productivity Press.

Chapter 15

Understanding and Utilizing ISO 9000 Standards

Introduction

So far we have discussed several ways that improvement may enter healthcare using a variety of methodologies and tools. In this chapter, we focus on the international standards for quality improvement. As we already have mentioned, all initiatives in quality are journeys toward improvement. Many tools, methodologies, and standards have been devised over the years for all different industries. Some are more applicable and useful than others. There is no magic tool or methodology that can guarantee improvement. However, some fundamental ways can improve the chances of success in any environment, including healthcare. One of these fundamental ways is the application of the International Organization for Standardization (ISO) 9000 standard. Generically, it can

- Improve existing quality systems
- Minimize auditing by accrediting organizations
- Improve subcontractors' and vendors' performances

In healthcare, with good planning, hard work, and a continual improvement attitude, healthcare providers and their organizations can use an ISO 9000 quality system to help them to

- Achieve better understanding of quality practices throughout the organization
- Ensure continued use of the required quality system
- Improve documentation and records
- Strengthen patient, supplier, and customer confidence and relationships
- Gain cost savings and improve profitability
- Form a foundation for ongoing total quality management

As important as the ISO standards are, complying with ISO 9000 standards does not ensure that every product or service meets patient requirements, but rather only that the organization's quality system is capable of meeting them. To do the former, organizations must continuously assess how satisfied patients are and improve the processes that create the services.

To be sure, ISO 9000 provides a quality management system that takes into account the measures, settings, services, and functions of both clinical and administrative activities within the healthcare industry. For those who are new to the standard, ISO 9001 provides basic definitions and guidelines that can help healthcare providers select and use the appropriate standard. In addition, it provides the system requirements that are auditable. ISO 9004, on the other hand, is a guideline that shows what a good system should include. Policies, procedures, job instructions, and documentation can be identified or created for each process and for each applicable clause within ISO 9001.

ISO is an excellent way to rationalize business processes in the healthcare industry; because the series is process based rather than compliance based, it is less complicated to implement than either of the Joint Commission on Accreditation of Healthcare Organizations (JCAHO) or National Committee for Quality Assurance (NCQA)/Healthcare Effectiveness Data and Information Set (HEDIS) accreditation systems. ISO 9000 works on the principle that an organization defines its own quality system based on processes that work best for it. Therefore, implementing ISO 9000 in all aspects of healthcare delivery requires unique approaches based on the individual practice, clinic, or hospital.

Consequently, healthcare organizations interested in implementing ISO 9000 and being effective with it must first identify the healthcare measures in a given program as well as the setting in which healthcare is delivered and the services provided. This means that the quality system ready to be implemented in a practice or a hospital environment must establish: (1) goals for performance and improvement, (2) program costs, and (3) parameters for patient satisfaction. Any successful program must address all three items; otherwise, improvement will fall short of expectations.

Healthcare is not as easy as manufacturing in defining and implementing quality systems primarily because healthcare's processes are overlapping much more than those in manufacturing. Healthcare services consist of many parts. In fact, services consist of many component parts, including institutional, ambulatory, long-term and home care; healthcare networks; clinical laboratories; and so on. However, for each delivery mode, it is possible to identify measures for specific settings, services provided, clinical conditions, health function status, customer satisfaction, administrative functions, and fiscal considerations.

In addition to these component parts, healthcare professionals and managers often face a split focus regarding process and outcomes. Clinicians stress outcomes with less concern for how they arrived at them; managers, on the other hand, stress processes. It is possible for both process and outcome to work together, if management and leadership are committed to an integrated healthcare quality management model using ISO 9000.

When implementing ISO 9000, every level of a healthcare organization contributes to the quality effort. Senior leaders participate in annual performance reviews, where they receive individual feedback from the board of trustees, employees, and peers. Included in this evaluation are measures such as effectiveness in meeting short- and long-term strategic goals and communicating quality values to employees and other stakeholders.

Senior leaders communicate and reinforce the organization's stakeholder focus and quality values to managers and supervisors. Communication methods can include job descriptions, bimonthly departmental and weekly individual meetings, and monthly reviews of a quality performance wheel.

Departments also can identify subprocesses, customers, measurements, and action plans that are aligned with performance and improvement. Stakeholder focus and quality values are communicated to the workforce and reinforced through personnel policies, training, staff meetings, departmental meetings, and newsletters. By means of a quality performance wheel (see Figure 15.1), overall organizational and work unit quality, as well as operational performance, is reviewed monthly with department managers.

An organization-wide sharing of quality knowledge, during which individuals and/or teams report on their progress, should also be held monthly. The agenda might include progress reviews, recognizing team and individual efforts, correlating improvement efforts to the strategic plan and the quality wheel, and verifying organizational learning.

Quality performance wheels can be used to monitor and improve virtually any aspect of a healthcare delivery program or system. We already have mentioned the three fundamental items for performance and improvement: performance measurement, program cost, and customer satisfaction. These represent the core for all programs.

The object of the performance wheel is to move measurement goals from the minimum acceptable ring to the outer or performance goal ring, forming a perfect

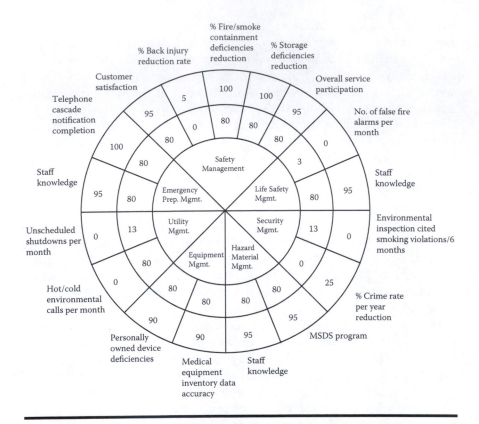

Figure 15.1 Partial wheel with goals added. (From Simmons, D. A. *Quality Digest*, March 1998 pp. 28–29. With permission).

circle. The process is continuous because new goals can then be set that improve on past performance. This is done through continual review and feedback.

The wheel displays system performance measures in relation to performance, which allows a balanced, comprehensive view of an organization's progress toward predetermined goals. These performance measures represent the top tier in a series of strategically important but increasingly specific documentation of process and outcome at the core process, department, work unit, and individual levels.

The performance wheel in Figure 15.1 shows measured and documented results of a recent survey and performance report for the JCAHO Environment of Care Standard. The inner circle includes seven key elements. Goals and minimum acceptable performance levels have been established. At least two target performance measures have been established for each of the seven key elements and are listed outside the outer ring. Figure 15.2 shows a hospital-based program.

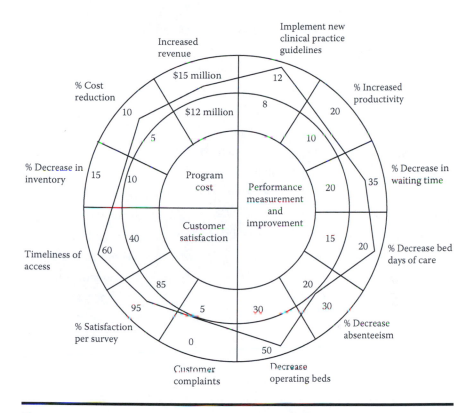

Figure 15.2 **Hospital-based performance model. (From Simmons, D. A.** ***Quality Digest,*** **March 1998 pp. 28–29. With permission).**

Statistical tools primarily identify causes of problems or situations. Analytical tools analyze and identify possible solutions to problems or situations that, for whatever reason, need to be corrected, changed, or modified. Frequently, the question arises over which tool is best suited to identify and solve a particular problem. From our experience the classic basic tools of quality (Pareto, histogram, scatter plot, control chart, process flowchart, brainstorming, check sheets) are used more often than any other tools, yet one is not limited to only those. No matter what tool is used the basic classic steps of problem solving must be followed. Table 15.1 shows the approach to problem solving and some tools.

When a practice or a hospital or a clinic is about to implement a quality management system using the ISO methodology, it must recognize that that implementation is going to be primarily process dependent and prevention oriented. This is very important because most of the medical professionals have

Table 15.1   Problem-Solving Approach and Typical Tools

Problem-Solving Approach	Basic Statistical Tools	Others
Prioritize problem	Data check sheets	Brainstorming
Analyze symptoms	Histograms	Affinity diagrams
Formulate theories	Pareto diagrams	Flowcharts
Test theories	Cause-and-effect diagrams	Nominal groups
Identify causes		Tree diagrams
Evaluate solutions	Run charts	Matrix diagram
Design solutions	Control charts	Pugh diagram
Address resistance	Process control	Plan-do-study-act
Implement solutions		Force field analysis
Check performance		And many more
Monitor controls		
Institutionalize solutions		

been used to satisfying the JCAHO requirements that are appraisal oriented—finding wrong things and correcting them. It is becoming more frequent that payers are beginning to show a preference for working with healthcare providers that provide information on process or, more specifically, the quality of treatment provided. For institutional and managed care providers, process is where most quality achievements can occur. Clinicians and direct healthcare providers, on the other hand, more often are concerned with outcomes. Strong support is growing on both sides to find ways to improve both process and outcome without compromising either. ISO is one way.

The integrated healthcare quality management model depicts a method for implementing ISO 9000 as both process quality management and outcome quality management. Both sides share the fundamental reasons for more quality management in healthcare:

- Increased public demand for performance data in healthcare delivery
- Potential decline in financial resources that would affect the quality of medical care
- Lack of sufficient evidence to support the effectiveness and reliability of many diagnostic and therapeutic methods
- Competition among providers for payer purchases of healthcare
- Financial concerns of third parties

ISO 9000 has been used successfully to address similar issues in industry, at both manufacturing and management levels. With many established models already in place, the healthcare industry can apply the garnered knowledge to its own challenges and look forward optimistically to the benefits of this adaptable standard within the various fields of care-giving.

To be sure, some practices, clinics, and hospitals may think that the ISO is not appropriate for them. However, from a generic perspective, four broad groups within the industry will find advantages in implementing an ISO 9000 quality system:

- *Institutional healthcare providers.* This group consists of hospitals, medical centers, and clinics that currently comply with standards set by the Joint Commission on Accreditation of Healthcare Organizations. Compliance to JCAHO standards enables institutional healthcare providers to obtain Medicare reimbursement for services to Medicare patients. The Medicare system is administered by the Federal Health Care Finance Administration, which bears primary survey responsibility and can delegate survey and compliance monitoring to state or other healthcare jurisdictional authority.
  - Caregivers typically invest 6–9 months preparing for a JCAHO survey. The number of hours converted into dollars is considerable, not to mention cost to the institution for the actual survey. With ISO 9000 compliance, there is relatively little interruption in healthcare delivery, as is experienced with the 3-year JCAHO accreditation cycle.
- *Managed care and health maintenance organizations.* These groups experience similar problems when preparing for the National Committee for Quality Assurance HEDIS report card system. NCQA performs both accreditation and performance measurement. Although the standards differ from JCAHO's, the process is essentially the same, with a long lead time and significant preparation and survey costs.
- *Physician group practices.* This group can benefit from registration for two reasons. First, implementing ISO 9000 can create a more efficient practice, allowing physicians to identify problems and initiate corrective action quickly while also monitoring, controlling, and reducing costs. Second, an ISO 9000-registered practice can point to its registration as a benchmark of an efficient and controlled operation. More and more, this is what larger institutional provider organizations and insurance companies look for in terms of stable physician group practices.
- *Medical equipment service providers.* This group includes original equipment manufacturers, in-house biomedical engineering programs, independent service organizations, and equipment remanufacturers. The U.S. Food

and Drug Administration, which requires medical equipment manufacturers to comply with federal requirements known as good manufacturing practices (GMPs), is petitioning for legislation requiring manufacturers to track equipment after sale. Given the large volume of medical equipment in use today as well as the equipment's portable nature, compliance would be virtually impossible. (Special note: After receiving significant protests, the FDA has told equipment providers to implement a quality systems standard or be faced with GMPs or equivalent legislation. ISO 9000 can solve the problem with less impact on service costs than any other quality management system can.)

New Accreditation Option for Hospitals: National Integrated Accreditation for Healthcare Organizations (NIAHO)

In addition to the ISO standard and the Joint Commission requirements, as of March 2009, hospitals had a new alternative to periodic no-charge surveys by state agencies for showing compliance with the Medicare program's conditions of participation. Det Norske Veritas (DNV) Healthcare Inc., with headquarters in Houston, is one of the first companies to offer a system (process) to accredit hospitals for participation in Medicare (NIAHO 2009).

This process would give three national accrediting organizations what federal regulations call "deeming authority" for hospitals: the Joint Commission; the American Osteopathic Association, which runs the Healthcare Facilities Accreditation program; and DNV Healthcare, which offers the comparatively new National Integrated Accreditation for Healthcare Organizations program. DNV Healthcare's accreditation program integrates ISO standard 9001 with Medicare's hospital conditions of participation.

The standard states generic requirements for how an organization implements its management system to accomplish its work and meet customers' needs, according to ISO's Web site. The need for this integration is to tie everything together. Whereas the ISO standard on quality management offered what the hospital's executives have sought for a long time, using the integration accreditation, the hospitals are now able to incorporate the Medicare conditions of participation and various accreditation and regulatory requirements into their quality management system and create a management systems manual. For an overview comparison of ISO and NIAHO, see Table 15.2.

Table 15.2   An Overview Comparison of ISO and NIAHO

ISO 9001 Quality Management System[a]	*National Integrated Accreditation for Health Care Organizations (NIAHO)*[b]	
Quality outline	**Governing body**	**Patient rights**
Management representative	Legal responsibility	Specific rights
Documentation and management reviews	Institutional plan and budget	Advance directive
	Contracted services	Language and communication
System requirements	**Chief executive officer**	Informed consent
		Grievance procedure
Measurement, monitoring, analysis	Qualifications	Restraint or seclusion
	Responsibilities	Restraint or seclusion: staff training requirements
Patient safety system	**Medical staff**	Restraint or seclusion: report of death
	Organized medical staff	**Infection control**
	Eligibility	
	Accountability	Infection control system
	Responsibility	
	Executive committee	**Medical records service**
	Medical staff participation	
	Medical staff bylaws	Organization
	Appointment	Complete medical record
	Performance data	
	Continuing education	Retention
	Governing body role	Confidentiality
	Clinical privileges	Record content
	Temporary clinical privileges	Identification of authors required
	Corrective or rehabilitation action	
	Admission requirements	

(Continued)

Table 15.2   An Overview Comparison of ISO and NIAHO (Continued)

ISO 9001 Quality Management System[a]	National Integrated Accreditation for Health Care Organizations (NIAHO)[b]	
	Medical records maintenance	**Discharge planning**
	History and physical	Written policies
	Consultation	Discharge planning evaluation
	Autopsy	Plan implementation
		Evaluation
	Nursing services	**Utilization review**
	Nursing service	Documented plan
	Nurse executive	Sampling
	Plan of care	Medical necessity determination
	Staffing management	Extended stay review
	Licensure or certification	**Rehabilitation services**
	Professional scope	Organization
	Department scope of service	Management and support
	Determining and modifying staffing	Treatment plan
	Job description	**Obstetric services**
	Orientation	Compliance
	Staff evaluations	Anesthesia services
	Medication management	**Emergency department**
	Management practices	Organization
	Formulary	Staffing

Table 15.2   An Overview Comparison of ISO and NIAHO (Continued)

ISO 9001 Quality Management System[a]	*National Integrated Accreditation for Health Care Organizations (NIAHO)[b]*	
	Scheduled drugs	Emergency services not provided
	Medication orders	
	Review of medication orders	Off-campus departments
	Oversight group	**Outpatient services**
	Available information	Organization
	Surgical services	Staffing
		Scope of service
	Organization	Organization
	Staffing and supervision	Services and diets
	Practitioner privileges	Diet manual
	History and physical	
	Available equipment	**Physical environment**
	Operating room register	Facility
	Postoperative care	Life safety management system
	Operative report	
	Immediate postoperative note	Safety management system
	Anesthesia services	Security management system
	Organization	Hazardous material (hazmat) management system
	Administration	
	Policies and procedures	Emergency management system
	Laboratory services	Medical equipment management system
	Organization	Utility management

(*Continued*)

Table 15.2 An Overview Comparison of ISO and NIAHO (Continued)

ISO 9001 Quality Management System[a]	*National Integrated Accreditation for Health Care Organizations (NIAHO)*[b]	
	Infectious blood and products	Organ, eye, and tissue procurement
	Patient notification	Process
	General blood safety	Organ procurement organization (OPO) written agreement
	Respiratory care services	
	Organization	Alternative agreement
	Physician order	Respect for patient rights
	Policies or protocols	
	Tests outside the lab	Documentation
	Radiation protection	Organ transplantation
	Equipment	Transplant candidates
	Order	
	Supervision	
	Staff	
	Records	
	Interpretation and records	
	Nuclear medicine services	
	Organization	
	Radioactive materials	
	Equipment and supplies	
	Interpretation	

[a] These are international standards that are updated every 4 years. They are not prescriptive but they do cover the essentials of a quality system.

[b] This NIAHO Interpretive Guidelines and Surveyor Guidance document is based upon the Centers for Medicare and Medicaid Services (CMS) Conditions of Participation for Hospitals 42 C.F.R. § 482 and State Operations Manual Regulations and Interpretive Guidelines for Hospitals. These interpretive guidelines are periodically updated based on notices distributed from CMS.

Because the ISO standard is not prescriptive, hospital departments such as pharmacy may seek out and incorporate best practices, as appropriate, and other standards into the hospital's management systems. The pharmacy, for example, looks at material from the Institute for Safe Medication Practices and the National Patient Safety Goals from the Joint Commission in determining standards of practice.

When the federal government established the Medicare and Medicaid programs in 1965, it decided that an institution "accredited as a hospital by the Joint Commission ... shall be deemed to meet the requirements" for participating in the Medicare program. With such an accreditation, the law said, the institution did not have to seek certification by a state survey agency. Until recently, the Joint Commission never had to apply to secure deeming authority for hospitals. However, federal law has required other national accrediting organizations to apply initially and then, if approved, reapply periodically. But, in July 2008, Congress revoked the Joint Commission's so-called unique deeming authority. Legislators have given the Joint Commission up to 24 months to apply for deeming authority and receive a decision from the Centers for Medicare and Medicaid Services (CMS).

Medical Devices

Surgically implanting a device, such as a pacemaker, has saved the lives of countless individuals battling with a compromised heart. Infusion pumps that automatically deliver consistent doses of drugs and eliminate the need for daily injections or pills are another example of how medical devices can drastically improve quality of life and treatment for patients. However, these same devices can pose a threat to human health unless a quality management system is in place to ensure that proper safety and quality procedures are being followed throughout their production.

The medical devices industry generated more than $230 billion in 2007, and that number is expected to grow to more than $285 billion by the end of 2012, according to the U.S. Department of Commerce's International Trade Administration. The increasing need for quality medical devices is matched by the need for quality management systems to ensure quality, standardize manufacturing, and ensure that these devices are safe for their intended use. The standard known as "ISO 13485: 2003—Medical Devices—Quality Management Systems—Requirements for Regulatory Purposes" has become the global standard for those involved in the manufacture of medical devices.

As in the traditional health industry, so in the medical devices industry there is a need for improvement. There are obviously many ways to improvement, including the Lean approach and the Six Sigma approach. An additional one, however, is coming from an international perspective: ISO 13485: 2003. It represents the requirements that medical device manufacturers must incorporate into their management systems. The current document supersedes its 1996 incarnation as well as EN 46001, EN 46002, and ISO 13488.

The standard is fundamentally based on ISO 9001. However, ISO 13485 removes ISO 9001's emphasis on continual improvement and customer satisfaction. In its place is an emphasis on meeting regulatory as well as customer requirements, risk management, and maintaining effective processes—namely, the processes specific to the safe design, manufacture, and distribution of medical devices. Specifically, however, ISO 13485: 2003 is based on eight quality management principles: customer focus, leadership, involvement of people, process approach, system approach to management, continual improvement, fact-based decision making, and mutually beneficial supplier relationships. When fully adopted, these principles have been proven to enhance organizational performance.

In essence, ISO 13485 is in part designed to produce a management system that facilitates compliance to the requirements of customers and—preeminently—various global regulators. What is of paramount importance is that a certification to ISO 13485 does not fulfill the requirements of either the FDA or foreign regulators. Rather, the certification aligns an organization's management system to the requirements of the FDA's quality system regulation (QSR) requirements as well as many other regulatory requirements found throughout the world. Therefore, ISO 13485 certification serves to create a management system that can be thought of as a framework on which to build compliance to various regulatory and customer requirements.

ISO 13485 dictates that risk management must be thoroughly documented and conducted throughout a product's entire life cycle, from initial concept to delivery and postdelivery. However, the standard leaves the specifics to a related standard, ISO 14971: 2001, Application of Risk Management for Medical Devices. While ISO 13485 states that a manufacturer's management team is charged with the management of device-related risks and the development of risk management plans, ISO 14971 defines a list of steps to be taken by management in order to fulfill risk-related requirements. While it is not mandatory that a manufacturer be ISO 14971 certified in order to attain ISO 13485 certification, being certified to the former standard can ease the attainment of certification to the latter.

To be precise here, we must, in no uncertain terms, declare that the purpose of ISO 13485 certification is sometimes misunderstood. ISO 13485 certification does not fulfill the requirements of ISO 9001; it is not equivalent to or have the ability to take the place of any country-specific requirement for medical device manufacturers. As previously mentioned, the standard is in part meant to serve as a means to the creation of a management system that aligns with the requirements of various regulators.

Medical device manufacturers also should realize the importance that risk management bears in an ISO 13485 management system. With this understanding, risk is now viewed as a continuum for the entire life cycle of the product or process. Risk assessments have become a key activity that manufacturers perform throughout the product life cycle, whether they are designing new products, choosing suppliers, inspecting finished goods, or performing corrective actions based on customer complaints. A combination of increased regulation and technological advances is forcing medical device manufacturers to couple their management systems with enterprise-wide risk management programs.

To be sure, the ISO 13485 is no longer thought of as pertaining solely to finished medical device manufacturers. Today, such manufacturers are requiring their subtier suppliers also to attain ISO 13485 certification. By cascading the requirements to the suppliers, medical device manufacturers want to realize better products and better services.

Identification and traceability also are an important theme in terms of product lots or batches, which carry with them supporting identification markings and records throughout the process. The ability to fine-tune in to a specific product lot or batch and all of its corresponding supporting records is a significant value to any medical device company, as well as the basis for many common audit trails.

Lastly, cleanliness or sterile conditions of the work environment are another main theme within the ISO 13485: 2003 standard. While ISO 9001: 2000 certainly elevated the importance of these types of requirements as they pertain to productivity, as well as an organized overall quality management system, ISO 13485: 2003 takes these requirements to the next level as many companies rely on these types of conditions as a matter of doing business altogether and also continually scrutinize their impact on the quality of the product.

Certification Process

Like any ISO certification, medical device manufacturers wishing to obtain ISO 13485 certification first need to educate themselves on the requirements of regulators and customers, as well as what an ISO 13485 compliant management system will entail. Then a management system that conforms to the standard's requirements needs to be implemented within the organization.

The first step to creating the management system should be drafting a quality manual that outlines an organization's goals, processes, and procedures for compliance and quality management. An employee with the know-how to develop and implement such a program can create the management system internally; otherwise, a hired consultant with an expertise in the ISO 13485 market can be used. After the quality manual has been written and a management system has been implemented, the organization needs to seek a certification body with which it is comfortable.

When seeking a certification body, the organization needs to be sure that the registrar is accredited by an accrediting body to include ISO 13485 certification in its scope. For example, in North America, certification bodies will be accredited through an organization such as ANSI/ASQ National Accreditation Board (ANAB). Accreditation boards in every major country review certification bodies to ensure that they meet requirements.

It also is important to keep the target market in mind. For instance, if a medical device manufacturer wants to sell in North America, it should seek certification through a registrar accredited by a North American accreditation body to ensure it will meet country-specific or customer requirements. If businesses are to be in other countries, then the appropriate registrar has to be found.

If a consultant is required, the organization needs to be sure that the prospect has expertise in ISO 13485; requesting referrals from an accredited registrar also can aid in finding the right match. It is important that the consultant understand the organization's business, has dealt with organizations of a similar size before, and has had experience with similar product lines. Always be wary of consultants that endeavor to radically change a management system that is already performing well. The consultant should come in and align his or her knowledge with the client's requirements and customer requirements, and that will work time after time.

The steps to attaining ISO 13485 certification are similar to those of ISO 9001, with some type of off-site document review followed by a preassessment and then assessment. After certification, an organization will be subject to ongoing surveillance by its certification body. The duration of the assessment is contingent on an organization's scope—its size, number of personnel, and type and complexity of products manufactured. Taking these elements into consideration, an organization can expect an assessment to last anywhere from a couple of days to more than a month.

The frequency of surveillance assessments will be determined by an organization's scope as well as its performance, though they will usually be conducted annually or semiannually. However, organizations should expect a complete reassessment 3 years after initial certification. A surveillance assessment takes into account concerns such as the fulfillment of management responsibilities, the execution of internal audits, and how an organization is performing in relation to the state of the industry and customer expectations.

Fundamentally, the benefits of following ISO 13485 may be summarized in the following:

- ISO 13485 emphasizes meeting regulatory as well as customer requirements, risk management, and maintaining effective processes.
- ISO 13485 is in part designed to produce a management system that facilitates compliance to the requirements of customers and global regulators.
- Benefits can be reaped from being both ISO 9001 and 13485 certified because ISO 9001 focuses on business aspects not found in ISO 13485 that are good for all businesses.

On the other hand, with a dual certification (ISO 9001 and 13485), medical device manufacturers can benefit from being both ISO 9001 and 13485 certified. While such manufacturers are not required to have ISO 9001 certification, it can bring further business benefits because it focuses on business aspects that are good for all businesses—for example, the emphasis on customer satisfaction and continuous process improvement that an ISO 13485 management system omits. Manufacturers of medical devices also will need to acquire ISO 9001 certification if they want to branch out to other industries because ISO 13485 certification will not be honored where ISO 9001 is required.

Summary

This chapter provided an overview of the international standards (ISO 9001 and 13485) for quality and introduced the NIAHO standards as they apply to healthcare. In the next chapter, we cover the Malcolm Baldrige National Quality Program as it applies to healthcare and focus on the guidelines for system improvement.

References

NIAHO. 2009. http://www.dnv.com/industry/healthcare/key_niaho_materials.asp (see NIAHO accreditation process [pdf]; NIAHO standards and interpretive guidelines [pdf]; NIAHO accreditation application [Word]). Retrieved on October 28, 2009.

Simmons, D. A. 1998. Examining ISO 9000 in health care. *Quality Digest* March: 27–29. http://www.qualitydigest.com/mar98/html/cover.html (retrieved on October 20, 2009).

Selected Bibliography

Nuhler, D., and T. Walters. 2009. Take a bite out of inefficiency: Dental practice uses ISO 9001:2000 to drill into equipment management. *Quality Progress* May: 45–51.

Schnoll, L. 2010. Under control: Medical device safety starts during the design stage. *Quality Progress* February: 58–60.

Stamatis, D. H. 1995. *Understanding ISO 9000 and implementing the basics to quality.* New York: Marcel Dekker.

West, J. 2009. Small change, big payoff; minor revisions in ISO 9001:2008 can lead to major benefits. *Quality Progress* April: 46–52.

Chapter 16

Understanding and Utilizing the Malcolm Baldrige National Quality Program

In the last chapter, we discussed International Organization for Standardization (ISO) 9000, ISO 13485, and the National Integrated Accreditation for Health Organizations (NIAHO) accreditation process. For the past year, the Institute for Healthcare Improvement (IHI) and several scientific partners have been hard at work developing a tool that will offer an alternative to the current state of affairs in which U.S. hospitals must figure out how to juggle and work on nearly 1,500 quality indicators and long lists of requirements from organizations such as the Joint Commission on Accreditation of Healthcare Organizations, the Leapfrog Group, the Centers for Medicare and Medicaid Services, and other payers. In addition to all these requirements, hospitals must participate in various quality assessment programs. While all are worthy in their intent and specificity, this ever expanding list of expectations and risks is creating more frustration and confusion than improvement.

It is not surprising that, when asked what they would value most, hospital quality leaders told IHI that they needed help making sense of all the demands and requirements, especially with tightening budgets for new projects and initiatives and less and less certainty about which programs can truly help patients, reduce waste, and create greater efficiencies.

Our suggestion is to generate a map based on the Malcolm Baldrige National Quality Award (MBNQA) for consistency, measurement, and improvement. The model of the Baldrige Award not only clarifies criteria for performance excellence but also helps health organizations (small and large) with a map for improvement on processes that lead to excellent patient care. It provides a way for them to design a customized path to achieve meaningful results.

Why is a map necessary for this improvement? A careful analysis of many healthcare facilities has identified many core items that could be helped with some kind of change in both easy and difficult situations to improve performance on important patient outcomes. The complexity of the clinical processes, in conjunction with regulatory requirements and individualized programs in different facilities, demands a somewhat standardized approach—at least for the generic healthcare processes (both clinical and managerial) that are the foundation of high performance.

According to Kabcenell (2009), typical key and generic processes in healthcare (hospital, clinics, physicians' practices, urgent care and nursing home facilities) are (1) patient care processes, (2) support processes, and (3) leadership and management processes. Kabcenell claims that if we focus on these three key processes, we will cover about 80% of most healthcare business. They are the high-volume and high-risk processes that have to be done reliably. For a detailed discussion of these, the reader can visit the Internet site IHI.org.

Fundamentally, there are three items of basic concern in generating this map. The first is to develop a focused quality agenda. It will help define the vision as well as the direction of where one wants to go. To be sure, most healthcare professionals in leadership positions are aware of which outcomes are crucial for the organization's success. However, an agenda will force the participants to sort and filter the processes that have been defined as important outcomes, whether they are mortality and harm, or costs and efficiency. By comparing the goals set for the organization with that of the current practice, one will be able to further sort the map by the degree of difficulty in implementing the processes or the financial implications. Ultimately, the map will help to create a sequential path for reaching important goals and will generate worthwhile projects.

The second item in generating a map of improvement is the notion of evaluation. This means that everyone in the organization must be cognizant of evaluating the improvement initiatives. If an active improvement program is already in place, check the activities against those identified by the overall agenda plan to confirm that the organization is on the path to the results it wants to achieve. It will be possible to identify important processes for reaching aims that may have been missed. For example, most organizations have active programs to improve the patient experience, but many do not know how important dietary and pain management programs are to improving that experience. Using the plan that has been generated can give more focused ideas for reaching stated goals.

The third and final item in generating a map for improvement is to find resources and information to boost overall performance improvement (however defined). The map in the form of the agenda that has been generated should contain a wealth of information about each process, including what requirements and aims are connected to the process, the prerequisites for success, measurement tools, and links to other information and resources for making the processes reliable. Any staff member can use the agenda to find the resources he or she needs to get started on improvement. And that includes executives, managers, and owners, who have their own leadership and management section on the agenda of improvement.

In an oversimplified manner, then, what we have been talking about is a path of identifying and resolving issues for improvement. This is shown in Table 16.1.

However this plan for improvement is identified and carried out, it is imperative that, above all, it be flexible. The need for flexibility is so essential that it will serve the organization with the ability to customize its needs. In order for this customization to be effective and efficient, it must be adaptable. "Adaptable" refers to a system for improvement that will be equally effective in a small physician's practice to a very large hospital. This is where the Baldrige Award guidelines come into play. Table 16.2 displays the criterion and points for each category. For the detailed description, requirements, and specific questions, the reader is encouraged to see MBNQA (2009–2010).

The evaluation of the Baldrige Award is based on a scoring of responses to criteria items (items), and award applicant feedback is based on two evaluation dimensions: (1) process and (2) results. Criteria users need to furnish information relating to these dimensions. Specific factors for these dimensions are shown in Table 16.2 and the scoring guidelines are shown in Table 16.3.

As we already have mentioned, the MBNQA is a primarily process-oriented system and it is the reason why it has gained acceptance in so many industries (small and large). "Process" in the MBNQA refers to the methods an organization uses and improves to address the item requirements in categories 1–6. The four factors used to evaluate process are approach, deployment, learning, and integration (ADLI).

Approach refers to

- Methods used to accomplish the process
- Appropriateness of the methods to the item requirements and the organization's operating environment
- Effectiveness of use of the methods

■ Degree to which the approach is repeatable and based on reliable data and information (i.e., systematic)

Deployment refers to the extent to which the approach is

■ Applied in addressing item requirements relevant and important to the organization
■ Applied consistently
■ Used (executed) by all appropriate work units

Learning refers to

■ Refining the approach through cycles of evaluation and improvement
■ Encouraging breakthrough change to the approach through innovation
■ Sharing refinements and innovations with other relevant work units and processes in the organization

Table 16.1   The Path to Improvement

Identify Process to Improve	Initiatives for That Improvement	Purpose for That Improvement
Acute myocardial infarction (AMI) care	Patient care processes	Reduce, minimize or eliminate waste and harm to the patients
End of life care	Support processes	Reduce or minimize mortality and cost per case
Intensive care	Leadership and management processes	Increase patient satisfaction
Emergency care		Increase equity to the organization
High hazard medications		Increase efficiency
Laboratory processes		Increase access
Time in patient care		
Transportation of patients		
Others		

Table 16.2   Malcolm Baldrige National Quality Award

Criteria	Items for Performance	Significant Inclusions of the Criteria	Points	Total
Leadership	1.1 Senior leadership 1.2 Governance and societal responsibilities	Includes an enhanced focus on sustainability and societal responsibilities and the senior leader's role	1.1: 70 1.2: 50	120
Strategic planning	2.1 Strategy development 2.2 Strategy deployment	Introduces core competencies as a strategic concept	2.1: 40 2.2: 45	85
Customer focus	3.1 Customer engagement 3.2 Voice of the customer	Has been redesigned around customer engagement and the voice of the customer	3.1: 40 3.2: 45	85
Measurement, analysis, and knowledge management	4.1 Measurement, analysis, and improvement of organizational performance 4.2 Management of information, knowledge, and information technology	Clearly separates but emphasizes both the importance of information and knowledge management and the management of information technology and systems	4.1: 45 4.2: 45	90
Workforce focus	5.1 Workforce engagement 5.2 Workforce environment	Has been simplified to add clarity and focus to important aspects of workforce engagement	5.1: 45 5.2: 40	85

(Continued)

Table 16.2 Malcolm Baldrige National Quality Award (Continued)

Criteria	Items for Performance	Significant Inclusions of the Criteria	Points	Total
Process management	6.1 Work systems 6.2 Work processes	Has been reorganized for a more logical flow of the questions	6.1: 35 6.2: 50	85
Results	7.1 Healthcare outcomes 7.2 Customer-focused outcomes 7.3 Financial and market outcomes 7.4 Workforce-focused outcomes 7.5 Process effectiveness outcomes 7.6 Leadership outcomes	Has been aligned with the changes in categories 1–6 to encourage the measurement of important and appropriate results	7.1: 100 7.2: 70 7.3: 70 7.4: 70 7.5: 70 7.6: 70	450
Total points				1,000

Notes: In the 2009–2010 version of the award, there was also an inclusion of a preface: organizational profile. There are two categories—P.1: organizational description; P.2: organizational situation. Neither of these categories is numerically evaluated; the intent is to identify and know the core competencies as a key characteristic of the organizational environment.

The core value in past versions of the award related to social responsibility has been retitled and rewritten to reflect the larger sustainability concepts embodied in societal responsibility.

Three terms were added to the glossary of key terms in the 2009–2010 version: customer engagement, voice of the customer, and work processes. In addition, the definition of sustainability was expanded to reflect societal aspects of organizational sustainability.

The results scoring guidelines have been modified specifically to address performance projection expectations in each scoring range. Also, performance projections have been included in the sample results figure presented in the guidelines for responding to results items.

Table 16.3   Scoring Criteria for the MBNQA

Score	Process
Used with categories 1–6	
0 or 5%	• No *systematic approach* to item requirements is evident; information is *anecdotal*. (A) • Little or no *deployment* of any *systematic approach* is evident. (D) • An improvement orientation is not evident; improvement is achieved through reacting to problems. (L) • No organizational *alignment* is evident; individual areas or work units operate independently. (I)
10, 15, 20, or 25%	• The beginning of a *systematic approach* to the *basic requirements* of the item is evident. (A) • The *approach* is in the early stages of *deployment* in most areas or work units, inhibiting progress in achieving the *basic requirements* of the item. (D) • Early stages of a transition from reacting to problems to a general improvement orientation are evident. (L) • The *approach* is *aligned* with other areas or work units largely through joint problem solving. (I)
30, 35, 40, or 45%	• An *effective, systematic approach,* responsive to the *basic requirements* of the item, is evident. (A) • The *approach* is *deployed,* although some areas or work units are in early stages of *deployment.* (D) • The beginning of a *systematic approach* to evaluation and improvement of *key processes* is evident. (L) • The *approach* is in the early stages of *alignment* with basic organizational needs identified in response to organizational profile and other process items. (I)
50, 55, 60, or 65%	• An *effective, systematic approach,* responsive to the *overall requirements* of the item, is evident. (A)

(Continued)

Table 16.3   Scoring Criteria for the MBNQA (Continued)

Score	Process
	• The *approach* is well *deployed*, although *deployment* may vary in some areas or work units. (D) • A fact-based, *systematic* evaluation and improvement *process* and some organizational *learning*, including *innovation*, are in place for improving the efficiency and *effectiveness* of *key processes*. (L) • The *approach* is *aligned* with organizational needs identified in response to the organizational profile and other process items. (I)
70, 75, 80, or 85%	• An *effective, systematic approach*, responsive to the *multiple requirements* of the item, is evident. (A) • The *approach* is well *deployed*, with no significant gaps. (D) • Fact-based, *systematic* evaluation and improvement and organizational *learning*, including *innovation*, are *key* management tools; there is clear evidence of refinement as a result of organizational-level *analysis* and sharing. (L) • The *approach* is *integrated* with organizational needs identified in response to the organizational profile and other process items. (I)
90, 95, or 100%	• An *effective, systematic approach*, fully responsive to the *multiple requirements* of the item, is evident. (A) • The *approach* is fully *deployed* without significant weaknesses or gaps in any areas or work units. (D) • Fact-based, *systematic* evaluation and improvement and organizational *learning* through *innovation* are *key* organization-wide tools; refinement and *innovation*, backed by *analysis* and sharing, are evident throughout the organization. (L) • The *approach* is well *integrated* with organizational needs identified in response to the organizational profile and other process items. (I)

Table 16.3   Scoring Criteria for the MBNQA (Continued)

Score	Process
Used with category 7	
0 or 5%	• There are no organizational *performance results* and/or poor *results* in areas reported. (Le) • *Trend* data either are not reported or show mainly adverse *trends*. (T) • Comparative information is not reported. (C) • *Results* are not reported for any areas of importance to the accomplishment of the organization's *mission. No performance projections* are reported. (1)
10, 15, 20, or 25%	• A few organizational *performance results* are reported, and early good *performance levels* are evident in a few areas. (Le) • Some *trend* data are reported, with some adverse *trends* evident. (T) • Little or no comparative information is reported. (C) • *Results* are reported for a few areas of importance to the accomplishment of the organization's *mission.* Limited or no *performance projections* are reported. (1)
30, 35, 40, or 45%	• Good organizational *performance levels* are reported for some areas of importance to the item requirements. (Le) • Some *trend* data are reported, and a majority of the *trends* presented are beneficial. (T) • Early stages of obtaining comparative information are evident. (C) • *Results* are reported for many areas of importance to the accomplishment of the organization's *mission.* Limited *performance projections* are reported. (I)
50, 55, 60, or 65%	• Good organizational *performance levels* are reported for most areas of importance to the item requirements. (Le) • Beneficial *trends* are evident in areas of importance to the accomplishment of the organization's *mission.* (T)

(Continued)

Table 16.3   Scoring Criteria for the MBNQA (Continued)

Score	Process
	• Some current *performance levels* have been evaluated against relevant comparisons and/or *benchmarks* and show areas of good relative *performance*. (C)
	• Organizational *performance results* are reported for most *key patient* and *stakeholder*, market, and *process* requirements. *performance projections* for some high-priority *results* are reported. (I)
70, 75, 80, or 85%	• Good to excellent organizational *performance levels* are reported for most areas of importance to the item requirements. (Le)
	• Beneficial *trends* have been sustained over time in most areas of importance to the accomplishment of the organization's *mission*. (T)
	• Many to most *trends* and current *performance levels* have been evaluated against relevant comparisons and/or *benchmarks* and show areas of leadership and very good relative *performance*. (C)
	• Organizational *performance results* are reported for most *key patient* and *stakeholder*, market, *process*, and *action plan* requirements, and they include some *projections* of future *performance*. (I)
90, 95, or 100%	• Excellent organizational *performance levels* are reported for most areas of importance to the item requirements. (Le)
	• Beneficial *trends* have been sustained over time in all areas of importance to the accomplishment of the organization's *mission*. (T)
	• Evidence of healthcare sector and *benchmark* leadership is demonstrated in many areas. (C)
	• Organizational *performance results* fully address *key patient* and *stakeholder*, market, *process*, and *action plan* requirements, and they include *projections* of future *performance*. (I)

Integration refers to the extent to which

- The approach is aligned with organizational needs identified in the organizational profile and other process items
- Measures, information, and improvement systems are complementary across processes and work units
- Plans, processes, results, analyses, learning, and actions are harmonized across processes and work units to support organization-wide goals

The idea of making sure that we focus on the process is to make certain our focus is on tangible improvements. To do that, we must know and understand the most intricate parts of the process under investigation. As important as the definition of the process is, it is meaningless unless we have some form of measuring the results of our efforts in the improvement endeavor. Therefore, the MBNQA provides for measuring the results. Results for the MBNQA refer to the organization's outputs and outcomes in achieving the requirements in items 7.1–7.6 (category 7). The four factors used to evaluate results are levels, trends, comparisons, and integration (LeTCI).

Levels refers to the current level of performance.

Trends refers to

- Rate of performance improvements or the sustainability of good performance (i.e., the slope of trend data)
- Breadth (i.e., the extent of deployment) of performance results

Comparisons refers to performance relative to

- Appropriate comparisons, such as competitors or organizations similar to one's organization
- Benchmarks or industry leaders

Integration refers to the extent to which results

- Measure (often through segmentation) and address important patient and stakeholder, health care service, market, process, and action plan performance requirements identified in the organizational profile and in process items
- Include valid indicators of future performance
- Are harmonized across processes and work units to support organization-wide goals

At this stage, the reader should have noticed that the item classification and scoring dimensions are based according to the kinds of information and data that have been collected relative to

■ *Process.* In process items, approach, deployment, learning, and integration are linked to emphasize that descriptions of approach should always indicate the deployment—consistent with the specific requirements of the item and the organization. As processes mature, their description also should indicate how cycles of learning (including innovation), as well as integration with other processes and work units, occur. Although the ADLI factors are linked, feedback to award applicants reflects strengths and opportunities for improvement in any or all of these factors.

■ *Results.* Results items call for data showing performance levels, trends, and relevant comparisons for key measures and indicators of organizational performance, and integration with key organizational requirements. Results items also call for data on the breadth of the performance results reported. This is directly related to deployment and organizational learning; if improvement processes are widely shared and deployed, there should be corresponding results. A score for a results item is thus a composite based on overall performance, taking into account the four results factors (LeTCI).

The two evaluation dimensions just described are central to evaluation and feedback. A critical consideration in evaluation and feedback is the importance of reported process and results to key organizational factors. The areas of greatest importance should be identified in the organizational profile and in items such as 2.1, 2.2, 3.1, 5.1, 5.2, and 6.1. The key patient and stakeholder requirements, competitive environment, workforce needs, key strategic objectives, and action plans are particularly important.

As with any evaluation, some guidelines should be observed in assigning scores to item responses. The MBNQA is no different. Here are some guidelines:

■ All areas to address should be included in the item response. Also, responses should reflect what is important to the organization.

■ In assigning a score to an item, first decide which scoring range (e.g., 50–65%) is most descriptive of the organization's achievement level as presented in the item response. "Most descriptive of the organization's achievement level" can include some gaps in one or more of the ADLI (process) or the LeTCI (results) factors for the chosen scoring range. An organization's achievement level is based on a holistic view of either the four process or four results factors in aggregate rather than on a tallying or averaging of independent assessments against each of the four factors. Assigning the actual score within the chosen range requires evaluating whether the item response is closer to the statements in the next higher or next lower scoring range.

- A process item score of 50% represents an approach that meets the overall requirements of the item, that is deployed consistently and to most work units, that has been through some cycles of improvement and learning, and that addresses the key organizational needs. Higher scores reflect greater achievement, demonstrated by broader deployment, significant organizational learning, and increased integration.
- A results item score of 50% represents a clear indication of good levels of performance, beneficial trends, and appropriate comparative data for the results areas covered in the item and important to the organization or mission. Higher scores reflect better trends and levels of performance, stronger comparative performance, and broader coverage and integration with the requirements of the organization or mission.

Baldrige Award applicants do not receive a single, final score as part of their feedback. Rather, they receive a scoring range for each criteria item, and they receive a score in two overall bands: one for process items and one for results items. The descriptors for these scoring bands portray the organization's overall progress and maturity in the process and the results dimensions. The scoring band descriptors are available at www.baldrige.nist.gov/Examiner_Resources.htm.

References

Kabcenell, A. October 13, 2009. Behind the health care improvement map. *Quality Digest.* http://www.qualitydigest.com/inside/health-care-article/behind-health-care-improvement-map.html (retrieved on October 21, 2009).

Malcolm Baldrige National Quality Award. 2009–2010. *Health care criteria for performance excellence.* Gaithersburg, MD: NIST.

Selected Bibliography

Dunn, P., and B. Santamour. 2003. How health care won its first Baldrige. *Hospitals & Health Networks* 77 (9): 67–74.

Goldstein, S. M. 2002. Empirical support for the Baldrige award framework in U.S. hospitals. *Health Care Management Review* 27 (1): 62–75.

Johnson, K. 2004. Two hospitals prescribe performance excellence. *Quality Progress* September: 46–55.

Leonard, D., and K. Reller. 2004. Simplify Baldrige for healthcare. *Quality Progress* September: 35–45.

Nielsen, D., M. Merry, P. Schyve, and M. Bisognano. 2004. Can the gurus' concepts cure healthcare? *Quality Progress* September: 25–34.

Ohldin, A., R. Taylor, A. Stein, et al. 2002. Enhancing VHA's mission to improve veteran health: Synopsis of VHA's Malcolm Baldrige Award application. *Quality Management in Health Care* 10 (4): 29–37.

Tiwari, A. 2009. Danger zones: The 10 toughest aspects of the Baldrige criteria. *Quality Progress* September: 42–47.

Epilogue

To be sure, healthcare in general is in need of reform. However, the reform may be from legal perspectives and internal processes in healthcare itself. In this book, we have focused on the latter.

However, we will miss the opportunity if we do not address the latest developments in healthcare reform the governmental way. On March 22, 2010, Congress passed a historic healthcare bill (H.R. 3200) by a vote of 219 to 212; they named it *health care reform,* although some have called it *Obama care.* The vote was strictly on party lines; no Republicans voted for the bill and only 34 Democrats voted against it. Everyone seems to have an opinion about Obama care; however, we thought we would stick to the facts and let you decide whether the bill is good or bad for the country, whether it is really a reform, whether it is a quality-driven improvement for all, and whether it meets minimum requirements for customer satisfaction:

In the Introduction and Chapter 1, we did mention that reform may be accomplished through some governmental intervention, but it was not recommended as an option for improvement. The fact of the matter is that what we ended up with is not reform from a quality perspective, but rather health rationing—total disregard of what the customer wants, needs, and expects, as well as redistribution of wealth at its best, imitating European systems. The changes are quite profound and not all are necessarily good. A summary follows.

Summary of New Healthcare Bill in 2010

In 2010, there are three major changes to health care. First, insurance companies are no longer allowed to deny coverage to children with preexisting illnesses. Second, children are able to stay on their parents' insurance policies until they turn 26 years old. Third, Medicare recipients who fall into a specific coverage gap will get a $250 rebate.

Other changes include an excise tax on indoor tanning, which will increase the cost of that service. Also, individuals who have not had health insurance for 6 months will receive a subsidy to enroll in high-risk insurance pools run by the states. All new insurance plans sold must exempt preventative care and screenings from deductibles. Finally, small businesses with fewer than 25 employees will receive up to a 35% tax credit for providing health insurance to their employees.

Summary of New Healthcare Bill in 2011

In 2011, the new health care bill will make changes focused mostly on preparing for later updates. The new bill will set up a long-term care insurance program. Individuals who pay premiums into this system for at least 5 years will become eligible to receive support with daily living assistance.

The senior citizens who fall into the "Medicare donut hole" (a coverage gap) will get a 50% discount on some drugs. In 2011, a new fee on drug makers will also be implemented to help pay for the upcoming changes. The fine on withdrawing funds from a health savings account for nonmedical expenses will increase by 5–10%. Employers will also need to start including the cost of healthcare on employees' W-2 forms.

Selected Specific Major Overall Changes

Because of the volume of information in the bill (over 2,000 pages), the following facts and figures have been assimilated here in a composite format from several sources (see selected bibliography) to make the governmental reform easily understood:

- *Cost:* The $940 billion cost over 10 years excludes the $150 billion that physicians will be reimbursed for low payment from Medicare.
- *Deficit:* The deficit is reduced by $143 billion over the first 10 years. This is an updated Congressional Budget Office (CBO) estimate. The first preliminary estimate said that it would reduce the deficit by $130 billion.
- *Coverage:* Coverage will be expanded to 32 million Americans who are currently uninsured.
- *Health insurance exchanges:* The uninsured and self-employed would be able to purchase insurance through state-based exchanges with subsidies available to individuals and families with income between 133 and 400% of poverty level.

- Separate exchanges would be created for small businesses to purchase coverage (effective 2014).
- Funding is available to states to establish exchanges within 1 year of enactment, until January 1, 2015.

■ *Subsidies:* Individuals and families who make between 100 and 400% of the federal poverty level (FPL) and want to purchase their own health insurance on an exchange are eligible for subsidies. They cannot be eligible for Medicare or Medicaid and cannot be covered by an employer. Eligible buyers receive premium credits and there is a cap for how much they have to contribute to their premiums on a sliding scale. As of this writing, *the federal poverty level for a family of four is $22,050.*

■ *Paying for the plan:* The plan will be paid for primarily through the following items:
- Medicare payroll tax on investment income: starting in 2012, the Medicare payroll tax will be expanded to include unearned income. That will be a 3.8% tax on investment income for families making more than $250,000 per year ($200,000 for individuals).
- Excise tax: beginning in 2018, insurance companies will pay a 40% excise tax on so-called "Cadillac" high-end insurance plans worth over $27,500 for families ($10,200 for individuals). Dental and vision plans are exempt and will not be counted in the total cost of a family's plan.
- Tanning tax: 10% excise tax on indoor tanning services.

■ *Medicare:* The Medicare prescription drug "donut hole" will be closed by 2020. Seniors who hit the donut hole by 2010 will receive a $250 rebate.
- Beginning in 2011, seniors in the gap will receive a 50% discount on brand-name drugs. The bill also includes $500 billion in Medicare cuts over the next decade.

■ *Medicaid:* Medicaid is expanded to include 133% of federal poverty level, which is $29,327 a year for a family of four.
- States will be required to expand Medicaid to include childless adults starting in 2014.
- The federal government pays 100% of costs for covering newly eligible individuals through 2016.
- Illegal immigrants are not eligible for Medicaid.

■ *Insurance reforms:* 6 months after enactment, insurance companies can no longer deny children coverage based on a preexisting condition.
- Starting in 2014, insurance companies cannot deny coverage to anyone with preexisting conditions.
- Insurance companies must allow children to stay on their parents' insurance plans until age 26.

- *Abortion:* The bill segregates private insurance premium funds from tax-payer funds. Individuals must pay for abortion coverage by making two separate payments; private funds must be kept in a separate account from federal and taxpayer funds.
  - No healthcare plan will be required to offer abortion coverage. States can pass legislation choosing to opt out of offering abortion coverage through the exchange.
    - *Even though anti-abortion Democrats worked out language with the White House separately on an executive order that would state that no federal funds can be used to pay for abortions except in the case of rape, incest, or health of the mother, there is still no agreement whether or not that would be enforceable. However, this mandate may be changed by the current president or future ones.*
- *Individual mandate:* In 2014, everyone must purchase health insurance or face a $695 annual fine. There are some exceptions for low-income people.
- *Employer mandate:* Technically, there is no employer mandate. Employers with more than 50 employees must provide health insurance or pay a fine of $2,000 per worker each year if any worker receives federal subsidies to purchase health insurance. Fines are applied to the entire number of employees minus some allowances.
- *Immigration:* Illegal immigrants will not be allowed to buy health insurance in the exchanges—even if they pay completely with their own money.
  - Over 10 years; this would reduce the deficit by $1.2 trillion in the second 10-year period.

These broad areas of coverage may be translated into numerical numbers as follows:

- An estimated *32 million* currently uninsured Americans will receive coverage under the bill
- The estimated cost of healthcare reform over the next 10 years is *$940 billion.*
- The estimated reduction in the deficit from the bill over the next 10 years is *$143 billion.*
- *$53 Billion:* This represents the portion of the $143 billion in deficit reduction that comes from Social Security payroll taxes that eventually will be paid out in the form of retirement benefits.
- *$70 Billion:* This represents the portion of the $143 billion in deficit reduction that comes from premiums to be collected as part of a new government-run, long-term care program for the elderly. These premiums eventually will be paid out in the form of benefits.

- *$88,000:* New health insurance subsidies will be provided to families of four making up to $88,000 annually or 400% of the federal poverty level.
- *Preexisting conditions:* Insurance companies will be prohibited from denying coverage based on preexisting conditions.
- *Age 26:* Insurers will be required to provide coverage for nondependent children up to age 26.
- *Donut hole:* Under current law, Medicare stops covering drug costs after a plan and beneficiary have spent more than $2,830 on prescription drugs. It starts paying again after an individual's out-of-pocket expenses exceed $4,550. Called the donut hole, this gap will be closed by 2020.
- *40% Tax:* A 40% tax will be imposed on insurance companies providing "Cadillac" health plans valued at more than $10,200 for individuals and $27,500 for families. The tax will kick in starting in 2018.
- *3.8% Medicare tax:* A 3.8% surcharge will be imposed on investment income for individuals making over $200,000 and couples making over $250,000. This tax increase is estimated to bring in $210 billion between 2013 and 2019.
- *$695 or 2.5%:* These amounts represent the potential amount of a fine for failure to purchase healthcare insurance. Starting in 2016, individuals will be required to purchase coverage or face a fine of up to $695 or 2.5% of income, whichever is greater. The plan includes a hardship exemption for poorer Americans.
- *50 Employees:* Companies with more than 50 employees will be required to pay a fee of $2,000 per worker if the company does not provide coverage and any of that company's workers receives federal healthcare subsidies. The first 30 workers will be subtracted from the payment calculation.
- *0.9%:* The Medicare Part A (hospital insurance) tax rate will be increased by 0.9%, to 2.35%.
- *$16 Billion:* Drug manufacturers will pay the United States this amount between 2011 and 2019.
- *$47 Billion:* Health insurers will pay this amount over the same period.
- *2.9% Excise tax:* Medical device manufacturers will pay a 2.9% excise tax on the sale of any of their products beginning January 1, 2013.
- *Tanning tax:* Healthcare reform established a tax of 10% on indoor tanning services. This will raise $2.7 billion between 2010 and 2019. As far as we know, getting a tan outside is still free.
- *$132 Billion:* Government payments to Medicare Advantage will be reduced by $132 billion over 10 years.

Now that we have addressed the overall effect and some specific changes in the bill, let us see which ones are the most important. The Patient Protection and Affordable Health Care Act, more commonly referred to as the "healthcare reform bill," has been a lightning rod for political debate because it effectively reshapes major facets of the country's healthcare industry. However, in all honesty, it does not improve the quality of healthcare.

- *One must have medical insurance:* Under the new law everyone will have to purchase health insurance or risk being fined. If the employer does not offer health insurance or if one cannot earn enough to purchase it, that individual may get assistance from the government. It is up to the individual to find if he or she is qualified for discounted health insurance. An additional 33 million people will be insured under this bill.
- *More healthcare jobs:* Looking for a job? This is your chance. With the new Bill, there will be additional 33 million insured. There is going to be huge demand for medical professionals across the nation. You can get a degree in several months with accelerated programs in a variety of health specialties. So you can be ready soon if you are thinking of changing your career. Colleges offer consultation for students who are interested at no cost. They also provide accelerated programs for many health fields.
- *Kids can stay on their parents' policy until age 26:* Currently, many insurance companies do not allow adult children to remain on their parents' plan once they reach 19. Companies cannot do that anymore.
- *Insurance cannot drop one's policy:* Your health insurance company will no longer be allowed to cancel your policy if you get sick.
- *Children can't be denied insurance:* Starting this year your child (or children) cannot be denied coverage simply because they have a preexisting health condition. If one does not have insurance, find it today.
- *No maximum limit on coverage:* Companies will be barred from instituting caps on coverage when your costs for treatments go up due to sickness.
- *No waiting time:* If one currently has preexisting conditions that have prevented that individual from being able to qualify for health insurance for at least six months, that individual now will have coverage options.

One can see from this cursory review that the governmental reform is not doing anything to control cost and certainly is not improving the quality of healthcare, especially customer satisfaction. It does, however, shift costs in the name of savings and completely ignores the principle of customer satisfaction that has been a pillar and a significant characteristic of quality for all industries and services, including healthcare, for many years. Furthermore, it lacks basic issues of improvement (such as understanding the needs of the customer, definition of a process, no recognition and utilization of specific tools that measure and improve quality) and tries to intervene with socialistic approaches (*i.e.* distribution of wealth and rationing) of solving some of the problems.

On the other hand, for this internal improvement in healthcare to take place, we all must come to recognize some realities, including the following:

■ Doctors are smart
■ Profit margins are falling
■ Work is case by case
■ Doctors are weak on business principles
■ Time is very limited
■ Lives are at stake
■ Safety is the number one concern
■ Insurance is complex

Given these realities, can we do anything about the reform? We believe that we can. We can provide proven tools of improvement to all healthcare institutions and providers. In fact, this help is needed now. However, the good news is that the help is available now and we know that it works. We can help in increasing efficiency and thereby improve quality in all areas of healthcare by:

■ Standardizing work (office and medical)
  – Eliminating waste
  – Relying on staff
  – Convincing those responsible to spend money (computers) for long-term gains
■ Improving quality skills
  – Taking commonsense approaches
  – Seeing and eliminating waste
  – Engaging in team- and data-based continuous improvement
■ Introducing quality Lean thinking as an everyday way of life through a three pronged-approach with (a) business strategy, (b) business improvement, and (c) business value stream analysis, as shown in summary form in Table E.1

We can start by

■ Exposing the biggest problem
  – Cost of current quality
  – Time for the physician

Table E.1 Lean Approach

Business Strategy	Business Improvement	Business Value Stream
Total quality control (TQC), just in time (JIT), drum–buffer–rope (DBR), simplified market pull (SMP), Lean accounting, flow of operations	Eliminate waste, visual cues, 5S, Six Sigma, error proofing, documented procedures, instructions	Define value, construct the VSM, make and understand the flow of activities, respond to customer demand, kaizen (continual improvement)

- Teaching *simple* methods to expose waste
  - It is very hard to be *simple*
  - It is very critical to quantify the waste
- Remembering that medical people are *smart* people and they have a different frame of reference. Therefore:
  - Do not talk jargon
    - We have weird terms:
    - Black belts and green belts (sound like injuries)
    - Spaghetti diagrams (sounds like overweight)
    - Value stream maps (Is this a cheap canoe trip?)
    - Cost of poor quality (poor quality is not here)
  - Do not have predisposed solutions
  - They need to self discover
  - Help them find their way
- Keys to success:
  - Be a coach and teacher
  - Teach the effective use of data. Every treatment recommendation should be based on evidence.
  - Show how process flows affect productivity
  - Solve their problems
  - You may see bigger issues
  - Solve their issues first

You may see bigger issues, but solve their issues first. Create time for healthcare institutions and providers; realize that they are "on the fly."

Selected Bibliography

Grier, P. http://www.csmonitor.com/USA/Politics/2010/0321/Health-care-reform-bill-101-Who-will-pay-for-reform (March 21, 2010)

Harshaw, T. http://opinionator.blogs.nytimes.com/2010/03/19/checking-the-math-on-health-care/?src=me (March 19, 2010)

http://aspe.hhs.gov/poverty/figures-fed-reg.shtmlnderstood (May 22, 2009)

http://candicemiller.house.gov/pdf/hr3200.pdf

http://kyl.senate.gov/legis_center/health.cfm

http://personalmoneystore.com/moneyblog/2010/03/22/new-health-care-bill-summary-basics-health-care-reform/ (May 29, 2010)

http://www.cnn.com/2010/POLITICS/03/18/health.compromise.highlights/index.html?hpt=T1

http://www.healthcare.gov/

http://www.healthreform.gov/

http://www.huffingtonpost.com/2010/03/17/american-public-divided-o_n_502439.html

http://www.healthcarebill2010.info/?ysmwa=5bT4-Sz3mslRd-PVw_BP4hPpbx5gFlzOlqOd_cYkRoMg1yvDYBQnHrLHiiosAl4O (March 24, 2010)

Jackson, J., and J. Nolan. http://www.cbsnews.com/8301-503544_162-20000846-503544.html (May 22, 2010)

Selected Bibliography

Agency for Healthcare Research and Quality. 2003. Executive summary. In *National health-care quality report,* 1–8. Rockville, MD: Agency for Healthcare Research and Quality.

Alderson, P. 2000. Noninterpretive skills for radiology residents: Customer service and satisfaction in radiology. *American Journal of Roentgenology* 175: 319–323.

Altpeter, T., K. Luckhardt, J. N. Lewis, A. H. Harken, and H. C. Polk, Jr. 2007. Expanded surgical time-out: A key to real-time data collection and quality improvement. *Journal of the American College of Surgeons* 204: 527–532.

American College of Medical Quality. 2005. *Medical quality management: Theory and practice.* Sudbury, MA: Jones and Bartlett Publishers.

American National Standard Institute. 1983. *Dimensioning and tolerancing.* Washington, D.C.: ANSI.

American Society of Mechanical Engineers. 1982. *YI4.5M–1982.* New York: American Society of Mechanical Engineers.

Bala, S. 2009. Lean triage for hospital ERs. *Quality Digest* March: 22–24.

Battles, J., and R. Lilford. 2003. Organizing patient safety research to identify risks and hazards. *Quality and Safety in Health Care* 12 (Suppl 2): ii2–ii7.

Beale, C., L. Brideau, K. Caldwell, et al. 2004. Trends in critical care planning and design. Panel discussion. *Health Facilities Management* 17 (1): 24–37.

Behm, D. July 19, 2003. A blueprint for patient safety. Planned layout of new facility near West Bend hailed as revolutionary. *JSOnline: Milwaukee Journal Sentinel.*

Bergeson, S. C., and J. D. Dean. 2006. A systems approach to patient-centered care. *Journal of the American Medical Association* 296 (23): 2848–2851.

Bergey, J., D. Smith, S. Tilley, et al. 1999. Why reengineering projects fail [technical report]. Carnegie Mellon University Software Engineering Institute, Pittsburgh, PA.

Berwick, D. M. 2004. *Escape fire: Designs for the future of healthcare.* Institute for Healthcare Improvement. San Francisco, CA: Jossey–Bass.

Berwick, D. M., A. B. Godfrey, and J. Roessner. 1990. *Curing health care.* San Francisco, CA: Jossey–Bass.

Bhalla, A. 2009. The right mix. *Quality Progress* May: 33–37.

Brinckloe, W. D. 1969. *Managerial operations research.* New York: McGraw–Hill.

Buckingham, M., and C. Coffman. 1999. *First, break all the rules: What the world's greatest managers do differently.* New York: Simon & Schuster.

Burke, R., and E. Greenglass. 2001. Hospital restructuring and nursing staff well-being: The role of personal resources. *Journal of Health and Human Services Administration* 24 (1): 3–26.

Burns, J. 1998. Performance improvement with patient service partners. *Journal of Nursing Administration* 28 (1): 31–37.

Carnell, M. 2010. Rediscovering true north. *Quality Progress* February: 52–53.

Carter, T. 2002. Hospitals and reengineering. *Journal of Hospital Marketing & Public Relations* 14 (1): 59–78.

Chassin, M., and E. Becher. 2002. The wrong patient. *Annals of Internal Medicine* 136 (11): 826–833.

Chassin, M. R., and R. W. Galvin. 1998. The urgent need to improve health care quality. Institute of Medicine National Roundtable on Health Care Quality. *Journal of the American Medical Association* 280 (11): 1000–1005.

Chrysler, Ford, and General Motors. 1995. *Potential failure mode and effect analysis.* Distributed by Automotive Industry Action, Southfield, MI.

Clarke, A., and M. Rao. 2004. Developing quality indicators to assess quality of care. *Quality and Safety in Health Care* 13 (4): 248–249.

Cleary, P. D. 2003. A hospitalization from hell: A patient's perspective on quality. *Annals of Internal Medicine* 138 (1): 33–39.

Cole, D. A. 1999. Creating outcomes with redesign efforts. *AORN Journal* 70 (3): 406–413.

Colwell, C., P. Pons, and R. Pi. 2003. Complaints against an EMS system. *Journal of Emergency Medicine* 25 (4): 403–408.

Conway, W. May 11, 2009. Hospitals: Admitting errors up front saves money in the long run. *Crain's Detroit Business,* p. 18.

Cook, A., H. Hoas, K. Guttmannova, et al. 2004. An error by any other name. *American Journal of Nursing* 104 (6): 32–43; quiz, 44.

Cronen, G., V. Ringus, G. Sigle, and J. Ryu. 2005. Sterility of surgical site marking. *Journal of Bone and Joint Surgery* 87 (10): 2193–2195.

Cullan, D. B., and M. D. Wongworawat. 2007. Sterility of the surgical site marking between the ink and the epidermis. *Journal of the American College of Surgeons* 205 (2): 319–321.

Denney, W., C. St. John, and L. Youngblood. 2009. Narrow healthcare's quality chasm. *Quality Progress* May: 39–45.

Denson, D. 1992. The use of failure mode distributions in reliability analysis. *RAC Newsletter* Spring: 1–3.

Dologite, K., K. Willner, D. Klepeiss, et al. 2003. Sharpen customer service skills with PCRAFT pursuit. *Journal for Nurses in Staff Development* 19 (1): 47–51.

Duckworth, W. E., A. E. Gear, and A. G. Lockett. 1977. *A guide to operational research.* 3rd ed. London: Chapman & Hall/Halsted Press.

Edmondson, J. 2009. Let's be clear: How to manage communication styles. *T+D* September: 30–31.

Epping-Jordan, J. E., S. D. Pruitt, R. Bengoa, et al. 2004. Improving the quality of care for chronic conditions. *Quality and Safety in Health Care* 13 (4): 299–305.

Epstein, A. M., J. S. Weissman, E. C. Schneider, et al. 2003. Race and gender disparities in rates of cardiac revascularization: Do they reflect appropriate use of procedure or problems in quality of care? *Medical Care* 41 (11): 1240–1255.

Ettinger, W., and M. Van Kooy. 2003. The art and science of winning physician support for Six Sigma change. *Physician Executive* 29 (5): 34–39.

First Consulting Group. 2003. Advanced technologies to lower heath care costs and improve quality. Massachusetts Technology Collaborative Innovation Outlook Series. Available at http://www.masstech.org/institute/health/STATFinal9_24.pdf.

Ford Motor Co. 1988. *Potential failure mode and effect analysis.* Dearborn, MI: Ford Motor Co.

———. 1989. *Potential failure mode and effect analysis.* Dearborn, MI: Ford Motor Co.

———. 2002. *Potential failure mode and effect analysis.* Dearborn, MI: Ford Motor Co.

Forrester, N. E. 2003. Accelerating patient-care improvement in the ED. *Healthcare Financial Management* 57 (8): 38–43.

Foster, L. 1982. *Modern geometric dimensioning and tolerancing.* Ft. Washington, PA: NTMA.

Galo, R. and D. Partin. (January 28, 2009). Health care: The hidden business killer. *Fortune: Small Business.* 47–54.

Galvin, R., and E. McGlynn. 2003. Using performance measurement to drive improvement: A road map for change. *Medical Care* 41 (1 Suppl): I48–I60.

Garcia, C. J., and D. P. St. Charles. 1988. Automating GD&T. *Quality* June: 56–58.

Gray, P. February 4, 2009. Health cure. *Fortune: Small Business* February: 57–65.

Greene, J. March 30, 2009. Success prompts Henry Ford medical to promote off-hour specialist program. *Crain's Detroit Business,* p. 4.

———. April 27, 2009. Hospitals target readmissions. *Crain's Detroit Business,* pp. 3, 22.

———. May 11, 2009. Hospitals find confession good for the bottom line. *Crain's Detroit Business,* p. 18.

Griffith, J. R. 2000. Championship management for healthcare organizations. *Journal of Healthcare Management* 45 (1): 17–30.

Halcom, C. April 6–12, 2009. Medicaid fraud, waste meet match from IT. *Crain's Detroit Business,* pp. 1, 20.

Hamilton, K., J. Kunkle, J. Levine, et al. 2003. The future of the facility. Executive dialog series. *Health Facilities Management* 16 (1): 23–37.

Hamilton, M., and B. Caruso. January 2003 High priority: Voice of the customer. *Quality Progress* 24–31.

Hansten, R., and M. Washburn. 1997. *Toolbook for health care redesign.* Gaithersburg, MD: Aspen Publishers.

Harrison, A. 2000. The war on waiting. *Health Care UK.* Winter: 52–60.

Harrison, M. I. 2005. *Diagnosing organizations: Methods, models and processes.* Thousand Oaks, CA: Sage Publications.

Haugh, R. May 2004. Administrative. In *The patient room,* ed. D. Scalise, T. H. Thrall, R. Haugh, et al. *Hospitals & Health Networks* 78 (5): 34–38, 40, 49–51.

Health Grades, Inc. 2004. *Health Grades quality study: Patient safety in American Hospitals.* Golden, CO: Health Grades, Inc.

Hibbard, J. H. 2003. Engaging health care consumers to improve the quality of care. *Medical Care* 41 (1): I61–I70.

Hobgood, C., A. Hevia, and A. Hinchey. 2004. Profiles in patient safety: When an error occurs. *Academic Emergency Medicine* 11 (7): 766–770.

Institute of Medicine. 2001. *Crossing the quality chasm: A new health system for the 21st century.* Washington, DC: National Academy Press.

———. 2001. *To err is human: Building a safer health system.* Washington, DC: National Academy Press.

Jing, G. 2009. A Lean Six Sigma breakthrough. *Quality Progress* May: 25–32.

Johnson, K. 2004. Two hospitals prescribe performance excellence. *Quality Progress* September: 46–56.

Jones, K., and R. Redman. 2000. Organizational culture and work redesign: Experiences in three organizations. *Journal of Nursing Administration* 30 (12): 604–610.

Josephs, F. 1987. *Production management: Concepts and analysis for operation and control.* New York: Ronald Press.

Karl, D. P., J. Morisette, and W. Taam. 1994. Some applications of a multivariate capability index in geometric dimensioning and tolerancing. *Quality Engineering* 6 (4): 649–665.

Kelly, K., and M. Mass. 1995. *SONA 7: Health care work redesign.* Thousand Oaks, CA: Sage Publications.

Koenigsaecker G. 2001. A manager's guide to implementing Lean. *Manufacturing and Technology News* 8 (9): 6–11.

Kotter, J. 2008. *A sense of urgency.* Boston, MA: Harvard Business Press.

Kotter, J. P. 1996. *Leading change.* Boston, MA: Harvard Business School Press.

Krulikowski, A. 1994. *Geometric dimensioning and tolerancing: A self study workbook.* Milwaukee, WI: Quality Press.

Kuisma, M., T. Maatta, T. Hakala, et al. 2003. Customer satisfaction measurement in emergency medical services. *Academic Emergency Medicine* 10 (7): 812–815.

Kwaan, M. R., D. M. Studdert, M. J. Zinner, and A. A. Gawande. 2006. Incidence, patterns, and prevention of wrong-site surgery. *Archives of Surgery* 141 (4): 353–357; discussion, 357–358.

Lee, S. Y., and J. A. Alexander. 1999. Managing hospitals in turbulent times: Do organizational changes improve hospital survival? *Health Services Research* 34 (4): 923–946.

Leonard, D., and M. K. Reller. 2004. Simplify Baldrige for healthcare. *Quality Progress* September: 35–45.

Lewis, B. December 4, 2003. Children's hospital designed for needs, comfort of anxious families. *The Tennessean* [online version].

Lewis, M. March 30, 2009. Henry Ford health system multicultural dermatology clinic. *Crain's Detroit Business,* p. 11.

Liker, J. K. 2004. *The Toyota way: 14 Management principles from the world's greatest manufacturer.* New York: McGraw–Hill.

Locock, L. 2003. Healthcare redesign: Meaning, origins and application. *Quality and Safety in Health Care* 12 (1): 53–57.

Malhotra, Y. 1998. Business process redesign: An overview. *IEEE Engineering Management Review* 26 (3): 27–31.

Malone, B. 2004. Pursuing patient safety. *Quality and Safety in Health Care* 13 (2): 86–87.

Mawji, Z., P. Stillman, R. Laskowski, et al. 2002. First do no harm: Integrating patient safety and quality improvement. *Joint Commission Journal on Quality Improvement* 28 (7): 373–386.

McGlynn, E. A., C. K. Cassel, S. T. Leatherman, et al. 2003. Establishing national goals for quality improvement. *Medical Care* 41 (1 Suppl): I16–I29.

Meinberg, E. G., and P. J. Stern. 2003. Incidence of wrong-site surgery among hand surgeons. *Journal of Bone and Joint Surgery* 85-A (2): 193–197.

Mello, M., and D. Hemenway. 2004. Medical malpractice as an epidemiological problem. *Social Science and Medicine* 59 (1): 39–46.

Miller, W. H. August 1, 1988. Changed focus: Technology fix to cost of quality control. *Industry Week*, p. 16.

Mitchell, G. 1993. *The practice of operational research*. Chichester, England: John Wiley & Sons Ltd.

Mitchell, P., C. L. Nicholson, and A. Jenkins. 2006. Side errors in neurosurgery. *Acta Neurochirurgica (Wien)* 148: 1289–1292.

Mody, M. G., A. D. Nourbakhsh, D. L. Stahl, M. Gibbs, M. Alfawareh, and K. J. Garges. 2008. The prevalence of wrong level surgery among spine surgeons. *Spine* 33: 194–198.

Moscynski, M. 2009. 3–2–1 Innovate. *T&D* July: 40–45.

National Health Information. 2003. Monitoring reduces hospital-acquired infections by 19%. *Performance Improvement Advisor* 7(8). National Health Information. Atlanta, GA.

Nelson, E., K. Nolan, T. Nolan, et al. 2004. *IHI's health system measures kit: Version 1.0*. Pursuing Perfection & IMPACT Network. Institute for Healthcare Improvement.

Nelson, E., M. Splaine, S. Plume, et al. 2004. Good measurement for good improvement work. *Quality Management in Health Care* 13 (1): 1–16.

Nelson, E. C., P. B. Batalden, K. Homa, et al. 2003. Microsystems in health care: Part 2. Creating a rich information environment. *Joint Commission Journal on Quality and Safety* 29 (1): 5–15.

Nelson, E. C., P. B. Batalden, T. P. Huber, et al. 2002. Microsystems in health care: Part 1. Learning from high-performing front-line clinical units. *Joint Commission Journal on Quality Improvement* 28 (9): 472–493.

Nichols, R., G. Segal, and D. Kessler. 2009. Linking training to care. *T+D*. October: 64–66.

Nielsen, D., M. Merry, P. Schyve, and M. Bisognano. 2004. Can the gurus' concepts cure healthcare? *Quality Progress* September: 25–34.

Norton, W. I., and L. Sussman. 2009. Team charters: Theoretical foundations and practical implications for quality and performance. *Quality Management Journal* 16 (1): 7–17.

Nuhfer, D., and T. Walters. 2009. Take a bite out of inefficiency. *Quality Progress* May: 46–51.

Olson, M. 2008. Compact risk: Controlling the perils of change. *T+D* September: 38–43.

Paradise, A. 2009. Talent management defined. *T+D* May: 58–69.

Patterson, R., ed. 2001. *Changing patient behavior: Improving outcomes in health and disease management.* San Francisco, CA: Jossey–Bass.

Pauly, D. 1986. *The cost of doing things better,* 196. Dearborn, MI: Society of Manufacturing Engineers.

Porter, M. E., and E. O. Teisberg. 2004. Redefining competition in health care. *Harvard Business Review* 82 (6): 64–76.

Prathibha, V., ed. 2010. *Medical quality management: Theory and practice.* Sudburry, MA: Jones and Bartlett Publishers.

Rakich J. S. 2001. Quality, CQI and reengineering in health services organizations. *Journal of Health & Social Policy* 13: 41–58.

Reason, J. 2000. Human error: Models and management. *British Medical Journal* 320: 768–770.

Revere, L., and K. Black. 2003. Integrating Six Sigma with total quality management: A case example for measuring medication errors. *Journal of Healthcare Management* 48 (6): 377–379; discussion, 392.

Richins, S. 2002. Customer service for step-down patients. *Journal of Nursing Administration* 32 (11): 558–560.

Rogers, E. M. 1995. *Diffusion of innovations,* 4th ed. New York: Free Press.

Rooney, J., O. K. Khoo, A. R. Higgs, T. J. Small, and S. Bell. 2008. Surgical site marking does not affect sterility. *ANZ Journal of Surgery* 78 (8): 688–689.

Rothman, G. 2006. Wrong-site surgery. *Archives of Surgery* 141 (10): 1049–1050.

Runy, L. May 2004. Universal rooms. In *The patient room,* ed. D. Scalise, T. H. Thrall, R. Haugh, et al. *Hospitals & Health Networks* 78 (5): 34–38, 40, 49–51.

Sahney, V. 2006. U.S. healthcare nonsystem: Major improvements are possible. *Technology Century* February–March: 26–29.

Sandrick, K. 2003. Tops in quality. *Trustee* 56 (8): 1, 12–16.

Scalise, D. 2003. Six Sigma in action: Case studies in quality put theory into practice. *Hospitals & Health Networks* 77 (5): 2, 57–62.

Schwab, R. 2000. Emergency department customer satisfaction: The point of view paradox. *Annals of Emergency Medicine* 35 (5): 499–501.

Schyve, P. M. 2000. The evolution of external quality evaluation: Observations from the Joint Commission on Accreditation of Healthcare Organizations. *International Journal for Quality in Health Care* 12 (3): 255–258.

Scott, T., R. Mannion, H. Davies, and M. Marshall. 2003. The quantitative measurement of organizational culture in health care: A review of the available instruments. *Health Services Research* 38 (3): 923–945.

Seago, J. 1999. Evaluation of a hospital work redesign: Patient-focused care. *Journal of Nursing Administration* 29 (11): 31–38.

Sherman, P. 2010. Get to the whole picture: Systems thinking. *Quality Progress* February: 33–38.

Shinde, S., and J. A. Carter. 2009. Wrong site neurosurgery—Still a problem. *Anaesthesia* 64 (1): 1–2.

Shine, K. I. 2001. Health care quality and how to achieve it. New York: Milbank Memorial Fund. Robert H. Ebert Memorial Lecture (available at http://www.milbank.org/reports/020130Ebert/020130Ebert.html).

Sirio, C., K. T. Segel, D. J. Keyser, et al. 2003. Pittsburgh regional healthcare initiative: A systems approach for achieving perfect patient care. *Health Affairs (Millwood)* 22 (5): 157–165.

Spackman, L. 2009. Change that sticks. *Quality Progress* April: 22–29.

Stamatis, D. H. 1996. Focus on the healthcare industry: A TQM practice update. *Financial Accounting Report* December: 8–10.

Stein, A. 2009. Work for change. *Fortune: Small Business* November: 25

Stump, L. S. 2000. Reengineering the medication error-reporting process: Removing the blame and improving the system. *American Journal of Health System Pharmacy* 57 (Suppl 4): S10–S17.

Tarantino, D. P. 2003. Process redesign. Part 1: Process selection. *Physician Executive* 29 (6): 71–73.

Teng, J. T. C., S. R. Jeong, and V. Grover. 1998. Profiling successful reengineering projects. *Communications of the ACM* 41 (6): 96–102.

Thrall, T. H. 2003. Work redesign. *Hospitals & Health Networks* 77 (3): 2, 34–38, 40.

Trisolini, M. G. 2002. Applying business management models in health care. *International Journal of Health Planning and Management* 17 (4): 295–314.

Valenti, W. M., and L. J. Bookhardt-Murray. 2004. Advanced access scheduling boosts quality, productivity and revenue. *Drug Benefit Trends* 16 (10): 510, 513–514.

Van Matre, J. G., and K. E. Koch. 2009. Understanding healthcare clinical process and outcome measures and their use in the Baldrige Award application process. *Quality Management Journal* 16 (1): 18–28.

Vincent, C., K. Moorthy, S. Sarker, et al. 2004. Systems approaches to surgical quality and safety: From conception to measurement. *Annals of Surgery* 239 (4): 475–482.

Walston, S. L. 1997. Reengineering hospitals: Evidence from the field. *Hospital and Health Services Administration* 2 (2): 143–163.

Walston, S. L., L. R. Burns, and J. R. Kimberly. 2000. Does reengineering really work? An examination of the context and outcomes of hospital reengineering initiatives. *Health Services Research* 34 (6): 1363–1388.

Walston, S. L., J. R. Kimberly, and L. R. Burns. 2001. Institutional and economic influences on the adoption and extensiveness of managerial innovation in hospitals: The case of reengineering. *Medical Care Research and Review* 58 (2): 194–228.

Walston, S. L., L. D. Urden, and P. Sullivan. 2001. Hospital reengineering: An evolving management innovation: History, current status and future direction. *Journal of Health and Human Services Administration* 23 (4): 388–415.

Warda, R. 2009. Know thyself. *Quality Progress* April: 30–37.

Wearing, C., and D. P. Karl. 1995. The importance of following GD&T specifications. *Quality Progress* February: 95–98.

Weaver, D., ed. 1999. *Patient care redesign: Lessons from the field.* American Organization of Nurse Executives. Chicago, IL: AHA Press.

West, J. E. 2009. Small change, big payoff. *Quality Progress* April: 47–52.

Whitmire, G. 1991. Why use GD&T. *Quality* March: 41–42.

Womack, J., and D. Jones. 1996. Beyond Toyota: How to root out waste and pursue perfection. *Harvard Business Review* 74 (5): 140–158.

———. 2003. *Lean thinking: Banish waste and create wealth in your corporation.* New York: Free Press.

Wong, D. A., J. H. Herndon, S. T. Canale, R. L. Brooks, T. R. Hunt, H. R. Epps, S. S. Fountain, S. A. Albanese, and N. A. Johanson. 2009. Medical errors in orthopedics—Results of an AAOS member survey. *Journal of Bone and Joint Surgery* 91 (3): 547–557.

Zahary, L. J. 2009. Filling in the blanks. *T+D* May: 62–67.

Zweig, G. 2009. Real-time x-ray inspection. *Quality Digest* March: 26–29.

Index